THE SPIRITUAL HERITAGE OF INDIA

SWAMI PRABHAVANANDA
with foreword by
Huston Smith

Vedanta Press
HOLLYWOOD, CALIFORNIA

ISBN 0-87481-035-3
Library of Congress Catalog Number 63-10517

Printed in the United States of America

If you wish to learn more about the teachings within this book, write to the Secretary, Vedanta Society of Southern California, 1946 Vedanta Place, Hollywood CA 90068-3996. Or phone 213/465-7114, fax 213/465-9568.

Nettesheim

THE SPIRITUAL HERITAGE OF INDIA

BOOKS BY SWAMI PRABHAVANANDA

Original Works

VEDIC RELIGION AND PHILOSOPHY

THE ETERNAL COMPANION (LIFE AND TEACHINGS OF SWAMI BRAHMANANDA)

THE SERMON ON THE MOUNT ACCORDING TO VEDANTA

RELIGION IN PRACTICE

YOGA AND MYSTICISM

Translations

THE WISDOM OF GOD (SRIMAD BHAGAVATAM)

SHANKARA'S CREST-JEWEL OF DISCRIMINATION (WITH CHRISTOPHER ISHERWOOD)

THE UPANISHADS (WITH FREDERICK MANCHESTER)

THE SONG OF GOD: BHAGAVAD-GITA (WITH ISHERWOOD)

HOW TO KNOW GOD, THE YOGA APHORISMS OF PATANJALI (WITH ISHERWOOD)

SWAMI PREMANANDA: TEACHINGS AND REMINISCENCES

CONTENTS

BOOK III

JAINISM AND BUDDHISM

BOOK IV

THE SIX SYSTEMS OF THOUGHT

BOOK V

VEDANTA AND ITS GREAT EXPONENTS

FOREWORD

Around the middle of this century Arnold Toynbee predicted that at its close the world would still be dominated by the West, but that in the twenty-first century "India will conquer her conquerors."[1] Preempting the place that is now held by technology, religion will be restored to its earlier importance and the center of world happenings will wander back from the shores of the Atlantic to the East where civilization originated five or six thousand years ago. His prediction provides an exceptionally forceful rationale, if one were needed, for reissuing the book in hand. For *The Spiritual Heritage of India* is one of the most useful summaries in print of the tradition Toynbee saw as destined to figure prominently in the long range human future.

The spiritual heritage of India is one of the world's standing miracles. It would rank among its greatest human achievements were it not that "achievement" isn't really the right word. It is more like a reception — the opening of a people to receive, through inspiration, the Breath of the Eternal. For the outbreathing of the Eternal is what India has taken truth to be — see *infra,* p. 28. We know that "Hinduism" is a label affixed by outsiders. Long ago, people to the west of the Indus River mispronounced its name and called those who lived on it or to its other side "Hindus," and in time "Hinduism" came to be used for their beliefs and practices. The Indians themselves knew no such word. There was no need for them to think of the truth by which they lived as other than the *sanatana dharma,* the Eternal Truth. It was Truth Itself — truth that had become incarnate in the tradition that sustained them.

How the incarnation was effected is itself an interesting point. In the West we tend to think of knowledge as cumulative: bits of information get joined into bodies of information that can grow indefinitely. India recognizes a kind of knowledge that fits this model, but she considers it "lower knowledge" — knowledge that is gained by reason and the senses playing over objective, finite particulars. Higher knowledge (*paravidya*) proceeds differently. Or rather, it doesn't proceed at all, for it enters history full-blown. It is futile to ask when this higher knowledge first appeared, for India has no notion of absolute beginnings — beginnings require time, and time for India is not absolute. The most we can say is that when a new cosmic cycle opens there are souls waiting in the wings, so to speak, with the higher wisdom already in store. Who these souls are is not a genetic accident: India has no place for chance or accident — the law of karma precludes it. The men and women who are born wise on the morning of a new creation are so because, though the world they enter is young, they themselves are not. Their *jivas* (individual psyches) having been held over from preceding cosmic cycles, they are already 'old souls' — old chronologically,

[1]Culturally, not politically. Toynbee's prediction appeared in an address he gave to The Philosophical Society of Edinburgh University in November, 1952.

to be sure, but more importantly in experience. Specifically they are yogis and yoginis who used their preceding lives to cultivate what might be regarded as a kind of 'night sight' — the night vision of the spirit by which fixed stars of eternity can be seen in broad daylight. Adepts in such vision, these seers stand poised on the brink of their final liberation when the new cycle begins. Their concluding legacy to the phenomenal world is to impregnate the new cycle with reflective knowledge of the truth they have assiduously shepherded. Keeping in touch with this truth through meditation, these *rishis* (seers) transmit it orally, direct from guru to disciple, until eventually their oral tradition gets committed to writing. In India the texts that result are the Vedas.

If we see the Vedas in this light, as apertures through which the Infinite entered conscious human awareness in South Asia in the present cosmic cycle, what word of the Infinite do the Vedas impart?

First the warning that on this topic words are unequal to their task. They can be useful, of course, or the Vedas themselves would not have been written, but a fundamental Vedic teaching concerns the limitations of words themselves when directed towards ultimates. Sooner or later these ultimates phase beyond language entirely. *Neti, neti,* not this, not this; the map is not the terrain, the menu is not the meal — the Vedas never tire of repeating this basic point. In this kind of knowing, words do not cause understanding; at best they occasion it: from spirit to spirit communion leaps. The word "Upanishads," denoting the culminating sections of the Vedas, makes this point in its very etymology. Deriving from roots which when conjoined mean to approach (*upa*) with utter (*ni*) firmness to loosen and destroy (*sad*) spiritual ignorance, it warns the reader right off that the topics he is about to encounter call for more than book learning. For their province is that 'higher mathematics' of the human spirit where knowing merges with being. Upanishadic truth is so subtle, so abstruse, that purely objective, rational intellects are likely to miss it entirely — off such intellects it rolls like water off oil. Only when discerned in a life that is living it — a life that incarnates it in its outlook, moods, and conduct — does truth of this order become fully convincing. It is like art. There comes a time when every master musician must say to his pupil, "Don't bother with what I say. Just watch how I take that passage."

To be able to perform as his teacher does, the student must become a changed person. The change begins with a change in his understanding — he now has some inkling of how the passage should sound — but other changes are required as well. Subtle muscular habits must be acquired and integrated, through feedback loops, with subliminal sensitivities to nuances of color and sound. The analogy helps us to see that the truths the Vedas deal with exceed language in a double sense. To the fact that the Infinite cannot be fitted into concepts which are finite by nature is joined the further fact that the knowledge in question resembles "knowing how" more than "knowing that"; it is more like knowing how to swim or ride a bicycle than like recognizing that these activities require certain movements of arms and legs. Vedantic epistemology involves yoga. To know, one must be; to deepen one's knowledge of the kind in question, one must deepen one's being.

These points must never be lost sight of, but provided they are kept in view, the mind may be given its due in the transformative process. Of the world's manifold traditions, none has held more firmly than India's to the double truth that (a) though the mind is intimately *meshed* with other components of the self, (b) it can take the lead in *changing* the self. First the student hears the truth, then he reasons on it. It is later, we are told, that he meditates on it to deepen his understanding and bring other components of himself abreast of where his mind, as advance scout, has already proceeded — see *infra,* p. 208.

The territory into which the mind is forever pressing is the Infinite, and if we were to look for the place where India most deserves to be credited for originality, it is perhaps here that we find it. The Chinese notion of the Tao is rich in its *sense* of the Infinite, but the Chinese were content to rest in that sense itself; they felt no compulsion to conceptualize it. The Greeks, on the other hand, tried to conceptualize everything they encountered, but this very penchant excluded them from ready access to a notion concepts could never close in on. Anaximander's Unbounded (*apeiron*) held promising possibilities, but instead of pursuing these his successors backed away from them — Greek philosophers were not about to give high marks to something that lacked determination. By the time of Aristotle, infinity had come to be associated with imperfection and lack (*Physics,* III:6–8); it meant the capacity for never-ending increase and was always potential, never completely actual.[2] Not until the Neo-platonists did a full-blown, positive view of the Infinite emerge in the West, and then in part, perhaps,

[2]As this difference between the Greek and Indian attitudes toward the infinite has not been sufficiently noticed, it will be well to document this last statement. In his *Thomism* (New York: Harper & Row, 1967), p. 71, Paul Grenet writes: "For the Greeks, 'finite' is complementary and synonymous with 'perfect.' (In French, *ouvrage fini* [a finished product]). 'Infinite' is pejorative and synonymous with 'imprecise,' and 'unformed.' . . . To-be-finite is for matter a perfection which comes to it from form." Frithjof Schuon concurs, noting that "the Greeks always have a certain fear of the Infinite, which is very visible even in their architecture: the Parthenon has real grandeur, but it expresses the religion of the finite and rational Perfect which, because it confuses the unlimited with the chaotic, the infinite with the irrational, is opposed to virgin nature" (*Islam and the Perennial Philosophy* [London: World of Islam Festival, 1976], p. 66). Leo Sweeney summarizes the matter as follows: "From whatever angle it was approached, infinity patently clashed with the dominant Greek notion of form as equivalent to perfection" (*Infinity in the Presocratics* [The Hague: Martinus Nijhoff, 1972], p. xvii).

through Indian influence.[3] If we look at a map of the world, Europe looks like an appendage growing out of a central, Asian body or trunk, and in this matter of the Infinite, capitalized because affirmatively conceived, the appearance seems accurate. For not only did India give that notion its earliest explicit articulation; it made the notion central to its history. This no other civilization has quite done. To speak only of ourselves, the modern West has an infinite of sorts, but it is of a largely mathematical variety which is not infinite at all in the complete sense of the word. For though a mathematical infinite is unlimited in certain respects — with regard to extension or number, for example — it is clearly not inclusive in all respects: sounds, colors, and other things that make our world substantial and concrete have no place within it. India's infinite is otherwise. It includes everything, which gave the Indian outlook right off a striking amplitude. When we think inclusively about the West the phrase that comes to mind is "the Western world." The comparable phrase that comes to mind when we think of India is "the Indian universe."

I have labored this point about the infinite because, though it is abstract in itself, it carries concrete implications. Everyone agrees that India is different, but what is it that *makes* her different? When a newcomer sets out to locate the elusive, distinctive ingredient the old-timers smile and wait. They wait for the moment they know well, each having encountered it in his turn. It is the moment when the visitor will throw up his hands and admit that India is indefinable, the reason being that it seems to include everything.

Which, of course, is precisely what the Infinite includes. "As above, so below" — I am suggesting that India's exceptional variety and inclusiveness derives from the fact that she saw the source of all things as Infinite in the all-inclusive and positive sense of that word: *sat,* Being in its totality, is endowed with consciousness (*chit*) and bliss (*ananda*). Philosophers know that to speak of such an Infinite requires paradoxes: because words and propositions are limited, every half truth they utter must be balanced by the other half they omit. The historical counterpart of this is the paradox of India herself — a whole host of paradoxes, actually, for wherever we turn, she confronts us with opposites so extreme they would have torn other civilizations apart but here are kept in creative tension. Bejewelled maharajas who receive as birthday presents their weight in precious stones from their starving subjects. Naked ascetics stretched on beds of nails, balanced by naked voluptuaries on temple friezes. Or the question of God: three hun-

[3]A. L. Basham says that "the possibility of Indian influence on Neoplatonism . . . cannot be ruled out" (*The Wonder that Was India* [New York: Grove Press, 1959], p. 486) and Rene Guenon goes further. "Among the Neo-Platonists," he writes, "Eastern influences were . . . to make their appearances, and it is there . . . that . . . the Infinite [is] met with for the first time among the Greeks" (*Introduction to Hindu Doctrines* [London: Luzac & Co., 1945], pp. 51–52).

dred and thirty million deities sounds like polytheism gone haywire until we hear that nothing other than the sole, indivisible Brahman even exists. What are we to make of such paradoxes? How can one possibly summarize such a geography of anomolies,

> this . . . world of high-soaring and deep-plunging thought, . . . of bewildering variety and rigidity of custom and behaviour, of startling ethical purity and equally startling licence, of seemingly immovable changelessness and supple flexibility, of incredible receptivity and unalterable self-identity, a jungle of life- and thought-patterns, . . . this . . . *complexio oppositorum* (combination of opposites)?[4]

Ninian Smart probably manages as much of a summary as is possible when he writes: "The genius of Hinduism is to combine divergent practices and beliefs into one overall system."[5]

This leads into the book in hand, for one of its many virtues is the way it integrates the variety in the Indian heritage which, left to itself, can be bewildering. Even Buddhism and Jainism, technically considered by Hindus to be unorthodox, are here shown to be authentic expressions of the basic Indian vision. Or the Six Systems of Indian Philosophy; often regarded as competitors, they are here shown to complement one another. And of course philosophy and psychology are not separated from theology as if they belonged in distinct compartments. It would be too weak to say that Indian thought as it emerges in the reading of this book is interdisciplinary. It is, rather, pre-disciplinary in the rich and holistic way that Biblical, Chinese and early Greek thought are.

As for the book's author, Swami Prabhavananda, few Indians have personally reached as many Western intellectuals as he did. As my own teacher in things Indian, Swami Satprakashananda of the Vedanta Society of St. Louis, was a brother monk of his in the Ramakrishna Order and is now, at 90, that Order's senior member, this Foreword provides an opportunity for me to acknowledge my indebtedness and express my gratitude, both to these men and to the Order they served so well. In these days when the walls that separated peoples are down and the world's traditions are being lavished on one another, the Ramakrishna Order stands as a model of cross-cultural sharing at its best.

—Huston Smith
Syracuse University
July 1978

[4]Hendrik Kraemer, *Religion and the Christian Faith* (Philadelphia: Westminster Press, 1956), p. 101.

[5]*Student's guide to THE LONG SEARCH (Miami: Miami-Dade Community College, 1978), p. 243.*

TRANSLITERATION OF SANSKRIT ALPHABET

VOWELS

short:	a i u e o ṛ
long:	ā ī ū ai au ṝ
anusvāra:	ṁ
visarga:	ḥ

CONSONANTS

gutturals:	k kh g gh ṅ
palatals:	c ch j jh ñ
cerebrals:	ṭ ṭh ḍ ḍh ṇ
dentals:	t th d dh n
labials:	p ph b bh m
semi-vowels:	y r l v
sibilants:	s as in *sit*
	ś palatal sibilant pronounced like the soft Russian *s*
	ṣ cerebral sibilant as in *show*
aspirate:	h

PREFACE

The Spiritual Heritage of India is a brief history of the philosophy of a country that has never distinguished philosophy from religion. The account extends from centuries of which there is no historical record to the recent Śrī Rāmakṛṣṇa revival of the ancient Vedānta.

In connection with each of the subjects taken up I have tried to supply sufficient quotation from the texts concerned, as incidental illustration and sometimes also as appended passages, to give body and force to the exposition.

My point of view is in one respect different from that of the Western scholar. I speak always as one born to the religious tradition of India, convinced of the profound truth of its essential message and familiar with its manifestations in the life of my people. Thus a religious phenomenon that to the Western scholar might well seem remote and merely curious, an item to be scientifically noted but not to be taken seriously—I refer to the transcendental consciousness—is to me a plain fact of supreme significance. I have dwelt in close association with most of the monastic disciples of Śrī Rāmakṛṣṇa, each of whom had attained that ultimate and blessed experience; and I have seen one of them, my spiritual master, Swami Brahmananda, living almost constantly—as a direct result of that experience—in a state of ecstatic communion with God.

I have just mentioned Śrī Rāmakṛṣṇa. As a representative of the monastic order founded more than half a century ago in his name, I may be forgiven for having often invoked him in this book. That I should do this was natural—indeed almost inevitable—since it is through Śrī Rāmakṛṣṇa, as reported by those who knew him, more than through anyone else, that I have come to whatever understanding I possess of the religion of India.

This religion has two aspects. There is its essential message, regarding which its leading representatives are in complete and obvious agreement. Then there are its many secondary elements, regarding which these same representatives often differ—or rather, as we shall see, appear to differ. Now in relation to this second aspect it may be well to anticipate briefly an important idea that will be set forth at greater length, again and again, in the course of the following chapters—an idea which constitutes a warning, especially to the Western reader. A Western reader, as he goes from one more or less intricate system of thought to another contrasting with it in detail after detail, may not unnaturally conclude that despite agreement in a few concepts these systems are mutually contradictory, and that one should speak not of Indian religion but of Indian religions. But this, to the Indian mind, would be to ignore the fact that finite views of the infinite are necessarily partial, and the further fact that they are relative to time and place, to individual temperament, and to the plane of consciousness that they reflect. When therefore one teaching seems to contradict another, it may in fact not so much contradict it as supplement it, the total truth residing not in any one theory but in a synthesis in which all theories have their part. The flexibility suggested is, and has always been, a primary characteristic of Indian religion.

The passages from the Upaniṣads are from the Prabhavananda–Manchester translation, and those from the Bhagavad-Gītā are from the Prabhavananda–Isherwood translation. Passages from the Bhāgavatam are from my translation entitled *The Wisdom of God*. The chapter on the Yoga Aphorisms of Patañjali has incorporated many of the comments on them contained in the book *How to Know God*, by Prabhavananda and Isherwood. The chapter on Śaṁkara was rewritten by Christopher Isherwood, and has been published as an introduction to the Prabhavananda–Isherwood translation, entitled Shankara's *Crest-Jewel of Discrimination*, of the *Vivekacūḍāmaṇi*. The teachings of Śrī Rāmakṛṣṇa (pp. 352 f.)—selected from Swami Brahmananda's *Śrī Śrī Rāmakṛṣṇa Upadeśa*—were translated by Swami Prabhavananda and Frederick Manchester.

Translations from Sanskrit and Bengali, throughout the volume, when not attributed to others, are by the present author.

Chapter and verse references for quotations from the Upaniṣads, the Bhagavad-Gītā, the Bhāgavatam, and the *Vivekacūḍāmaṇi* are to the Sanskrit originals.

Grateful acknowledgements are due to a number of publishers for permission to reprint material from their books: to Advaita Ashrama, Mayavati, India, for passages from *The Complete Works of Swami Vivekananda*; to George Allen & Unwin, Ltd., and the Macmillan Co., New York, for passages from S. Radhakrishnan's *Indian Philosophy* and *Outlines of Indian Philosophy*, by M. Hiriyanna; to the Sri Aurobindo Ashram, Pondicherry, India, for passages from *Essays on the Gita*, by Sri Aurobindo Ghose; to the Cambridge University Press for a passage from *What is Life?*, by Erwin Schrödinger; to Ganesh & Co. Ltd., Madras, for passages from *Śakti and Śākta*, by Sir John Woodroffe; to Longmans, Green & Co. Ltd., for a passage from *Ramanuja's Idea of the Finite Self*, by P. N. Srinivasachari; to the Sri Ramakrishna Centenary Committee, Belur Math, Calcutta, for passages from *The Cultural Heritage of India*; and finally to the Vedanta Society of Southern California, Hollywood, for passages from the following works, all mentioned above: Shankara's *Crest-Jewel of Discrimination*, the *Bhagavad-Gita* (translated by Prabhavananda and Isherwood), *How to Know God*, *The Upanishads* (translated by Prabhavananda and Manchester), and *The Wisdom of God*.

I am happy to record my obligation to several persons who have given assistance in the production of this work. To the late Percy H. Houston I am indebted for editing a considerable portion of the original manuscript; and to the late V. Subrahmanya Iyer for reading a large section of it and making valuable suggestions. To the memory of those two scholars, one of the West, one of the East, I offer my homage. To the physicist Joseph Kaplan I am indebted for a series of notes showing the parallelism between the cosmological ideas of Kapila, the Sāṁkhya philosopher, and the findings of modern science.

By special arrangement, the final draft of this history has had much attention, as regards form, from Frederick Manchester. He has rewritten the Preface, chapters 1–4, 10, 24, and 25; and—except of course for matter previously published and here reproduced unaltered—he has edited the remainder of the book.

Finally, for much painstaking labour in preparing the manuscript for the press, I am indebted to a member of my immediate household, Brahmacharini Usha.

P.

December 1960

INTRODUCTION

The word *darśana*, which is usually translated 'philosophy', means in Sanskrit seeing or experience. From this we may gather that Indian philosophy is not merely metaphysical speculation, but has its foundation in immediate perception. God and the soul are regarded by the Hindu mind, not as concepts, speculative and problematical, as is the case in Western philosophy, but as things directly known. They can be experienced not merely by a chosen few, but, under right conditions, by all humanity.

This insistence upon immediate perception rather than on abstract reasoning is what distinguishes the Indian philosophy of religion from philosophy as Western nations know it. Immediate perception is the source from which springs all Indian thought.

This perception, it must be made clear, is not of the senses, nor must it be confused with the operations of the intellect, nor of the emotions; it is supersensuous, transcendental—something not to be fully explained in rational terms.

The Māṇḍūkya Upaniṣad speaks of three states of consciousness—waking, dreaming, and dreamless sleep.[1] These are common to all men. In addition, there is turīya (The Fourth), the transcendental state—known also as samādhi—which may be described as the ultimate consciousness. Though it is realizable by all men, they do not experience it in their spiritually ignorant condition. Indian philosophers call the transcendental state by various names, but all of the names unmistakably point to the same concept.

Turīya, or samādhi, is a phenomenon well known throughout the history of Indian life. Today, as well as in earliest times, it is experienced. Śrī Rāmakṛṣṇa, the greatest saint of modern India, though not a learned man, attained samādhi, and having realized the highest illumination spoke words of solace and wisdom to all men. The state is conceivably attainable by anyone who strives hard to free himself from the dross of worldliness.

The Hindu, however, is careful not to confuse reveries, dreams, hallucinations, and hypnotic spells with transcendental experience. Before a state is recognized as genuinely transcendental, it must pass certain tests.

[1] The Upaniṣads are a portion of the Vedas, the authoritative scriptures of India. Why the Vedas are regarded as authoritative will be explained in Chapter 1.

First, the revelation it brings must be related (as was said by Jaimini, founder of the Pūrva Mīmāṁsā school of thought) to arthe anupalabdhe—something which is otherwise unknown and unknowable. The transcendental revelation is therefore not a revelation of things or truths normally perceived or generally known, nor of truths capable of ordinary perception or of apprehension through the ordinary instruments of knowledge. And yet it must be universally understandable in relation to human experience, and must be communicable to us in human terms.

Second, the truth it reveals must not contradict other truths. It is necessarily beyond and above reason, but it must not contradict reason.

Thus Indian religion, though having its foundation in supernatural revelation, gives a legitimate place to logic and reason, and it has never been an obstacle to the growth of philosophic thinking. In fact, no race has produced a succession of more subtle or more rigidly logical thinkers than the Hindus—and yet, without exception, they have declared that reason, unaided by transcendental experience, is blind. Those who are called orthodox philosophers accept the Vedic scriptures as recording revealed truths; and they make these scriptures the basis of their reasoning. Śaṁkara, one of the foremost philosophers of India, has this to say concerning the limitations of reason in the investigation of truth:

> 'As the thoughts of man are altogether unfettered, reasoning which disregards the holy texts and rests on individual opinion only has no proper foundation. We see how arguments, which some clever men have excogitated with great pains, are shown, by people still more ingenious to be fallacious, and how the arguments of the latter again are refuted in their turn by other men; so that, on account of the diversity of men's opinions, it is impossible to accept mere reasoning as having a sure foundation.'[1]

[1] Śaṁkara's commentary on the Vedānta Sūtras, trans. George Thibaut, *Sacred Books of the East*, vol. XXXIV, pp. 314–15 (II. i. 11). Explaining the final cause and substance of the universe, Śaṁkara further remarks as follows: 'Perfect knowledge has the characteristic mark of uniformity, because it depends on accomplished actually existing things; for whatever thing is permanently of one and the same nature is acknowledged to be a true or real thing, and knowledge conversant about such is called perfect knowledge, as, for instance, the knowledge embodied in the proposition "Fire is hot". Now, it is clear that in the case of perfect knowledge a mutual conflict of men's opinions is impossible. But that cognitions founded on reasoning do conflict is generally known; for we continually observe that what one logician endeavours to establish as perfect knowledge is demolished by another, who, in his turn, is treated alike by a third. How, therefore, can knowledge, which is founded on reasoning, and whose object is not something permanently uniform, be perfect knowledge? . . . Nor

The systems of Indian philosophy fall into two main divisions according as they do or do not accept the authority of the Vedas. All systems except Buddhism and Jainism are pronounced āstika—meaning, in effect, orthodox; these two, which deny the authority of the great primary scriptures, are nāstika—unorthodox. If, however, we interpret āstika literally—belief in existence after death—then all systems of thought, with the exception of the system attributed to Cārvāka, are āstika.

What Cārvāka really taught, or whether there was a philosopher named Cārvāka at all, it is difficult to know, for we hear of him only through the refutation, by various other schools of thought, of a philosophy of sensualism attributed to him. This philosophy was, in effect, but the simple philosophy of scepticism which appears as a crosscurrent in every age and every country. The name Cārvāka literally means sweet word.

Some Oriental scholars translate nāstika as atheist. But if this meaning of the word is applied to Buddhism and Jainism because they reject an anthropomorphic God, then it should be applied also to many of the orthodox schools. The Sāṁkhya philosophy, for example, denies God as creator, yet it is held to be orthodox.

Curiously, there is no equivalent in Sanskrit for the word atheism. In the Gītā mention is made of those who do not believe in God, the intelligent principle, but these are spoken of merely as of 'deluded intellect'.

As we have intimated, the Vedas, or Śrutis (revealed truths), stand as an absolute authority behind which the orthodox schools cannot go. In this sense their authority might seem to resemble that of the Holy Bible in many periods of Christian thought; but in the words of Dr S. Radhakrishnan, 'The appeal to the Vedas does not involve any reference to an extra-philosophical standard. What is dogma to the ordinary man is experience to the pure in heart.'[1] With the exception of Buddhism and Jainism, all Indian schools of thought regard the

can we collect at a given moment and on a given spot all the logicians of the past, present, and future time, so as to settle (by their agreement) that their opinion regarding some uniform object is to be considered perfect knowledge. The Veda, on the other hand, which is eternal and the source of knowledge, may be allowed to have for its object firmly established things, and hence the perfection of that knowledge which is founded on the Veda cannot be denied by any of the logicians of the past, present, or future. We have thus established the perfection of this our knowledge which reposes on the Upanishads, and as apart from it perfect knowledge is impossible, its disregard would lead to "absence of final release" of the transmigrating souls. Our final position, therefore, is that on the ground of Scripture, and of reasoning subordinate to Scripture, the intelligent Brahman is to be considered the cause and substance of the world.' (*Ibid.*, pp. 316–17.)

[1] *Indian Philosophy*, vol. I, p. 51.

Vedas as recording the transcendental experience of the first mighty seers of India. This experience cannot and should not contradict similar experience in any age or country. Furthermore, it is accessible to all. For these reasons, all Hindus believe that the Vedas are eternal—beginningless and endless—and that in them transcendental experience has had its standard manifestation.

What then of Buddhism and Jainism? Shall we exclude them from the highest expressions of Indian thought? The fact is that they accept the authority of revealed knowledge and transcendental experience, though they deny the authority of the Vedas, particularly of the ritualistic portions, as a result of certain historical circumstances. They were born at a time when the spirit of the Vedas had been lost, when the Hindus held faithfully only to the letter of the law, and when priestcraft reigned supreme. Religion confined itself to sacrificial rites. The yearning to know the truth of the Self, or Brahman in one's own soul, which is attained only by the pure in heart, was absent. Buddha, though he denied the authority of the Vedas, actually impressed their spirit upon his followers by urging them to live the pure life in order to free themselves from the burden of sorrow. And he showed the way by himself attaining nirvāṇa—another name for samādhi, the transcendental state.

Thus the teachings of Buddha do not contradict the spirit of the Vedas but are in entire harmony with it; and the same is true of the teaching of Mahāvīra, founder of Jainism.

From the foregoing it can be readily seen that the Indian philosophy of religion is fundamentally mystic and spiritual. Says Professor M. Hiriyanna:

'. . . Indian philosophy aims beyond Logic. This peculiarity of the view-point is to be ascribed to the fact that philosophy in India did not take its rise in wonder or curiosity as it seems to have done in the West; rather it originated under the pressure of a practical need arising from the presence of moral and physical evil in life. It is the problem of how to remove this evil that troubled the ancient Indians most, and mokṣa in all the systems represents a state in which it is, in one sense or another, taken to have been overcome. Philosophic endeavour was directed primarily to find a remedy for the ills of life, and the consideration of metaphysical questions came in as a matter of course.'[1]

This, then, is central in Indian philosophy—an overmastering sense of the evil of physical existence combined with a search for

[1] *Outlines of Indian Philosophy*, pp. 18 f.

release from pain and sorrow—and by these two things it is distinguished from the philosophies of any other race or country.

We are led here to a consideration of the charge of pessimism brought against Indian philosophy by the West—the charge that it springs, as has been asserted, 'from lassitude and a desire for rest'. This criticism by those who, as is so much done in the West, seek fulfilment through positive, aggressive action, arises from a misunderstanding of the purpose of Indian philosophy. This philosophy is pessimistic if by pessimism is meant acknowledgement of the true nature of life in this world—that it is a strange mingling of good and evil, that on the plane of the senses it yields but a doubtful happiness, and that physical and moral evils continue to the end of our mortal existence. The distinctive characteristic of Indian philosophy lies in the fact, not merely that it is dissatisfied with existing suffering, but that it points out the path towards the attainment of mokṣa, or release, which is a state of unalloyed and infinite bliss.

Philosophers differ, however, with respect to the exact nature of mokṣa; and the differences make up the substance of Hindu thought. These are due in part to varying grades of experience in realizing the transcendental life; and of course they are due above all to the attempt to express the inexpressible.

In one thing, however, the philosophers all agree. That is, that spiritual perfection can be attained here and now. 'Man's aim', says Professor Hiriyanna, 'was no longer represented as the attainment of perfection in a hypothetical hereafter, but as a continual progress towards it within the limits of the present life.'[1] Mokṣa, or the attainment of freedom from the limitations and sufferings of physical life, is the supreme aspiration of all Indian philosophy.[2]

Śaṁkara, speaking of the supreme goal of human life, says: 'A man is born not to desire enjoyments in the world of the senses, but to realize the bliss of jīvanmukti [liberation while living].' And the Upaniṣads over and over again emphasize this truth: 'Blessed is he who attains illumination in this very life; for a man not to do so is his greatest calamity.'[3] But in these same scriptures it is pointed out

[1] *Outlines of Indian Philosophy*, p. 19.

[2] The Pūrva Mīmāṁsā, one of the six philosophical systems of India, is an apparent exception to what I have just said; for it does not speak of mokṣa, or release, but rather teaches work and sacrifices as a means of reaching heaven and realizing the enjoyments thereof. But, though this philosophy does not directly specify mokṣa as the goal of its striving, indirectly it does. For work, as taught by Jaimini, brings purification of the heart, which leads one to mokṣa. If, however, we take Pūrva and Uttara Mīmāṁsā as forming one system of thought, then we may declare that, without exception, Indian philosophies set forth mokṣa as the ultimate goal, and affirm that it may be attained in this life. (Pūrva and Uttara Mīmāṁsā are discussed in detail in Chapters 13 and 14.)

[3] Kena, II. 5.

that if a man fails to attain the supreme goal in this life he can attain it in some other life, for he will be given unlimited opportunities, by rebirths, to reach the goal of perfection.

The failure to attain direct experience of the truth, and consequently of freedom, is due to man's spiritual ignorance, which is all but universal, and which forms the chief cause of sin and suffering. It can be dispelled by direct knowledge of ultimate truth obtained through purification of the heart, and through a constant striving for detachment of the soul from worldly desires. By transcending the limitations of the body, the mind, and the senses, one may enter the superconscious state.

The methods of attaining this highest state of consciousness are hearing about, reasoning about, and meditating upon the ultimate reality. One must first hear about it from the Śruti, or Vedas, and from the lips of a guru, an illumined teacher. Then one must reason about it. Finally comes meditation upon it in order to realize the truth for oneself. Different schools offer different methods of attaining the same goal, but all agree in recommending the practice of yoga, or the exercises prescribed in the art of concentration and meditation.

To tread the path of philosophy is to seek after truth and follow a way of life. Before a man sets out on the quest after truth, he must fulfil certain conditions. Śaṁkara sums them up as follows: First, there must be discrimination between the real and the unreal. This statement means, not that a man must possess complete knowledge of absolute reality, which is attained only after long practice of meditation, but that he must unfailingly subject the nature of things to a rigid analysis by discriminating between what is transitory and what is abiding, or between what is true and what is false. The second condition is detachment from the selfish enjoyments of life. The aspirant must learn that the highest good is realized not through worldly pleasure, but through a continuous search for the infinite, the enduring joy. This ideal of renunciation must be realized by a gradual purification of the seeker's heart and mind. A third condition is that the student must acquire tranquillity of mind, self-control, patience, poise, burning faith in things of the spirit, and self-surrender. These are called the six treasures of life. The thirst for mokṣa, or release, is the fourth condition.[1]

Deliverance from spiritual darkness, entrance upon the path of illumination, comes only through annihilation of the false ego. 'When the ego dies, all troubles cease', says Śrī Rāmakṛṣṇa. Such a condition of being does not imply the loss of one's individuality, but rather the attainment of a greater individuality, for we can lose nothing that is

[1] See Śaṁkara's Commentary on the Brahma Sūtras, Athāto Brahma jijñāsā, I. i. 1.

real. Kālidāsa, the great Hindu poet and dramatist, has beautifully expressed this truth. He says that the ideal of renunciation consists in owning the whole world while disowning one's own self.

What then is the relation of psychology and ethics to Indian religious philosophy? The science of psychology, as Westerners know it, is man's attempt to explain the behaviour of his mind with reference to his body and the stimuli received through his senses. Ethics is the formulation of the science of conduct in relation to society as man faces his multifarious activities as a social being. Are these interpretations of man's ordinary nature and life considered by the philosophies of India?

They are, in a very definite way. As a matter of fact, Indian philosophy and Indian psychology are not merely allied subjects, but the latter is actually an integral part of the former. To the Hindu mind, psychology has its inception in the thinking self and not in the objects of thought. It is not content with merely observing the workings of the mind in the normal planes of consciousness, as is the case with the modern system called behaviourism, but points out how the mind ranges beyond the conscious plane of psychic activity, and how the resulting experience is even more real than experience of the objective world. It differs also from the psychoanalysis of Freud, in that, though it accepts the subconscious mind, it holds that man is capable of controlling its impressions as well as those of his conscious mind, and of attaining to the superconscious state, which no school of Western psychology has yet taken into consideration. By teaching the normal mind methods of restraining its own vagaries, with the aim of gaining supreme mastery over itself, and of ultimately rising above itself, Indian philosophy distinguishes its beliefs from those of all other known systems of philosophy or psychology. The Yoga system of Patañjali deals specifically with the process of mind control.

Ethics also has a role in Indian philosophy. Though not identical with it, ethics is its very foundation. Philosophy seeks by ethics to transcend the mere life of conduct, so that ethics supplies the means for making itself superfluous. Moreover, Hindu ethics not only concerns itself with outer human activity, but extends to the inner life as well. Every teaching is conditioned by the phrase 'in thought, word, and deed'. Ways of achieving right conduct are explicitly revealed—ways which, if followed, will enable one instinctively to live the ethical life. Emphasis is laid upon ultimately transforming the whole being and rising above the injunctions of moral codes. The wise man is not troubled, we read in the Upanisads, by thoughts like these: 'Have I not done right?' 'Have I done wrong?' Bhavabhuti, a Sanskrit poet, says, appropriately: 'An ordinary man is truthful when the words follow the fact. But the saint's words are followed by the fact.'[1] Such is the relation between saintliness and truthfulness.

Indian philosophy is thus not a mere way of thinking but a way of life, a way of light, and a way of truth. To become a philosopher is to become transformed in life, renewed in mind, and baptized in spirit.

[1] *Uttara-Rāmacaritam.*

BOOK I

THE VEDAS AND THE UPANIṢADS

PEACE CHANT

May my speech be one with my mind, and may my mind be one with my speech.
O thou self-luminous Brahman, remove the veil of ignorance from before me, that I may behold thy light.
Do thou reveal to me the spirit of the scriptures.
May the truth of the scriptures be ever present to me.
May I seek day and night to realize what I learn from the sages.
May I speak the truth of Brahman.
May I speak the truth.
May it protect me.
May it protect my teacher.

Om . . . Peace—peace—peace.

Ṛg-Veda

CHAPTER 1

THE VEDAS: GENERAL ASPECTS

The oldest scriptures of India, and the most important, are the Vedas. Orthodox Hindus, who include all schools of Indian thought past and present except Buddhists and Jains, recognize in them the origin of their faith and its highest written authority. Buddhists and Jains reject them, though in varying degree: the Buddhists renouncing them altogether, the Jains acknowledging their spiritual validity but denying that they are in any peculiar sense sacred. Of Jains there are in India today about a million and a quarter; of Buddhists, in India proper, there are virtually none. For the vast majority of modern Hindus, therefore, amongst all their sacred writings, the Vedas are supreme.

This does not, however, suggest the whole story. For the term Vedas, as used by the orthodox, not only names a large body of texts composed in times indefinitely remote, and handed down by generation after generation to our own day, but in another sense stands for nothing less than Divine Truth itself, the inexpressible truth of which the Vedic texts are of necessity but a pale reflection. Regarded in this second aspect, the Vedas are infinite and eternal. They are that perfect knowledge which is God.

Even more than the other scriptures of the world, the Vedas make a special claim to be divine in their origin. The Bible, the Koran, and other revelations of the word of God owe their authority to delivery of the sacred message through an angel, or prophet, or other special messenger from God to certain chosen persons. And these revelations must be accepted on faith. No question is raised as to whether any human being today can verify these revelations in his own experience. The Vedas, on the other hand, are said to be apauruṣeya, which means divine in origin. In fact, in the words of Sāyanācārya, the learned commentator on the Vedas, Yo vedebhyaḥ akhilam jagat nirmame—God created the whole universe out of the knowledge of the Vedas. That is to say, Vedic knowledge existed even before the creation of mankind. The authority of the Vedas does not depend upon anything external. They themselves *are* authority, being the knowledge of God. And, as we shall see later, their truth is verifiable by any spiritual aspirant in transcendental consciousness.

But it is the Vedas in the concrete sense of scriptures with which alone we are henceforth concerned. As such, they are divided into four major parts, and each of these, in turn, is further divided and subdivided—as may be conveniently seen in the following table:

- Ṛk
  - Work
    - Saṁhitās
    - Brāhmaṇas
    - Āraṇyakas
  - Knowledge (Upaniṣads)
- Sāma
  - Work
    - Saṁhitās
    - Brāhmaṇas
    - Āraṇyakas
  - Knowledge (Upaniṣads)
- Yajur
  - Work
    - Saṁhitās
    - Brāhmaṇas
    - Āraṇyakas
  - Knowledge (Upaniṣads)
- Atharva
  - Work
    - Saṁhitās
    - Brāhmaṇas
    - Araṇyakas
  - Knowledge (Upaniṣads)

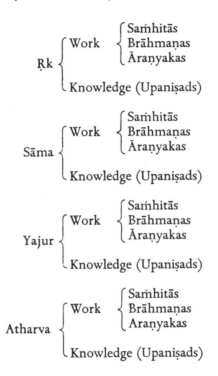

Many questions suggested by this classification we shall pass by for the moment, while we inquire how, in the view of orthodox Hindus, this body of sacred texts came into being. The answer involves certain Hindu beliefs with which, if only in preliminary fashion, we should now become acquainted. To the Hindu, creation is beginningless and endless. That it is beginningless he proves by a simple process of logic. If creation had a beginning, then must the creator also have had a beginning, since until there is a creation there can be no creator; but to admit that the creator had a beginning would be to admit that God had a beginning, since God is not God until he creates—and to think of God as having had a beginning would, to the Hindu, be a manifest absurdity. God, who contains within himself the seed, the material cause, of the universe, first brings forth the universe out of his own being, and then in due time takes it back again to himself. This process of creation and dissolution goes on for ever and ever, for it is as endless as it is beginningless. Eternity is witness, not of one universe only—that, for example, of which we are now a part—but of an infinite succession of universes. The birth, life, and destruction of a universe constitutes a cycle. To say that there was never a first cycle, and will never be a last, is only a way of affirming that the creative function of God is, like himself, eternal.

Further beliefs concern the stuff of which the successive universes are composed. This stuff is simply an immense multitude of beings, some animate, some inanimate. Plants, animals, and men are animate; rocks and stones are inanimate. But all are alike beings. These, by their nature, are involved in a process the final goal of which is their complete absorption into God—in his quiescent, or noncreative, aspect. When an individual being is thus absorbed he is free forever from the cycles of finite existence; but the process leading to this blessed state may be a long one. Not only may a being be born, live, and die, and then be born again, live, and die, indefinitely, within the bounds of a single universe, but he may also be born again and again into an indefinite series of universes. The history of a particular individual, the number of times he experiences rebirth, or reincarnation as it is called, depends entirely upon the quality of his will, upon the moral effort he puts forth. As he rises in moral and spiritual stature he is born into an ever higher plane of existence until at last he returns to the world as man. Birth as a human being is extolled as a sacred birth, not because to be born as man necessarily leads to immediate liberation—far from it—but because the achievement of liberation is possible to man alone.

Against the background of these conceptions the orthodox view of the origin of the Vedas may be quickly sketched. At the very beginning of each cycle, holy seers are born into the world, men who in previous universes have ascended far towards the supreme goal and are therefore especially capable of perceiving divine truth. These blessed saints—ṛṣis, the Hindus call them—meditate on God, and while so meditating discern the everlasting laws of the spirit; and it is the concrete record of these laws, so discerned, that constitutes, in each cycle, the most authoritative or sacred writings. The record of the meditations of the ṛṣis born at the beginning of our own cycle is, then, what we know as the Vedas.

Thus far the account is, to orthodox eyes, literal truth. However, around the origin and early development of the Vedas are clustered many myths and symbols. Some of these we may now glance at—

though in so doing we should realize that the gods of the Hindu, or devas as he calls them, must always be sharply distinguished from God. God is the one supreme being, the uncreated; while the gods, though supernatural, belong (together with many other orders of supernatural beings) among the creatures. Like the Christian angels, they are much nearer to man than to God.

'As smoke and sparks arise from a lighted fire kindled with damp fuel'—runs one account—'even so, Maitreyi, have breathed forth from the Eternal all knowledge and all wisdom—what we know as the Ṛg-Veda,[1] the Yajur Veda, and the rest. They are the breath of the Eternal.'[2] And another, more circumstantial: 'The gods performed a sacrificial rite, meditating on the transcendental being as the sacrifice itself. From out that sacrifice came Ṛk, Sāma, and Yajur.'[3] (The Atharva—see the Table, above—which was probably later than the others, and of minor importance, is not here mentioned.) And another relates, with still more circumstance, how the god Brahmā was once meditating on his creator when there was manifested within the shrine of his heart the eternal word Om—the seed of all knowledge and of all thought. One by one were also manifested the sounds of all the letters, and through these letters there became known unto Brahmā the wisdom of the Vedas. Then in order to spread this knowledge through the world he taught it to his disciples —to Marīci, Atri, Aṅgiras, and others—and these in turn to the world around them. In this fashion did the Vedas become known to all mankind.

By way of accounting for certain subdivisions of the Yajur a story is told[4] which has about it, like so many of the ancient scriptural narratives, a quaint, childlike humour. On a certain occasion the ṛṣis, it seems, planned a conference. 'Whoever fails to attend', they announced, 'will commit a great sin—equal to that of killing a brāhmin.'[5] Now Vaiśampāyana failed to attend, and, as a consequence, the curse of all the other ṛṣis fell upon him. In order to expiate his offence he requested his disciples to practise austerities. One disciple, however, Yājñavalkya by name, remonstrated thus: 'Master, how can you expiate your sin by the austerities of these thy worthless disciples? I am the one amongst them who alone can bring good unto thee by my practices.' At this Vaiśampāyana grew angry, and said: 'How dare you speak thus? I want no such hot-headed,

[1] Ṛk, when joined with Veda, becomes Ṛg, by a regular change of consonant.

[2] Bṛhadāraṇyaka Upaniṣad, II. iv. 10.

[3] Ṛg-Veda, x. 90: Puruṣa Sūkta, 9.

[4] From the Sanskrit quoted in the Introduction to Durgacharan Samkhya-Vedanta Tirtha's Bengali translation of the Īśa Upaniṣad with Śaṁkara's commentary (Calcutta: Kshirode Chandra Majumdar).

[5] A member, that is, of the brāhmin, or priestly, caste.

egotistical disciple as you! Give back what you have learned from me, and be off!'

So the egotist Yājñavalkya spewed from his mouth all that he had learned, and departed. His fellow disciples, unable to endure this insult to their knowledge, assumed the form of tittiri birds and gathered up the lore that had been ejected and taught it to their pupils. Thus it was that the branch of the Yajur called the Black Yajur, or, with reference to the birds, the Taittirīya, came into being.

Now Yājñavalkya, having cast away his knowledge of the Vedas, felt how empty he was, and realized what a very beast a man becomes who is destitute of this wisdom. But where might he find a teacher? Then it occurred to him that the sun-god never separates himself from the Vedas; for in the morning he is adorned with the Ṛg-Veda, at noon with the Yajur Veda, and in the evening with the Sāma Veda. And so, accepting the sun-god as his master, Yājñavalkya prayed to him for knowledge. The sun-god, pleased with the ardour of his new votary, did according to his desire, and the portion of the Vedas which he taught him was henceforth known as the White Yajur. Yājñavalkya then, in his turn, taught this to his disciples.

For the study of the Vedas, according to long tradition, and even according to the Vedas themselves, one must have—as Yājñavalkya had—a master, or guru: 'Approach a teacher', says the Muṇḍaka,[1] 'with humility and with a desire to serve.' Elsewhere we read: 'To many it is not given to hear of the Self. Many, though they hear of it, do not understand it. Wonderful is he who speaks of it; intelligent is he who learns of it. Blessed is he who, taught by a good teacher, is able to understand it.'[2]

The function of the 'good teacher', as Hinduism conceives it, is twofold. He of course explains the scriptures, the spirit as well as the letter; but, what is more important still, he teaches by his life—by his little daily acts, by his most casual words, sometimes even by his silence. Only to be near him, only to serve and obey him in humility and reverence, is to become quickened in spirit; and the purpose of the study of the Vedas is not merely or primarily to inform the intellect, but to purify and enrich the soul:

> Pleasant indeed are the study and teaching of the Vedas!
> He who engages in these things attains to concentration of
> mind,
> And is no longer a slave to his passions;
> Devout, self-controlled, cultivated in spirit,
> He rises to fame and is a blessing to mankind.[3]

[1] I. ii. 12.
[2] Kaṭha, I. ii. 7.
[3] Śatapatha Brāhmaṇa, Mādhyandinī śākhā, XI. v. 7, Swādhyāya praśaṁsā, 1.

We have said that the orthodox Hindu regards the Vedas as his highest written authority. Any subsequent scripture, if he is to regard it as valid, must be in agreement with them: it may expand them, it may develop them, and still be recognized, but it must not contradict them. They are to him, as nearly as any human document can be, the expression of divine truth. At the same time it would be a mistake to suppose that his allegiance to their authority is, in the final analysis, blind and automatic. If he considers them the word of God, it is because he believes their truth to be verifiable, immediately, at any moment, in his own personal experience. If he found on due examination that it was not so verifiable, he would reject it. If he found that any part of it was not so verifiable, he would reject that. In short, he conceives that his faith in the Vedas is as well founded, and on grounds exactly as critical, as is the natural scientist's belief in any physical law. And in this position these very scriptures themselves, he will tell you, uphold him. The real study, they say, is—not study of themselves—but study of that 'by which we realize the unchangeable'. In other words, the real study, in religion, is first-hand experience of God.

The Vedas teach the knowledge of God, and lay down work as a means to that knowledge—the word work here signifying both sacrificial rites and unselfish performance of secular duty. When through work our hearts are purified, we are ripe for divine knowledge. Work and knowledge—these two are the subjects of the Vedas, and name the parts into which (as a Table has already indicated) Rk, Sāma, Yajur, and Atharva are each divided.

The two following chapters will deal, respectively, with the work portion of the Vedas and with the knowledge portion—the latter and much the more important being universally known as the Upaniṣads.

CHAPTER 2

SAṀHITĀS, BRĀHMAṆAS, ĀRAṆYAKAS

The work portion of the Vedas, immensely important though it has been to the concrete practice of religion in India, has less interest for us today than the knowledge portion. Still, we must not fail to obtain some further idea of it, and especially of the first of its three divisions—the Saṁhitās.

Saṁhitās

The Saṁhitās are collections of mantras, or hymns, most of which sing the praises of one or another personal god. Sometimes the god is conceived as little more than a magnified man. In one hymn, for example, Indra, the god of rain, has a body clad in golden armour, is very strong, and descends to earth, where he lives and eats with his votaries, fights and overcomes their enemies the demons, and establishes his dominion. Similarly Varuṇa, in another hymn, is described as a mere nature god, presiding in anthropomorphic form over air and water. But, again, the god—even at times the same god that was just now so much a man—becomes nothing less than the Supreme Being, omniscient, omnipresent, omnipotent—and that within which the visible world is contained. Thus Varuṇa:

Wherever two together plot, and deem they are alone,
King Varuṇa is there, a third, and all their schemes are known.
This earth is his, to him belong these vast and boundless skies;
Both seas within him rest, and yet in that small pool he lies.
Whoever far beyond the sky should think his way to wing,
He could not there elude the grasp of Varuṇa the king.
His spies descending from the skies glide all this world around;
Their thousand eyes all-scanning sweep to earth's remotest bound.
Whate'er exists in heaven and earth, whate'er beyond the skies,
Before the eyes of Varuṇa, the king, unfolded lies.
The ceaseless winkings all he counts of every mortal's eyes:
He wields this universal frame, as gamester throws his dice.[1]

[1] John Muir (trans.); Atharva Veda, iv. 16. 1–5.

In Varuṇa, in his more exalted manifestation, dwells Ṛta—conceived as the principle of universal law and order, physical and spiritual. Existing forever in Varuṇa, in complete perfection, this principle is but palely reflected in the created world. Yet it is because of it that there exists a moral order, because of it that the sun, moon, and stars, morning and evening, day and night, keep their appointed times. 'The dawn follows the path of Ṛta, the right path—as if knowing it before. Never does she lose her way. The sun follows the path of Ṛta.'[1]

Perhaps highest in conception of the gods with concrete names is Hiraṇyagarbha:

'Before the universe appeared, there first appeared Hiraṇyagarbha. He, being manifest, became the one lord of the manifested universe. Out of himself came the invisible world, out of himself came the sky and this earth. Unto him whose being is unknown and unknowable, whose desire it was that this universe be created, who is the source of happiness—unto him we offer our sacrifice! Unto him who is the purifier of our hearts, who is the giver of strength, whose command all beings, together with the gods, obey, whose shadow is immortality as well as mortality, whose being is unknown and unknowable, whose desire it was that this universe be created, who is the source of happiness—unto him we offer our sacrifice!'[2]

In the following famous hymn, the Puruṣa Sūkta, the Supreme Being, or God, is represented as at once concrete ('infinite heads', 'unnumbered eyes') and in the highest degree abstract—'beyond all predicates'. He both is and is not the created universe, for while the created universe is a part of his being it is not the whole of it:

'The Universal Being has infinite heads, unnumbered eyes, and unnumbered feet. Enveloping the universe on every side, he exists transcending it. All this is he—what has been and what shall be. He is the lord of immortality. Though he has become all this, in reality he is not all this. For verily is he transcendental. The whole series of universes—past, present, and future—express his glory and power; but he transcends his own glory. All beings of the universe form, as it were, a fraction of his being; the rest of it is self-luminous, and unchangeable. He who is beyond all predicates exists as the relative universe. That part of him which is the relative universe appears as sentient and insentient beings. From a part of him was born the body of the universe, and out of this body were born the gods, the earth, and men.'[3]

[1] Ṛg-Veda, i. 24. [2] *Ibid.*, x. 121. 1–2. [3] *Ibid.*, x. 90. 1–5.

In the passage, it may be observed in passing, there is a definite rejection of pantheism: 'Though he has become all this, in reality he is not all this.' The words are characteristic of all Indian thought, and will be echoed and re-echoed in later pages of this book. There is, properly speaking, whatever appearances may sometimes suggest to the contrary, no pantheism in India. The Hindu sees God as the ultimate energy in and behind all creation, but never, either in ancient or in modern times, as identical with it.

It is a far cry from the rain-god Indra, with his golden armour, to a Universal Being who envelops and transcends the world; but a step still remained to be taken, and this also the Saṁhitās took. Indra and the Universal Being had one thing in common: they were both personal gods. It is true that the Universal Being was said to be 'beyond all predicates', but also, in almost the same breath, he was said to possess heads, and eyes, and feet, and to transcend 'his own glory'.

'Who has seen the first-born, when he that had no bones bore him that has bones? Where is the life, the blood, the self of the universe? Who went to ask of any who knew?'[1] Thus from the conception of God as a personal being the Vedic seers passed on to almost their final conception of him as utterly impersonal, so remote indeed from resemblance to anything human that no longer will they refer to him as 'he' or 'him', but only as TAD EKAṀ—in English, THAT. It is under this designation that he appears in the hymn of creation, called the Nāsadīya hymn:

> Existence was not, nor its opposite,
> Nor earth, nor heaven's blue vault, nor aught beyond.
> The subtle elements that are the veil
> Of this so insubstantial world, where then
> Might they find out a place? by whom be known?
> The deep abyss of waters—where was that?
> Death was not yet, nor deathlessness; the day
> Was night, night day, for neither day nor night
> Had come to birth. Then THAT, the primal font
> Of life—breathless—to its own maya joined—
> Brooded eternally. Itself beside,
> In the wide universe there nothing was.
> In the beginning gloom—gloom hidden in gloom!
> From its cause undistinguished stood the world:
> But lo, thereafter, from its darkling state—
> Yet undistinguished from its cause—it rose,
> By the pure will of THAT made manifest.

[1] Ṛg-Veda, i. 4. 164. Quoted by S. Radhakrishnan, *Indian Philosophy*, vol. I, p. 93 (London, Allen & Unwin, 1923).

Whence came this will? From out a seed it came
Asleep within the heart of THAT—the seed
Of vanished worlds that have in order wheeled
Their silent courses from eternity:
The manifest in the unmanifest they found—
The sages, searching deep within themselves. . . .
Ah, what are words, and what all mortal thought!
Who is there truly knows, and who can say,
Whence this unfathomed world, and from what cause?
Nay, even the gods were not! Who, then, can know?
The source from which this universe hath sprung,
That source, and that alone, which bears it up—
None else: THAT, THAT alone, lord of the worlds,
In its own self contained, immaculate
As are the heavens, above, THAT alone knows
The truth of what itself hath made—none else![1]

This famous hymn has provided the basis for a great deal of philosophic speculation. For in it God is represented (it may be observed) as both the material and the efficient cause of the universe—both that out of which it was made, and that by which it was made. In it also is that extraordinary conception of the universe, alluded to in the preceding chapter, as continually alternating between the phase of expression and the phase of potentiality: birth, existence, destruction—then a state of quiescence—then again birth, existence, destruction; and so on forever.

The preceding brief survey of the varying conceptions of God in the Saṁhitās quite naturally raises two questions. The first is this: Why is it that now one god, now another, is lifted to the loftiest position and celebrated as the supreme divinity? Professor Max Müller has observed this phenomenon, and named it henotheism, but has done little to fathom its mystery. Its true explanation is to be found in the hymns themselves; 'and it is a grand explanation,' declares Swami Vivekananda, 'one that has given the theme to all subsequent thought in India and one that will be the theme of the whole world of religions: Ekaṁ sat viprā bahudhā vadanti[2]—"That which exists is One: sages call it by various names".'[3]

The subject is worth pausing with, for in the quoted words lies the secret not only of an aspect of the Vedic hymns but also—as Swami Vivekananda suggests—of an aspect of the religious life of India throughout her long history. Casual visitors to this ancient land

[1] Ṛg-Veda, x. 129. 1–7. Swami Prabhavananda and Frederick Manchester (trans.), *Voice of India*, vol. III, no. 1.

[2] *Ibid.*, i. 164.

[3] *Complete Works of Swami Vivekananda*, vol. I, p. 347.

carry away with them the impression of an elaborate polytheism. True it is that India has always had many gods—but in appearance only. In reality she has had but one god, though with prodigal inventiveness she has called him 'by various names'. Indra, Varuṇa, Hiraṇyagarbha—Rāma, Kṛṣṇa, Śiva: What does it matter? Whichever of these or of many others the Hindu chooses for his adoration, that one becomes for him God himself, in whom exist all things, including, for the time being, all other gods. It is because India has been so permeated with the spirit of Ekaṁ sat viprā bahudhā vadanti that she has known relatively little of religious fanaticism, of religious persecution, of religious wars. Characteristically she has sought the truth in every faith—even in faiths not her own.

But there was a second question: Why is it that in the Vedic hymns we find elementary ideas of God as well as the most advanced? To the Western scholar there is here no mystery; for he is accustomed to think of all things in terms of evolution, as he conceives evolution, and in the simpler anthropomorphic notions he sees the first stages of a growth which slowly ripens to abstraction. But not so the orthodox Hindu. What he sees in the graduated scale of Vedic conceptions is a beneficent correspondence to varied stages of religious attainment. Some men are but barbarians in spiritual things; others are seers and sages. The Vedas (and this, say the orthodox, was a clear purpose of the exalted ṛṣis) minister to all according to their needs. Some they teach to fly; some they must first teach to walk. To those at a low stage they offer polytheism, even at times materialism; to those at a higher stage monotheism; and to those at the top of the scale a notion of God so utterly impersonal, so devoid of anything describable in human terms, as to be suited only to the greatest saints, and to these only in their most strenuous moments.

For it would appear, in general, that even the greatest of Hindu saints have found the conception of God as abstract reality too rarefied for constant use. Occasionally they rise to it, but not for long. Like more ordinary mortals they too have yearned for a notion of divinity close to their minds and hearts, something they could readily love, and meditate upon, and worship.

In the contrasting spiritual levels of the Vedic hymns, as interpreted by the orthodox, we touch on a general aspect of Indian thought to which we must often return: its variety and flexibility, despite its extraordinary central oneness—its remarkable genius for adaptation.

Brāhmanas

The Brāhmaṇas, in comparison with the Saṁhitās, are concerned with practical, everyday things—with the details of sacrificial rites and with specific duties and rules of conduct.

Brāhmaṇāḥ vividiṣanti yajñena dānena—The brāhmins desire to know, with the sacrifices and charity as the means. That is, when the heart becomes purified by the performance of sacrifices and charity, there arises the knowledge of Brahman. Thus is acknowledged the need for the performance of sacrifices and for the ceremonials and rites of religion. But it is true that at times undue importance was laid on these things, as well as on the mere chanting of the words of the Vedas, so much so that the sacrifices themselves often took the place of a living religion—a circumstance that occurs in the development of all religious institutions.

Under such conditions, prayer and supplication before the object of worship becomes unnecessary; for by the performance of elaborate and fixed sacrifices the gods may be forced to grant one's desires. Professor Das Gupta believes that in these sacrificial rites is to be found the germ of the law of karma (which Manu later systematized philosophically): 'Thou canst not gather what thou dost not sow. As thou dost sow, so wilt thou reap.'[1]

This hardening of the institutional part of religion exalted in time the power of the priests; and it was in opposition to this externalizing and crystallizing of what should have remained living symbols of truths behind appearances, and also in opposition to the tyranny of a rising priesthood, that Buddha rose in revolt. The Bhagavad-Gītā had already condemned the tendency to attribute undue importance to ritualistic sacrifices.

The duties and rules of conduct prescribed by the Brāhmaṇas are largely those common to all religious creeds. Self-control is emphasized, and love, and kindness; theft, murder, and adultery are forbidden. We are all deep in debt, declare the Brāhmaṇas, the most important of our obligations being those to the gods, to the seers, to the spirits of the dead, to living men, and to animals. Our debt to the gods we must pay with sacrifices; to the seers with feelings of admiration and devotion; to departed spirits with prayers in their behalf; to living men with love and kindness; to animals with food and drink—and to all of these, whenever we partake of nourishment, we must tender a portion to the accompaniment of fitting prayers.

By the due discharge of these our moral debts we achieve no merit, but if we neglect them we become unworthy of our privileged status as human beings. Our duties must be performed, moreover, with no thought of self or selfish ends, but simply because they are, for a righteous man, duties—and because they purify the heart.

[1] Cf. 'Whatsoever a man soweth, that shall he also reap' (Gal. vi. 7).

Āraṇyakas

The Āraṇyakas, or forest treatises, need detain us but a moment. They may most simply be regarded as a supplement to the Brāhmaṇas—and a corrective. Like the Brāhmaṇas, they deal much in rites and ceremonies, but unlike the Brāhmaṇas they do not rest in them. They are vividly aware that not in rites and ceremonies, but in the truths they stand for, lies their real importance; and so from the fruit or flesh of the sacrifice they pass to its spiritual interpretation.

In so doing, in so occupying themselves less with the outward symbol than with the inner reality, they come close to the chief and central glory of all the Vedas—the universally admired Upaniṣads.

Before we come to deal with the Upaniṣads, a few remarks regarding the division of each of the Vedas seem pertinent. Professor Paul Deussen has rightly declared that this division into Saṁhitās, Brāhmaṇas, Āraṇyakas, and lastly Upaniṣads is based on the principle of dividing life into āśramas, or stages. According to Vedic teachings, man's life is divided into four stages. First is the brahmacarya, or student life, when a boy lives with his teacher and receives both religious and secular instruction. The youth is trained in self-control and acquires such virtues as chastity, truthfulness, faith, and self-surrender. The next stage is gārhasthya, or married life. The chief injunction for this stage is to practise the ritualistic sacrifices as explained in the Brāhmaṇas. At the stage of vāṇaprastha, or retirement, a man is no longer required to adhere to ritualism, but is instructed to follow the Āraṇyakas and engage in symbolic meditation. Finally he enters upon the life of renunciation, in which he is bound neither by work nor by desire, but is dedicated wholly to acquiring knowledge of Brahman.

Thus the general plan of life as taught in the Vedas is, successively, student life, married life, the life of retirement, and the life of renunciation. Each of these periods of a man's mortal existence has its special duties and observances, though it is also true that through a special Vedic declaration a person may enter immediately into the life of renunciation, and not pass through the intermediate stages of probation.

Through the institution of monasticism a man may begin early the life of renunciation. When one enters a monastery, one passes through a Vedic ritual, meanwhile meditating upon the truths of the Upaniṣads. According to Vedic teaching, monastic life is the highest stage a man may attain. Modern India retains this idea, and there are not wanting today men highly trained in Western science and literature who are willing to assume monastic vows. Thus the influence of the Vedas has been perpetuated through the ages.

Parenthetically it may be said that the daily life and conduct of the people of India even today are guided by the injunctions of the Vedas. This is particularly true of the ceremonies connected with birth, marriage and death. In the words of Professor S. N. Das Gupta, 'The laws which regulate the social, legal, domestic and religious customs and rites of the Hindus even to the present day are said to be but mere systematized memories of old Vedic teachings, and are held to be obligatory on their authority.' Every brāhmin repeats daily the Vedic prayer called the Gāyatrī mantra, which is a verse from the Ṛg-Veda. It runs as follows:

Om bhur bhuvaḥ swaḥ tat savitur vareṇyam, bhargo devasya dhīmahi, dhiyo yo naḥ pracodayāt, Om. (May we meditate on the effulgent Light [or power] of him who is worshipful, and who has given birth to all worlds. May he direct the rays of our intelligence towards the path of good.)

CHAPTER 3

UPANIṢADS

Preliminary Considerations

The Sanskrit title Upaniṣads is the plural of Upaniṣad, which is in itself a very interesting word. Literally, it means sitting near devotedly, and so brings concretely to mind an earnest disciple learning from his guru, his spiritual master. It also means secret teaching—secret, no doubt, because a teaching vouchsafed only to those who are spiritually ready to receive it and profit by it. Still another interpretation of the word is sponsored by the great commentator Śaṁkara: knowledge of God. In this sense it points to the central subject of that portion of the Vedas which it has named. It is this portion, the so-called knowledge portion, that we are now to examine.

Since they brought to a close each of the four Vedas, the Upaniṣads came to be spoken of often as the Vedānta—the anta or end of the Vedas. The word anta, like the related *end* (Sanskrit and English belonging to the same family of languages), has, in addition to its literal meaning, the figurative meaning of goal or purpose. Thus it is that when a modern Hindu speaks of the Vedānta he may have both senses more or less in mind, the scriptures referred to being for him the last part of the Vedas and at the same time their ultimate reason for existence, their perfect culmination—in a word, their highest wisdom.

How many Upaniṣads once existed is unknown. One hundred and eight have been preserved, these ranging in length from a few hundred to many thousands of words, some in prose, some in verse, some part one, part the other. In style and manner they vary widely, often within the same Upaniṣad, being now simply and concretely narrative, now subtly and abstractly expository, often assuming, in either case, a dialogue form. Their tone too fluctuates, the characteristic seriousness and elevation finding occasional relief in homely humour. Who wrote them, no one knows, nor, with any accuracy, when they were written. The ṛṣis (sages) whose insight they embody remain wholly in the background, impersonal as the truth they stood for, their individual lives lost forever, and even their names—

In the dark backward and abysm of time.

Of the one hundred and eight extant Upaniṣads sixteen were recognized by Śaṁkara as authentic and authoritative. In his commentary on the Vedānta Aphorisms he included quotations from six. On the other ten he wrote elaborate commentaries. It is these ten which, partly on account of their intrinsic importance, but mainly no doubt because of Śaṁkara's commentaries, have come to be regarded as the principal Upaniṣads. Together they constitute, and will probably always constitute, the primary object of attention for all who would know the Hindu religion. Following are their names: Īśa, Kena, Kaṭha, Praśna, Muṇḍaka, Māṇḍūkya, Chāndogya, Bṛhadāraṇyaka, Aitareya, and Taittirīya.

These will be our main concern in the rest of this chapter. But before we begin a study of their ideas, we should note carefully certain characteristics, thus far unmentioned, of the Upaniṣads as a whole.

One of these is their essential homogeneity. Many apparently differing conceptions are to be found in them, but these are, roughly speaking, to be found in all of them, not distributed, one in one Upaniṣad, another in another. It is true that one Upaniṣad may emphasize certain ideas, or a certain view, more than the rest, or may specialize as it were in a particular topic; but such distinctions often seem purely accidental, and are never important. The partitions between the Upaniṣads might therefore, for all practical purposes, be completely done away with, the whole hundred and eight being reduced to one. Accordingly, in our own brief analysis of the ten chief Upaniṣads, none will receive separate scrutiny.

Another and more important characteristic arises from the fact that the Upaniṣads are the work of saints and seers. Their authors were concerned with reporting insights which came to them in thought or vision, not with making these insights superficially coherent. They were not builders of systems but recorders of experience. We must be prepared, therefore, for apparent inconsistency, for obliviousness to one conception through temporary absorption in another. Nowhere must we expect to find the whole truth gathered together once for all in easy, triumphant, conscious formulation.

Still another characteristic of the Upaniṣads has to do with their form. Never were ideas set down—an expositor might suspect—with less regard for his convenience. Nowhere is there a logical beginning, nowhere a logical end. Such basic order, therefore, as appears in the following summary of their thought is an order which is imposed upon them, not discovered in them. Furthermore, attention at all points is not upon parts, clearly recognized as parts, but upon wholes —upon brief, comprehensive, unanalysed statement, it may be, or upon such particular elements as round out, when taken together, a momentary conception. Accordingly, the reader must be prepared to find, in passages adduced to illustrate a given detail, not only the expected matter, but often other matter having no immediate connection. Sometimes, moreover, for the same reason, an outstanding passage must more than once make its appearance.

Brahman

Like all mortals, before and since, the ṛṣis looked out upon a world in motion—wind and wave, waxing and waning moon, growth and decay, birth and death. But was that all there was? Was there nothing that stayed the same, and could therefore be felt as real—in contrast with the things that changed? Yes, answered the ṛṣis, there was something; and they called it Brahman—God.

Still if Brahman was conceived as the permanent, the enduring, that was evidently because of the existence, in some sense, of the transient. On the one hand there was Brahman; on the other hand there was the universe. What was the relation between them?

To this question the Upaniṣads give what may appear to be three separate answers.

Often they speak of Brahman *and* the universe: two things, not one, and both possessed of a permanent reality. Not that the two are really separate, however, and unrelated: distinctly not. The connection between them is expressed in a great variety of ways. Sometimes they are referred to as soul and body, Brahman being the soul, the universe the body—Brahman the indwelling life, light, force, energy; the universe that in which Brahman resides. But this is an image which must be interpreted in the light of other images—as, for example, that in which Brahman is clay, the universe individual vessels into which clay has been moulded. The universe, in this view, is of the same ultimate substance as Brahman, though Brahman is and remains distinct from the vessels into which some of it has been shaped. In the following illustrative passages many other images will be met with—the language of the Upaniṣads is often richly inventive; but what is to be especially observed is that in each of them the seer has before his mind a duality—Brahman on the one hand, the universe on the other—and that this duality persists.

'In the heart of all things, of whatever there is in the universe, dwells the Lord.'[1]

[1] Īśa, 1.

'This is the truth of Brahman in relation to nature: whether in the flash of the lightning, or in the wink of the eyes, the power that is shown is the power of Brahman.'[1]

'This is the truth of Brahman in relation to men: in the motions of the mind, the power that is shown is the power of Brahman.'[2]

'The Imperishable is the Real. As sparks innumerable fly upward from a blazing fire, so from the depths of the Imperishable arise all things. To the depths of the Imperishable they again descend.

'Self-luminous is that Being, and formless. He dwells within all and without all. He is unborn, pure, greater than the greatest, without breath, without mind.

'From him are born breath, mind, the organs of sense, ether, air, fire, water, and the earth, and he binds all these together.

'Heaven is his head, the sun and moon his eyes, the four quarters his ears, the revealed scriptures his voice, the air his breath, the universe his heart. From his feet came the earth. He is the innermost Self of all.'[3]

'Self-luminous is Brahman, ever present in the hearts of all. He is the refuge of all, he is the supreme goal. In him exists all that moves and breathes. In him exists all that is. He is both that which is gross and that which is subtle. Adorable is he. Beyond the ken of the senses is he. Supreme is he. Attain thou him!

'He, the self-luminous, subtler than the subtlest, in whom exist all the worlds and all those that live therein—he is the imperishable Brahman. He is the principle of life. He is speech, and he is mind. He is real. He is immortal. Attain him, O my friend, the one goal to be attained!'[4]

In the following passages again the duality has been resolved by identifying Brahman with the universe—'yet is he still the same'.

Thou art the fire,
Thou art the sun,
Thou art the air,
Thou art the moon,
Thou art the starry firmament,
Thou art Brahman Supreme:
Thou art the waters—thou,
The creator of all!

[1] Kena, IV. 4.
[2] *Ibid.*, 5.
[3] Muṇḍaka, II. i. 1–4.
[4] *Ibid.*, ii. 1–2.

Thou art woman, thou art man,
Thou art the youth, thou art the maiden,
Thou art the old man tottering with his staff;
Thou facest everywhere.

Thou art the dark butterfly,
Thou art the green parrot with red eyes,
Thou art the thunder cloud, the seasons, the seas.
Without beginning art thou,
Beyond time, beyond space.
Thou art he from whom sprang
The three worlds.[1]

Filled with Brahman are the things we see;
Filled with Brahman are the things we see not;
From out of Brahman floweth all that is;
From Brahman all—yet is he still the same.[2]

Let us note in passing the relation of these last lines to the question, already touched upon, of pantheism in India. If the universe emanated from Brahman, then clearly he—or rather some portion of him—*is* the universe; and to that extent the idea is pantheistic. But observe that despite this emanation Brahman 'is still the same'—in which case it is evident, whatever else may be true, that the universe and Brahman are not identical; and it is precisely the identity of the two that the West understands by pantheism.[3]

It was on such passages as we have just been reading that the great commentator Rāmānuja, as we shall see later, based his interpretation of the Upaniṣads, and consequently his own religious philosophy.

According to a second conception, for which there is ample apparent support in the text of the Upaniṣads, there is no longer question of Brahman *and* the universe; there is only Brahman. Brahman is completely transcendent—if such an expression can be used when there is no longer anything to transcend.

'This is Brahman, without cause and without effect, without anything inside or outside.'

In the course of his teaching, the sage Yājñavalkya says:

[1] Śvetāśvatara, IV. 2–4.
[2] Peace chant in the Upaniṣads of the White Yajur Veda.
[3] Pantheism, says Webster, is 'the doctrine that the universe, taken or conceived of as a whole, is God; the doctrine that there is no God but the combined forces and laws which are manifested in the existing universe'.

'My beloved, let nothing I have said confuse you. But meditate well the truth that I have spoken.

'As long as there is duality, one sees *the other*, one hears *the other*, one smells *the other*, one speaks to *the other*, one thinks of *the other*, one knows *the other*; but when for the illumined soul the all is dissolved in the Self, who is there to be seen by whom, who is there to be smelt by whom, who is there to be heard by whom, who is there to be spoken to by whom, who is there to be thought of by whom, who is there to be known by whom? Ah, Maitreyi, my beloved, the Intelligence which reveals all—by what shall it be revealed? By whom shall the Knower be known? The Self is described as *not this, not that*. It is incomprehensible, for it cannot be comprehended; undecaying, for it never decays; unattached, for it never attaches itself; unbound, for it is never bound. By whom, O my beloved, shall the Knower be known?'[1]

In a view in which Brahman is 'without effect', or in which Brahman is assumed but there is declared to be no duality, there is manifestly no provision for a universe. In other passages of similar purport, of which the following is an example, the figure of clay is used—and the many forms it takes from the hand of the potter:

'In words or speech alone the modification originates and exists. In reality there is no such thing as modification. It is merely a name, and the clay alone is real.'[2]

So the universe of name and form is in name and form alone, for Brahman is the only reality. On this point the Muṇḍaka Upaniṣad speaks thus:

'As rivers flow into the sea and in so doing lose name and form, even so the wise man, freed from name and form, attains the Supreme Being, the Self-luminous, the Infinite.'[3]

It was from such sayings as these that the greatest of Hindu commentators, Śaṁkara, drew the philosophy for which he is known. This, like that of Rāmānuja, we shall examine later.

Still a third conception of Brahman is hinted in the Upaniṣads. No affirmation whatever regarding Brahman, the ṛṣis sometimes felt, can be made. He escapes all definition, all description.

'Brahman is he whom speech cannot express, and from whom the mind, unable to reach him, comes away baffled.'[4]

[1] Bṛhadāraṇyaka, IV. v. 14–15. [2] Chāndogya, VI. i. 5.
[3] Muṇḍaka, III. ii. 8. [4] Taittirīya, II. 4.

'That which cannot be expressed in words but by which the tongue speaks—know that to be Brahman. Brahman is not the being who is worshipped of men.

'That which is not comprehended by the mind but by which the mind comprehends—know that to be Brahman. Brahman is not the being who is worshipped of men.

'That which is not seen by the eye but by which the eye sees—know that to be Brahman. Brahman is not the being who is worshipped of men.

'That which is not heard by the ear but by which the ear hears—know that to be Brahman. Brahman is not the being who is worshipped of men.

'That which is not drawn by the breath but by which the breath is drawn—know that to be Brahman. Brahman is not the being who is worshipped of men.'[1]

And again, in a passage preserved only in Śaṁkara's commentary:

'"Sir," said a pupil to his master, "teach me the nature of Brahman." The master did not reply. When a second and a third time he was importuned, he answered: "I teach you indeed, but you do not follow. His name is silence."'

This last paradoxical view of Brahman seems the more worth noting because of the possibility that it too, like the others we have defined, had an important place in later Hindu philosophy—perhaps indeed a more important place than either of the other two. For who can say whether the apparent agnosticism of Buddha, often miscalled atheism, his refusal to make any affirmation whatever regarding Brahman, or God, may not have come from his attention to such passages as we have just quoted? For nobody doubts that Buddha made the most thorough study of the ancient scriptures.

Three views of Brahman, then, to sum up, all have a basis in the text of the Upaniṣads, the first two of which, primarily associated respectively with Rāmānuja and Śaṁkara, have for centuries divided the allegiance of orthodox saints and scholars. Must they continue to do so? Is there no means by which they can be reconciled?

None, it is clear, if reconciliation is to depend upon a discovery of identity between passages which on a natural interpretation are plainly dissimilar in meaning. That the relation of Brahman to the universe is variously represented in the Upaniṣads there can be no manner of doubt; and if a student is forced to make a choice between one formulation and another, then he will naturally lean to that one

[1] Kena, I. 5–9.

which seems to him the best supported and the least productive of difficulties. But is he forced to choose? May not each of the three principal interpretations be correct—and at the same time, taken by itself, incomplete?

Such a view tends to seem natural and plausible the more one comes to realize a general characteristic of the Upaniṣads which has already been mentioned. They are not calculated constructions of logic but spontaneous records of mystic experience, and mystic or transcendental experience is not a static thing but a process. With one stage of this experience there corresponds one view of reality, with another stage another view, and the truth is that each of the three views we have encountered can be explained as a simple reflection of a particular stage of mystic experience. This will be clearer on closer analysis.

The primary step towards mystic experience is the negation or denial of all external things. Brahman (or Ātman) is neither 'this' nor 'that'—neti neti Ātmā. As the sages became absorbed in meditation, as they rose above the plane of physical perception, the universe of finite objects and the universe of ideas were both obliterated from their consciousness. 'Who is there to be seen by whom, who is there to be smelt by whom, who is there to be heard by whom, who is there to be spoken to by whom, who is there to be thought of by whom, who is there to be known by whom?'[1] In that ineffably exalted state, time and space and causation, which are the conditions of objective experience, entirely cease to exist. Here there is no thought, here there is no theory. What now is the relation between Brahman and the universe? . . . But what Brahman? But what universe? Śāntoyam Ātmā—His name is silence.

Thus may we account, in terms of inexpressible experience, for that view or no view which amounts, in finite formula, to something like agnosticism.

Let us follow further the mystic cycle. On his return from the peak of unitary consciousness, the sage, now enlightened with regard to the ultimate nature of reality, may find himself either in the normal state of consciousness or in bhāvamukha, an intermediate state in which his consciousness is both normal and transcendental.

If he is in the normal state, he will clearly perceive finite objects, but—the memory of the transcendental vision of Reality being present in his consciousness—the finite mist that veils the Infinite dissolves before his eyes as fast as it appears. The clay vessels—to revert to the familiar figure—are seen to be all of one substance, what makes them apparently separate being but name and form. Name and form, which give us the appearance of a finite universe, are

[1] Bṛhadāraṇyaka, IV. v. 15.

realized as appearance only. If then the sage, while in such a state, is moved to give an account of his experience, he will depict God as the only reality and the world as māyā, an appearance.

If, on the other hand, as he descends from the height of meditation, he finds himself in bhāvamukha, he will again perceive what we call finite objects, being partly in a normal state of consciousness; but since the transcendental vision is still also present, with its all-enveloping unity, he will be vividly aware that in reality they emanate from God and share in his being. Giving expression to this experience, he will supply the basis for the first view to which attention has been drawn.

All three views, then, are actually present in the Upaniṣads. On this point there need be no controversy. All three views are true—for each corresponds with and exactly expresses a typical stage of transcendental experience. As to which is the highest, the truest truth, probably no mystic would doubt, since that for him must be the one which best interprets the culmination of his vision.

Śrī Rāmakṛṣṇa from his own personal experience of Brahman described the different stages of perception of God:

'When one attains samādhi [transcendental consciousness] then only comes to him the knowledge of Brahman. Then only does he attain the vision of God. In that ecstatic realization all thoughts cease. One becomes perfectly silent. There is no power of speech left by which to express Brahman.'[1]

'The jñāni, or follower of the path of knowledge, analyses the universe of the senses, saying, "Brahman is not this, not that", and gives up worldliness. Thus does he attain to knowledge of Brahman. He is like the man who, climbing a stairway, leaves each step behind, one after another, and so reaches the roof. But the vijñāni, who gains an intimate knowledge of Brahman, has his consciousness further extended. He knows that roof and steps are all of the same substance. First he realizes, "All is not, God is." Next he realizes, "All is God."

'Few can stay long on the roof. Those who reach samādhi and attain Brahman soon return to the normal plane of consciousness, and then they realize that he has become everything. They then see God in the heart of all.'[2]

Ātman

If the ṛṣis, looking outward, saw a world in motion, so also when they looked within. Within themselves, also, they found incessant change—sensations, emotions, images, thoughts, fancies—fancies, thoughts, images, emotions, sensations—forever succeeding one

[1] *Śrī Śrī Rāmakṛṣṇa Kathāmṛta*, vol. III, pp. 9–10. [2] *Ibid.*, 11, 12.

another, like restless waves upon a shoreless sea. But was that all there was? Did nothing midst all this ceaseless phantasmagoria stay the same? Again the searching question, as before in relation to the external world; again the answer of confident affirmation. Yes, somewhere within or behind the tumult, apart from it, superior to it, there was, the ṛṣis said, a silent and constant witness. This they called the Ātman, or Self.

The Ātman exists equally, they said, in all beings, inanimate as well as animate, rocks and stones and trees as well as birds and beasts and men. 'At the heart of all—whatever there is in the universe—abides the Self.'[1] Beings differ enormously, however, in the degree to which the Ātman, present in all, has come to be realized—to be known, in other words, for what it really is. At the bottom of a vast scale are inanimate objects; at the top (and this is his most sacred privilege) is man. In all beings, at whatever point in the scale they may be, a spiritual process goes on:

'He who is aware how that the Self gradually unfolds within him obtains for himself a greater development. Herbs and trees and animals he sees, and he knows that in them too the Self is gradually revealed. For in herbs and trees there is only sap, but in animals there is mind. Among animals, moreover, it can be seen that the Self is manifested little by little, for in some of them thought is present as well as sap, but in others there is sap only. And in man, especially the Self by degrees unfolds itself, for he of all beings is most endowed with consciousness. He says what he has known, he sees what he has known, he knows what is to happen tomorrow, he knows the gross and the subtle. In his mortality he desires the immortal. Thus is he endowed. In other animate beings understanding goes no further than hunger and thirst: they do not say what they have known, nor do they see what they have known. They do not know what is to happen tomorrow, nor do they know the gross and the subtle. To a certain point they go—but they go no further.'[2]

Here, plainly enough, there is a theory of evolution, though a theory very different from that now current in the West. According to the Western conception only animate things evolve, and in these the development implies radical changes in the organism as a whole. Nowhere within the organism is there a permanent element standing apart from the change. According to the Upaniṣads, on the other hand, all creation evolves, inanimate as well as animate, and the development in which alone they are interested is interpreted not as a process of radical change but rather as a gradual uncovering or

[1] Īśa, 1.

[2] Aitareya Āraṇyaka, II. ii. 1–5.

bringing to light of a quintessence originally present and incapable of modification. Here, as everywhere else, Indian philosophy holds fast to an immutable element at the very heart of the flux.

To uncover the Ātman, to come to know it for what it really is, is to see that it is separate and distinct from its dwelling place; and the individual being in which the perception of this distinctness is perfect —and this can only be a man in his highest spiritual development— exists no longer. For, according to the Upaniṣads, all individual beings had their origin in a mistaken identification of the Ātman with body, senses, mind. As the moon, shining, appears itself to be a source of light, though in reality it but reflects the sun, so body, senses, mind, reflecting without knowing it the power of the Ātman, imagine themselves to have an independent and separate being. The whole process of spiritual evolution is only a process of undoing this prodigious original error.

The relation of the Ātman to the individual being in which it resides is dramatically set forth in the following story—in which, as often, the Ātman is referred to as the Self or the true Self, and the individual being, by implication, as the other, or ordinary, self.

'It was said of old: "The Self, which is free from impurities, from old age and death, from grief, from hunger and thirst, which desires nothing but what it ought to desire, and resolves nothing but what it ought to resolve, is to be sought after, is to be inquired about, is to be realized. He who learns about the Self and realizes it obtains all the worlds and all desires."

'The gods and demons both heard of this truth, and they thought to themselves: "Let us seek after and realize this Self, so that we may obtain all the worlds and all desires."

'Thereupon Indra from the gods, and Virochana from the demons, went to Prajapati, the renowned teacher. For thirty-two years they lived with him as pupils. Then Prajapati asked them why they had both lived with him so long.

'"We have heard", they replied, "that one who realizes the Self obtains all the worlds and all desires. We have lived here because we want to learn of this Self."

'Then said Prajapati: "That which is seen in the eye, that is the Self. That is immortal, that is fearless, and that is Brahman."

'"Sir," inquired the disciples, "is that the Self which is seen reflected in the water, or in a mirror?"

'"The Self is indeed seen reflected in these," was the reply.[1]

'Then Prajapati added: "Look at yourselves in the water, and whatever you do not understand, come and tell me about it."

[1] Chāndogya, VIII. vii. 1–3.

'Indra and Virochana gazed on their reflections in the water, and returning to the sage, they said: "Sir, we have seen the Self; we have seen even the hair and the nails."

'Then Prajapati bade them don their finest clothes and look again in the water. This they did, and returning to the sage, they said: "We have seen the Self, exactly like ourselves, well adorned and in our finest clothes."

'To which Prajapati rejoined: "The Self is indeed seen in these. The Self is immortal and fearless, and it is Brahman." And the pupils went away well pleased.

'But Prajapati, looking after them, lamented thus: "Both of them departed without analysing or discriminating, and without truly comprehending the Self. Whosoever follows a false doctrine of the Self will perish."

'Now Virochana, satisfied for his part that he had found out the Self, returned to the demons and began to teach them that the body alone is to be worshipped, that the body alone is to be served, and that he who worships the body and serves the body gains both worlds, this and the next. Such doctrine is, in very truth, the doctrine of the demons![1]

'But Indra, on his way back to the gods, realized the uselessness of this knowledge. "As this Self", he reasoned, "seems to be well adorned when the body is well adorned, well dressed when the body is well dressed, so will it be blind when the body is blind, lame when the body is lame, deformed when the body is deformed. When the body dies, this same Self will also die! In such knowledge I can see no good."

'So he returned to Prajapati and asked for further instruction. Prajapati required him to live with him for another thirty-two years, after which time he taught him thus:

'"That which moves about in dreams, enjoying sensuous delights and clothed in glory, that is the Self. That is immortal, that is fearless, and that is Brahman."

'Pleased with what he had heard, Indra again departed. But before he had reached the other gods he realized the uselessness of this knowledge also. "True it is", he thought to himself, "that this Self is not blind when the body is blind, nor lame or hurt when the body is lame or hurt. But even in dreams it is conscious of many sufferings. So in this doctrine also I can see no good."'[2]

Thus it was that Prajāpati started his disciple step by step on the long process of thinking out his problem. The theory that the body was the Self was clearly not tenable. Nor was the second hypothesis

[1] Chāndogya, VIII. viii. 1–5. [2] *Ibid.*, ix. 1–2.

much more satisfactory, though in dreams one does indeed attain a freer state of mind than in waking, and though the dream self therefore seems above the physical self. Again the disciple approached the master, whereupon Prajāpati gave still a third explanation:

'When a man is sound asleep, free from dreams, and at perfect rest—then is he the Self. The Self is immortal and fearless, and it is Brahman.'[1]

It was to make clear to Indra that the mind is not the Self, because the Self continues to exist without the mind, that Prajāpati wished his disciple to analyse the state of deep sleep; and now the inquiring god, who had ignorantly identified the mind with the Self, did indeed discover that he had not known the Self—for in dreamless sleep mind, he found, is 'almost annihilated'.

'For even before he had reached home, he felt the uselessness also of such a teaching. "In reality," thought he, "one does not know oneself as this or as that while asleep. One is not conscious, in fact, of any existence at all. The state of one in deep sleep is next to annihilation. I can see no good in this knowledge either."'[2]

Once more Indra approached his teacher and asked to be taught. And this time Prajāpati gave him the highest truth of the Self:

'This body is mortal, always gripped by death, but within it dwells the immortal Self. This Self, when associated in our consciousness with the body, is subject to pleasure and pain; and so long as this association continues, freedom from pleasure and pain can no man find. But as this association ceases, there cease also the pleasure and the pain. Rising above physical consciousness, knowing the Self to be distinct from the senses and the mind—knowing it in its true light—one rejoices and is free.'[3]

'The gods, the luminous ones, meditate on the Self, and by so doing obtain all the worlds and all desires. In like manner, whosoever among mortals knows the Self, meditates upon it, and realizes it—he too obtains all the worlds and all desires.'[4]

Deep, then, within us all—if we may attempt a simple restatement of the last few pages—resides the Ātman, the Self. Often it remains so deep within that we are unaware of its existence, and so falsely imagine that we consist only of body, senses, and mind. We imagine, further, that this individual being we call ourselves has a separate and independent existence, whereas in fact it is only an appearance—a light

[1] Chāndogya, xi. 1. [2] *Ibid.*, xi. 2. [3] *Ibid.*, xii. 1. [4] *Ibid.*, 5.

upon a screen, the source of which, the Ātman, we do not see. Once we turn away from the screen and face the Ātman—once we uncover it, bring it within our vision—we discern what is unreal and what alone is real. This process of realizing the Ātman for what it is, the Reality, and our individual being for what it is, a mere appearance, is the process of spiritual growth.

It is evident that the ṛṣis were deeply concerned with what we should now call psychology, and it may be of interest to pursue somewhat further their ideas in this field.

The senses they regarded as the gateways to finite experience. These are ten in number, five being known as the senses of knowledge (sight, hearing, touch, smell, and taste), and five as senses of action (speech, grasping, moving, excretion, and generation). As the senses come into contact with their objects, countless sensations arise, but only a part of them reach the field of consciousness. Further, as Western psychology likewise points out, the senses do not of themselves give a total picture; for this the 'points of sensation' must be gathered together and made into a whole.

Now the mind in its relation to the materials provided by the senses is known as antaḥkaraṇa, the 'internal instrument', and also by three other names according as it is thought of as performing one or another of its three several functions.

When it receives impressions of the outer world through the senses, it is called manas.

When it is engaged in identifying an object, in distinguishing one object from another, or in classifying or relating objects, it is called buddhi.

When it is engaged in establishing the stream of incoming sense data as belonging to itself—in annexing it, in other words, as the experience of a particular person—it is called ahaṁkāra, the ego-sense.

The Ātman is of course beyond the mind in all its aspects. It is in no sense an instrument: it is the user of instruments. Says the Kaṭha Upaniṣad:

'Above the senses is the mind. Above the mind is the intellect. Above the intellect is the ego. Above the ego is the unmanifested seed, the Primal Cause. And verily beyond the unmanifested seed is the Self, the unconditioned, knowing whom one attains to freedom and achieves immortality.'[1]

In one passage the Ātman is described as enclosed in a series of sheaths.

First, there is the annamaya, the food-body. This is the sheath of

[1] II. vi. 7–8.

the physical self, named from the fact that it is nourished and maintained by food.

Second, and 'different from this body of food, there is another and subtle sheath, which is prāṇamaya'. Prāṇamaya means composed of prāṇa; and prāṇa is the vital principle, the force which vitalizes and holds together the body and the mind. It pervades the whole organism, and its gross manifestation is breath. As long as this vital principle exists in the organism, life continues.

Third, and 'different from the sheath composed of prāṇa, there is the manomaya'. Manomaya means composed of manas; and with the function of manas, an aspect of the mind, we are already acquainted.

Fourth, and 'subtler than the sheath composed of manas, there is another sheath, called vijñānamaya'. Vijñānamaya means composed of vijñāna; and vijñāna means intellect, and refers to the faculty which discriminates, determines, or wills.

Fifth, and 'different from the sheath made up of vijñāna, there is the ānandamaya'. Ānandamaya means composed of ānanda; and ānanda means bliss, and the sheath refers to the ego. In the Upaniṣads the sheath is known also as the 'causal body'. In deep sleep, when the senses and the mind cease functioning, there still stands the causal body between the finite world and the blissful Self. As this fifth sheath is nearest of all to the blissful Self, its name in the Upaniṣads is ānandamaya.

Such are the five sheaths which are said to cover the Self. The true Self, or Ātman, is obviously none of these—nor can its true nature be known as long as it is identified with them.[1]

The Upaniṣads identify, in all, three states of consciousness, to which we have already been introduced by the story of Indra and Prajāpati.

The first is the waking state, characterized by the awareness of things external to the body, sensual enjoyment of gross objects, and conviction as to the identity of consciousness and the physical body. When a man is in this state he is known as vaiśwānara, because he is then 'lord of his physical body'.

The second is the dreaming state. When in this a man is known as taijasa. He is aware of internal phenomena and enjoys mental impressions. This is a condition intermediate between waking and deep sleep. The mind is now active, though independently of the sense organs, and is without consciousness of the gross body. In this state a man is a purely mental being.

The third state is that of deep sleep. When in this a man is known as prājña. He is entirely unaware of the external world, and also of the internal world. As when the darkness of night covers the day,

[1] See Taittirīya Upaniṣad.

and with the day the objects before us seem to disappear, similarly the gloom of ignorance in deep sleep covers up consciousness, and thoughts and knowledge apparently vanish. With this third state we reach the ego, or 'causal sheath', so-called because it contains the root of ignorance.

Besides these three states there is the Pure Consciousness, which should not be called a state because it transcends all states. It is known simply as The Fourth—turīya. Of a different order from the three preceding, having no connection with the finite mind, it comes into being only when in meditation the ordinary self is left behind and the Ātman, or true Self, is fully realized. It is thus described:

'The Fourth, say the wise, is not subjective experience, nor objective experience, nor experience intermediate between these two, nor is it a negative condition which is neither consciousness nor unconsciousness. It is not the knowledge of the senses, nor is it relative knowledge, nor yet inferential knowledge. Beyond the senses, beyond the understanding, beyond all expression, is The Fourth. It is pure unitary consciousness, wherein awareness of the world and of multiplicity is completely obliterated. It is ineffable peace. It is the supreme good. It is one without a second. It is the Self. Know it alone!'[1]

Turīya, The Fourth, is, in short, the supreme mystic experience.

Such is the conception of the Ātman to be found in the Upaniṣads, and also of various phenomena with which it is associated. But does the Ātman actually exist, or is it only a figment of the imagination? What proof do the Upaniṣads offer of its reality?

None directly, explicitly, it must be said, nothing in the way of definite, conscious, philosophical reasoning. Still, implied in their revelations, are the following arguments.

If, first of all, there is no Ātman, if there is nothing beyond body and mind, what is it, then, that bridges the gap occasioned by the obliteration of mind in deep sleep and so affords continuity to our individual existence? The Ātman supplies the answer.

Again, it is evident that the motion of any object can be known only in relation to an object that is comparatively static; the movement of this in turn must be known in relation to a third object moving still more slowly; and so on indefinitely until one arrives at something completely at rest. The body, the mind, everything we experience, we know to be in motion; beyond them, therefore, there must be something which stands fast. This something is the Ātman.

Finally, our minds, egos, senses, bodies, we recognize as objects.

[1] Māṇḍūkya, 7.

But objects imply a subject: if these things are objects, then a subject must be assumed. This subject, the silent witness, is the Ātman.

Thoughts such as these, suggested by the Upaniṣads, may thus be given the shape of argument; but it must always be remembered that it was not upon argument, however seemingly conclusive, that the ṛṣis based their convictions. For, once more, the ṛṣis were seers, reporters of direct experience, not dialecticians. If they affirmed the existence of the Ātman, it was primarily for the most immediate of all reasons—they had discovered it within themselves.

Identity of Brahman and Ātman

Endless change without, and at the heart of the change an abiding reality—Brahman. Endless change within, and at the heart of the change an abiding reality—Ātman. Were there then two realities?

No, answered the ṛṣis, Brahman and Ātman are one and the same. And they summed up the prodigious affirmation in the words Tat Tvam asi—That thou art.

Of the Hindu identification of Brahman and Ātman, Paul Deussen, best known perhaps of all Western students of the Upaniṣads, has said:

'It was here for the first time the original thinkers of the Upaniṣads, to their immortal honour, found God. They recognized one Ātman, one inmost individual being, as the Brahman, the inmost being of universal Nature and of all her phenomena.'

The tribute is an impressive one, though in the implication that the startling discovery was the climactic point in a development of reason or experience, it is scarcely in keeping with the texts of the Upaniṣads—at least as these are interpreted by Hindu orthodoxy. For in this interpretation the identity of Ātman and Brahman was a vital portion of the wisdom known to the ṛṣis from the beginning. Certain it is that in the Upaniṣads the idea is nearly everywhere either stated or implied—though nowhere perhaps more simply and attractively than in the following famous story. We shall find a title for it in words already quoted.

'That Art Thou'

When Svetaketu was twelve years old, his father Uddalaka said to him, 'Svetaketu, you must now go to school and study. None of our family, my child, is ignorant of Brahman.'

Thereupon Svetaketu went to a teacher and studied for twelve years. After committing to memory all the Vedas, he returned home full of pride in his learning.

His father, noticing the young man's conceit, said to him: 'Svetaketu, have you asked for that knowledge by which we hear the unhearable, by which we perceive the unperceivable, by which we know the unknowable?'

'What is that knowledge, sir?' asked Svetaketu.

'My child, as by knowing one lump of clay, all things made of clay are known, the difference being only in name and arising from speech, and the truth being that all are clay; as by knowing one nugget of gold, all things made of gold are known, the difference being only in name and arising from speech, and the truth being that all are gold—exactly so is that knowledge, knowing which we know all.'

'But surely those venerable teachers of mine are ignorant of this knowledge; for if they possessed it, they would have taught it to me. Do you therefore, sir, give me that knowledge.'

'Be it so,' said Uddalaka, and continued thus:[1]

'In the beginning there was Existence, one only, without a second. Some say that in the beginning there was nonexistence only, and that out of that the universe was born. But how could such a thing be? How could existence be born of nonexistence? No, my son, in the beginning there was Existence alone—one only, without a second. He, the One, thought to himself: Let me be many, let me grow forth.[2]

'Thus out of himself he projected the universe: and having projected out of himself the universe, he entered into every being and every thing. All that is has its self in him alone. He is the truth. He is the subtle essence of all. He is the Self. And that, Svetaketu, That art Thou.'

'Please, sir, tell me more about this Self.'

'Be it so, my child.[3]

'As the bees make honey by gathering juices from many flowering plants and trees, and as these juices reduced to one honey do not know from what flowers they severally came, similarly, my son, all creatures, when they are merged in that one Existence, whether in dreamless sleep or in death, know nothing of their past or present state because of the ignorance enveloping them—know not that they are merged in him and that from him they came.

'Whatever these creatures are, whether a lion, or a tiger, or a boar, or a worm, or a gnat, or a mosquito, that they still are when they come back from dreamless sleep.

'All these have their self in him alone. He is the truth. He is the subtle essence of all. He is the Self. And that, Svetaketu, That art Thou.'

1. Chāndogya, VI. i. 1–7. 2. *Ibid.*, ii. 1–3. 3. *Ibid.*, viii. 7.

'Please, sir, tell me more about this Self.'

'Be it so, my son.[1]

'The rivers in the east flow eastward, the rivers in the west flow westward, and all enter into the sea. From sea to sea they pass, the clouds lifting them to the sky as vapour and sending them down as rain. And as these rivers, when they are united with the sea, do not know whether they are this or that river, likewise all those creatures that I have named, when they have come back from Brahman, know not whence they came.

'All those beings have their self in him alone. He is the truth. He is the subtle essence of all. He is the Self. And that, Svetaketu, That art Thou.'

'Please, sir, tell me more about this Self.'

'Be it so, my child.[2]

'If someone were to strike once at the root of this large tree, it would bleed, but live. If he were to strike at its stem, it would bleed, but live. If he were to strike at the top, it would bleed, but live. Pervaded by the living Self, this tree stands firm, and takes its food; but if the Self were to depart from one of its branches, that branch would wither; if it were to depart from a second, that would wither; if it were to depart from a third, that would wither. If it were to depart from the whole tree, the whole tree would wither.

'Likewise, my son, know this: The body dies when the Self leaves it—but the Self dies not.

'All that is has its self in him alone. He is the truth. He is the subtle essence of all. He is the Self. And that, Svetaketu, That art Thou.'

'Please, sir, tell me more about this Self.'

'Be it so. Bring a fruit of that Nyagrodha tree.'

'Here it is, sir.'

'Break it.'

'It is broken, sir.'

'What do you see?'

'Some seeds, extremely small, sir.'

'Break one of them.'

'It is broken, sir.'

'What do you see?'

'Nothing, sir.'

'The subtle essence you do not see, and in that is the whole of the Nyagrodha tree. Believe, my son, that that which is the subtle essence—in that have all things their existence. That is the truth. That is the Self. And that, Svetaketu, That art Thou.'

'Please, sir, tell me more about this Self.'

'Be it so. Put this salt in water, and come to me tomorrow morning.'

[1] Chāndogya, ix. 1–4.
[2] *Ibid.*, x.

Svetaketu did as he was bidden. The next morning his father asked him to bring the salt which he had put in the water. But he could not, for it had dissolved. Then said Uddalaka:

'Sip the water, and tell me how it tastes.'

'It is salty, sir.'

'In the same way,' continued Uddalaka, 'though you do not see Brahman in this body, he is indeed here. That which is the subtle essence—in that have all things their existence. That is the truth. That is the Self. And that, Svetaketu, That art Thou.'

'Please, sir, tell me more about this Self,' said the youth again.

'Be it so, my child.

'As a man may be blindfolded, and led away, and left in a strange place; and as, having been so dealt with, he turns in every direction and cries out for someone to remove his bandages and show him the way home; and as one thus entreated may loose his bandages and give him comfort; and as thereupon he walks from village to village, asking his way as he goes, and arrives home at last—just so does a man who meets with an illumined teacher obtain true knowledge.

'That which is the subtle essence—in that have all beings their existence. That is the truth. That is the Self. And that, O Svetaketu, That art Thou.'

'Please, sir, tell me more about this Self.'

'Be it so, my child.

'When a man is fatally ill, his relations gather round him and ask, "Do you know me? Do you know me?" Now until his speech is merged in his mind, his mind in his breath, his breath in his vital heat, his vital heat in the Supreme Being, he knows them. But when his speech is merged in his mind, his mind in his breath, his breath in his vital heat, his vital heat in the Supreme Being, then he does not know them.

'That which is the subtle essence—in that have all beings their existence. That is the truth. That is the Self. And that, O Svetaketu, That art Thou.'[1]

'That art Thou' (where 'Thou' means, of course, not the ordinary self, the individual being, but the Ātman) is one of the mahāvākyas, or great sayings—concise utterances in which the Upaniṣads sum up their whole teaching. Others are Aham Brahmāsmi[2] (I am Brahman), Prajñānaṁ Brahma[3] (Pure Consciousness is Brahman), Ayam Ātmā Brahma[4] (This Self is Brahman). It is interesting to note that the ten orders of monks of the school of Śaṁkara are differentiated to this day by the particular mahāvākya upon which they meditate.

[1] Chāndogya, xi-xv.
[2] Bṛhadāraṇyaka, I. iv. 10.
[3] Aitareya, III. i. 3.
[4] Bṛhadāraṇyaka, II. 5.

In the story just summarized, the identity of Brahman and Ātman is explicitly and repeatedly asserted, but nearly everywhere, as has been already indicated, it is at least implied. Observe, for example, the following passages:

'What is within us is also without. What is without is also within. He who sees difference between what is within and what is without goes evermore from death to death.'[1]

'The wise man who sees him revealed in his own soul, to him belongs eternal peace; to none else, to none else.'[2]

'That being, of the size of a thumb, dwells deep within the heart.[3] He is the lord of time, past and future. Having attained him, one fears no more. He, verily, is the immortal Self.'[4]

'That being, of the size of a thumb, is like a flame without smoke. He is the lord of time, past and future, the same today and tomorrow. He, verily, is the immortal Self.'[5]

'The supreme person, of the size of a thumb, the innermost Self, dwells forever in the heart of all beings. As one draws the pith from a reed, so must the aspirant after truth, in his mind, with great perseverance, separate That from his body. Know That to be pure and immortal—yea, pure and immortal.'[6]

'The Self, who understands all, who knows all, and whose glory is manifest in the universe, lives within the shrine of the heart, the city of Brahman.'[7]

'Brahman is supreme; he is self-luminous, he is beyond all thought. Subtler than the subtlest is he, farther than the farthest, nearer than the nearest. He resides in the shrine of the heart of every being.'[8]

'The Self is not known by the weak, nor by the thoughtless, nor by those who do not rightly meditate. But by the rightly meditative, the thoughtful, and the strong, he is fully known.'[9]

'Smaller than a grain of rice is that Self; smaller than a grain of barley, smaller than a mustard seed, smaller than a canary seed, yea, smaller even than the kernel of a canary seed. Yet again is that Self within the shrine of my heart greater than the earth, greater than the heavens, yea, greater than all the worlds.'[10]

[1] Kaṭha, II. iv. 10. [2] *Ibid.*, v. 12.

[3] The sages ascribe a definite, minute size to the Self in order to assist the disciple in meditation.

[4] Kaṭha, II. iv. 12. [5] *Ibid.*, iv. 13. [6] *Ibid.*, vi. 17.

[7] Muṇḍaka, II. ii. 7. [8] *Ibid.*, III. i. 7. [9] *Ibid.*, ii., 4.

[10] Chāndogya, III. xiv. 3.

'Formless is he, though inhabiting form. In the midst of the fleeting he abides forever. All-pervading and supreme is the Self. The wise man, knowing him in his true nature, transcends all grief.'[1]

'Like two birds of golden plumage, inseparable companions, the individual self and the immortal Self are perched on the branches of the selfsame tree. The former tastes of the sweet and bitter fruits of the tree; the latter, tasting of neither, calmly observes. The individual self, deluded by forgetfulness of its identity with the divine Self, grieves and is sad. But when he recognizes the worshipful Lord as his own true Self, and beholds his glory, he grieves no more. When the seer beholds the Effulgent One, the Lord, the Supreme Being, then, transcending both good and evil, and freed from impurities, he unites himself with him.'[2]

In the following ancient fable the popular imagination found its own way of illustrating the oneness of the Ātman, the Self within, and Brahman. It is here given in the words of Swami Vivekananda, who had it from Śrī Rāmakṛṣṇa, who, in turn, had heard it from Totā Purī, his early friend and master.

'A lioness in search of prey came upon a flock of sheep, and as she jumped at one of them, she gave birth to a cub and died on the spot. The young lion was brought up in the flock, ate grass and bleated like a sheep, and it never knew that it was a lion. One day a lion came across this flock and was astonished to see in it a huge lion eating grass and bleating like a sheep. At his sight the flock fled and the lion-sheep with them. But the lion watched his opportunity and one day found the lion-sheep asleep. He woke him up and said, "You are a lion." The other said, "No," and began to bleat like a sheep. But the stranger lion took him to a lake and asked him to look in the water at his own image and see if it did not resemble him, the stranger lion. He looked and acknowledged that it did. Then the stranger lion began to roar and asked him to do the same. The lion-sheep tried his voice and was soon roaring as grandly as the other. And he was a sheep no longer.'[3]

Realization of Brahman

At the heart of the world without is Brahman. At the heart of the world within is Ātman. And Brahman and Ātman are one. But the Upaniṣads do not end with a mere theory of existence. They do not even begin with it. For everywhere their ultimate appeal is not to

[1] Kaṭha, I. ii. 22.
[2] Muṇḍaka, III. i. 1–3.
[3] *Complete Works of Vivekananda*, vol. I, pp. 324–5.

the intellect but to the will. They would have men not only understand, though that is important, but do. And the one thing they would have them do is to realize God.

And what is it to realize God? Put most simply, it is to enter into union with him. And when does one achieve this union? It is when one reaches the supreme state of consciousness—called, as we have seen, turīya (The Fourth), since it differs from the three states which we ordinarily experience.

Turīya, the final, all-embracing goal of the spiritual life, is sometimes conceived by the Upaniṣads as a state of knowledge, sometimes as a state of liberation.

Of course the knowledge referred to, when the goal is conceived as knowledge, is not what we ordinarily understand by the word. Here a sharp distinction is made.

'There are two kinds of knowledge, the higher and the lower. The lower is knowledge of the Vedas (the Rik, the Sama, the Yajur, and the Atharva), and also of phonetics, ceremonials, grammar, etymology, meter, and astronomy. The higher is knowledge of that by which one knows the changeless Reality. By this is fully revealed to the wise that which transcends the senses, which is uncaused, which is indefinable, which has neither eyes nor ears, neither hands nor feet, which is all-pervading, subtler than the subtlest—the everlasting, the source of all.'[1]

The lower knowledge, being of the intellect and the senses, is limited to the objective, finite world. With Brahman or Ātman, 'unseen but seeing, unheard but hearing, unperceived but perceiving', it can in the nature of things have nothing to do. 'None beholds him with the eyes, for he is without visible form. Yet in the heart is he revealed through self-control and meditation. Those who know him become immortal.'[2] 'The Self is not known through study of the scriptures, nor through subtlety of the intellect, nor through much learning. But by him who longs for him is he known. Verily unto him does the Self reveal his true being.'[3] Elsewhere the Ātman is described as 'that from which speech, along with the mind, turns away—not able to comprehend'.[4]

Knowledge of the Ātman, of Brahman, is of course the higher knowledge—parāvidyā. It is neither objective knowledge, taking cognizance of the external world, nor subjective experience of concepts and emotions; it transcends indeed all the three categories of empirical knowledge—the knower, the thing known, and the act of knowing. Yet it is by no means a condition of emptiness or

[1] Muṇḍaka, I. i. 4–6.
[2] Kaṭha, II. vi. 9.
[3] *Ibid.*, I. ii. 23.
[4] Taittiriya, II. 4.

darkness; on the contrary it is associated with fullness of joy and with infinite illumination. When the Self appears, all is light. 'He shining, everything shines.'[1] And with the light comes peace. 'The wise man who sees Him revealed in his own soul, to him belongs eternal peace; to none else, to none else.'[2]

To achieve the higher knowledge is the ultimate purpose of all beings, and the immediate and principal purpose of man. 'Blessed is he who attains to this supreme wisdom in this very life; if he does not, he has lived in vain.'[3]

Conceived as liberation—mokṣa—turīya is the state which results when the bonds of ignorance have been burst asunder, and implies freedom not only from all imperfections and limitations, but also from birth and death.

Mokṣa, say the Upaniṣads, may be attained either during the course of one's life or at the moment of death.

For him who has achieved liberation during life the vision of the world has changed into the vision of the final reality—Brahman. He is then called 'the living free'. For him delusion is gone forever. He is free from all selfish desire, for all sense of want in him is extinguished by the ineffable experience of the Self. His only delight is in God. 'Having fully ascertained and realized the truth of Vedanta, having established themselves in purity of conduct by following the yoga of renunciation, these great ones attain to immortality in this very life.'[4]

For him who has not achieved mokṣa during life there is the possibility of obtaining it at death—provided that during his life he has disciplined and prepared himself for it, making it his sole aim.

But whether achieved during life or at its close, the attainment of mokṣa is the attainment of immortality, though not in the sense in which the word is sometimes understood. Immortality as taught in the Upaniṣads does not imply a survival to all eternity of the individual self, of what we know in this world as an individual man or personality. This self has no absolute reality, and can therefore have no absolute or permanent existence. When mokṣa is achieved, it altogether disappears. Furthermore, the immortality of the Upaniṣads, in contrast with a common Western conception, cannot properly be regarded as in any sense a continuance in time. As a matter of fact, the very word time, as well as the word eternity, is, strictly speaking, out of place in the present context—although its use is inevitable. For the immortality of the Upaniṣads is nothing but the coming into its own of the divine Self, and this Self is beyond time, which, with space and a thousand other conditions of human life, belongs only to the finite world.

[1] Kaṭha, II. v. 15. [2] *Ibid.*, 12. [3] Kena, II. 5. [4] Muṇḍaka, III. ii. 6.

'The Self is the omniscient Lord. He is not born. He does not die. He is neither cause nor effect. This Ancient One is unborn, eternal, imperishable; though the body be destroyed, he is not killed. If the slayer think that he slays, if the slain think that he is slain, neither of them knows the truth. The Self slays not, nor is he slain. . . . Soundless, formless, intangible, undying, tasteless, odourless, eternal, without beginning, without end, immutable, beyond nature, is the Self. Knowing him as such, one is freed from death. Smaller than the smallest, greater than the greatest, this Self forever dwells within the hearts of all. When a man is free from desire, his mind and senses purified, he beholds the glory of the Self and is without sorrow.'[1]

In words that may stand as a commentary on the well-known passage just quoted, Swami Vivekananda says:

'. . . as a man having a book in his hands reads one page and turns it over, goes to the next page, reads that, turns it over, and so on, yet it is the book that is being turned over, the pages that are revolving, and not he—he is where he is always—even so with regard to the soul. The whole of nature is that book which the soul is reading. Each life, as it were, is one page of that book; and that read, it is turned over, and so on and on, until the whole of the book is finished, and the soul becomes perfect, having got all the experiences of nature. Yet at the same time it never moved, nor came nor went; it was only gathering experiences. But it appears to us that we are moving. The earth is moving, yet we think that the sun is moving instead of the earth, which we know to be a mistake, a delusion of the senses. So is also this delusion that we are born and that we die, that we come or that we go. We neither come nor go, nor have we been born. For where is the soul to go? There is no place for it to go. Where is it not already?'[2]

The conception of immortality to be found in the Upaniṣads runs counter, it must be admitted, to a common human desire. Most of us cling fondly to what we call our individuality, or personality, and we long to retain it through what we think of as an infinite extension of earthly time. Against this prepossession there lies implicit in the Upaniṣads the following argument. This so-vaunted individuality of ours—what is it, after all? Born as it is of the false identification of the Self with the non-Self, it is but the illusory product of a radical misunderstanding. It has no genuinely real, no ultimate, existence. And, further, if only we will but observe and reflect, we shall realize that everything which pertains to this particularized self, whether of body or mind, is in a state of incessant change. To cherish our finite

[1] Kaṭha, I. ii. 18–20. [2] *Complete Works of Vivekananda*, vol. VI, pp. 21 f.

individuality is therefore to expend our affections on what, moment by moment, we are losing forever. But on the other hand, beside this elusive, ever-vanishing self, there is another Self, the Ātman, the real man, motionless behind the flux. In that, and only in that, lies our higher and truer individuality, which, so long as we continue in our blindness, we can never know. It is only when we have achieved mokṣa that we come to know it; and then we realize it in its fullness.

The Path to Realization

To experience turīya, to become a knower of Brahman, to be liberated from every finite bond—in short to realize God: such is the all-important purpose of life. But how is this purpose to be achieved?

It is to be achieved, say the Upaniṣads, through two types of spiritual discipline, both of which are essential: observation of moral laws and the practice of meditation.

The moral laws are summed up in the single principle of self-control—a check on selfish impulses, passions, and desires. This it is that finds imaginative expression in the following famous passage:

'Know that the Self is the rider and the body the chariot; that the intellect is the charioteer, and the mind the reins. The senses, say the wise, are the horses; the roads they travel are the mazes of desire. The wise call the Self the enjoyer when he is united with the body, the senses, and the mind. When a man lacks discrimination, and his mind is uncontrolled, his senses are unmanageable, like the restive horses of a charioteer. But when a man has discrimination and his mind is controlled, his senses, like the well-broken horses of a charioteer, lightly obey the rein. He who lacks discrimination, whose mind is unsteady, and whose heart is impure, never reaches the goal, but is born again and again. But he who has discrimination, whose mind is steady, and whose heart is pure, reaches the goal, and having reached it is born no more. The man who has a sound understanding for charioteer, a controlled mind for reins—he it is that reaches the end of the journey, the supreme abode of Vishnu, the all-pervading.[1]

'The Self, deep-hidden in all beings, is not revealed to all; but to the seers, pure in heart, concentrated in mind—to them is he revealed. The senses of the wise man obey his mind, his mind obeys his intellect, his intellect obeys his ego, and his ego obeys the Self.'[2]

Elsewhere the Upaniṣads enter somewhat more fully into details of conduct:

'Let your conduct be marked by right action, including study and

[1] Kaṭha, I. iii. 3–9.

[2] *Ibid.*, 12–13.

teaching of the scriptures; by truthfulness in word, deed, and thought; by self-denial and the practice of austerity; by poise and self-control; by performance of the everyday duties of life with a cheerful heart and an unattached mind.

'Speak the truth. Do your duty. Do not neglect the study of the scriptures. Do not cut the thread of progeny. Swerve not from truth. Deviate not from the path of good. Revere greatness.

'Let your mother be a god to you; let your father be a god to you; let your teacher be a god to you; let your guest also be a god to you. Do only such actions as are blameless. Always show reverence to the great.

'Whatever you give to others, give with love and reverence. Gifts must be given in abundance, with joy, humility, and compassion.

'If at any time there is any doubt with regard to right conduct, follow the practice of great souls, who are guileless, of good judgment, and devoted to truth.

'Thus conduct yourself always. This is the injunction, this is the teaching, and this is the command of the scriptures.'[1]

The ultimate moral ideal of the Upaniṣads is complete self-abnegation, the utter renunciation of all selfish and personal desires. To one in such a state of inner purity there is no longer thought of 'me' and 'mine', the individual self to which such words pertain being wholly absorbed and extinguished in the infinite oneness of God.

Once a man has achieved turīya, his ultimate goal, he has no further concern with moral laws. 'When the seer beholds the Effulgent One, the Lord, the Supreme Being, then, transcending both good and evil, and freed from impurities, he unites himself with him.'[2] To be 'beyond both good and evil' is not of course to be able to do evil with impunity, but rather to be incapable of it.

The practice of meditation, the second and more important of the two types of spiritual discipline, must, say the Upaniṣads, be led up to by hearing and reflection.

We must first hear the truth of Brahman, and we must hear it—this idea we have before encountered—from a guru, or teacher—one to whom it has been fully revealed.

'To many it is not given to hear of the Self. Many, though they hear of it, do not understand it. Wonderful is he who speaks of it: intelligent is he who learns of it. Blessed is he who, taught by a good teacher, is able to understand it.'[3]

'The truth of the Self cannot be fully understood when taught by an

[1] Taittirīya, I. xi. [2] Muṇḍaka, III. i. 3. [3] Kaṭha, I. ii. 7.

ignorant man, for opinions regarding it, not founded on knowledge, vary one from another. Subtler than the subtlest is this Self, and beyond all logic. Taught by a teacher who knows the Self and Brahman as one, a man leaves vain theory behind and attains to truth.'[1]

'Words cannot reveal him. Mind is unable to reach him. The eyes do not see him. How then can he be comprehended save when taught by those seers who indeed have known him?'[2]

'Arise! Awake! Approach the feet of the master and know THAT. Like the sharp edge of a razor, the sages say, is the path. Narrow it is, and difficult to tread.'[3]

But hearing is not enough. No true teacher demands blind acceptance of his doctrine. In order to reach intellectual conviction, we must therefore reflect. As aids to reflection we may engage in the study of logic or of natural science, and in independent philosophical speculation.[4]

Having heard the truth of God, and having duly reflected upon it, we are ready for meditation. And what is meditation? In its highest form, say the Upaniṣads, it is concentration upon the truth Aham Brahmāsmi (I am Brahman).[5] As aids to meditation, various symbols of Brahman are accepted, of which the most important is the mystic syllable Om.

'Affix to the Upanishad, the bow incomparable, the sharp arrow of devotional worship; then, with mind absorbed and heart melted in love, draw the arrow and hit the mark, the imperishable Brahman. Om is the bow, the arrow is the individual being, and Brahman is the target. With a tranquil heart, take aim. Lose thyself in him, even as the arrow is lost in the target. In him are woven heaven, earth, and sky, together with the mind and all the senses. Know him, the Self alone. Give up vain talk. He is the bridge of immortality. Within the lotus of the heart he dwells, where, like the spokes of a wheel, the nerves meet. Meditate on him as Om. Easily mayest thou cross the sea of darkness.'[6]

Scattered hints on the technique of meditation, such as that mentioned in the passage just quoted, are found in the Upaniṣads, but no full and adequate information. That is because in ancient

[1] Kaṭha, I. ii. 8. [2] *Ibid.*, II. vi. 12. [3] *Ibid.*, I. iii. 14.

[4] It was as aids to reflection that six main schools of thought within Hinduism were developed. These we shall consider later.

[5] Bṛhadāraṇyaka, I. iv. 10. [6] Muṇḍaka, II. ii. 3–6.

times, as at present and throughout the intervening centuries, the exact methods to be followed were communicated directly from master to disciple and were never formally set down in writing. For this practice the Hindu would offer several reasons. One is that, as the Upaniṣads indicate, such details can have no use or meaning for one who is not spiritually prepared for them, and another is that in actual practice they are infinitely varied to suit the needs of individual disciples. The guru has perhaps no more important duty than to study carefully the personality and temperament of the pupils committed to his charge, and to prescribe to each, according to his nature, an appropriate method of meditation.

Meditation is the last step on the path of realization.

'None beholds him with the eyes, for he is without visible form. Yet in the heart is he revealed, through self-control and meditation. Those who know him become immortal. When all the senses are stilled, when the mind is at rest, when the intellect wavers not—then is known, say the wise, the highest state. The calm of the senses and the mind has been defined as yoga. He who attains it is freed from delusion.'[1]

Of this 'highest state'—samādhi, mokṣa, turīya—we shall continue to hear in later chapters, sometimes under still other names. For it is the shining sun to which all Hindu religion points. It is this that is meant by the *realization of God.*

Karma and Reincarnation

For those who fully realize God, whether during the course of their lives or at the point of death, finite existence is at an end. But not so with those who fall short of the goal. What happens to these after death is set forth in a number of passages.

'When a man is about to die, the subtle body, mounted by the intelligent Self, groans—as a heavily laden cart groans under its burden.

'When his body becomes thin through old age or disease, the dying man separates himself from his limbs, even as a mango or a fig or a banyan fruit separates itself from its stalk, and by the same way he came he hastens to his new abode, and there assumes another body, in which to begin a new life.'[2]

'When his body grows weak and he becomes apparently unconscious, the dying man gathers his senses about him and completely

[1] Kaṭha, II. vi. 9–11.

[2] Bṛhadāraṇyaka, IV. iii. 35–6.

withdrawing their powers descends into his heart. No more does he see form or colour without.

'He neither sees, nor smells, nor tastes. He does not speak, he does not hear. He does not think, he does not know. For all the organs, detaching themselves from his physical body, unite with his subtle body. Then the point of his heart, where the nerves join, is lighted by the light of the Self, and by that light he departs either through the eye, or through the gate of the skull, or through some other aperture of the body. When he thus departs, life departs; and when life departs, all the functions of the vital principle depart. The Self remains conscious, and, conscious, the dying man goes to his abode. The deeds of this life, and the impressions they leave behind, follow him.

'As a leech, having reached the end of a blade of grass, takes hold of another blade and draws itself to it, so the Self, having left this body behind it unconscious, takes hold of another body and draws himself to it.

'As a goldsmith, taking an old gold ornament, moulds it into another, newer and more beautiful, so the Self, having given up the body and left it unconscious, takes on a newer and better form, either that of the fathers, or that of the celestial singers, or that of the gods, or that of other beings, heavenly or earthly.

'The Self is verily Brahman. Through ignorance it identifies itself with what is alien to it, and appears to consist of intellect, understanding, life, sight, hearing, earth, water, air, ether, fire, desire and the absence of desire, anger and the absence of anger, righteousness and the absence of righteousness. It appears to be all things—now one, now another.

'As a man acts, so does he become. A man of good deeds becomes good, a man of evil deeds becomes evil. A man becomes pure through pure deeds, impure through impure deeds.

'As a man's desire is, so is his destiny. For as his desire is, so is his will; as his will is, so is his deed; and as his deed is, so is his reward, whether good or bad.

'A man acts according to the desires to which he clings. After death he goes to the next world, bearing in his mind the subtle impressions of his deeds; and after reaping there the harvest of his deeds, he returns again to this world of action. Thus he who has desire continues subject to rebirth.

'But he in whom desire is stilled suffers no rebirth. After death, having attained to the highest, desiring only the Self, he goes to no other world. Realizing Brahman, he becomes Brahman.

'When all the desires which once entered into his heart have been driven out by divine knowledge, the mortal, attaining to Brahman, becomes immortal.

'As the slough of a snake lies cast off on an anthill, so lies the body of a man at death; while he, freed from the body, becomes one with the immortal spirit, Brahman, the Light Eternal.'[1]

'Those who offer sacrifices and do deeds of charity go to the region of shade; from shade to night, the world of the fathers; from the world of the fathers to the realm of ether; from ether to soma.'[2]

Certain ideas emerge with more or less clearness from these several passages.

First of all, it is evident that the fortunes that await a man after death depend entirely upon his moral quality, and that this in turn depends upon his deeds. Simple as this statement may appear, it yet leaves room for considerable misunderstanding.

By deeds, for example, we are to understand not merely external action—this gift of food to the hungry, that theft of money from the till—but also every thought, feeling, impulse, imagination. Again, the deeds referred to are not wholly the deeds done in this present life, but also the deeds done in all past lives; and yet even such a statement is far less complex than the facts—as these are envisaged by the ancient ṛṣis.

For one's moral worth at death is not determined by a simple casting up of the long account of actions done through a succession of lives: these actions, from the first to the last, are interrelated as cause and effect—each action a cause of other actions to follow, and these again a cause of others, in an endless series. Notice '*a* cause', not '*the* cause'. A new action is not a product merely of the action that precedes it; rather it is the product of a state of moral character which itself is the cumulative product of all past deeds. Your nature at this moment is infinitely more complex a compound than ever chemist achieved by the successive addition to an original element of any number of other elements each interacting with the rest. Only—for the figure is not perfect—in the moral alchemy each new element is the product of the total compound that precedes it.

Even yet one factor has been completely ignored—and that the most important of all, tragically important, for upon it depends nothing less than man's hope of salvation. Thus far each new action has been spoken of as if it were simply the product of the compound of character that came before it. Sometimes—far too often the ṛṣis would say—this is indeed the case: events take their natural course, and what follows is an inevitable sequence upon what precedes. But, happily, not always. For that would mean that men are as

[1] Bṛhadāraṇyaka, iv. 1–7. [2] Chāndogya, V. x. 3–4.

helpless to mould their own destiny as a leaf in the stream or a feather in the wind. Indian philosophy is at no time, or in any sense, fatalistic. The will as conceived by the Upaniṣads, and other Indian scriptures, has in it an element of complete freedom, a power sufficient to enable a man to act in direct opposition to the spontaneous tendency of his accumulated character—and therefore to control his future.

An element of complete freedom—observe. The will, to an indeterminate extent, is itself caught in the hard chain of cause and effect, is itself formed and modified by deeds. The outward act you perform today, the thought you think, qualify your will of the next moment, your will of tomorrow. They make it better, or they make it worse; still in the next moment, or tomorrow, there still remains that particle of ineluctable liberty that permits you to remake your life.

In this region we meet again with a word universally associated with Indian philosophies—karma.[1] It is the word translated as deeds in a passage lately quoted: 'A man of good *deeds* becomes good, and a man of evil *deeds* becomes evil.' Karma, then, in the sense with which we are here concerned, means, first of all and most simply, deeds. But it is deeds with a special connotation not present in the English word—deeds conceived not only as isolated acts beginning and ending in themselves, but also as acts in a stream of causation, each one being at once an effect and a cause, or, in a common image, at once a fruit and a seed. When we use the word karma correctly, referring to the moral law, we should have in mind all the ideas with which the present section has dealt.

If at death a man's karma is good, then one of two paths is possible for him, the path of the fathers or the path of the gods. If his spiritual growth has almost enabled him to attain liberation in this life, then he enters the path of the gods, the path of no return. Following that path from 'light' to 'light' (higher planes of existence, or, perhaps, states of consciousness), and finally to Brahman, he gradually becomes one with the divine Being in his impersonal aspect and so reaches at last the end of his journey. If his goodness is of a lower order, then he enters the path of the fathers, so-called, where by 'fathers' are meant those souls of the departed who must return to earth. Taking this path, he goes to one or another heaven, where he enjoys the fruits of the good deeds which he has done in the body—the pleasures being rarer but not essentially different from those known on earth; and when these fruits are no more, he is born again. It appears that whichever path is taken by the good man after death, he walks that

[1] Karma is a singular noun, the plural being karmāṇi (deed, deeds); but in the philosophical sense only the singular is used. Strictly, for linguistic conformity, the passage above might be rendered: 'A man of good conduct . . .'

path clothed in a new body appropriate to a new and higher realm of being.

If at death the quality of his karma is evil, then a man goes to the regions of the wicked, there to eat the bitter fruits of his deeds. These fruits once exhausted, he too returns to earth.

Two aspects of the subject, above all, must not be lost sight of. First, it is on this earth that a man determines his spiritual destiny and achieves his final realization. The other worlds are only places where what is done here is given its reward of happiness or of misery. Even the good man whose privilege it is to take the path of no return owes his blessed fortune, not to anything he does after he leaves this earth, but to what he did when he was here—in his latest and in his previous lives. If he does not return to earth, that is only because his realization was already virtually achieved. And, as for the vile man, nothing that he experiences in another world after death either advances or retards his progress. Earth, and earth alone, then, is the scene of man's spiritual struggle.

A second aspect is at most implied rather than stated in the passages quoted above. That is the fact that ultimately all men will achieve liberation, however long, for some, may be the struggle, and however many returns, lower and higher in the scale of being, may be in store for them. The Upaniṣads know no such thing as eternal damnation—and the same is true of every other Hindu scripture.

SELECTED PASSAGES FROM THE UPANIṢADS

Know the Self and Be Free

The Self is not to be known through study of the scriptures, nor through subtlety of the intellect, nor through much learning. But by him who longs for him is he known. Verily unto him does the Self reveal his true being.

The Self is not to be known by the weak, nor by the thoughtless, nor by those who do not rightly meditate. But by the rightly meditative, the thoughtful, and the strong, he is fully known.

Having known the Self, the sages are filled with joy. Blessed are they, tranquil of mind, free from passion. Realizing everywhere the all-pervading Brahman, deeply absorbed in contemplation of his being, they enter into him, the Self of all.

Having fully ascertained and realized the truth of Vedanta, having established themselves in purity of conduct by following the yoga of renunciation, these great ones attain to immortality in this very life; and when their bodies fall away from them at death, they attain to liberation.[1]

[1] Muṇḍaka, III. ii. 3–6.

Eternal Truth

'The Infinite is the source of joy. There is no joy in the finite. Only in the Infinite is there joy. Ask to know of the Infinite.'

'Sir, I wish to know of it.'

'Where one sees nothing but the One, hears nothing but the One, knows nothing but the One—there is the Infinite. Where one sees another, hears another, knows another—there is the finite. The Infinite is immortal, the finite is mortal.'

'In what does the Infinite rest?'

'In its own glory—nay, not even in that. In the world it is said that cows and horses, elephants and gold, slaves, wives, fields, and houses are man's glory—but these are poor and finite things. How shall the Infinite rest anywhere but in itself?

'The Infinite is below, above, behind, before, to the right, to the left. I am all this. This Infinite is the Self. The Self is below, above, behind, before, to the right, to the left. I am all this. One who knows, meditates upon, and realizes the truth of the Self—such an one delights in the Self, revels in the Self, rejoices in the Self. He becomes master of himself, and master of all the worlds. Slaves are they who know not this truth.'[1]

The City of Brahman

As one not knowing that a golden treasure lies buried beneath his feet, may walk over it again and again, yet never find it, so all beings live every moment in the city of Brahman, yet never find him, because of the veil of illusion by which he is concealed.

The Self resides within the lotus of the heart. Knowing this, consecrated to the Self, the sage enters daily that holy sanctuary.

Absorbed in the Self, the sage is freed from identity with the body and lives in blissful consciousness. The Self is the immortal, the fearless; the Self is Brahman. This Brahman is eternal truth.[2]

The Self within the heart is like a boundary which divides the world from THAT. Day and night cross not that boundary, nor old age, nor death; neither grief nor pleasure, neither good nor evil deeds. All evil shuns THAT. For THAT is free from impurity: by impurity can it never be touched.

Wherefore he who has crossed that boundary, and has realized the Self, if he is blind, ceases to be blind; if he is wounded, ceases to be wounded; if he is afflicted, ceases to be afflicted. When that boundary is crossed, night becomes day; for the world of Brahman is light itself.[3]

[1] Chāndogya, VII. 23, 24, 25. [2] *Ibid.*, VIII. iii. 2–4. [3] *Ibid.*, VIII. iv. 1–2.

Satyakāma Tells the Truth

One day the boy Satyakama came to his mother and said: 'Mother, I want to be a religious student. What is my family name?'

'My son,' replied his mother, 'I do not know. In my youth I was a servant and worked in many places. I do not know who was your father. I am Jabala, and you are Satyakama. Call yourself Satyakama Jabala.'

Thereupon the boy went to Gautama and asked to be accepted as a student. 'Of what family are you, my lad?' inquired the sage.

Satyakama replied: 'I asked my mother what my family name was, and she answered: "I do not know. In my youth I was a servant and worked in many places. I do not know who was your father. I am Jabala, and you are Satyakama. Call yourself Satyakama Jabala." I am therefore Satyakama Jabala, sir.'

Then said the sage: 'None but a true brahmin would have spoken thus. Go and fetch fuel, for I will teach you. You have not swerved from the truth.'[1]

For the Sake of the Self

Yajnavalkya (addressing his wife): 'Maitreyi, I am resolved to renounce the world and begin the life of renunciation. I wish therefore to divide my property between you and my other wife, Katyayani.'

Maitreyi: 'My lord, if this whole earth belonged to me, with all its wealth, should I through its possession attain immortality?'

Yajnavalkya: 'No. Your life would be like that of the rich. None can possibly hope to attain immortality through wealth.'

Maitreyi: 'Then what need have I of wealth? Please, my lord, tell me what you know about the way to immortality.'

Yajnavalkya: 'Dear to me have you always been, Maitreyi, and now you ask to learn of that truth which is nearest my heart. Come, sit by me. I will explain it to you. Meditate on what I say.

'It is not for the sake of the husband, my beloved, that the husband is dear, but for the sake of the Self.

'It is not for the sake of the wife, my beloved, that the wife is dear, but for the sake of the Self.

'It is not for the sake of the children, my beloved, that the children are dear, but for the sake of the Self.

'It is not for the sake of wealth, my beloved, that wealth is dear, but for the sake of the Self.'[2]

The Light for Man

Once when Yajnavalkya came to the court of King Janaka, the king welcomed him with a question.

[1] Chāndogya, IV. iv. 1–5.

[2] Bṛhadāraṇyaka, II. iv. 1–5.

Janaka: 'Yajnavalkya, what serves as the light for man?'

Yajnavalkya: 'The light of the sun, Your Majesty; for by the light of the sun man sits, goes out, does his work, and returns home.'

Janaka: 'True indeed, Yajnavalkya. But when the sun has set, what serves then as his light?'

Yajnavalkya: 'The moon is then his light.'

Janaka: 'When the sun has set, O Yajnavalkya, and the moon has set, what serves then as his light?'

Yajnavalkya: 'The fire is then his light.'

Janaka: 'When the sun has set, O Yajnavalkya, and the moon has set, and the fire has gone out, what serves then as his light?'

Yajnavalkya: 'Sound is then his light; for with sound alone as his light, man sits, goes out, does his work, and returns home. Even though he cannot see his own hand, yet when he hears a sound he moves towards it.'

Janaka: 'True indeed, O Yajnavalkya. When the sun has set, and the moon has set, and the fire has gone out, and no sound is heard, what serves then as his light?'

Yajnavalkya: 'The Self indeed is his light; for by the light of the Self man sits, moves about, does his work, and when his work is done, rests.'

Janaka: 'Who is that Self?'

Yajnavalkya: 'The self-luminous being who dwells within the lotus of the heart, surrounded by the senses and sense organs, and who is the light of the intellect, is that Self.'[1]

To None Else

As fire, though one, takes the shape of every object which it consumes, so the Self, though one, takes the shape of every object in which it dwells.

As air, though one, takes the shape of every object which it enters, so the Self, though one, takes the shape of every object in which it dwells.

As the sun, revealer of all objects to the seer, is not harmed by the sinful eye, nor by the impurities of the objects it gazes on, so the one Self, dwelling in all, is not touched by the evils of the world. For he transcends all.

He is one, the lord and innermost Self of all; of one form, he makes of himself many forms. To him who sees the Self revealed in his own heart belongs eternal bliss—to none else, to none else![2]

[1] Bṛhadāraṇyaka, IV. iii. 1–7.

[2] Kaṭha, II. v. 9–12.

The Blessed Sages

Having known the Self, the sages are filled with joy. Blessed are they, tranquil of mind, free from passion. Realizing everywhere the all-pervading Brahman, deeply absorbed in contemplation of his being, they enter into him, the Self of all.

Having fully ascertained and realized the truth of Vedanta, having established themselves in purity of conduct by following the yoga of renunciation, these great ones attain to immortality in this very life; and when their bodies fall away from them at death, they attain to liberation.[1]

The Knower of Brahman

He who knows Brahman becomes Brahman. No one ignorant of Brahman is ever born in his family. He passes beyond all sorrow. He overcomes evil. Freed from the fetters of ignorance, he becomes immortal.[2]

[1] Muṇḍaka, III. ii. 5–6. [2] *Ibid.*, 9.

BOOK II

THE AUXILIARY SCRIPTURES

CHAPTER 4

THE AUXILIARY SCRIPTURES

The Vedas, whose acquaintance we have been making, are the principal, ultimate, and basic scriptures of India. They alone are conceived of as Śruti—which is to say, 'direct from God' or 'God reveals it'. But they are by no means the only writings held sacred by the orthodox Hindu. Indeed, to an extent seldom if ever paralleled elsewhere, literature and scripture have been in India one and the same thing. The Vedas, as we have seen, are often abstract and difficult. To be comprehended by the multitude they required simplification, expansion, illustration—in a word, popularization. Thus it was that alongside of the Vedas there gradually came into being a large body of writings, sometimes half-secular in nature, sometimes almost wholly religious, which are appropriately known as Auxiliary Scriptures. These, in contrast with the Vedas, are thought of as of merely human origin. They are man-made, not God-made. Some preliminary notion of them may be obtained from the following brief account:

Epics. Of these there are two principal works, the Rāmāyaṇa and the Mahābhārata, together with many others that are subordinate or derivative. These are all known in India as itihāsa, or history, and are accepted as true records of the events they narrate. One brief portion of the Mahābhārata, known as the Bhagavad-Gītā (often referred to simply as the Gītā), has emerged from its context to become virtually an independent work, and to assume such importance as to be called the Bible of India. (See the reference to the Gītā below, under Smṛtis.)

Smṛtis. The Sanskrit word smṛti means memory, and, accordingly, the Smṛtis are writings devised to fix in remembrance, for practical use, the spiritual laws and precepts stated or implied in the Vedas. The resemblance is such between the Smṛtis proper and the Bhagavad-Gītā that it has become customary with Indian commentators to speak of the latter not as 'history', which by origin it really is, but as 'Smṛti'. To bear this fact in mind is to avoid much possible confusion.

Purāṇas. Of these there are eighteen. They are long narratives in verse, the chief of which is the Bhāgavatam. After the Vedas and the Bhagavad-Gītā, the Bhāgavatam is now regarded by Hindus as the most authoritative of their scriptures.

Tantras. Tantra literally means that which saves by that which spreads; or, loosely rendered, spread the scriptures and save mankind.

The Epics in Indian Culture

Our concern in the present chapter is with the two chief epics—exclusive, however, of the Bhagavad-Gītā, whose importance is such as to demand for it a separate and detailed consideration.

From the beginning the Rāmāyaṇa and the Mahābhārata have exercised a profound influence upon India. The legends which compose them, the national heroes whom they celebrate, and the truths of which they are the imaginative expression, have supplied poets and dramatists, theologians and political thinkers, painters and sculptors, with their principal themes and their never-failing inspiration. Thus indirectly, as well as directly, they have permeated the national consciousness, from the highest classes to the lowest. Uneducated as well as educated have been familiar with them, even during British rule, when literacy was at its lowest ebb. In the quiet hours of evening, when work is finished, men, women, and children meet together in villages throughout the land, and listen eagerly to recitations from them by specially trained storytellers. Thus are brought to the humblest cottage the essential moral lessons and the great spiritual truths of an immemorial tradition. The beneficent effect upon the vast masses of the Indian population can scarcely be exaggerated. By virtue of it one may say that even the lowest Indian peasant or labourer, though illiterate, is still in a deep sense cultivated. Though he may be ignorant in all else, he is spiritually informed.

Much of the appeal of the two great epics is suggested in the following words of Swami Vivekananda:

'The internal conflicts between righteousness and filial affection in the mind of the God-fearing yet feeble old blind King Dhritarashtra; the majestic character of the grandsire Bhisma; the noble and virtuous nature of the royal Yudhisthira and of the other four brothers, as mighty in valour as in devotion and loyalty; the peerless character of the women, the stately queen Gandhari, the loving mother Kunti, the ever devoted and all-suffering Draupadi—these and hundreds of other features of this epic and of the Ramayana have been the cherished heritage of the whole Hindu world for the last several thousands of years, and form the basis of its thoughts and of its moral and ethical ideas.'[1]

[1] *Complete Works of Vivekananda*, vol. IV, pp. 96–7.

To understand well the Rāmāyaṇa and the Mahābhārata is in large measure to understand India.

The Rāmāyaṇa

The Rāmāyaṇa (Life of Rāma) is generally regarded as the first poetical work of purely human origin in the literature of India, and its traditional author, Vālmīki, as the first Indian poet. The general style in which the poem is composed differs from that of the verse portions of the Vedas by its greater diffuseness, simplicity, and charm.

Legends, as was natural, grew up concerning Vālmīki and his work. The poet, we hear, was originally an ignorant man and a highway robber, whose life and character were transformed through the mediation of the great saint Nārada. Having been instructed by the sage in the worship of Rāma, he fell one day into such deep meditation that he lost all consciousness of the external world and remained in this condition even when ants built their mounds all about him. From this incident he received his name, for Vālmīki signifies 'born of an ant hill'.

On another occasion, as he was about to bathe in a river, he saw amid the branches of a tree a pair of doves wheeling and billing. The sage—for he was now become such—was greatly pleased at the sight, but in a moment an arrow whisked past him and buried itself in the body of the male bird. As the dove fell to the ground, his mate whirled about him in deep grief, whereupon Vālmīki, looking about and seeing the hunter, exclaimed in righteous anger:

> For endless years to come, O hunter, never shall thy soul find peace,
> Since for love itself thou wouldst not from thy cruel slaying cease.[1]

As soon as he became conscious of what he had said, he remarked to himself: 'What is this? What am I saying? I have never before spoken like this!' Now it happened that the words he had uttered were arranged in meter—the very same pattern in which he afterwards wove his story of Rāma.

The substance of his poem, we are told, he learned from Nārada. Following is a brief summary of its central narrative.

Story of the Rāmāyaṇa

Daśaratha, the high-souled royal sage, was the beloved ruler of the beautiful city of Ayodhyā. Three queens were his, Kauśalyā, Kaikeyī,

[1] The passage is here given the form chosen by Romesh C. Dutt for his condensed versions of the Indian epics. In the original the verse has eight feet but, as in the *Iliad* and the *Odyssey*, there is no rhyme.

and Sumitrā, but none of them had borne him children. So, yearning for sons, he performed a sacrifice, to which he invited all the great sages, with Vaśiṣṭha at their head. The ceremony was not without effect. From the sacred fire on the altar there arose a celestial being of matchless beauty, holding in his arms a certain food which when eaten causes conception. This was divided among the three queens. In due time, Queen Kauśalyā gave birth to Rāma, revered by all, and possessed of all virtues. Kaikeyī brought forth Bharata, rich in valour, and Sumitrā bore the bright and bold twins Lakṣmaṇa and Śatrughna. As the boys grew in years they received the education befitting princes of the blood.

When they had arrived at their sixteenth year, Viśwāmitra, greatest of ascetics, came to the court of their father in search of aid against ferocious demons who were disturbing the peace of his hermitage. All four brothers were ready to come to his assistance, but it was Rāma that he chose, for he knew the lad's miraculous powers and recognized him as a divine man, being himself a pure soul steadfast in his vows. So Rāma, the lotus-eyed, with his loving brother Lakṣmaṇa followed Viśwāmitra and overpowered and killed the demons.

Then Viśwāmitra brought Rāma and Lakṣmaṇa to the kingdom of Mithilā to attend the sacrificial rite performed by King Janaka in order to find a suitable husband for his foster daughter, the beautiful Sītā. King Janaka addressed the sage in these words: 'O best of ascetics, this is the famous effulgent bow. If Rāma succeeds in stringing it, I will offer him in marriage my daughter Sītā, not born of mortals.' Thereupon Rāma took the mighty bow, and having fixed its string, easily and gracefully bent it, and even broke it in twain, so great was his strength. Many a prince before him had put forth his best effort to accomplish the feat—but in vain.

When Rāma took his bride Sītā to his home, his father decided that the time had come when he should give up his power and install Rāma as prince regent. With the consent of his subjects, therefore, he arranged that Rāma should the next day be anointed ruler. While the whole kingdom rejoiced because of the approaching ceremony, a wicked maid in the service of Queen Kaikeyī aroused in her mistress a furious jealousy of Rāma, and advised her to take advantage of two boons which the king had once offered her. Let her now demand that they be granted, for the king could not break his word. Let her ask that her son, Bharata, be placed upon the throne, and that Rāma be exiled for fourteen years.

When Queen Kaikeyī insisted upon the fulfilment of his promise, the king was overwhelmed, but Rāma gladly offered to renounce the throne and go into exile. Shortly afterward he departed from the court in company with his loving wife, Sītā, and his devoted brother,

Lakṣmaṇa. As Rāma took leave of his mother, Kauśalyā, she said to him: 'May the law of truth and righteousness, to which you adhere so strictly, protect you always.' When Rāma begged Sītā not to follow him, she replied: 'Wherever Rāma goes, there goes Sītā. The sufferings and hardships of a forest life, O Rāma, if I have your love, become experiences of joy. Where you are, it is heaven, and where you are not, everything is darkness.' And Rāma answered: 'Even heaven will not be heaven to me without you by my side.'

Immediately after Rāma's departure, King Daśaratha, whose very life and soul Rāma had been, passed away, unable to bear the grief of separation.

Now Bharata, having been absent on a visit to his maternal uncle, was unaware of what had occurred in Ayodhyā. When he learned of his father's death and of the exile of his beloved brother, he straightway went into the forest, sought out Rāma, and entreated him to return and accept the throne; but Rāma, rather than allow his father's promise to be broken, refused. Obliged to go back disappointed, Bharata yet carried with him Rāma's sandals. These he kept on the throne while he ruled as Rāma's regent.

Meanwhile Rāma, Sītā, and Lakṣmaṇa journeyed southward along the bank of the River Godavari, and as they went they built little cottages for shelter and lived by hunting deer and gathering fruit. One day, as Sītā sat alone, Rāvaṇa, the king of Ceylon, appeared disguised as a beggar and abducted her. He entreated her to become his queen, but Sītā, who was the very embodiment of chastity and purity, and who was forever devoted to her beloved Rāma, refused even to look at him. So Rāvaṇa, the demon king, who had conquered gods and men—in fact almost the entire world—took her in an 'air chariot' to Ceylon, and there imprisoned and tortured her to force her to his will—but without success.

When Rāma and Lakṣmaṇa returning to the cottage found Sītā missing, their grief was boundless. In vain they sought for her everywhere, until finally, from a dying bird, they learned of her fate. Sītā, they were told, was in Ceylon; but how were they to reach the island and fight the demon king? At least they could set out towards that far-off place, and this they immediately did. Fortunately, on their way, they met a mighty race of monkeys,[1] who under their holy leader, Hanumān, proved to be most friendly and most desirous of giving aid.

In the end Hanumān and his people joined Rāma in waging war on Rāvaṇa. A bridge was built by the monkeys connecting the

[1] The monkeys and demons are imaginative transformations of the aboriginal tribes of India. Hanumān is regarded as the greatest of devotees, one who completely surrendered himself to the divine Rāma.

southernmost point of the mainland of India with Ceylon—a little squirrel, according to legend, helping in the work. 'Blessed art thou,' said Rāma to the squirrel, 'for thou dost act to the best of thy ability.' Then he gently stroked the back of his little friend, and squirrels to this day bear the marks of Rāma's fingers.

The bridge completed, Rāma and his army entered Ceylon and gave battle to King Rāvaṇa. After several months' warfare the demon king was conquered and killed, his throne given to his brother Bibhīṣaṇa (who was devoted to Rāma), and Sītā rescued. In the very moment of their triumph, however, Rāma and Sītā had to face a new ordeal. Murmurs were heard among their followers touching Sītā's virtue. 'How do we know', they questioned, 'that Sītā continued pure during all the time she lived in the household of the demon king?' To this Rāma replied, simply: 'Sītā is purity and chastity itself.' But the complaints of the people were not stilled. 'We want the test,' they cried. Finally, to meet their demand, Sītā plunged into sacrificial fire. No sooner did this happen than from out the flames there rose up the god of fire himself, bearing on his head a throne—and there, seated upon the throne, was the slandered Sītā, unharmed.

At the expiration of his term of exile Rāma returned with Sītā and Lakṣmaṇa to the kingdom of Ayodhyā, where, to the great satisfaction of all, he was at last crowned king.

Thereafter many years passed pleasantly with Sītā, until at last evil whispers regarding her began again to be heard. She had been stolen and carried off by a demon, people said, and the proof that had been given of her chastity was not enough. She must submit to a further test, or she must be driven from the court.

Now a king must bow before public opinion. Though it was like tearing out his own heart to do it, Rāma forced himself to banish his beloved and faithful wife. Into the forest she went, and dwelt in the hermitage of the sage and poet Vālmīki. There she gave birth to twin boys, who were brought up in ignorance of their identity. Vālmīki, meanwhile, composed his poem, the Rāmāyaṇa—or rather the part of it preceding the exile of Sītā—and taught the youths, now his pupils, to sing it.

The time came when Rāma was called upon to perform a sacrificial rite which could not be completed without a wife by his side. Accordingly, his subjects begged him to marry, but this he refused to do. For the first time in his life he held out firmly against their wishes. 'This', he said, 'cannot be. My life is Sītā's.' So a golden statue of Sītā was made in order that Rāma might complete his sacrifice, and for the pleasure of the guests who should attend the sacred ceremony a dramatic entertainment was arranged. To it came Vālmīki, together with Lava and Kuśa, the unrecognized sons of Rāma and Sītā. At the bidding of the sage the two boys sang the life story of their parents in the presence of Rāma and a vast audience of his subjects. When they came to tell of Sītā's exile, Rāma's grief was beyond control. Beholding his anguish, Vālmīki thus addressed him: 'Grieve not. I will bring Sītā here.' Then, to the unspeakable joy of Rāma, his wife appeared upon the stage. But suddenly from the assembled multitude, even at this moment, there arose a murmur: 'The test! The test!' Hearing this, Sītā appealed to the gods to exonerate her. As if in answer, the earth instantly opened at her feet; and crying out 'Here is the test!' she disappeared into the bosom of her mother. (For Sītā was born of Earth, her very name meaning 'furrow'.) Overwhelming was Rāma's sorrow, and loud the people's lamentation.

Presently a messenger from the gods appeared and announced that Rāma's mission, which was to bring peace and happiness to all the world, was fulfilled; whereupon Rāma, realizing to the full his true Self, departed out of his body and joined his beloved Sītā in his celestial abode.

Interpretation of the Rāmāyaṇa

Only an occasional hint would lead the reader of this short synopsis to think of the Rāmāyaṇa as in the least a sacred scripture, and indeed if he were to read the entire seven books of the epic he would find in them but an inadequate suggestion of its full meaning to the devout Hindu. For the Hindu brings to it a spiritual interpretation which has been a tradition for centuries, almost one might say for ages.

The tradition finds especially complete expression in one of the Smṛtis, a subordinate, derivative epic known as the Adhyātma Rāmāyaṇa. This poem, whose authorship and date are alike unknown, tells over again in briefer form Vālmīki's tale, and in doing so, makes perfectly plain, throughout, its second or symbolic meaning. Rāma and Sītā are revealed as avatārs, divine incarnations, the first in a series which will include Kṛṣṇa and Buddha. In Rāma and Sītā, according to the Adhyātma Rāmāyaṇa, we behold the embodiment of Brahman in his dual aspect, the unmanifest and the manifest: Rāma representing him as impersonal absolute existence, quiescent, contained within himself; Sītā (the 'furrow', symbol of fertility) representing him as personal, creative, self-projecting. Both are recognized as God by all the characters in the poem, and as such are devoutly worshipped. Rāvaṇa, even, hating Rāma as he does, robbing him of Sītā and fighting against him—even Rāvaṇa worships them. Indeed, his very enmity is a form of worship.

This idea of worshipping God as enemy, peculiar to the Auxiliary Scriptures, may seem at first mere paradox. It is explained as follows. Salvation is union with God—a union brought about by constantly dwelling on his name, by keeping him always in one's consciousness. To think of God is to come closer to him. Now ordinarily concentration upon him arises, of course, from love; but it may also arise from hate, since hate too, as all men know, fastens one's mind upon its object.

Rāma, regarded as a mortal, is of course the embodiment of all the virtues, but especially of the virtue of truthfulness—both in its primary sense and in the sense of faithfulness to the given word. It is for the sake of truth that he loses his kingdom. His father had promised rashly, but the promise had nevertheless to be kept. This extreme devotion to truth is to be understood in the light of the characteristic Hindu belief that it is this quality by which God himself is chiefly known. God is, above all, truth. The man who loves truth must therefore in the end love God; the man who does not love truth will never love God—until his nature has suffered radical change. All other crimes can be forgiven, for they represent faults that can be overcome, but not so untruthfulness. This alone, for the Hindu, is the unpardonable sin.

Not only are the main characters of the Rāmāyaṇa interpreted by the Adhyātma Rāmāyaṇa[1] as religious symbols, but also all the main incidents. The carrying off of Sītā, for example, is viewed as a vivid expression of that profound hatred for Rāma which for Rāvaṇa is, as we have seen, the paradoxical substitute for love.

The Yoga-Vāśiṣṭha

There is a second subordinate, derivative Rāmāyaṇa, known as the Yoga-Vāśiṣṭha, the reputed author of which was the sage Vaśiṣṭha, chief priest of King Daśaratha. In this poem it is related how there awakened in the heart of Rāma, while he was still very young, a feeling of detachment from the world. He realized that the world is a vain shadow, that life is transitory, that everything we sense or experience today is and tomorrow is not, that everywhere and always there is suffering, that no state of existence is free from pain and grief, and that nothing is unconditionally good. Such were the thoughts of Rāma as he brooded on human fate. So Vaśiṣṭha instructed him regarding the unchangeable Reality, by way of illustration telling many interesting stories. The philosophy of the poem may be summed up in few words:

Life as it is known to most men is fleeting and filled with sorrow. This sorrow has its root in ignorance. In ignorance we foolishly think the transitory world to be real, not perceiving that our present

[1] It is interesting to note that Śrī Rāmakṛṣṇa was especially fond of the Adhyātma Rāmāyaṇa, and warmly recommended it to his devotees and disciples.

consciousness and all our daily experiences are but the stuff of dreams. Let us then awake betimes to the true Self, the universal Self, the one immutable Reality behind the change. Once awake, we shall know suffering and death no more.

By right thinking and diligent discrimination we attain to the truth of Brahman.

The Mahābhārata

The Mahābhārata—as its name hints—tells the story of the noble descendants of King Bharata. Its reputed author was Vyāsa.

In its original form it consisted of twenty-four thousand verses, in its final form of more than two hundred thousand. It is a rich collection of many histories and many legends. It has been truly said of it that it 'represents a whole literature rather than a single homogeneous work', and that 'it constitutes a veritable treasure house of Indian lore, both secular and religious, and gives, as does no other single work, an insight into the innermost depths of the soul of the people of Hindustan'[1]—where 'Hindustan' is merely another word for India.

The scene of the poem is the ancient kingdom of the Kurus; and the central story—the germ of which is to be found in the Vedas—concerns a great dynastic war. Following is a sketch—of course the merest sketch—of this central story.

Story of the Mahābhārata

After the death of King Pāṇḍu, his brother Dhṛtarāṣṭra became king, and brought up the five sons of Pāṇḍu along with his own hundred sons. As they grew up, the five sons of Pāṇḍu—the Pāṇḍavas—distinguished themselves for their valour, their piety, and their heroic virtues. In consequence Duryodhana, the eldest son of King Dhṛtarāṣṭra, burned with jealousy, and together with his brothers and his evil counsellors plotted in many ways against the lives of his noble cousins. On one occasion the Pāṇḍavas were prevailed upon to visit with their mother a distant town called Vāraṇāvata, on the plea that a religious festival was being held there. There they were accommodated in a palace built, by Duryodhana's direction, of inflammable materials. But the Pāṇḍavas were warned of the plot by a good man; and so they managed to escape before the house was set afire. When Duryodhana and his brothers learned that the palace had been reduced to ashes, they felt that all obstacles were now removed from their path.

The Pāṇḍavas had fled to the forest with their mother, where they

[1] *Cultural Heritage of India*, vol. I, p. 98.

lived in the guise of brāhmins. Many were the adventures they had, but their fortitude of mind, physical strength, and extraordinary valour made them overcome all dangers. By chance, in course of time, they heard of the approaching marriage festival of the princess of a neighbouring country. Kings and princes were to assemble at the court of her father, and the princess was to choose for her husband that one among them who could string a bow of great magnitude and pierce a difficult target. The Pāṇḍavas decided to go to the ceremony in their role as brāhmins.

At last the day came when suitors gathered from the four corners of India, all anxious to win the hand of the princess. Among them was Duryodhana. One after another they tried their skill, and every one failed even to bend the bow. But finally Arjuna, the third born of the Pāṇḍavas, arose, quietly approached the arena, and with ease and skill both strung the bow and hit the target. Then the princess, Draupadī, threw the garland of flowers over Arjuna's head, accepting him as her husband. The other kings and princes there assembled, however, could not bear the idea that a princess should be won by a poor brāhmin, and they tried to prevent the marriage by force of arms. The five brothers fought all these warriors, won the battle, and carried away the bride in triumph.

The five brothers now returned with Draupadī to their home in the forest, where they had been living on alms, as was the custom of brāhmins, and said to their mother, in jest: 'Mother, we have today brought home a most wonderful gift.' To this the mother replied: 'Enjoy the gift in common, my children, all of you.' Then, seeing the princess, she cried out: 'Oh, what have I said! It is a girl!' But what could be done? The mother's word was spoken once for all and could not be disregarded. So Draupadī became the common wife of all the Pāṇḍavas.

Dhṛtarāṣṭra the king and his jealous son now learned not only that the Pāṇḍavas were alive, but that they had married Draupadī, thus forming a strong alliance with a powerful neighbouring king. Though Duryodhana conceived of fresh plots to destroy them, King Dhṛtarāṣṭra was prevailed upon by the wise counsels of his uncle Bhīṣma and other elders to send for the Pāṇḍavas and offer them half of his kingdom. Accordingly the kingdom was divided. Duryodhana took possession of the richer eastern portion, with its ancient capital Hastināpur, on the Ganges, and Yudhiṣṭhira, the eldest of the Pāṇḍavas, was given the western portion of the kingdom, which was then a wilderness.

The Pāṇḍavas cleared a space in the forest and there built for themselves a beautiful city. This they called Indraprastha. Their kingdom thus happily established, they made plans to hold the rājasūya, or Imperial Sacrifice, in order to crown the eldest, Yudhiṣṭhira, as king. But in the interim, by the advice of Kṛṣṇa, their cousin (but not a brother of Duryodhana), the Pāṇḍavas decided to attack and conquer a tyrant king, Jarāsandha by name, who held captive many other kings with the intention of killing them. After fourteen days of continuous battle Jarāsandha was killed, and the captive kings were set free.

To the Imperial Sacrifice came the liberated kings with rich offerings. Other kings came to pay tribute. Dhṛtarāṣṭra and his sons, having been duly invited, were present, and also Kṛṣṇa. Amidst great rejoicing Yudhiṣṭhira was crowned.

The vast splendour and wealth of the Pāṇḍavas and the great honours shown them at the sacrifice caused the heart of Duryodhana to burn anew with intense jealousy, and when he came back to his own kingdom he devised a new plan for their destruction. King Yudhiṣṭhira, esteemed for his piety, truthfulness, and upright conduct, had but one weakness—his love of gambling. Taking advantage of this, Duryodhana challenged him to play at dice with Śakuni, a crafty gambler, and Yudhiṣṭhira regarded it as a point of honour to accept the challenge. Śakuni played dishonestly, and the king lost everything he possessed, including even his kingdom. Then maddened by the game, he staked his brothers, himself, and, finally, the fair Draupadī—and lost all. The Pāṇḍavas were now completely at the mercy of Duryodhana, who heaped insults upon them and subjected Draupadī to most inhuman treatment.

At length Dhṛtarāṣṭra intervened, set the brothers and Draupadī free, and gave Yudhiṣṭhira back his kingdom.

But again Duryodhana, with the permission of his father, challenged Yudhiṣṭhira to play at dice, this time under a strange condition. The loser would have to give up his kingdom and retire to the forest for twelve years, thereafter live unrecognized in a city for one year, and if he were found out during that year the same term of exile would have to be endured again. This game also Yudhiṣṭhira lost, and with his brothers and Draupadī went to live in the forest. There they dwelt for twelve years, practising many virtues and austerities and performing many deeds of valour. The part of the epic dealing with this period in their lives is replete with interesting stories and with ethical and spiritual teaching.

Once, while wandering in the forest, the Pāṇḍavas felt very thirsty, whereupon Yudhiṣṭhira sent one of the younger of them, Nakula, to search for water. Nakula found a crystal lake, but as he was about to drink from it, he heard a voice say: 'Stop, child. First answer my questions, and then drink of the water.' But Nakula in his thirst gave no heed to the words, drank of the water, and dropped down dead.

Since he failed to return, another brother, Sahadeva, took up the quest—and, as it chanced, came to the same lake, and there discovered Nakula's lifeless body. In his great thirst he was about to drink of the water when he heard the same warning voice that Nakula had heard before him. But he too gave no heed to it, took of the water, and at once fell dead. One by one, Arjuna and Bhīma followed in the footsteps of their brothers, acted in every respect as they had done, and suffered the same fate.

At last came Yudhiṣṭhira. He beheld his four brothers lying dead, and while lamenting his sudden unaccountable loss, he heard a voice crying: 'Yudhiṣṭhira, my child, answer my questions, and your grief and thirst will be over.'

'I will answer your questions according to my understanding,' replied Yudhiṣṭhira. 'Ask of me.'

Now the voice was the voice of Dharma, or Virtue, which had assumed the form of a crane.

'What', asked the crane, 'is the path to heaven?'

'Truthfulness.'

'By what means does one find happiness?'

'By right conduct.'

'By subduing what do men escape grief?'

'By subduing their minds.'

'When is a man loved?'

'When he is without vanity.'

'Of all the wonderful things in the world what is the most wonderful?'

'That no man, though he sees people dying all around him, believes that he will die.'

'By what path does one reach religion?'

'By argument it cannot be reached. Of scriptures and doctrines there are many, but they avail not. The path to religion is that trodden by the saints.'

Dharma, well pleased, revealed himself to Yudhiṣṭhira and brought back to life the dead brothers.

Since Dharma knew that the thirteenth year of the exile to which the Pāṇḍavas were doomed had just begun and that it was required of them that they should live in a city unrecognized, he helped them all to change their appearance and advised them to go to the kingdom of Virāṭ. Many were the incidents that befell them during the year in which, disguised, they served the king of Virāṭ, but their identity was discovered only at its close. Thus were all the conditions of the wager finally fulfilled, and their ordeal was past.

Then Yudhiṣṭhira asked Duryodhana to restore to him his half of the kingdom. But to this the evil prince would not listen. Then

Yudhiṣṭhira said he would be content if only he and his brothers were each given a village. But even this proposal Duryodhana rejected. 'Without a struggle,' he cried, 'I will not yield even so much land as can be covered by the point of a needle.'

Elders of the hostile families did their utmost to settle the quarrel, even Kṛṣṇa exerted all his influence—but Duryodhana was adamant. In the end preparations were begun for inevitable war.

Kṛṣṇa, though both sides desired his aid, would take no active part in the strife, but he gave his army to Duryodhana and offered himself as charioteer to Arjuna, prince of warriors and leader of his brothers' forces.

Neighbouring kings were drawn into the conflict, and even remote ones, until the whole of India was involved.

The war was fought in one great contest on the plain of Kurukṣetra. Here it was, in the space between the opposing armies, before the fight was begun, that Kṛṣṇa, who is the avatār of the Mahābhārata, as Rāma was the avatār of the Rāmāyaṇa, gave to Arjuna the immortal teachings of the Bhagavad-Gītā.

The battle lasted eighteen days, and ended, with the death of Duryodhana, in favour of the Pāṇḍavas.

Yudhiṣṭhira now became undisputed emperor and ruled India for thirty-six years. At his death Parīkṣit, the grandson of Arjuna, was placed on the throne; and the Pāṇḍavas, together with Draupadī, retired to the Himalayas. There, far withdrawn from the cares of the world, they practised many austerities.

The epic ends with the story of their great journey to the abode of God—God, that is, in his personal aspect. All set out together, the five brothers and the queen; but one by one all fell dead by the way, because they were not sufficiently pure to be able to enter heaven in their human bodies—no, not quite all, for Yudhiṣṭhira was without fault and so reached heaven while yet alive. Awaiting him there were Queen Draupadī, his four brothers, and others, relatives and friends, who had died on earth. Thus, as we last glimpse the characters whose fortunes we have followed through so many sorrowful adventures, they are reunited in joy.

An incident near the close of the poem must hardly go unrecorded, for it is a touching example of the simple appeal, the homely humanity, that is characteristic of India's epics.

Yudhiṣṭhira is accompanied on his last journey by his faithful dog Dhruba. When, together, they come to heaven, Yudhiṣṭhira is freely granted admission—but not Dhruba.

'Without Dhruba', declares Yudhiṣṭhira, 'I will not enter!'

When at length Yudhiṣṭhira goes to his happiness, Dhruba is by his side.

Comment on the Mahābhārata

The Mahābhārata, like the Rāmāyaṇa, is—we recall—an auxiliary scripture. That is to say, it follows, expands upon, illustrates, the all-important Vedas. Necessarily, however, in so brief a sketch as has here been given of so monumental a work, this quality has been inadequately suggested. Still some signs of it have appeared. The barest outline of the action of the poem cannot conceal that in its main course it is an illustration of the Vedic doctrine—the doctrine indeed of all religions—that right prevails. In it virtue and truth, though sorely tried, triumph at last over vice and wickedness. And the dialogue between Dharma and Yudhiṣṭhira is of course explicitly didactic.

The burden of any discussion of the subject, however, must centre in a study of the sublime episode called the Bhagavad-Gītā. This is true for two reasons: first, because it is in the Gītā alone that the poem gives a systematic exposition of religious ideas, and second, because even certain topics that are elsewhere taken up, or that implicitly pervade the narrative, are here given their most complete and analytic treatment.

So important is the Gītā that it will be reserved for a separate chapter. What follows here is a miscellaneous collection of passages of an ethical or religious nature, all drawn from other parts of the poem.

The first is the circumstantial statement of a rule of morals that has been universally acknowledged—though not, unhappily, universally practised:

'Treat others as thou wouldst thyself be treated.'[1]

'Do nothing to thy neighbour which hereafter thou wouldst not have thy neighbour do to thee.'[2]

'He who is always a friend of others and by his word, thought, and deed is continually engrossed in doing good to others—he, O Jājali, knows the meaning of dharma.'[3]

From the mouth of Yudhiṣṭhira comes the following group of moral maxims, some in no respect peculiar to India, others bearing traces, in idea or emphasis, of its characteristic thought:

'Alms-giving is the way to fame, truthfulness is the way to heaven,

[1] Śānti parva, 167. 9. This and the following passages from the Mahābhārata have been translated from *Śrīman-Mahābhāratam* (Gorakhpur: Gita Press).

[2] Anuśāsana parva, 113. 8.

[3] Śānti parva, 262. 9.

right conduct is the way to happiness. The best of gains is the gaining of health, and the best of happiness is contentment.'[1]

'There is no greater virtue than kindness. They who have their minds under control never come to grief. Friendship with the holy never ages.'[2]

'He who gives up vanity is loved by all. He who gives up anger never grieves. He who gives up greed becomes happy.'[3]

'Kindness is desiring happiness for all. Straightforwardness is mental poise. Holy is he who is kind to all. Wicked is he who is cruel.'[4]

With the exception of three excerpts from the Anuśāsana parva, the remaining passages are from the Śānti parva, one of the most beautiful of the eighteen cantos of the poem, and easily the longest. The scene is at the bedside of Bhīṣma, affectionately known as the 'grandsire', though a celibate—the ideal celibate of the poem. He was revered for his pure life, his devotion to truth, his great wisdom, and his incomparable heroism. Old though he was, he fought valiantly at Kurukṣetra, only at last to go wounded from the field. Then it was that Kṛṣṇa, desirous that his friends and disciples should learn the words of truth from the lips of the sage, came to him, accompanied by the Pāṇḍavas and others, and asked him to give of his wisdom. Many were the things he talked of, from the duties of a monarch to the secrets of philosophy, illustrating his remarks with endless tales of kings and saints and gods. His teachings, occupying nearly one-fourth of the entire epic, constitute an immemorial storehouse of Hindu laws, moral codes, and spiritual practices.

These, then, are words of the holy sage, as he lay dying on his 'bed of arrows':

'Man should always worship God with devotion—this I consider the greatest of all truths.'[5]

'The blessed ones who love the Lord and are devoted to him are free from anger, malice, avarice, and evil thought.'[6]

'Meditating on thee, O Kṛṣṇa, the energy of youth has come back to me. By thy grace I am able to speak out what would bring good to all.'[7]

'I consider human endeavour greater than dependence on fate. He who depends on fate confounds himself.'[8]

[1] Vana parva, 313. 70. [2] *Ibid.*, 76. [3] *Ibid.*, 78. [4] *Ibid.*, 90.
[5] Anuśāsana parva, 149. 8. [6] *Ibid.*, 149. 133.
[7] Śānti parva, 54. 23. [8] *Ibid.*, 56. 15.

'There is no sight equal to learning, no austerity equal to truthfulness, no misery like passion, and no happiness equal to following the ideal of renunciation.'[1]

'The secret meaning of the Vedas is truth; of truth, self-control; of self-control, freedom from all limitations. This is the sum of all scriptures.'[2]

'Purity of conduct is the greatest purity. To think of God continuously, to worship him, to chant his name and sing his praises—this is the best way of attaining the highest good.'[3]

'The Mahābhārata', says Ānandavardhana, perhaps the greatest of Sanskrit literary critics, as he sums up the philosophy of the poem—'The Mahābhārata teaches man ultimately to renounce the vanity of earthly glories and attain dharma [truth and righteousness], vairāgya [renunciation], śānti [eternal peace], and mokṣa [salvation]. Vyāsa himself remarks in his epic that he has sung the glory of the Lord and that his epic is the Nārāyaṇa Kathā, "The Story of the Lord", thus clearly indicating what the message of his epic is; for the story of the Pāṇḍavas is only an occasion, the purpose being to reveal the greatness of the Lord. Shun, therefore, all worldliness and love the Lord.'[4]

[1] Śānti parva, 176. 35.
[2] *Ibid.*, 251. 11.
[3] Anuśāsana parva, 108. 12.
[4] Dhvanyaloka.

CHAPTER 5

THE BHAGAVAD-GĪTĀ

The Teacher and the Disciple

Embedded in one book of the great Indian epic the Mahābhārata occurs the Bhagavad-Gītā, or Song of God, the most popular work in all the religious literature of India. This great document is assigned by scholars to a time somewhere between the fifth and the second centuries before Christ. Its influence upon the minds of prophets, reformers, and ascetics, and upon the laity—indeed upon the whole of Hindu life and thought through countless generations—is recognized by all students of Indian culture. Without fear of contradiction it may be said to be the Holy Bible of India, though, unlike the Upaniṣads, it is not regarded as Śruti,[1] or revealed scripture, but only as Smṛti, or tradition elaborating the doctrines of the Upaniṣads.

The following passage from the Invocation prefixed to the poem expresses the same idea thus: 'All the Upaniṣads are the cows, the son of the cowherd [Kṛṣṇa] is the milker, Pārtha [Arjuna] is the calf, men of purified intellect are the drinkers, and the supreme nectar known as the Gītā is the milk.'

The Song of God is written in the form of a dialogue between Kṛṣṇa, who may be called the Christ of India, and his friend and disciple, Arjuna. This Kṛṣṇa is the Divine One, the 'Lord who abides within the heart of all beings'. He represents a conception which is the basis of all Indian religious thought, namely, that all existence is a manifestation of God, and that God exists in all beings as the innermost Self. In every heart Kṛṣṇa is concealed, and when the veil of ignorance which covers the inner sanctuary is withdrawn, we hear the voice of Kṛṣṇa, the very voice of God. In the Gītā, Kṛṣṇa openly

[1] The Śruti, or revealed scripture, as has before been noted, is regarded as having originated in God himself. The Smṛti embodies the teachings of divine incarnations, prophets, saints, and sages. It derives its authority from the Śruti, which it must in no way contradict. The distinction emphasized is that between revealed scripture on the one hand, and religious commentary and tradition on the other.

declares himself to be one with Brahman, the Infinite Self, and urges Arjuna to attain to 'my being'.

Flying from fear,
From lust and anger,
He hides in me
His refuge, his safety:
Burnt clean in the blaze of my being,
In me many find home.[1]

Thus Kṛṣṇa of the Gītā as a historical personage has but a secondary importance.[2] Therein he differs from the Christ of the New Testament, at least the Christ upon whose personality is based the whole religion of Christianity. The Gītā is mainly concerned with Kṛṣṇa the teacher, who is identical with the divine Self, or the Infinite in man. Indeed, to those who seek spiritual illumination, it matters little, in the case of either Kṛṣṇa or Christ, whether the figure ever existed as a historical personage, so long as it is possible for them to attain through him their heart's desire, namely, union with God—the Universal Self.

And in the Gītā we find stress laid not on Kṛṣṇa as an individual personality, but on Kṛṣṇa in his transcendental aspect, as the Soul of all souls, the great 'I AM'—a fact illustrated by Arjuna's vision of the Universal Form in the body of Kṛṣṇa, described in the eleventh chapter.

Arjuna, the disciple and friend of whom Kṛṣṇa is the constant companion, is typically human, being neither a saint nor a sinner, but a struggling soul seeking to escape from grief and misery. He is represented in the Gītā as a man of action, a fighter—a man living

[1] IV. 10.

[2] 'The historical Krishna, no doubt, existed. We meet the name first in the Chhandogya Upanishad where all we can gather about him is that he was well known in spiritual tradition as a knower of the Brahman, so well known indeed in his personality and the circumstances of his life that it was sufficient to refer to him by the name of his mother as Krishna son of Devaki for all to understand who was meant. In the same Upanishad we find mention of King Dhritarashtra son of Vichitravirya, and since tradition associated the two together so closely that they are both of them leading personages in the action of the Mahabharata, we may fairly conclude that they were actually contemporaries and that the epic is to a great extent dealing with historical characters and in the war of Kurukshetra with a historical occurrence imprinted firmly on the memory of the race. . . . There is a hint also in the poem of the story or legend of the Avatar's early life in Vrindavan which, as developed by the Puranas into an intense and powerful spiritual symbol, has exercised so profound an influence on the religious mind of India. We have also in the Harivansha an account of the life of Krishna, very evidently full of legends, which perhaps formed the basis of the Puranic accounts.' Sri Aurobindo Ghose, *Essays on the Gita* (First Series), pp. 19–21.

in the world, but confused as to his duty and the true meaning and goal of life, and eager to find a way to peace and freedom.

The Gītā is, then, in the form of a conversation between Kṛṣṇa, who is Nārāyaṇa, or God, and Arjuna, who represents nara, or man. The Gītā is the song of God chanted in thrilling notes to human ears.

The Teachings of the Gītā

The commentaries upon the Gītā are numerous. Each school of philosophy in India has found in it the source of its metaphysical system, and from it every philosopher or saint has drawn inspiration. So the Gītā contains the germs of all forms and systems of Indian religious thought, but it cannot itself be limited to any particular system of metaphysics or religion. For it is not a metaphysical treatise, nor is it the fruit of the traditional religious thinking of any particular sect; rather, one should say, it contains metaphysical truths in their diverse aspects, and embodies every form of religious thought, practice, and discipline. Conflicting ideas apparently lie side by side unreconciled. A person who holds to one religion as exclusively true will find in the Gītā, as some Western critics hold, 'different streams of tradition becoming confused in the mind of the author'.

The spirit of catholicity is a prominent feature of all Indian teachings. They evince a spirit of harmony rather than of conflict, of synthesis and toleration rather than of opposition and sectarianism. Infinite is God, infinite are his aspects, and infinite are the ways to reach him. In the Atharva Veda we read: Ekaṁ jyotir bahudhā bibhāti—The one Light appears in diverse forms. This ideal of harmony has held its own in India down to the present time. The Gītā carries it to its logical conclusion in blending, synthesizing, and reconciling conflicting metaphysical theories and opposed conceptions of spiritual discipline. We read in its pages:

> Whatever wish men bring me in worship,
> That wish I grant them.
> Whatever path men travel
> Is my path:
> No matter where they walk
> It leads to me.[1]

Sri Aurobindo has rightly remarked: 'The Gita is not a weapon for dialectical warfare; it is a gate opening on the whole world of spiritual truth and experience, and the view it gives us embraces all the

[1] IV. 11.

provinces of that supreme region. It maps out, but it does not cut up or build walls or hedges to confine our vision.'[1]

Fundamentally the Gītā insists upon knowledge of the Self, or God, as the only goal of life. All religions, all doctrines spring from God; and yet no religion or doctrine can encompass his being; any one religion has value only inasmuch as it helps man to attain to him. The conflicts of doctrines cease only when he shines in our hearts. 'When the whole country is flooded, the reservoir becomes superfluous. So, to the illumined seer, the Vedas are all superfluous.'[2]

In his last utterance Śrī Kṛṣṇa, the divine teacher, clearly and definitely states the 'supreme word' of the poem, the highest note of the discourse: Hear thou again my supreme word, he says, the profoundest of all—

Give me your whole heart,
Love and adore me,
Worship me always,
Bow to me only,
And you shall find me:
This is my promise
Who love you dearly.

Lay down all duties
In me, your refuge.
Fear no longer,
For I will save you
From sin and from bondage.[3]

This 'supreme word' of the Gītā, though a simple utterance, is not easy to obey and realize. Self-surrender, knowingly 'to live, move, and have our being in God', is central in all religious teachings—or yogas, as they are called in the Gītā.

These yogas, which are peculiar to Indian life, are fully expounded in the Gītā. The word yoga literally means union—union with God. Its secondary meaning, a path to union with the Godhead, applies to the different disciplines. These paths of attainment may be found in the earliest Indian scriptures, and they have always been known to the sages and scholars of the land. They are principally four: jñāna yoga, or the path of union through knowledge; rāja yoga, or the path of realization through meditation and psychic control; bhakti yoga, or the path of realization through love and devotion; and karma yoga, or the path of union through work. Not only have all of these been expounded in the Gītā as the various methods of attaining union with God, but in its teachings they stand reconciled, blended, and harmonized.

[1] Ghose, *op. cit.* (First Series), p. 10. [2] II. 40. [3] XVIII. 65, 66.

Most commentators, however, stress one or another yoga as the characteristic teaching of Śrī Kṛṣṇa. Formerly, either jñāna yoga or bhakti yoga—attainment by means of knowledge or devotion—was stressed; today much emphasis is put on karma yoga, or the path of work. But the fact is that whenever Śrī Kṛṣṇa speaks of one of them, he naturally attaches extreme importance to that particular one—so much so that each of the yogas in turn assumes the pre-eminent place. The perfect man of the Gītā, with some resemblance to the Aristotelian conception of the ideal man as the harmonious embodiment of all the virtues, is one who is active as well as meditative, who is full of devotion, and who at the same time possesses the knowledge of the Self.

The Gītā is divided into eighteen chapters, which can be grouped into three sections, or books. The first of these three books deals with karma yoga, the path of work, and here the insistence is upon action. The second book is an exposition of jñāna yoga, the path of knowledge, and here the insistence is upon knowledge of the Self. The subject of karma is not entirely dismissed, but is harmonized with the path of knowledge. The last of the books discusses bhakti yoga, or the path of love and devotion, and the insistence here is on worship and love of the one Supreme Lord. Jñāna (knowledge) and karma (work) do not disappear, but are both harmonized with devotion. As Sri Aurobindo has beautifully expressed it: 'The double path [jñāna and karma] becomes the triune way of knowledge, works and devotion. And the fruit of the sacrifice, the one fruit still placed before the seeker, is attained—union with the divine Being and oneness with the supreme divine nature.'[1] And in and through this triune way of knowledge, works, and devotion, runs the thread of rāja yoga, or the path of meditation, which insists on poise, self-control, tranquillity, and the meditative life.

From another angle, the first book, comprising the first six chapters, deals with the true nature of Tvam, or Thou (i.e. the true nature of the Self), a word that appears in the great Vedāntic saying Tat Tvam Asi—Thou art That.[2] The second book explains the nature of Tat, or That; and the last book brings out the identity of Thou with That. Thus the great Vedāntic truth embodied in the saying Thou art That forms the subject-matter of the Gītā, and the whole poem is only an exposition of its meaning.

The Doctrine of Renunciation

Once, when Śrī Rāmakṛṣṇa was asked, 'What does the Gītā teach?' he replied, 'If you utter the word "Gītā" a few times, you begin to say

[1] Ghose, *op. cit.* (First Series), p. 54. [2] Chāndogya, VI. xiii. 3.

"tāgi, tāgi"—meaning one who has renounced. The call to renunciation pervades the Gītā.'

Renunciation is indeed the beginning, the middle, and the end of spiritual life. It is inseparable from any of the yogas taught in the Gītā. It does not necessarily imply, however, adoption of the monastic life. For it is a discipline that has to be practised by all, by monks no more than by men of the world. Otherworldliness, in spite of the associations of the word, does not imply escaping into the forest and shunning the duties of everyday life. Throughout, the Gītā insists on the performance of the duties of life, though with a heart free from attachment and thoughts of worldly gain, and devoted entirely to the adoration of God.

It is interesting to note that the Gītā condemns in unmistakable terms acceptance of monastic life if the spirit of renunciation is lacking in the heart.

The failure to grasp the true spiritual outlook of the Gītā has led many in modern times to read the ideals of modern secularism into the pages of this ancient Indian scripture. Instead of the ideal of renunciation—the denial of 'me' and 'mine' and the conversion of the lusts of the flesh into a passionate love of God—they find in it only a condemnation of otherworldliness and an insistence on living in the world for the performance of the world's works. The ideal of knowledge, devotion, meditation, and nonattachment, they aver, is subservient to karma, according to them the central doctrine of the Gītā. So the Western ideals of humanitarian service and social uplift, besides political activity and family life, have been identified with the karma yoga of the Gītā. All of these objectives and ideals may of course be laudable, and the Gītā does not condemn them, but it is also certain that it does not teach them as karma yoga. Granting that these ideals are recognized in the Gītā, unless they are spiritualized they have no relation to karma yoga. Not karma, mere action, but karma yoga, union with God through action, is the essence of the teaching of the Gītā on this subject.

Thus, not sacrifice for humanity, but service to humanity as a sacrifice unto God, whose image we learn to see in man, is the true ideal. No political activities undertaken with a selfish motive, but such activities performed as worship of God; not merely family life and the performance of the ordinary domestic duties, but a life of nonattachment in the midst of these duties, combined with knowledge of the nature of one's immutable, eternal Self—this is the real message of the Bhagavad-Gītā. It is only as worldly affairs are spiritualized and transformed that they become a part of karma yoga. In short, temporal life and spiritual values stand in a relation of harmony; they constitute one divine life—as the Gītā tells us.

Insistence on the performance of svadharma, or one's secular duty, in the spirit of yoga, is indeed often met with in the Gītā, but this insistence ceases to have force and meaning with the growth of higher knowledge. Sri Aurobindo makes this issue abundantly clear when he says:

'An inner situation may even arise, as with the Buddha, in which all duties have to be abandoned, trampled on, flung aside in order to follow the call of the Divine within. I cannot think that the Gita would solve such an inner situation by sending Buddha back to his wife and father and the government of the Sakya State, or would direct a Ramakrishna to become a Pundit in a vernacular school and disinterestedly teach little boys their lessons, or bind down a Vivekananda to support his family and for that to follow dispassionately the law or medicine or journalism. The Gita does not teach the disinterested performance of duties, but the following of the divine life, the abandonment of all dharmas, *sarvadharmān*, to take refuge in the Supreme alone, and the divine activity of a Buddha, a Ramakrishna, a Vivekananda is perfectly in consonance with this teaching.'[1]

The Battlefield of Kurukṣetra

The great poem opens with a description of two armies arrayed against each other. The scene is laid in the field of Kurukṣetra, where, accompanied by his divine charioteer, Kṛṣṇa, stands Arjuna, the hero, about to give battle to the host of the Kauravas. As Arjuna views both the armies he is filled with melancholy. The horrors of war and the terror of death overwhelm him, and he turns to Kṛṣṇa, who urges him to carry on the fight against his enemies, the enemies of righteousness and truth. Arjuna's feeling of revulsion against useless slaughter meets with Kṛṣṇa's stern rebuke. 'Arjuna,' he says, 'is this hour of battle the time for scruples and fancies? Are they worthy of you, who seek enlightenment? Any brave man who merely hopes for fame or heaven would despise them.'[2]

So, at the very beginning of the great book, we are astonished to see one of the supreme teachers of spiritual truth supporting war. How is this to be explained?

As we proceed, we discover that the way of realizing the divine consciousness, and attaining eternal life and infinite peace, is through complete detachment and self-surrender. We can understand the Gītā as a holy scripture and Kṛṣṇa as a divine teacher only when we consider that this war is but an occasion for bringing spiritual truths to our attention. But it is still difficult to understand how the actual war, and Kṛṣṇa's urging to wage it to the end, can be reconciled with

[1] Ghose, *op. cit.* (First Series), pp. 45–6.

[2] II. 2.

any spiritual teaching. The Gītā's ideal man is certainly not the superman of Nietzsche's imagination, who would crush all opposition in his struggle for power. Quite the contrary, it is he 'who delights in God', like a yogi (one who practises yoga), whose spiritual practices correspond to the life of contemplation which Aristotle considers the highest attainment of man. Yoga, or union with God, has been defined in the Gītā as follows:

' "The light of a lamp does not flicker in a windless place": that is the simile which describes a yogi of one-pointed mind, who meditates upon the Atman. When, through the practice of yoga, the mind ceases its restless movements, and becomes still, he realizes the Atman. It satisfies him entirely. Then he knows that infinite happiness which can be realized by the purified heart but is beyond the grasp of the senses. He stands firm in this realization. Because of it, he can never again wander from the inmost truth of his being.'

Now that he holds it
He knows this treasure
Above all others:
Faith so certain
Shall never be shaken
By heaviest sorrow.

'To achieve this certainty is to know the real meaning of the word yoga. It is the breaking of contact with pain.'[1]

But we are still facing the problem of war and the destruction it involves. This Gordian knot can easily be cut if we read a symbolic meaning into the battlefield of Kurukṣetra. Many commentators say that Kurukṣetra is not an external battlefield but one of our own making, within ourselves. It is the battlefield of life. It is not the scene of a war in the world outside, but of one which we continually wage within us against the evil forces of passion, prejudice, and evil inclination, in order that we may hold dominion over ourselves. Arjuna was awakened enough to realize the need of struggling against these forces; but then despondency and weakness of will got the upper hand, and he longed to fall back to the familiar ways of pleasure, which are the ways of least effort. At this point of weak despair, Kṛṣṇa, the voice of God, urged him to struggle further against his evil nature and win the kingdom of heaven.

This explanation is in entire harmony with the teachings of the Gītā. If the Gītā had been a book independent of the Mahābhārata, we need not have concerned ourselves with the question whether or not the war was actually fought. But since it forms a chapter of the

[1] VI. 19–23.

great epic, dealing with the war between the Pāṇḍavas and the Kauravas, we are forced to find a means of reconciling the fact of war with the aspiration after spiritual life with which it is permeated. Ancient commentators such as Śaṁkara, Rāmānuja, and Śrīdhara took the actual war for granted. None of them made any attempt either to explain the war away or to establish harmony between the spirit of war and the spirit of peace; for they all took it for granted that the readers of the Gītā were familiar with the dharma of India based on caste, or gradation of life and duties. But the modern mind is not familiar with this ancient tradition, and, moreover, it knows the worst horrors of war. Hence it finds it difficult to justify Kṛṣṇa's urging Arjuna to fight.

In order, therefore, that we may perceive more clearly just why Kṛṣṇa bade Arjuna fight, and how by fulfilling his duty as a warrior Arjuna could attain to the highest peace and beatitude, we must familiarize ourselves with the caste system of India. This was rooted in the Vedas, and was known as Varṇāśrama dharma, or religion and duty based on the different orders of life. The democratic West, at least theoretically, does not believe in caste. 'All men are born equal' is the central doctrine in its social philosophy. Equal opportunities will bring equal results. But has this theory any foundation in the facts of life? Even supposing equality to be established, would this world then remain a world? Variety and unity in variety make up the universal law of creation. Take away the variety, and this world would cease to be. The facts of birth and death, and of life itself, contradict the theory of equality and uniformity. Since individuals are born with different temperaments, they cannot grow and succeed in the same way and to the same extent, however equal might be the opportunities afforded them.

Indian philosophy recognizes the variety as well as the unity. In the soul of man there is no distinction either of sex or caste, and the one God dwells in the hearts of all beings alike. In the Gītā, as well as in the Upaniṣads, God is described as Puruṣa—one who resides in the temple of the body. But God is not expressed equally in all beings, and all beings are not living equally in God; nor is God's power equally manifest in nature and in man.

Śrī Kṛṣṇa on the one hand, declares that

> Seeing all things equal,
> The enlightened may look
> On the brahmin, learned and gentle,
> On the cow, on the elephant,
> On the dog, on the eater of dogs.[1]

[1] V. 18.

On the other hand, he points out the difference between man and beast, as well as between man and man. And this difference is caused by the 'differentiation of guṇa and karma'.[1]

Most Indian philosophers accept the view of the Sāṁkhya philosophy that the whole of nature is composed of three forces, or guṇas, called in Sanskrit sattwa, rajas, and tamas. In the world of mind and matter these correspond, respectively, to equilibrium, activity, and inertness. Sattwa, or equilibrium, expresses itself in calmness, purity, and tranquillity; rajas, or activity, in desire, power, and energy; tamas, or inertia, in dullness, laziness, and weakness.[2]

Every man has in him these three forces. At times tamas prevails, and we are lazy; we lack incentive, and our wills grow weak. Again rajas prevails, and we become active, hopeful, and ambitious; we want to be up and doing. Or sattwa possesses us, as a result of which we grow calm and serene, and high and noble thoughts fill our minds. Though all three guṇas work in each man, always one or another predominates over the other two; and the one that predominates determines the group, or caste, to which he belongs.

There is no denying that human society is a graded organization. Since men have different mental constitutions, they cannot all follow one and the same ideal. Swami Vivekananda has made this wise remark upon the subject:

'Two ways are left open to us—the way of the ignorant, who think that there is only one road to truth and that all the rest are wrong—and the way of the wise, who admit that, according to our mental constitution or the plane of existence in which we are, duty and morality may vary. The important thing is to know that there are gradations of duty and morality, that the duty of one state of life, in one set of circumstances, will not and cannot be that of another.'[3]

All this does not mean, however, that the universal ideal of nonresistance, purity, nonattachment, tranquillity, and the like—in short, the ideal of living in the consciousness of God—has to be adapted to the individual temperament; for the high spiritual goal of life must be kept in view by all men.

But at the same time different levels of being must be recognized,

[1] IV. 13.

[2] Cf. Plato's threefold division of the soul (*Republic*, IV) into the rational, the spirited, or concupiscent, and the temperate. These are reconciled by justice, or righteousness. Plato may have arrived at his conclusions through study of Hindu philosophy.

[3] *Complete Works of Vivekananda*, vol. I, p. 35.

so that everyone may be enabled, step by step, sooner or later, to attain to supreme good.

Indian systems of morality and religion have stressed this fact from the earliest times, and in the Hindu scriptures and books on ethics different rules of conduct are formulated for different types of men. The Gītā insists that a man should shape his ideals according to the type to which he belongs, and thus endeavour to follow his svadharma—to do his duty according to the state of his growth. This is a surer way to progress than that of taking up other men's ideals, when these are so unsuited to one's temperament that they can never be fully realized. One should not be expected to perform a task beyond one's strength. 'For instance,' to quote Swami Vivekananda, 'we take a child and at once give him the task of walking twenty miles; either the little one dies, or one in a thousand crawls the twenty miles to reach the end exhausted and half dead.'[1]

Nonresistance is recognized by all the great teachers as the highest virtue. The Gītā also regards it as the highest virtue, but does not say that all people under all circumstances must practise it. On the contrary, it points out that for some it is necessary to learn to resist evil in order that by this means they may grow into a state in which they have the moral strength to endure it. Consider the man who does not resist because he is weak or lazy and will not make the effort to do so. Is this the virtue of nonresistance? Then consider another who knows that he can strike an irresistible blow if he likes, and yet does not strike, but blesses, his enemy. In the words of Swami Vivekananda: 'The one who from weakness does not resist commits a sin, and therefore cannot receive any benefit from his nonresistance; while the other would commit a sin by offering resistance.'[2] That is to say, we must gather the power to resist; then, having gained it, we must renounce it. Then only will nonresistance be a virtue. If, merely lacking in will, we deceive ourselves into the belief that we are actuated by the highest motives, we do not merit praise. Says Swami Vivekananda, speaking of meritorious resistance:

'. . . this nonresistance is the highest manifestation of power in actual possession, and what is called the resisting of evil is but a step on the way towards it.'[3]

'Arjuna became a coward at the sight of the mighty army arrayed against him; his "love" made him forget his duty towards his country and king. That is why Sri Krishna told him that he was a hypocrite, and said, "Thou talkest like a wise man, but thy actions betray thee to be a coward; therefore stand up and fight".'[4]

[1] *Complete Works of Vivekananda*, vol. I, p. 39.
[2] *Ibid.*, pp. 36–7.
[3] *Ibid.*, p. 37.
Ibid.

Paul Elmer More, reviewing the teachings of Christ, such as nonresistance, humility, and renunciation, remarks: 'The doctrines of Christ, if accepted by the world in their integrity—the virtues, that is, of humility, nonresistance and poverty—would . . . simply make an end of the whole social fabric . . . ; and there is every reason to believe that he [Christ] looked to see only a few chosen souls follow in his footsteps.'[1]

Only a few can follow in his steps, because only a few are ideal brāhmins, endowed with sattwa. All others must seek graded ideals, graded standards and duties, in order that in time they also may become ideal brāhmins and so attain to the highest.

More, making a distinction between worldly and spiritual virtues, adds: 'To apply the laws of the spirit to the activities of this earth is at once a desecration and denial of religion, and a bewildering and unsettling of the social order.' He declares, in effect, that as we meet other men who are not inspired by religious virtues—a particularly common experience—we cannot, in our relations with them, practise virtues like humility, purity, poverty, chastity, and nonresistance in their highest form; for if we did, the very structure of society would be undermined. In place of these, he would have us practise the Aristotelian or cardinal virtues of justice, temperance, prudence, and fortitude.

The Gītā and all Hindu books on ethics meet this central problem of conduct in a somewhat different way. Instead of drawing a sharp line of distinction between virtues, worldly and spiritual, they indicate the existence of graded virtues—virtues different according to the different types of humanity and their varying conditions in life. But they insist that each is a step leading to a virtue higher in the scale of life, and that the ultimate goal is the attainment of spiritual consciousness.

To quote the Gītā:

> All mankind
> Is born for perfection
> And each shall attain it,
> Will he but follow
> His nature's duty.[2]

Śrī Kṛṣṇa asserts that people are differentiated 'according to the guṇas, born of their own nature'.

He says in the Gītā:

[1] *Shelburne Essays*, 'The Religious Ground of Humanitarianism', p. 243.
[2] XVIII. 45.

Seer and leader,
Provider and server:
Each has the duty
Ordained by his nature
Born of the gunas.

The seer's duty,
Ordained by his nature,
Is to be tranquil
In mind and in spirit,
Self-controlled,
Austere and stainless,
Upright, forbearing;
To follow wisdom,
To know the Atman,
Firm of faith
In the truth that is Brahman.

The leader's duty,
Ordained by his nature,
Is to be bold,
Unflinching and fearless,
Subtle of skill
And open-handed,
Great-hearted in battle,
A resolute ruler.

Others are born
To the tasks of providing:
These are the traders,
The cultivators,
The breeders of cattle.

To work for all men,
Such is the duty
Ordained for the servers:
This is their nature.[1]

Since, as the Gītā teaches, a man must perform the duties and practise the virtues suitable to his individual being, he should learn to worship God by so doing. This will ultimately help him to rise above both duty and virtue. To rise above the guṇas, says the Gītā, is the highest ideal of man. Hence, though Śrī Kṛṣṇa does urge Arjuna to fulfil his duty as a kṣatriya (a member of the warrior caste), he

[1] XVIII. 41–44.

wishes him also to be nistraiguṇya—one above the three gunas. The state of such a man is identical with union with Brahman, or God.

In his commentary on the Gītā, Swami Swarupananda remarks:

'The highest worship of the Lord consists in the closest approach to him. Māyā, which includes Karma, or habits, tendencies and actions, prevents a man from nearing the Lord, i.e., realizing his own Self. By working out one's Karma alone, according to the law of one's being, can this veil be rent and the end accomplished.'[1]

The Gītā furthermore explains how, by fulfilling the law of one's being, and by offering the Lord all work and duties and virtues as worship, one may attain purity of heart, self-control, and dispassionateness of spirit. Then it is that one

> . . . casts from him
> Vanity, violence,
> Pride, lust, anger
> And all his possessions,
> Totally free
> From the sense of ego
> And tranquil of heart;
> That man is ready
> For oneness with Brahman.[2]

Thus human society becomes a graded organization. Though the highest goal of life is the same for all men, and certain truths are universal, these matters of highest import cannot be attained by all in precisely the same way. The special requirements of individuals—varying with their natures, tendencies, temperaments—must be recognized; and man has to be treated as a spiritual being in the process of formation. Hence the necessity of an accepted scripture or a teacher to enable a person to know what particular ideals are suited to the law of his own life and being, and will therefore best help him to move towards perfection.[3]

[1] *Srimad-Bhagavad-Gita* (trans. Swami Swarupananda [Calcutta: Advaita Ashrama, 1956]), p. 387.

[2] XVIII. 53.

[3] The subject should perhaps not be dropped without a further word to prevent any possibility of misunderstanding on an extremely important point. In the Hindu idea of a man's proper conduct there is unquestionably an element of relativity; one man's moral requirements and responsibilities may not in all respects be the same as another man's. But it is important to realize that there are sharp limits to this relativity. The allowable differences between one man's conduct and another man's all fall within a comparatively narrow and innocuous zone. No man, whatever his temperament or condition in life, may lie or steal or murder. The Ten Commandments of Moses, on which Western morality is based, are as absolutely and universally valid in India as they are in America.

Is Nirvāṇa Compatible with Work in the World?

As we have already learned, in our study of the Upaniṣads, the supreme goal of human life is mokṣa, or liberation. It is release from the wheel of birth and death through attainment of knowledge of the true Self, which is one with Brahman. It is also complete cessation of pain and sorrow. As already explained, our suffering is an immediate experience, and, as such, it can be got rid of only through immediate experience of the Self in union with the blissful Brahman. Mokṣa is called in the Gītā Brahma-nirvāṇa—extinction in Brahman, or union with Brahman. It exactly corresponds to attaining the kingdom of heaven within. Christ teaches us: 'Be ye therefore perfect, even as your Father which is in heaven is perfect.' The same ideal of perfection is taught in the Gītā. Mokṣa, or Brahma-nirvāṇa, is not an experience to be had only after death, but one that can be attained here and now. Every age produces living souls that do experience nirvāṇa in this life. Thus the Gītā, speaking of the knower of God:

> Absorbed in Brahman
> He overcomes the world
> Even here, alive in the world.
> Brahman is one,
> Changeless, untouched by evil:
> What home have we but Him?
>
> The enlightened, the Brahman-abiding,
> Calm-hearted, unbewildered,
> Is neither elated by the pleasant
> Nor saddened by the unpleasant.
>
> His mind is dead
> To the touch of the external:
> It is alive
> To the bliss of the Atman.
> Because his heart knows Brahman
> His happiness is for ever.[1]
>
> All consumed
> Are their imperfections,
> Doubts are dispelled,
> Their senses mastered,
> Their every action
> Is wed to the welfare

[1] V. 19–21.

Of fellow-creatures:
Such are the seers
Who enter Brahman
And know nirvana.[1]

Only that yogi
Whose joy is inward,
Inward his peace,
And his vision inward
Shall come to Brahman
And know nirvana.[2]

Thus the Gītā teaches that through yogic practices of nonattachment, and through freedom from lust and anger, one attains purity and perfection and everlasting peace (the peace that passeth all understanding) while still living in this world.

Nirvāṇa, or self-extinction in Brahman, clearly implies extinction of the ego, the false self, in the higher Self—the source of all knowledge, of all existence, and of all happiness. One who experiences it no longer identifies himself with the limitations of the body, the senses, and the mind, but unites himself in consciousness with Brahman, the all-pervading and divine Being. This consciousness is the transcendental consciousness; it is the samādhi of the yogis, the nirvāṇa of the Buddhists, and the kingdom of heaven of the Christians. One does not dwell continuously, however, in that state of complete absorption. One returns to normal consciousness when one is in contact with what we may call outer world consciousness, but the illumination which one experienced in the transcendental state never again leaves one. Though one is now experiencing the world, and is vividly conscious of the manifold universe, one knows one's true Self, and the sense of the divine presence is ever with one. Of one in this state we read in the Gītā:

His heart is with Brahman,
His eye in all things
Sees only Brahman
Equally present,
Knows his own Atman
In every creature,
And all creation
Within that Atman.

'That yogi sees me in all things, and all things within me. He never loses sight of me, nor I of him. He is established in union with me,

[1] V. 25. [2] V. 24.

and worships me devoutly in all beings. That yogi abides in me, no matter what his mode of life.'[1]

Thus we realize that the illumination derived from the transcendental experience is not confined to the state of actual absorption, but extends beyond into the normal state, in which one perceives the multiplicity of the changing world. But one who has had that transcendental experience looks upon the relative universe with a calm, penetrating eye; for, though one sees multiplicity and relativity, and the concomitant play of joys and sorrows, of life and death, yet one glimpses behind the relativity and the multiplicity the one, immutable, blissful Brahman. It is then, affirms the Gītā, that one discovers a love for all one's fellows and nourishes the will to do them good.

Clearly nirvāṇa is philosophically compatible with worldly activity. In practice also we see, in Kṛṣṇa, Buddha, Christ, Śaṁkara, Rāmakṛṣṇa, Vivekananda, and many others, how, having attained to transcendental consciousness, one may continue to live an illumined life in the service of humanity. But this humanitarian service is founded first of all on the love of God—a love which perceives all men as partakers of his being.

More than all the other sacred scriptures of the world, the Gītā insists on action in the world, and exhorts men never to turn away from activity and the doing of good to others. We shall see, when we come to discuss karma yoga, how works aid in self-purification and the attainment of Brahma-nirvāṇa. Having reached perfection in yoga, with nothing more to gain from works, one still does not cease from action.

The charge brought against Indian religions, especially Buddhism, that they inculcate passivity and inaction, is without any real basis. Both Hinduism and Buddhism have as their ideal nirvāṇa, or the attainment of the kingdom of heaven, which is an experience of unalloyed bliss in God while one continues to live a life of intense activity in this world.

One very pertinent question, however, arises in this connection. The Brahma-nirvāṇa of the Gītā, as well as the nirvāṇa of Buddhism, clearly means the extinction of the ego in the realization of the transcendental consciousness; but as one returns from the transcendental to the normal state, does not one's former ego-consciousness return to one? Without this consciousness, how is it possible again to perceive the multiple universe or perform any service to humanity?

Śrī Rāmakṛṣṇa, to whom samādhi, or transcendental consciousness, may be said to have been as natural as is normal consciousness to us,

[1] VI. 29–31.

and who yet continued to live for the good of humanity, explained this problem as follows:

'Some retain the sense of ego as "the servant I" or "the devotee I"—the sense "Thou art the Lord, I am Thy child"—even after attaining samādhi. The "I" of a devotee does no harm to any living creature. It is like a sword which, after touching the philosopher's stone, is turned to gold. The sword retains the same form, but it does not cut or injure anyone.[1] The dry leaves of the coconut tree drop off in the wind, leaving marks on the trunk; those marks only show that there were leaves there at one time. Similarly, only the form or mark of ego is left in one who has reached God. Also his passions remain only as empty forms. He becomes simple and pure like a child.'[2]

'Śaṁkara and spiritual teachers like him came down to the consciousness of "ego" for the teaching and good of humanity. . . . The bee buzzes until it alights in the heart of the flower. It becomes silent as soon as it begins to drink the honey. Then again, after it has drunk its fill, it makes a sweet humming sound.'[3]

'Few can stay long on the roof. Those who reach samādhi and attain Brahman return to the lower plane of consciousness and then realize that it is he who has become man and the universe. The singer cannot hold to the highest note very long. He comes down to the lower notes. Similarly, the man of realization comes back from the transcendental consciousness and perceives the world of relativity, and, though he sees the world, he sees Brahman everywhere.'[4]

A liberated man overcomes the world of karma, and though he continues to live and work, he is not bound or tainted by it. He lives only to exhaust what are known as the prārabdha karmas.[5] After he has exhausted his prārabdha, his body falls away, and he attains what is known as absolute freedom. The state of mind of the free soul at death is thus described in the Gītā:

'At the hour of death, when a man leaves his body, he must depart with his consciousness absorbed in me. Then he will be united with me. Be certain of that. Whatever a man remembers at the last, when

[1] *Kathāmṛta*, vol. I, p. 146.
[2] *Ibid.*, vol. I, p. 91.
[3] *Ibid.*, vol. III, p. 10.
[4] *Ibid.*, vol. III, p. 11.
[5] In the teachings of the Gītā, however, a distinction is made between the avatārs, or divine incarnations, such as Kṛṣṇa, Christ, and others on the one hand, and ordinary souls, who attain nirvāṇa through struggles of their own, on the other. The former have no prārabdha karmas (the stored-up karmas of the past which unfold in the present life), and have never been subject to the law of karma; the latter free themselves from all karma except the prārabdha.

he is leaving the body, will be realized by him in the hereafter; because that will be what his mind has most constantly dwelt on, during this life.'[1]

This is the general law: a man's next life is guided by his present one. The sum total of his deeds in the present life, that attachment or desire that has been his, comes to his mind before death and determines his immediate future existence. And this same law applies to a free soul, whose only attachment has been to God. He goes, not to another life, but, as it is said, to him.

Thus we read in the Gītā:

> What fashion His form has, who shall conceive of it?
> He dwells beyond delusion, the dark of maya.
> On Him let man meditate
> Always, for then at the last hour
> Of going hence from his body he will be strong
> In the strength of this yoga, faithfully followed:
> The mind is firm, and the heart
> So full, it hardly holds its love.
>
> Thus he will take his leave: and now, with the life-force
> Indrawn utterly, held fast between the eyebrows,
> He goes forth to find his Lord,
> That light-giver, who is greatest.

'Now I will tell you briefly about the nature of Him who is called the deathless by those seers who truly understand the Vedas. Devotees enter into Him when the bonds of their desire are broken. To reach this goal, they practise control of passions.

'When a man leaves his body and departs, he must close all the doors of the senses. Let him hold the mind firmly within the shrine of the heart, and fix the life-force between the eyebrows. Then let him take refuge in steady concentration, uttering the sacred syllable Om and meditating upon me. Such a man reaches the highest goal. When a yogi has meditated upon me unceasingly for many years, with an undistracted mind, I am easy of access to him, because he is always absorbed in me.

'Great souls who find me have found the highest perfection. They are no longer reborn into this condition of transience and pain.'[2]

The Gītā raises one more problem, this time with reference to the man who struggles to attain perfection and fails to realize it in this life. Arjuna says:

[1] VIII. 6. [2] VIII. 9–15.

'Suppose a man has faith, but does not struggle hard enough? His mind wanders away from the practice of yoga and he fails to reach perfection. What will become of him then?

'When a man goes astray from the path to Brahman, he has missed both lives, the worldly and the spiritual. He has no support anywhere. Is he not lost, as a broken cloud is lost in the sky?

'This is the doubt that troubles me, Krishna; and only you can altogether remove it from my mind. Let me hear your answer.'

Sri Krishna:

'No, my son. That man is not lost, either in this world or the next. No one who seeks Brahman ever comes to an evil end.

'Even if a man falls away from the practice of yoga, he will still win the heaven of the doers of good deeds, and dwell there many long years. After that, he will be reborn into the home of pure and prosperous parents. He may even be born into a family of illumined yogis. But such a birth in this world is more difficult to obtain.

'He will then regain that spiritual discernment which he acquired in his former body; and so he will strive harder than ever for perfection. Because of his practices in the previous life, he will be driven on toward union with Brahman, even in spite of himself. For the man who has once asked the way to Brahman goes further than any mere fulfiller of the Vedic rituals. By struggling hard, and cleansing himself of all impurities, that yogi will move gradually toward perfection through many births, and reach the highest goal at last.'[1]

The Ultimate Reality: God and Avatār

In its analysis of the ultimate reality, the Gītā brings out explicitly what is implied in the direct experiences of the seers and sages of the Upaniṣads. Behind the objects of this phenomenal world lies a changeless, permanent reality, the supreme Brahman; and behind the fleeting senses and mind of an individual human being is the Self, also a changeless, permanent reality; and the supreme Brahman and this Self are one. Every individual houses within himself the Eternal Spirit, the immutable, timeless self-existence; and though this Eternal Spirit dwells within all, and all beings exist in him, he is not tainted or affected by the thoughts and actions, good or evil, of individual men.

> The Lord is everywhere
> And always perfect:
> What does He care for man's sin
> Or the righteousness of man?

[1] VI. 37–45.

The Atman is the light:
The light is covered by darkness:
This darkness is delusion:
That is why we dream.

When the light of the Atman
Drives out our darkness
That light shines forth from us,
A sun in splendour,
The revealed Brahman.[1]

Knowledge of the immutable, eternal, timeless self-existence is called, as we have seen, Brahma-nirvāṇa. It is not to be confused with intellectual concepts, nor with a method of thinking. It is a direct, immediate experience, in which, as Śrī Rāmakṛṣṇa once told his disciple Vivekananda, the spiritualized consciousness sees God more directly, more intimately, than the physical consciousness sees the objective world.[2]

Is it then possible to give an account of this experience of God? The Gītā affirms that this svarupa, or true being, is unthinkable, indefinable, and yet realizable. That it is realizable is plain, for, says the Gītā,

Utterly quiet,
Made clean of passion,
The mind of the yogi
Knows that Brahman,
His bliss is the highest.[3]

Srī Rāmakṛṣṇa says:

'When one attains samādhi, then alone comes the knowledge of Brahman, and one attains the vision of God. In that ecstatic realization, all thoughts cease, and one becomes perfectly silent. There is no power of speech left by which to express Brahman. For verily is he beyond thought and speech.'[4]

The method commonly adopted by the philosophic mind of India to describe the Indescribable has been that of negation—neti neti Ātmā (The Atman is neither this nor that). Buddha did not attempt even this negative way of describing. When questioned about the Indescribable, he always remained silent. But the Gītā admits that the

[1] V. 15–16.
[2] Cf. Plato's distinction between knowledge and opinion. (*Republic*, IV.)
[3] VI. 27.
[4] *Kathāmṛta*, vol. III, pp. 9–10.

abstract and difficult method of negation can be adopted only by a select few of exceptional nature and training.

'As for those others, the devotees of God the unmanifest, indefinable and changeless, they worship that which is omnipresent, constant, eternal, beyond thought's compass, never to be moved. They hold all the senses in check. They are tranquil-minded, and devoted to the welfare of humanity. They see the Atman in every creature. They also will certainly come to me.

'But the devotees of the unmanifest have a harder task, because the unmanifest is very difficult for embodied souls to realize.'[1]

So, because of the arduous nature of the path of God, we find in the Gītā as well as in the Upaniṣads, not merely the abstract notion of an absolute who is merely the Beyond, but a God who is 'the Father, the Mother, the Sustainer of the world'.[2] In the Gītā we find God portrayed as 'the Goal, the Supporter, the Lord, the Witness, the Abode, the Refuge, the Friend, the Origin, the Dissolution, the Substratum, the Storehouse, the Seed immutable'[3]—a conception answering the need of the human heart, the need for love, and work, and worship.

This idea of an impersonal-personal God which we find in the teachings of the Indian scriptures is not the fruit of human reason. Indeed, most Hindu thinkers do not believe that proof of the existence of God lies in the realm of reason, but rather in the fact that he is realized, in the experience of actually seeing him and knowing him in his fullness. Both aspects of the Godhead—the personal and the impersonal—are realized and experienced by those whose eyes have been opened.

Śrī Rāmakṛṣṇa, the greatest mystic philosopher of our age, having realized God in all his aspects, utters this truth concerning the conception of an impersonal-personal Godhead—a conception present also in the Gītā:

'The jñāni, or one of philosophic mind, analyses the universe of the senses, saying "Brahman is not this, not that", and gives up all worldliness. Thus does he reach the knowledge of Brahman, just as the man who climbs a stairway leaves each step behind and so reaches the roof. But the vijñāni, who gains an intimate knowledge of him, has his consciousness extended. He knows that the roof and the steps are all made of the same substance. He who is realized as Brahman by the process of elimination is also realized as becoming man and the universe. The vijñāni knows that he who is without attributes

[1] XII. 3–5. [2] Gītā, IX. 17. [3] *Ibid.*, IX. 18.

in one aspect is, in another aspect, the repository of all blessed attributes.

'The true knower knows that he who is Brahman is the personal God; that he who is impersonal, attributeless, and beyond the guṇas, is again the personal God, the repository of all blessed qualities. Man, the universe, mind, intelligence, love, dispassion, knowledge—these are the expressions of his power and glory.'[1]

The conception of a personal God contained in the Gītā has been identified by certain modern Indian thinkers with theism, whereas some Western writers have called it pantheism. But it would be a great mistake to identify the teachings of the Gītā with any Western system. God, to traditional Hindu thinkers, is not a mere intellectual abstraction, nor a mode of thinking; he is a being realized and realizable. Western theism and pantheism are at their best intellectual concepts, or convictions of the mind, whereas God, as has been clearly asserted in all Hindu scriptures, is beyond mind and thought. When this being beyond thought is given by the seers a name within the domain of thought, this name may resemble theism or pantheism, yet it signifies something vastly different from any intellectualized God of the West. Sri Aurobindo, who perhaps of all modern interpreters of the Gītā has best caught the spirit of the poem, says of the Gītā's concept of God:

'. . . it is no shrinking and gingerly theism afraid of the world's contradictions, but one which sees God as the omniscient and omnipotent, the sole original Being, who manifests in himself all, whatever it may be, good and evil, pain and pleasure, light and darkness as stuff of his own existence, and governs himself what in himself he has manifested. Unaffected by its oppositions, unbound by his creation, exceeding, yet intimately related to this Nature and closely one with her creatures, their Spirit, Self, highest Soul, Lord, Lover, Friend, Refuge, he is ever leading them from within them and from above through the mortal appearances of ignorance and suffering and sin and evil, ever leading each through his nature and all through universal nature towards a supreme light and bliss and immortality and transcendence. This is the fullness of the liberating knowledge. It is a knowledge of the Divine within us and in the world as at the same time a transcendent Infinite. An Absolute who has become all that is by his divine Nature, his effective power of Spirit, he governs all from his transcendence. He is intimately present within every creature and the cause, ruler, director of all cosmic happenings and yet is he far too great, mighty and infinite to be limited by his creation.'[2]

[1] *Kathāmṛta*, vol. III, pp. 11 f. [2] Ghose, *op. cit.* (Second Series), pp. 133 f.

The ideal of a personal God is certainly present in the Gītā, but it is the ideal of an impersonal-personal Deity, expressing ultimate oneness in which there exists no 'I' or 'Thou' but only the one indivisible, self-luminous, blissful Existence. Absorption in the absolute and perfect union, from which the devotee, preoccupied too exclusively with some divine personality and with the values of the finite world, may at first shrink, is borne witness to by the mystic experiences of the saints and sages. A St. Francis of Assisi or a Śrī Caitanya of Bengal, though he may begin his life of devotion by loving and worshipping a personal God, concludes it by realizing his oneness with the Eternal and by being absorbed in him.

In the same way the teachings of Christ or of the Bible as a whole cannot be reconciled with any of the theological conceptions of Godhead, either theistic or pantheistic. When Christ bids us pray to the Father in heaven, we can give his words a theistic or deistic interpretation; but when he indicates that the kingdom of God is within, and that 'I and my Father are one', he implies a mysticism not usually associated with the word theism. And in the 139th Psalm occur the following words, of great mystic significance:

> 'Whither shall I go from thy spirit? Or whither shall I flee from thy presence? If I ascend up into Heaven, thou art there; if I make my bed in hell, behold, thou art there. If I take the wings of the morning and dwell in the uttermost parts of the sea, even there shall thy hand lead me, and thy right hand shall hold me.'

Just as the idea of one immutable God, personal and yet impersonal in his nature, pervades all advanced religions, so the conception of an avatār, the Supreme Being descending upon earth in human form, seems also to be universal. This conception finds its place for the first time in Indian philosophy in the Gītā, though its basis is laid in certain passages of the Upaniṣads. That God dwells in the heart of all beings as their innermost Self is the fundamental truth of both these scriptures. To know that innermost Self is to become one with God. 'A knower of Brahman becomes Brahman',[1] declare the seers of the Upaniṣads. Since God exists in all beings, every being in a sense represents a descent from God into the finiteness of name and form, and only the veil of ignorance hides from him his essentially divine nature; and when a being is born with the full knowledge of the Self, and with the divine consciousness not veiled by ignorance, that being is a full embodiment of the Godhead. Such a man is known as an avatār.

The Gītā doctrine of the avatār is parallel and almost identical with

[1] Muṇḍaka, III. ii. 9.

the conception of the Word made flesh, 'full of grace and truth', as we find it in the Gospel according to St John,[1] but with this difference, that Jesus of Nazareth is alone identified with the Logos; he is called the only begotten Son of God,[2] whereas in the Gītā it is clearly stated that God is made flesh many times, in different ages and in different forms. It is thus easy for the Hindus to accept Christ as an avatār and to worship him unreservedly, exactly as they worship Kṛṣṇa. They cannot accept him, however, as the *only* Son of God.

Kṛṣṇa, the teacher of the Gītā, openly declares himself to be an incarnation of the Godhead, asserting that he appears whenever he is needed upon earth. His birth, however, was not similar to that of Arjuna and other embodied souls, who were born in consequence of their past karmas, are tied by the fetters of ignorance, and remain under the thralldom of māyā. The birth of a Kṛṣṇa or a Christ is the result of free choice; for the Incarnation does not yield to the domination of māyā, but rather puts māyā under subjection, does not live in ignorance but in full consciousness of his divinity. Kṛṣṇa speaks:

> I am the birthless, the deathless,
> Lord of all that breathes.
> I seem to be born;
> It is only seeming,
> Only my maya.
> I am still master of my Prakriti,
> The power that makes me.[3]
>
> He who knows the nature
> Of my task and my holy birth
> Is not reborn
> When he leaves this body:
> He comes to me.[4]

Compare with these last lines the words of the Bible: 'But as many as received him, to them gave he power to become the sons of God; even to them that believe on his name.'[5]

To know a Kṛṣṇa or a Christ is to know God; for verily these are the children of Light—indeed, they are Light themselves. Though God dwells everywhere, to see him one must look through these divine incarnations. To worship a Kṛṣṇa or a Christ is not, however, to worship a man as God, is not to worship a person; it is to worship God himself, the impersonal-personal Existence, in and through a

[1] 'In the beginning was the Word, and the Word was with God, and the Word was God.'
[2] John iii. 16. [3] IV. 6. [4] IV. 9. [5] John i. 12.

man-god. Śrī Rāmakṛṣṇa said that the divine incarnations are like so many doors through which we peep into or touch the Infinite.

The Hindus have a theory, demonstrated by historical events, that spiritual culture moves in cyclic waves. An upward movement is followed by a downward one, the downward one by an upward one, and so on—an alternation which may be described as the dilation and contraction of the higher life of society. When the pendulum swings low and truth and righteousness are forgotten, the necessity arises for the birth of an avatār. The Gītā says:

> When goodness grows weak,
> When evil increases,
> I make myself a body.
>
> In every age I come back
> To deliver the holy,
> To destroy the sin of the sinner,
> To establish righteousness.[1]

From time to time, then, a divine incarnation is needed to re-establish the eternal truth, the eternal spirit of religion, by his living example. God descends upon earth in the form of a man to instruct man how to ascend towards him. Thus does the avatār really become the way, the truth, and the life.

Swami Saradananda, one of the foremost disciples of Śrī Rāmakṛṣṇa, has beautifully summarized the characteristics of avatārs:

'. . . first and foremost, . . . they [the avatārs] are born free. The endless struggle and hardship which they undergo to discover the hitherto unknown path to superconsciousness are prompted to them always by their desire to enrich the lives of their fellow beings, and not by any selfish motive whatsoever. Indeed, every action in their lives proceeds from a beneficent motive. Secondly, they are born endowed with perfect memory. This enables them to remember their former births and the deeds which they accomplished in those. It helps them besides to remember always the utterly transitory nature of human life and its enjoyments, and makes them run to the goal as fast as possible. And by means of this power they are able moreover to compare the present with the past and find out the direction along which the development of people's minds has proceeded hitherto, and the means which would help them to grow and reach the goal quickly in the future. Thirdly, they are the discoverers of new paths in the field of religion. Fourthly, they are able to transmit knowledge

[1] IV. 7, 8.

to their fellow beings simply by a touch or even by an act of will. Fifthly, they are able to perceive clearly, at the very first sight, the samskaras, or tendencies, produced by past karmas of their fellow beings, although they are never eager to make a show of that power to others; and this ability helps them to know instantly what would aid one to reach easily the highest stage of superconsciousness. Thus they are the born spiritual guides of humanity. And, lastly, they are conscious of their mission throughout their lives.'[1]

Ethics and Moral Disciplines

We have already seen that the purpose of life should be to break down the barrier of the ego and realize Brahman, the innermost Self in all beings, and that the means to this end is to see the one Self revealed in all and to love all equally. So the man who aspires to the divine state devotes his life to the service of God in humanity.

> Who burns with the bliss
> And suffers the sorrow
> Of every creature
> Within his own heart,
> Making his own
> Each bliss and each sorrow:
> Him I hold highest
> Of all the yogis.[2]

And we find this truth echoed in a different setting, and amongst a different race, when Jesus of Nazareth declared: 'Therefore all things whatsoever ye would that men should do to you, do ye even so to them; for this is the law and the prophets.'[3]

The inner life of man must possess perfect tranquillity—complete freedom from passions and passionate desires—in order that he may realize the blissful Brahman. This tranquillity is not, in the words of Sri Aurobindo, 'an indolence, incapacity, insensibility, inertia; it is full of immortal power, capable of all action, attuned to deepest delight, open to profoundest love and compassion and to every manner of intensest Ananda (bliss)'.

To gain this tranquillity requires the practice of self-control. By self-control are not meant the repressions and inhibitions so much talked about in the recent psychology of the West, for these very things are condemned by Śrī Kṛṣṇa in unmistakable terms:

[1] Saradananda, *Sri Ramakrishna the Great Master* (Madras: Ramakrishna Math, 1920), vol. I, pp. 25–6.

[2] Gitā, VI. 32.

[3] Matt. vii. 12.

'A man who renounces certain physical actions but still lets his mind dwell on the objects of his sensual desire is deceiving himself. He can only be called a hypocrite. The truly admirable man controls his senses by the power of his will. All his actions are disinterested. All are directed along the path to union with Brahman.'[1]

But the behaviouristic alternative of giving free play to all impulses and all desires, which is creating a condition of moral chaos among the youth of today, is not the alternative offered by the Gītā.

Even a mind that knows the path
Can be dragged from the path:
The senses are so unruly.
But he who controls the senses
And recollects the mind
And fixes it on me,
I call him illumined.[2]

This alternative is in short the direction of the thoughts and energies of the mind towards God. Direction, rather than repression, is the method of the Hindus for achieving self-control.

The uncontrolled mind
Does not guess that the Atman is present:
How can it meditate?
Without meditation, where is peace?
Without peace, where is happiness?
The wind turns a ship
From its course upon the waters:
The wandering winds of the senses
Cast man's mind adrift
And turn his better judgment from its course.
When a man can still the senses
I call him illumined.[3]

A further distinction is made in the Gītā between the divine man and the asura, or demoniac man. The one moves towards the attainment of liberation, while the other moves away from God to plunge down to lower births and deeper sufferings.

'A man who is born with tendencies toward the Divine, is fearless and pure in heart. He perseveres in that path to union with Brahman which the scriptures and his teacher have taught him. He is charitable.

[1] III. 6, 7. [2] II. 60, 61. [3] II. 66–8.

He can control his passions. He studies the scriptures regularly, and obeys their directions. He practises spiritual disciplines. He is straightforward, truthful, and of an even temper. He harms no one. He renounces the things of this world. He has a tranquil mind and an unmalicious tongue. He is compassionate toward all. He is not greedy. He is gentle and modest. He abstains from useless activity. He has faith in the strength of his higher nature. He can forgive and endure. He is clean in thought and act. He is free from hatred and from pride. Such qualities are his birthright.

'When a man is born with demonic tendencies, his birthright is hypocrisy, arrogance, conceit, anger, cruelty and ignorance.'[1]

Describing evil qualities further, the teacher concludes:

'Hell has three doors: lust, rage and greed. These lead to man's ruin. Therefore he must avoid them all. He who passes by these three dark doors has achieved his own salvation. He will reach the highest goal at last.'[2]

One more point is to be considered regarding self-control and the moral life. The Gītā lays great stress on self-exertion for the sake of self-improvement, and at the same time exalts divine grace and the need for us to surrender ourselves to God. 'The self is to be saved by one's own self'; so must one 'exert oneself'. Buddha laid stress on self-exertion, and Christ on divine grace. But these two stand reconciled in the life of a man who has become absorbed in a godly life. He is aware that he must strive, but through his strivings he ultimately learns that all the success he gains is only by divine grace, that in the end he must rely upon a higher will. But the preliminary striving is essential. Says Śrī Rāmakṛṣṇa: 'The breeze of divine grace is blowing upon all. But one needs to set the sail to feel this breeze of grace.'

The Yogas

The Gītā is considered a handbook of practical living as well as a guide to spiritual attainment. In fact, practical life, if rightly pursued, follows one of the paths towards the spiritual goal. These paths, known as yogas, we have already briefly discussed.

The word yoga literally means yoking, or union (the two words yoga and yoke are derived from the same root). In this it resembles the word religion, which has at its core the ideal of binding together. The distinction between individuals, with their finiteness and limitedness, is caused, as we have noted again and again, by ignorance, and does not represent the true nature of man. Until the barrier of ego

[1] XVI. 1–4. [2] XVI. 21, 22.

is broken down, and union with the true Self is consummated, one cannot attain to the inward state described as the kingdom of God. The word yoga defines the methods by which man's union with God is made possible. Many are the paths by which one may travel to reach this one destination. 'Many religions, many paths.' Hindu philosophy recognizes four main paths (yogas) to attainment. They are, as previously indicated, jñāna yoga, the path of knowledge; karma yoga, the path of action; bhakti yoga, the path of devotion, or love; and rāja yoga, the path of meditation.

Each of these yogas is an independent path to God, and when the end is attained, all four seem to join together in one. Supreme love, divine knowledge, true meditation, and true and divine action are at last identical and cannot be differentiated from one another. The Gītā insists that they must all be practised. Man is a complex of faculties—reason, will, emotion, and the impulse to action—and he must seek union with God through all of them. He must be active as well as meditative; he must cultivate his intelligence and seek the supreme knowledge as well as cultivate love for the Divine Being—such, in short, is the yoga ideal as taught in the Gītā.

Jñāna yoga literally means the path of union through knowledge. It has come to connote intellectual analysis leading to the immediate perception (anubhuti) of God, who is both transcendent and immanent, who is the inner reality of both man and the external universe. Philosophic reasoning does not imply mere natural ratiocination, but something more, for man's unaided intellect cannot lead him to God. There must be in addition a transformation of life and conduct, a conversion of the soul, before the knowledge of God, or the Self, can be attained. Thus says the Gītā:

> 'There are some who have actually looked upon the Atman, and understood It, in all Its wonder. Others can only speak of It as wonderful beyond their understanding. Others know of Its wonder by hearsay. And there are others who are told about It, and do not understand a word.'[1]

For immediate realization and understanding of the Self, jñāna yoga advocates that reasoning about God be followed by certain disciplines.

First of all, the philosopher must learn to discriminate between the real and the unreal. The opening chapters of the Gītā explain this process of discrimination:

> 'That which is nonexistent can never come into being, and that

[1] II. 29.

which is can never cease to be. Those who have known the inmost Reality know also the nature of is and is not.'[1]

The only abiding reality—the immutable, the illimitable, the indestructible Reality—is that by which the whole universe is pervaded. It is the same as the Self in man. Whatever we perceive or sense or experience has both beginning and end; therefore must our faculty of discrimination lead us to hold fast to the enduring reality, the Self, or God, in the midst of fleeting objects and the experiences of life and death.

'A serene spirit accepts pleasure and pain with an even mind, and is unmoved by either. He alone is worthy of immortality.'[2]

Since we know the Self alone to be real, we should learn to realize in it the great source of happiness and renounce the desire for pleasure.

> When he has no lust, no hatred,
> A man walks safely among the things of lust and hatred.
> To obey the Atman
> Is his peaceful joy:
> Sorrow melts
> Into that clear peace:
> His quiet mind
> Is soon established in peace.[3]

To follow the path of philosophy is also to follow the path of self-control, directing the mind towards the Reality. Says the Gītā:

> So, with his heart serene and fearless,
> Firm in the vow of renunciation,
> Holding the mind from its restless roaming,
> Now let him struggle to reach my oneness,
> Ever-absorbed, his eyes on me always,
> His prize, his purpose.[4]

Jñāna yoga is the very declaration of neti, neti (not this, not this), which we considered in our study of the Upaniṣads. The Self must not be identified with impermanent entities like the body, the mind, and the senses, nor with any object or instrument of experience. When a person has become an adept in detaching his true Self from the non-Self, he becomes blessed with the vision of the Divine, and

[1] II. 16. [2] II. 15. [3] II. 64, 65. [4] VI. 14.

there dawns upon him the knowledge of the Self in all and of all in the Self.

Following the path of knowledge and discrimination does not imply giving up the normal activities of life. What one is required to do is to regard the body as the house which one inhabits, and the mind and the senses as the instruments of living—to all of which the Lord is the witness. A person so doing acts but does not identify himself with his actions. He experiences the objective universe, but from this universe he has learned to detach himself.

Action, we have already noted, is not opposed to the highest wisdom. An individual who has attained the highest knowledge and the supreme peace, though he has nothing to gain by action, nor anything to lose by inaction, yet works, not however for his ordinary self, but, through exercise of mind, senses, and body, for his true Self, which he has identified with the Lord of the universe. Never forgetful of his true Self, he is forever one with God; and knowing that the Self exists in all, he engages in the service of God in all mankind. Such a man, steady in wisdom, experiences intense rest in the midst of intense action.

'He who sees the inaction that is in action, and the action that is in inaction, is wise indeed. Even when he is engaged in action he remains poised in the tranquillity of the Atman.'[1]

Thus a perfected soul, though active in the world of impermanence, unites his consciousness with God, and, says the Gītā, achieves this union through his very activity. This is just what is meant by karma yoga. Before the advent of Śrī Kṛṣṇa there came a period in the spiritual life of India when the teachings of the Upaniṣads were misinterpreted. We have seen that, according to the scriptures, knowledge alone can give freedom or salvation, but knowledge cannot be acquired through action. Karma, moreover, creates bondage. And over and above all concern with life in the world is the ideal of renunciation of worldly things—an ideal with which the Upaniṣads are permeated. This, in course of time, when not thoroughly understood, led to the belief in passivity as the supreme state. As we have seen, the opening chapters of the Gītā tell how the disciple Arjuna, confused as to the path and the conduct to choose, turned to Kṛṣṇa for counsel. Kṛṣṇa, God incarnate, then gave the correct interpretation of the teachings of the Upaniṣads. Renunciation, he pointed out, is renunciation not of the world but of worldliness, not of actions but of desires. Karma leads to bondage if it increases the weight of desires and magnifies the ego; it leads to

[1] IV. 18.

freedom if it helps to deny the self or to free one from attachment to the fruits of action. Śrī Rāmakṛṣṇa, in our own time, has illustrated this interpretation of karma yoga and the ideal of renunciation by a simile of a boat resting on the water. 'Let the boat rest on the water,' he said, 'but let not the water come into the boat. Let a man live in the world, but let not the world live in him.'

That is, be in the world but not of it. The Gītā says:

> 'You have the right to work, but for the work's sake only. You have no right to the fruits of work. Desire for the fruits of work must never be your motive in working. Never give way to laziness either.'[1]

The Upaniṣads teach that knowledge alone can give freedom, and that infinite knowledge is stored in the soul of man. The very nature of the Self implies not only immortality and perfect bliss but also cit, or pure consciousness. Says the Gītā: 'The Atman is the light. The light is covered by darkness. This darkness is delusion.'[2] The poem clarifies the issue by teaching the secret of work, namely, that we must so work that every act will help to unfold the knowledge of the Self by removing the ignorance of the ego. The one aim and the true goal of karma yoga is the union of one's self with God through action. Not through any special actions do we accomplish this, but through our svadharmas—the particular duties proceeding from the law of our individual natures.

> Whatever your action,
> Food or worship;
> Whatever the gift
> That you give to another;
> Whatever you vow
> To the work of the spirit:
> O son of Kunti,
> Lay these also
> As offerings before me.[3]

In order to effect this union with God through activity, we must possess tranquillity and the peace that comes through meditation. Since to the unmeditative man no peace will come, the Gītā puts emphasis upon the practice of meditation, technically known as rāja yoga. Patañjali explains rāja yoga as an eightfold path consisting of yama (moral disciplines), niyama (religious disciplines), āsana (posture), prāṇāyāma (breathing exercises), pratyāhāra (releasing

[1] II. 47. [2] V. 15. [3] IX. 27.

the mind from the thralldom of the senses), dhāraṇā (concentration), dhyāna (meditation), and samādhi (the superconscious state). The Gītā does not systematically explain these eight steps, yet they are implied in its teachings. The main stress is laid on stilling the restless mind and becoming absorbed in the consciousness of the divine Self.

'Patiently, little by little, a man must free himself from all mental distractions, with the aid of the intelligent will. He must fix his mind upon the Atman and never think of anything else. No matter where the restless and unquiet mind wanders, it must be drawn back and made to submit to the Atman only.'[1]

Utterly quiet,
Made clean of passion,
The mind of the yogi
Knows that Brahman,
His bliss is the highest.[2]

In connection with the practice of yoga, the Gītā counsels moderation in eating, drinking, sleeping, and recreation. Extremes must be avoided. In unmistakable terms Śrī Kṛṣṇa condemns the excessive practice of austerities in the name of yoga. 'You may know', says the Gītā, 'those men to be of demonic nature who mortify the body excessively, in ways not prescribed by the scriptures. They do this because their lust and attachment to sense-objects has filled them with egotism and vanity. In their foolishness, they weaken all their sense-organs, and outrage me, the dweller in the body.'[3]

Knowledge is not of the dry intellectual kind; neither is meditation directed to some dry or abstract principle; rather, they are knowledge of, and meditation upon, Him who is rasa, or full of bliss, and who is love itself. The pursuit of a spiritual ideal is always accomplished in an atmosphere of joy. In this atmosphere sorrow itself, which for an aspirant can be only the sorrow of separation from the beloved Lord, loses much of its sting, for along with it there is always the expectancy of union with him. In separation from God, as in union with him, the aspirant, as well as the perfected soul, lives in continuous adoration of the Infinite. Bhakti yoga, or the path of love, is this adoration, and worship is constant worship of the Lord, who is the inner being, the Self in man, and the embodiment of love and all blessed qualities. The teachings of the Gītā emphasize a 'whole-souled devotion' to the Supreme. As this devotion grows, the sinner becomes a saint.

[1] VI. 25–6. [2] VI. 27. [3] XVII. 5, 6.

Though a man be soiled
With the sins of a lifetime,
Let him but love me,
Rightly resolved,
In utter devotion:
I see no sinner,
That man is holy.

Holiness soon
Shall refashion his nature
To peace eternal;
O son of Kunti,
Of this be certain:
The man that loves me,
He shall not perish.[1]

The culmination of bhakti yoga, and in fact of all the yogas, is the complete unconditional surrender of the lower self, or ego, to God, or the Supreme Self. When the barrier of the ego is removed, by following the path either of knowledge, or of work, or of love, or of meditation, or by following all of them at once, the omnipresent, omniscient, immortal Lord of the universe becomes revealed as the Lord of the heart—the Supreme Self.

SELECTIONS FROM THE BHAGAVAD-GĪTĀ

Arjuna

Is this real pity that I feel, or only a delusion? My mind gropes about in darkness. I cannot see where my duty lies. Krishna, I beg you, tell me frankly and clearly what I ought to do. I am your disciple. I put myself into your hands. Show me the way.[2]

Sri Krishna

Your words are wise, Arjuna, but your sorrow is for nothing. The truly wise mourn neither for the living nor for the dead.[3]

Just as the dweller in this body passes through childhood, youth and old age, so at death he merely passes into another kind of body. The wise are not deceived by that.[4]

[1] IX. 30, 31. [2] II. 7. [3] II. 11. [4] II. 13.

Worn-out garments
Are shed by the body:
Worn-out bodies
Are shed by the dweller
Within the body.
New bodies are donned
By the dweller, like garments.[1]

Arjuna

Krishna, how can one identify a man who is firmly established and absorbed in Brahman? In what manner does an illumined soul speak? How does he sit? How does he walk?[2]

Sri Krishna

He knows bliss in the Atman
And wants nothing else.
Cravings torment the heart:
He renounces cravings.
I call him illumined.[3]

The tortoise can draw in its legs:
The seer can draw in his senses.
I call him illumined.[4]

The recollected mind is awake
In the knowledge of the Atman
Which is dark night to the ignorant:
The ignorant are awake in their sense-life
Which they think is daylight:
To the seer it is darkness.[5]

He knows peace who has forgotten desire.
He lives without craving:
Free from ego, free from pride.
This is the state of enlightenment in Brahman:
A man does not fall back from it
Into delusion.
Even at the moment of death
He is alive in that enlightenment:
Brahman and he are one.[6]

[1] II. 22.
[2] II. 54.
[3] II. 55.
[4] II. 58.
[5] II. 69.
[6] II. 71, 72.

Arjuna

But, Krishna, if you consider knowledge of Brahman superior to any sort of action, why are you telling me to do these terrible deeds?

Your statements seem to contradict each other. They confuse my mind. Tell me one definite way of reaching the highest good.[1]

Sri Krishna

I have already told you that, in this world, aspirants may find enlightenment by two different paths. For the contemplative is the path of knowledge: for the active is the path of selfless action.[2]

The world is imprisoned in its own activity, except when actions are performed as worship of God. Therefore you must perform every action sacramentally, and be free from all attachment to results.[3]

Perform every action with your heart fixed on the Supreme Lord. Renounce attachment to the fruits. Be even-tempered in success and failure; for it is this evenness of temper which is meant by yoga.[4]

The yoga of action, say the ignorant,
Is different from the yoga of the knowledge of Brahman.
The wise see knowledge and action as one:
They see truly.[5]

Take either path
And tread it to the end:
The end is the same.
There the followers of action
Meet the seekers after knowledge
In equal freedom.

It is hard to renounce action
Without following the yoga of action.
This yoga purifies
The man of meditation,
Bringing him soon to Brahman.[6]

Arjuna

Tell me, Krishna, what Brahman is. What is the Atman, and what is the creative energy of Brahman? Explain the nature of this relative world, and of the individual man.[7]

[1] III. 1. [2] III. 3. [3] III. 9. [4] II. 48.
[5] V. 4. [6] V. 5, 6. [7] VIII. 1.

Sri Krishna

Brahman is that which is immutable, and independent of any cause but Itself. When we consider Brahman as lodged within the individual being, we call Him the Atman. The creative energy of Brahman is that which causes all existences to come into being.[1]

He is all-knowing God, lord of the emperors,
Ageless, subtler far than mind's inmost subtlety,
Universal sustainer,
Shining sunlike, self-luminous.

What fashion His form has, who shall conceive of it?
He dwells beyond delusion, the dark of Maya.
On Him let man meditate
Always . . .[2]

Make a habit of practising meditation, and do not let your mind be distracted. In this way you will come finally to the Lord, who is the light-giver, the highest of the high.[3]

Arjuna

Some worship you with steadfast love. Others worship God the unmanifest and changeless. Which kind of devotee has the greater understanding of yoga?[4]

Sri Krishna

Those whose minds are fixed on me in steadfast love, worshipping me with absolute faith. I consider them to have the greater understanding of yoga.[5]

Quickly I come
To those who offer me
Every action,
Worship me only,
Their dearest delight,
With devotion undaunted.[6]

A man should not hate any living creature. Let him be friendly and compassionate to all. He must free himself from the delusion of 'I' and 'mine'. He must accept pleasure and pain with an equal tranquillity. He must be forgiving, ever-contented, self-controlled, united constantly with me in his meditation. His resolve must be

[1] VIII. 3. [2] VIII. 9. [3] VIII. 8. [4] XII. 1. [5] XII. 2. [6] XII. 6.

unshakable. He must be dedicated to me in intellect and in mind. Such a devotee is dear to me.[1]

Now I have taught you that wisdom which is the secret of secrets. Ponder it carefully. Then act as you think best. These are the last words that I shall say to you, the deepest of all truths. I speak for your own good. You are the friend I chose and love.

Give me your whole heart,
Love and adore me,
Worship me always,
Bow to me only,
And you shall find me:
This is my promise
Who love you dearly.

Lay down all duties
In me, your refuge.
Fear no longer,
For I will save you
From sin and from bondage.[2]

Arjuna

By your grace, O Lord, my delusions have been dispelled. My mind stands firm. Its doubts are ended. I will do your bidding.[3]

[1] XII. 13, 14. [2] XVIII. 63–6. [3] XVIII. 73.

CHAPTER 6

THE SMṚTIS, THE PURĀṆAS, THE TANTRAS

The Smṛtis

The Smṛtis embody the laws formulated by saints and sages—Manu, Yājñavalkya, and others.

No date can be definitely assigned to these scriptures, since Oriental scholars differ by as much as several centuries in their estimates. The Code of Manu, for instance, is assigned by Sir William Jones to 1250 BC, and by Sir Monier Williams to as late as 500 BC. We can be safe in asserting that the Smṛtis are post-Vedic, inasmuch as the code of laws found in them is traditionally supposed to be based on the Vedas.

Since to the Hindu mind only the Vedas are wholly sacrosanct, it follows that the Smṛtis at best possess but a secondary authority. They record civil laws, social obligations, and ceremonies performed at the birth of a child, during initiation into Vedic mantra, at marriage, and at the moment of death. They comprise, in short, the daily duties, usages, and customs to be observed by the several castes and by people in different stages of life; and their avowed purpose is to aid all men to attain the highest spiritual development.

The extraordinary thing about these ceremonies, usages, and customs, for daily observance and for special occasions, as practised in every part of India, is their infinite variety and yet their substantial underlying unity. The variety is accounted for by the fact that they were given many different forms, each developing independently of the rest in a particular part of the country; their unity by their common source in the Vedic religion.

For centuries the authority of the Smṛtis has held sway over the minds of the people of India, who have rigidly followed the social laws of these codes. At the present time, however, there is discernible a certain laxity in their observance, due to the revolutionary changes that have everywhere occurred. Orthodox Hindus do not feel unduly alarmed at this, for they have always regarded the Smṛtis as of secondary importance. Swami Vivekananda once remarked to a disciple that a new Smṛti ought to be written for the guidance of modern India. It has already been observed that a distinction is made between Smṛti, or traditions, and Śruti, or revelations. The Śrutis are direct, immediate experience of Reality; the Smṛtis are man-made laws. The latter embody, to be sure, certain eternal truths, but they are truths capable of adaptation to changing times.

Of all the Smṛtis, the Code of Manu possesses the highest authority. Manu, according to the orthodox view, was the first man.[1] Tradition declares that Brahmā gave him a code of laws in one hundred thousand verses, which for practical purposes he reduced to four thousand.

Among the duties and disciplines prescribed by the Laws of Manu are conquest of the senses, freedom from lust and greed, study of the sacred scriptures, and detachment from the world. One must speak only when necessary, honour old age, respect one's parents, and injure no one, whether in thought, word, or deed. In the twelve books of Manu there is an account of creation, and there are teachings regarding education, marriage, domestic life, laws of the state, punishments, reincarnation, and ultimate freedom. The main purpose of the code was to preserve a fixed society, and it has actually maintained during many centuries the racial integrity of the Indian people.

Fundamentally, the code insists upon the intelligent exercise of the will in conformity to the will of God. The principles involved, not necessarily the laws as crystallized by long and formal application, are universal in their truth and in their acceptability. Self-control, for example, receives great stress. A man must subdue his lust, and even while he is a student he must not consciously lapse from strict continence. All this is in preparation for marriage and for the ultimate state of sannyās, or renunciation.

The Purāṇas[2]

The word purāṇa literally means ancient, the name being applied to certain scriptures to mean 'that which lives from of old' or 'that

[1] See the story of creation in the next section.

[2] 'A Purāṇa or sacred poetical work, supposed to be compiled or composed by the poet Vyāsa; and comprising the whole body of Hindu theology; each Purāṇa should treat of five topics especially: the creation, the destruction and renovation of worlds; the genealogy of gods and heroes; the reigns of the Manus, and the transaction of their descendants; but great variety prevails in this respect and few contain historical or genealogical matter. There are eighteen acknowledged Purāṇas.' (*Shabda-Sagara* [*Sanskrit-English Dictionary*] by Pandit-Kulapati Jivananda Vidyasagara [Calcutta: Bhattacharyya, 1900].)

which is ever new though old'. The Purāṇas were written mainly to popularize the abstract ethical and spiritual truths of the Vedas and the Upaniṣads by means of concrete illustrations from the lives of avatārs, saints, sages, kings, and devotees, whether historical or legendary. K. S. Ramaswami, the Indian scholar, has thus described them:

'. . . the Purāṇas are a vital portion of the scriptures of the Hindus. They are primarily an extension, amplification and illustration of the spiritual truths declared in the Vedas. Outsiders may call them legends like the works of fiction current today. Some insiders too may regard them as mere illustrative fictions or allegories, or as relating to yogic realities unconnected with the external material world. But the bulk of the Hindus and the main body of traditional opinion attribute to the Purāṇas a double character, viz. illustrative value and impressive actuality. They have largely moulded public life, belief and conduct in our land for thousands of years, and they must be fully utilized by us if we are to realize the truths of the Vedas. Herein lies their permanent and supreme value to us.'[1]

Altogether there are eighteen Purāṇas, six devoted to Viṣṇu, six to Brahmā, and six to Śiva. All of them are written in verse, and all are usually attributed to Vyāsa, the reputed author of the Mahābhārata and editor of the Vedas. Their date may safely be assigned to the somewhat uncertain Epic Period.

At this time the Vedic gods, such as Indra, Mitra, Varuṇa, and Skanda, were transformed into the three divinities Brahmā, Viṣṇu, and Śiva; and these in turn were conceived as but manifestations of the one Primeval Spirit, the Lord adored by all, the one undecaying Brahman.[2] Brahmā, Viṣṇu, and Śiva (the last of these being also called Rudra, Mahādeva, and Maheśwara) are known as the Trimūrti, or Trinity, of the Hindus. In the words of the Viṣṇu Purāṇa: 'The Lord God, though one without a second, assumes the three forms respectively of Brahmā, Viṣṇu, and Śiva for creation, preservation and dissolution of the world.' And in the Padma Purāṇa we read: 'Brahmā, Viṣṇu, and Śiva, though three in form, are one entity. No difference between the three exists except with respect to attributes.' Moreover, the votaries of this Trimūrti make no distinction between them, as they identify one with another. Viṣṇu, for example, is described as Śiva's arrow, and Śiva as Kṛṣṇa's flute. Kṛṣṇa, again, is regarded as the incarnation of Viṣṇu.

[1] *Cultural Heritage of India*, vol. I, pp. 181 f.

[2] Brahman (neuter) denotes the impersonal God, and Brahmā (masculine) is the personal Creator, one of the Trimūrti.

The Purāṇas, then, popularize the abstract teachings of the Upaniṣads by means of stories concerning saints, sages, and kings. Some of these legends and tales are common to all the Purāṇas, though in details and in method of presentation they differ widely. The principal beauty of the Purāṇas lies in the fact that they reconcile knowledge and devotion. Śrī Rāmakṛṣṇa, speaking of the Bhāgavata Purāṇa, quaintly but suggestively remarks, 'It is fried in the butter of knowledge and steeped in the honey of love.'

The Bhāgavatam is not only the most popular of all the Purāṇas but is regarded by the Vaiṣṇavas as one of the genuinely authoritative scriptures.[1] For these reasons we shall choose it for special attention.

Vyāsa, according to legend, wrote the Bhāgavatam and taught it to Śuka his son, who in turn made it public.

As an introduction to the Bhāgavatam, the narrator tells an interesting story concerning this Śuka, who is regarded by all Hindus as one of the greatest saints of all the ages.

'Suka, the son of Vyasa, was indeed a great yogi, a knower of Brahman, who realized unity in the midst of diversity. His mind and consciousness were always united with God. We have heard about him, and how, after beginning the life of renunciation, having no consciousness of his body, he would walk about naked. One day, while thus walking in the wood, he passed by a lake in which some nymphs were bathing. They watched him pass, feeling no shyness in his presence; but as Vyasa, who was following his son, approached, they hastily got out of the water and clothed themselves. This surprised the great sage, and he asked the nymphs, "Why do you act so strangely, my children? You did not shrink from the young Suka, who was naked, yet you feel shy before me, an old man, fully clothed." To this the nymphs replied: "Revered sir, in you there lingers a trace of the consciousness of sex, but in your son Suka there is none."'[2]

Following is Śuka's prayer to the Lord as recorded in the Bhāgavatam. It is typical of the Hindu mind.

O thou Lord supreme, I bow down to thee!
For thy sole pleasure and play didst thou bring forth this universe.
Thou art the highest in the highest! Who can sing thine infinite glory?
Thou art the innermost ruler of every heart;
Thy paths are mysterious;
Thy ways are blessed.

[1] Vaiṣṇavism, which teaches the ideal of love for God and complete self-surrender to him, is sometimes called the Bhāgavata religion.

[2] I. iv. 1–5.

Thou dost wipe away all the tears of thy devotees;
Thou dost destroy the wickedness of the wicked.
Thy form is purity itself, and thou dost give purity and Self-knowledge to those who seek thee.
Salutations to thee again and again, O Lord of hosts!

I praise thee, O Lord!
Thou art the strength and support of all thy worshippers;
Thou art manifest in the hearts of all true yogis;
The evildoer findeth thee not.
Thou art one without a second.
Thou dost shine in thine own glory, in thy resplendent, blissful Self.

What sweetness is in thy name,
What joy is in thy remembrance!
Those who chant thy holy name, and meditate on thee, become forever free from all evils;
The wise, worshipping thy feet, conquer all fear of life and death:
Thus do they realize thee, thou supreme goal of all true seekers.

Before thee there is no barrier of caste, or race, or creed:
All thy children attain purity through thy holy name.
Calm souls worship thee, knowing that they are one with thee.
Thou art the Lord supreme,
Thou art indeed the Vedas,
Thou art the Truth,
Thou art the goal of all discipline;
Thy lovers meditate on thy blissful form, and become lost in the joy thereof.

Shower thy grace upon me, O Lord, and in thy mercy look upon me!
Thou art the Lord of wealth,
Thou art the Lord of all creation,
The Lord of all thy lovers and devotees.
Look upon all beings with thy mercy!
Blessed are they that meditate on thy Lotus Feet,
For they shall be purified;
Blessed are they that are purified,
For they shall attain Self-knowledge.
The wise call thee the impersonal, without attributes;
They also call thee the personal God with divine attributes;
Thou art both, and thou dost manifest thyself as the one or the other,
According to our understanding.
O Lord, forever look in mercy upon me![1]

[1] II. iv. 11–24.

Cosmology has a definite place in all of the Purāṇas. The following is a résumé of the story of creation as we find it recounted in the Bhāgavatam.

'Creation has no absolute beginning. The present universe is but one of a series of worlds that are past and of worlds that are to be. The cosmic energy alternates between periods of potentiality and of expression. The phase of potentiality is known as dissolution; the phase of expression is known as creation.

'Created things are of different kinds. The avyakta, or cosmic energy, consists of three gunas. When the equilibrium of the gunas is disturbed, there are manifested universal intelligence, universal ego, the mind, the senses and the organs of sense, the subtle principle of the elements, and the elements themselves. As these combine and recombine in various ways, all beings attain to existence.

'Among them there are sthavara, or stationary beings, such as herbs, shrubs, creepers, and plants. They have unmanifested consciousness. In them the sense of touch alone has evolved.

'Then there are the brute species, the animals, in which the sense of smell is highly developed.

'Next comes man.

'Lastly, there are the devas, the pitris, the gandharvas, and the kinnaras. These are gods, demigods, angels, and spirits.

'All things whatsoever were created by Brahma.

'Thus it was that Creation came to pass:

'While the world was yet submerged beneath the ocean, God lay brooding on Naga, king of the serpents, as Naga floated upon the waters. God was resting with eyes closed, but his consciousness was fully awake. He was completely merged in the bliss of his own Self.

'As the time of creation drew nigh, God felt a stir within his being, and there issued forth from the centre of his person a full-blown Lotus. Its light was dazzling, and the whole ocean was illumined by its splendour.

'Within this Lotus were all the materials for creation.

'Immediately Brahma came forth from the Lotus, and, seating himself upon it, turned his head in all directions to see whether any other beings were present. Hence he is called the four-faced Brahma.

'Brahma did not recognize himself, and had no recollection of his previous creations. After a time he became restless and felt a desire for knowledge. Looking about him and seeing in the external world no hope for the fulfilment of this desire, he sought in meditation for the knowledge which he realized must be within himself, and at last he found the Truth, and God himself, within his own heart. He then saw God everywhere, and felt blest indeed.

'Then God spoke to him, saying:

'"Oh Brahma, I command thee: again create the world, as thou hast often done in times past. To create is to thee not new. Whatsoever is to be created is already within me, as thou well knowest. Creation is only the projection into form of that which already exists."

'While God was yet speaking, a strong wind arose and lashed the water into a fury. With the knowledge and power which he had acquired through the practice of tapas, Brahma withdrew into himself the wind and all the waters of the sea; and then finding himself floating on the water, still seated on the Lotus, he re-entered the heart of the Lotus, and dividing it into three sections created the three spheres—heaven, earth, and sky.

'Brahma also gave to the world the four Vedas: the Rik, the Sama, the Yajur, and the Atharva.

'Brahma is the personification of what the philosophers call the Sphota, the word Om. He is called the first-born of God.

'Brahma's first human creations were saints, who, immediately upon being created, fell into deep meditation, finding no interest in the things of the world. Thus, through them, Brahma saw no possibility of propagation of their species. While he was meditating upon what course he should pursue, his own form divided itself; one half became man and the other half became woman.

'The man was called Manu, and the woman Shatarupa; and from them have sprung all mankind.'[1]

As we have already seen, neither the Purāṇas nor the other scriptures of the Hindus, nor the philosophers of India at any time, declare in favour of an absolute beginning or an absolute end of creation. Rather, they believe that the cosmic universe passes through phases of potentiality and manifestation. The Purāṇas assert, moreover, that the universe moves in cycles. They describe the historic evolution of life by a division of these into four, called the four yugas—satya, tretā, dwāpara, and kali. The duration of kali yuga, which is the present age, is 432,000 years. That of satya, tretā, and dwāpara is respectively, four times, three times, and twice the duration of kali yuga. All four yugas combined form a mahāyuga, or great cycle.

The peculiar characteristics of each of the four are named in the Purāṇas. In satya yuga, for example, virtue is in the ascendant, and it grows progressively less through the cycles until in kali yuga it is practised least. After kali yuga, however, satya yuga again appears, and so on through eternity.

According to the orthodox view, Rāma, the hero of the Rāmāyaṇa,

[1] See *The Wisdom of God*, Bk. III, chap. 2, pp. 42–5.

lived in tretā yuga, and Kṛṣṇa lived near the end of dwāpara yuga. At Kṛṣṇa's passing, kali yuga came into existence, and about 400,000 years of this cycle have already elapsed. The final impression left on the mind by this vast procession of numbers is that this world of ours is very, very old. Many a civilization has appeared and in time disappeared, and still human life continues.

Of the twelve books into which the Bhāgavatam is divided, the tenth and the eleventh are the most important. The tenth tells the life story of Kṛṣṇa, and the eleventh contains the instructions he gave to his disciple and friend Uddhava.

The chief part of Śrī Kṛṣṇa's story is the rāsa-līlā, his play with the shepherdesses; and this part is most glaringly misrepresented by Western scholars, who have failed to understand the meaning of the original. A brief summary of the episode will help us to interpret correctly the significance of Śrī Kṛṣṇa to the Hindu mind.

He embodies the quality of love. Love is divine, and love finds expression in many forms. To Yaśodā, God was her own baby Kṛṣṇa. To the shepherd boys he was Kṛṣṇa, their beloved friend and playmate, and to the shepherd girls he was Kṛṣṇa, their beloved friend, lover, and companion.

When Kṛṣṇa played on his flute, the shepherdesses forgot everything, even their own bodies, and ran to him for the sake of his great, compelling love. Once Kṛṣṇa, to test their love for him, said to them, 'Oh, ye pure ones, your duties must first be to your husbands and children. You do not need to come to me, for if you only meditate on me you will gain salvation.' The shepherdesses replied, 'Oh, thou cruel lover, we aspire to serve only thee. Thou knowest the scriptural truths, and thou dost advise us to serve our husbands and our children. Yes, we will abide by thy teaching. But thou art in all, and thou art all. By serving thee we serve all.'

Kṛṣṇa, who gives delight to all and is blissful in his own being, divided himself into as many Kṛṣṇas as there were gopīs, or shepherdesses, and danced and played with them. Each gopī felt the divine presence and the divine love of Śrī Kṛṣṇa. Each one felt herself most blessed, and each one's love for him was so absorbing that she felt herself one with him—each one even realized that she *was* Kṛṣṇa.

Truly has it been said that those who meditate on the divine love of Śrī Kṛṣṇa, and upon this sweet relationship with the gopīs, become free from lust and sensuality.

Swami Vivekananda has made some pertinent remarks upon the idyl of the shepherdesses in the life of Kṛṣṇa:

'Ah, that most marvellous passage of his life, the most difficult to understand, and which none ought to attempt to understand until he has become perfectly chaste and pure, that most marvellous expansion of love, allegorized and expressed in that beautiful play in Brindaban, which none can understand but he who has become mad with, and drunk deep of, the cup of love. Who can understand the throes of the love of the gopis—the very ideal of love, love that wants nothing, love that does not care even for heaven, love that does not care for anything in this world or the world to come?[1]

'The historian who records this marvellous love of the gopis is one who was born pure, the eternally pure Suka, the son of Vyasa. So long as there is selfishness in the heart, so long is love of God impossible; it is nothing but shopkeeping.[2]

'Aye, forget first the love for gold, and name and fame, and for this little trumpery world of ours. Then, only then, you will understand the love of the gopis, too holy to be attempted without giving up everything, too sacred to be understood until the soul has become perfectly pure. . . .

'That is the very essence of the Krishna incarnation. Even the Gita, the great philosophy itself, does not compare with that madness, for in the Gita the disciple is taught slowly how to walk towards the goal, but here is the madness of enjoyment, the drunkenness of love, where disciples and teachers and teachings and books, all these things, have become one, even the ideas of fear and God and heaven! Everything has been thrown away. What remains is the madness of love. It is forgetfulness of everything, and the lover sees nothing in the world except that Krishna, and Krishna alone—the face of everything becomes a Krishna, his own face looks like Krishna, his own soul has become tinged with the Krishna colour. That was the great Krishna.'[3]

The eleventh book contains the teachings of Kṛṣṇa regarding love, knowledge, service, and meditation. They are essentially the teachings of the Upaniṣads and the Gītā. Perhaps they are best summarized in the following words of Kṛṣṇa, addressed to Uddhava, from the eleventh book:

'The first requisites for spiritual life are these: doing no injury; being truthful, honest, nonattached, modest; abstaining from wealth; maintaining faith in an after-life; practising continence, silence, patience, forgiveness, fearlessness, physical and mental purity, austerity, self-reliance, hospitality; chanting the name of the Lord; performing sacrifices; surrendering the self to me; making pilgrimages; working for the good of others; and serving the teacher. These are known in yoga as the practices of yama and niyama. These, my friend, if rightly followed, bring great spiritual unfoldment.

[1] *Complete Works of Vivekananda*, vol. III, p. 257. [2] *Ibid.*, p. 258. [3] *Ibid.*, p. 259.

Calmness is a steady flow of the mind toward God.
Self-restraint is control of the organs of sense.
Patience is bearing the burden of life cheerfully.
Steadiness is overcoming the palate and the impulse of sex.
The highest charity is refraining from violence.
Austerity is the giving up of desire.
Valour is the conquest of one's own self.
To know the truth is to see the oneness of the Self with God.
Truthfulness is true and agreeable speech as exemplified by the sages.
Purity is nonattachment to work.
Renunciation is overcoming the world.
Virtue is the treasure which men covet.
I, the supreme Lord, am the sacrifice.
The greatest gift is the gift of knowledge.
The greatest strength is the control of prana.
Fortunate is he who meditates on my divine powers.
The highest profit is in devotion to me.
Wisdom is removing false ideas of multiplicity and realizing the unity of the Self.
Modesty is abhorrence of evil deeds.
Excellence of character arises from disregard of worldly considerations.
Happiness is the transcending of both pleasure and pain.
Misery is hankering after pleasures of sense.
Learned is he who discriminates between bondage and freedom.
Ignorant is he who identifies himself with the body.
The right path is that which leads to me.
The wrong path is that which causes restlessness of the mind.
Heaven is the domination of sattwa in the mind.
Hell is the predominance of tamas.
The teacher who has realized his oneness with me is the true friend.
He indeed is rich who is rich in virtues.
Poor is he who is discontented.
Mean is he who is not master of his senses.
Godly is he who is not attached to objects of sense.
Divine is he who has overcome both good and evil.'[1]

The Tantras

The Tantras are the scriptures by means of which knowledge is spread in order to save humanity from ignorance.[2] They are also

[1] Bhāgavatam, XI. xix. 32–45.

[2] Of all Indian scriptures, the Tantras are most often misunderstood by Western scholars, and even native scholars are not altogether free from error in dealing

known as Āgamas—revelations, in conformity, that is, with the revelations of the Vedas. Their authorship is unknown, though there is a tradition that Śiva uttered them to his divine consort Śakti (the Divine Mother), and that through her they reached mankind. Their date is uncertain, but since Buddha was familiar with them they are obviously pre-Buddhistic. Buddhistic Tantras exist, however, belonging to the Tibetan school of Buddhism.

The original Tantras are divided into three main groups according as the deity chosen for worship is Viṣṇu, Śiva, or Śakti. Thus there are Vaiṣṇava Āgamas (or Pañcarātra), the Śaiva Āgamas, and the Śākta Āgamas, besides the later Buddhistic Āgamas composed in Tibet. The Śākta group is the most popular, so much so that the word Tantra has come to mean, generally though mistakenly, only the Śākta Āgamas. It is to these that we shall give our attention.

The Tantras are all broadly divided into three parts: sādhanā, which includes spiritual practices and disciplines and ritualistic forms of worship; siddhi, or attainments from such practices; and philosophy. Let us examine the last of these first.

The philosophy of the Tantras is based on the Upaniṣads. It is nondualistic, upholding the identity of the individual soul with Śiva-Śakti—that is, in the language of the Upaniṣads and of Śaṁkara, the identity of the individual self with Brahman, or the Universal Self. Śaṁkara calls the creative power of the universe māyā, or illusion, the universe for him possessing in itself no absolute reality, whereas the Tantras call this creative power Śakti, or God the Mother, and regard the universe as her play when she has become mind and matter. Here, in their interpretation of reality, the Tantras apparently approach the philosophy of Rāmānuja, who looked upon the universe of mind and matter as a transformation of Brahman—as, in effect, the body of God.

This Śakti, or God the Mother, is not distinct from Śiva, or Brahman, the Absolute of the Upaniṣads, but is the power of the Absolute. In the transcendental plane, which is static, where there is but one

with them. But I must declare in this connection that in recent years one Western student of Eastern philosophy, Sir John Woodroffe, an Englishman and at one time Chief Justice of the High Court of Calcutta, has, through a lifetime devoted to the study of Tāntric literature, done yeoman service in the cause of a proper understanding of these difficult scriptures, both through translations of original manuscripts and through correct interpretations of their spirit. 'Tantra Shastra [scriptures]', he says, '—(is) generally spoken of as a jumble of "black magic", and "erotic mysticism", cemented together by a ritual which is "meaningless mummery". A large number of persons who talk in this strain have never had a Tantra in their hands, and such Orientals as have read some portions of these scriptures have not generally understood them, otherwise they would not have found them to be so "meaningless". They may be bad, or they may be good, but they have a meaning. Men are not such fools as to believe in what is meaningless.'

undivided, absolute existence, and where there is no universe, the truth is known as Śiva, or the Absolute Existence-Knowledge-Bliss; but in the active, immanent plane, that is, the plane in which the universe is known, there is experienced by the seer the play of Śakti, of God the Mother. Śrī Rāmakṛṣṇa was wont to say that just as fire and its burning power are inseparable, so inseparable are Brahman and Śakti. 'When I meditate upon Reality as at rest,' he once remarked, 'that is, without the activities of creation, preservation, and dissolution, I call it Brahman. When I meditate upon Reality as creative, I call it Śakti. In either case I am concerned with one and the same truth, the difference being only in name and aspect.'[1]

According to the Tantras, God the Mother has within herself the seeds of creation. At the end of a cycle she gives birth to a new world and lives within it. In the Upaniṣads a figure is given of the female spider and her web. The spider weaves her thread out of herself and then lives upon it. God the Mother is both the container and the contained.

'It is the desire for the life of form [writes Sir John Woodroffe, in explaining the philosophy of the Tantras] which produces the universe. This desire exists in the collective Vāsanās [thirst or desires], held like all else in inchoate state in the Mother-Power, which passing from its own (Svarūpa) formless state gives effect to them. Upon the expiration of the vast length of time which constitutes a day of Brahmā the whole universe is withdrawn into the great Causal Womb (Yoni) which produced it. The limited selves are withdrawn into it, and again, when the creative throes are felt, are put forth from it, each appearing in that form and state which its previous Karma had made for it. Those who do good Karma but with desire and self-regard (Sakāma) go, on death, to Heaven and thereafter reap their reward in good future birth on earth—for Heaven is also a transitory state. The bad are punished by evil births on earth and suffering in the Hells which are also transitory. Those, however, who have rid themselves of all self-regarding desire and work selflessly (Niṣkāma Karma), realize the Brahman nature which is Sacchidānanda. Such are liberated, that is never appear again in the World of Form, which is the world of suffering, and enter into the infinite ocean of Bliss Itself. This is Mokṣa or Mukti or Liberation. As it is freedom from the universe of form, it can only be attained through detachment from the world and desirelessness. For those who desire the world of form cannot be freed of it. Life, therefore, is a field in which man, who has gradually ascended through lower forms of

[1] *Kathāmṛta*, vol. I, p. 49.

mineral, vegetable and animal life, is given the opportunity of heaven-life and Liberation. The universe has a moral purpose, namely the affording to all existence of a field wherein it may reap the fruits of its actions. The forms of life are therefore the stairs (Sopāna) on which man mounts to the state of infinite, eternal, and formless Bliss. This then is the origin and the end of man. He has made for himself his own past and present condition and will make his future one. His essential nature is free. If wise, he adopts the means (Sādhanā) which lead to lasting happiness, for that of the world is not to be had by all, and even when attained is perishable and mixed with suffering.'[1]

This quotation adequately summarizes the attitude not merely of the Tantras but of the whole body of the Hindu scriptures toward the origin and end of man.

The teachings of the Tantras are never at variance with those of the Upaniṣads. Even the worship of God the Mother is not new in the Tantras. In the Kena Upaniṣad we find, for example, when the gods grew arrogant because of their victory over the demons, that it was Umā, God the Mother, who brought them to their senses and offered them the supreme knowledge. (Correspondingly, the Tantras hold that by worship of God in the aspect of Mother supreme knowledge and liberation can be achieved. 'She brings to light and freedom those with whom she is well pleased.') Further, there is a hymn in the Ṛg-Veda in honour of God the Mother, which reads: 'I spread the heavens over the earth. I am the energy in Brahman, I am the mother of all. It is for me that Brahman resides in all intellects, and it is I who have penetrated all the worlds with my power and am holding them in their places. . . . Again, apart from the heavens and apart from this earth, I remain always the all-intelligent primal energy, as well as the one intelligent being, perfect and untouched by my magic creation.'[2]

Sādhanā and Siddhi

The Tantras are primarily and fundamentally practical scriptures on sādhanā. The word sādhanā means a striving or discipline for the attainment of a certain prescribed goal. And that goal, or siddhi (attainment), as may be guessed, is mokṣa, liberation from the bondage of ignorance, and from the chain of recurring birth and death, through knowledge of the true Self as one with Śiva, or Brahman. The attainment of this knowledge, though possible only through effort, must be direct and immediate. According to the Tantras and all the other Hindu scriptures, infinite knowledge,

[1]. *Śakti and Śākta*, pp. 11 f.

[2] Ṛg-Veda, x. 125. 3, 7.

power, and bliss are latent in every man. The object of sādhanā is just to unfold this knowledge and power and to realize this bliss.

The authority of the scriptures does not depend upon mere belief in them as revelations, but upon the fact that their truths can be revealed in one's own soul. In other words, the test of their validity is primarily a positive one. They contend, moreover, that the spiritual practices they inculcate will bring the promised results to all who follow them. Briefly, they insist that one must act in order to experience the truth of God.

The sādhanās, or spiritual disciplines, however, should be undertaken only with the help of a guru, or spiritual teacher. All Hindu schools of thought, in fact, maintain that submission to the direction of a competent teacher is essential if one is to attain to knowledge of God, for religion is a practical science to which neither books nor scriptures can be a complete guide. The aspirant must therefore associate himself with one who is competent and holy, who has demonstrated the truths of religion in his own life, and who can therefore initiate the disciple into the secrets of spiritual unfoldment. The Tantras define two kinds of dīkṣa, or initiation: śāmbhavī (or śāktī) and māntrī. Śāmbhavī occurs when the disciple immediately experiences divine vision, attaining the supreme knowledge by the mere wish or touch of the guru. Though to us this sudden transformation may seem fantastic, we may see it substantiated in the lives of Kṛṣṇa, Christ, and Rāmakṛṣṇa. Christ said to his disciple, 'Be thou whole [perfect]', and the disciple instantly attained perfection; Kṛṣṇa by a word gave divine sight to Arjuna, and the realization of God; and within living memory Rāmakṛṣṇa by a touch gave illumination to his disciples.[1]

But this form of initiation is possible only through supreme teachers. Lesser teachers must have recourse to the other form of initiation, namely, māntrī. In this the guru initiates the disciple by presenting him with a mantra, or sacred word or formula. In the Tantras the philosophy involved in the mantras is given detailed explanation, the underlying principle being that words and thoughts are inseparable, and that a person may effect a complete change in his character by meditating upon a thought with the help of a word and by repeating the word. The root of initiation, declare these scriptures, is the mantra; the mantra is the body of God; and God is the root of siddhi, or attainment of knowledge and perfection.

Men vary in capacity, temperament, and level of growth in the

[1] I myself had the blessed fortune to live in the society of many of Śri Rāmakṛṣṇa's disciples, each one of whom testified to the fact that he had attained samādhi through the Master's touch. The effects of that touch one could perceive in their lives and their characters.

intellectual, moral, and spiritual spheres. Accordingly, the Tantras classify humanity into three general categories: divya, or divine; vīra, or heroic; and paśu, or animal. The paśus, in whom animal passions predominate, must avoid all objects of temptation and regularly observe the ritualistic forms of worship and meditation. The vīras, in whom there is a greater love for spiritual than for material things, may abide in the midst of the objects of temptation, while they learn to maintain their equanimity and self-control by devoting their thoughts more and more to God. And the divyas, who have become established in self-control, whose minds are absorbed in the thought of God, and in whom is to be found an expression of all divine qualities, such as love, kindness, and truthfulness—like the emanation of fragrance from a flower—these are beyond all need of spiritual discipline.

Four forms of worship and meditation are prescribed in the Tantras. The highest is Brahma-sadbhāva—meditating on the identity of the inner Self of man with Brahman as he exists in all and all exist in him. The second in this scale is constant meditation on the chosen ideal of God within one's own heart. The third is japa, repetition of the mantra (the word corresponding to the chosen ideal of God) and prayer. And the last and lowest is external worship of an image or a symbol.

Those who are advanced enough to meditate on the identity of the inner Self with God do not need the aid of external symbols or rituals, but for others symbols and rituals are always very helpful and in most cases are needed. Says Sir John Woodroffe:

> 'Brāhmanism thus sagely resolves the Western dispute as to the necessity or advisability of ritual. It affirms it for those who have not attained the end of all ritual. It lessens and refines ritual as spiritual progress is made upwards; it dispenses with it altogether when there is no longer need for it. But until a man is a real "Knower", some sādhana is necessary if he would become one. . . . What may be suitable for the unlettered peasant may not be so for those more intellectually and spiritually advanced. It is however a fine general principle of Tāntric worship that capacity, and not social distinction such as caste, determines competency for any particular worship.'[1]

The Tantras developed elaborate rituals and symbols for those who needed them, and supplied most of the temple rituals in India. In the worship of something outside the Inner Self—for example, a Chosen Deity—an external symbol, such as an image, a picture, an emblem, or a geometrical design called yantra, may be used. In

[1] *Śakti and Śākta*, p. 514.

practising ritualism worshippers must also practise inward meditation and adoration. Those who follow the ritualist path are falsely accused by the ignorant of being idolators, for if one will only learn their form of worship, one may perceive for oneself what disciplines are involved. As a matter of fact, in this process of external worship there is a wonderful harmony and blending of jñāna (knowledge), bhakti (love), karma, and rāja yoga. Sir John Woodroffe has correctly explained the matter:

'According to Hindu views, primary importance is attached to mental states, for as the Divine Thought made the world, man makes his character therein by what he thinks. If he is always thinking on material things and has desires therefore he himself becomes material and is given over to lust and other passions. If, on the contrary, he has always his mind on God, and associates everything with the thought of Him, his mind becomes pure and divine.'[1]

As we have already noted, the Śākta Tantra teaches the Motherhood of God—God as Śakti, or the power which creates and preserves the universe and dissolves it into herself. The concept Mother, indeed, takes many forms, has many aspects, and what is experienced as terror and death and destruction is included in her play. These three—terror, death, and destruction—are but the obverse of bliss, life, and creation. The tender Mother shows her benign aspect to those who are her votaries, in whatever form or aspect they may worship her. And she is to be seen and realized everywhere in the universe. A beautiful prayer occurs in the Caṇḍī, a prayer book of the Śākta Tantras:

'O Mother, thou art the embodiment of all knowledge. Wherever there are intelligence and learning, there art thou manifest. All women are thy forms. Thou hast thy being in the universe, filling and permeating all things.'

Thus spiritual aspirants are taught to look upon all women as the embodiment of Śakti, or Mother.[2]

[1] *Śakti and Śākta*, pp. 530 f.

[2] It should be noted that there evolved a school of thought amongst the Śāktas known as vāmācāra. Its ritual of wine and women, apparently a pure sensualism, gained some notoriety. If, however, we penetrate a little into the meaning of the accessories used we shall find no ground for condemnation. The symbols of wine and women were employed in order to teach freedom from lustful passions by trying to see everywhere the Divine Mother. In course of time, it is true, the original spirit of the ritual was forgotten, and degeneration of the whole form of worship ensued. The idea involved was an admirable one, but in its application it became dangerous and actually evil.

A most important portion of the Tantras is that which deals with what is technically known as kuṇḍalinī yoga. The word kuṇḍalinī literally means the coiled up. According to the scriptures, the divine energy remains unmanifested within us, and to the yogi's eye it has a form like that of a coiled serpent. The object of spiritual practices is to awaken this sleeping power in man. There are, assert the Tantras, seven centres of consciousness, the seventh of which is located in the brain. These centres, resembling lotuses, are technically known as cakras. Through certain prescribed exercises the kuṇḍalinī, or Divine Energy, rises through the centres until it reaches the seventh, and in this seventh occurs a mystic union with the Supreme Lord, who there resides. Then it is that one attains transcendental consciousness.

This kuṇḍalinī and these seven cakras or lotuses are not physical but subtle and vital, and the mystic with his divine sight opened sees them. He also experiences various psychic and spiritual visions as his sleeping energy awakens to full life.

Once Śrī Rāmakṛṣṇa spoke of the centres of energy in this way:

'In the scriptures mention is made of the seven centres of consciousness. When the mind is attached to worldliness, consciousness dwells in the three lower centres, the plexus sacro-coccygeal, sacral, and solar. Then there are in it no high ideals or pure thoughts. It remains immersed in lust and greed. The fourth centre of consciousness is the region of the heart. Spiritual awakening comes when the mind rises to this centre. At this stage man has a spiritual vision of the Divine Light and is struck with wonder at its beauty and glory. His mind then no longer runs after worldly pleasures. The region of the throat is the fifth centre of consciousness. When the mind rises to this centre, man becomes free from nescience and ignorance. He then talks only on subjects relating to God and grows impatient if any worldly topic is discussed. He avoids hearing about worldly subjects. The sixth centre is between the eyebrows. When the mind rises to this centre, man becomes merged in divine consciousness. There is still left in him, however, the consciousness of a separate ego. Seeing the beatific vision of God he becomes mad with joy and longs to come closer to him and be united with him. But he cannot, for there is still the ego which stands between them. One may compare God to the light in a lantern. You seem to feel its warmth; yet though you wish to do so, you cannot touch it, on account of the glass intervening. The centre in the brain is the seventh centre. When one rises to this plane, there is samādhi. That is the transcendental consciousness, in which one realizes his oneness with God.'[1]

[1] *Kathāmṛta*, vol. I, pp. 72–3.

SELECTED PASSAGES FROM THE MAHĀNIRVĀṆA TANTRA

The Lord of this universe becomes pleased with him who is engaged in doing good to the world, since the Lord is its soul and refuge.

He is one. He ever is. He is the Truth, one without a second. He is the supreme Being. He is self-effulgent, ever shining. He is eternal consciousness and bliss.[1]

He is unchangeable, self-existent, and serene, and he is beyond all predicates. He is the witness of all, the Self of all, pervading everything; he is the omnipresent.

He, the eternal, dwells concealed in the heart of all beings. Though himself devoid of senses, he is the illuminator of all the senses, the source of their powers.[2]

He knows all, but none knows him.[3] The world of forms appears real because he, the ground of all existence, is real.[4]

Through fear of him the wind blows, the sun gives heat, the clouds shower rain, and the trees in the forest flower.[5]

All gods and goddesses—nay, the whole universe from Brahma to a blade of grass—are his forms.[6] If he be pleased, the universe is pleased.[7]

Just as the pouring of water at its root nourishes the branches and leaves of a tree, so by worshipping him all the gods and goddesses attain bliss.[8]

As all rivers must go to the ocean, so all acts of worship reach him as the ultimate goal.[9]

For the attainment of liberation with ease and delight, there is no way but to worship him, to meditate upon him, and to pray to him.[10]

[1] II. 33–4. [2] *Ibid.*, 35–6. [3] *Ibid.*, 37. [4] *Ibid.*, 38. [5] *Ibid.*, 44.
[6] *Ibid.*, 46. [7] *Ibid.*, 47. [8] *Ibid.*, 48. [9] *Ibid.*, 50. [10] *Ibid.*, 52.

BOOK III

JAINISM AND BUDDHISM

CHAPTER 7

JAINISM

What is Jainism?

The words Jain and Jainism are derived from the Sanskrit root ji, which means to conquer. A Jain is one who believes in conquering the flesh in order to attain to that supreme purity which leads to infinite knowledge, infinite happiness, and infinite power—the same conquering the flesh and the same self-liberation that all other religions of India have taught. It is said that Jainism is as old as the Vedic religion. Vardhamāna, known also as Mahāvīra, or the supreme spiritual hero, whose name has come to be identified with Jainism, is but the last in a long series of inspired prophets, or seers.[1]

According to its tradition, Jainism goes back to the beginning of time and its truths were gradually revealed to certain divine men called tīrthaṅkaras. Its cosmogony has paralleled that of other Indian faiths in that it postulates a series of cosmic cycles, consisting of utsarpiṇī, or ages of expansion, and avasarpiṇī, or ages of contraction, or decay—our own age being one of the latter. During the present period of contraction, twenty-four tīrthaṅkaras have appeared from time to time, Ṛṣabha being the first and Mahāvīra the last.

Ṛṣabha is, then, the founder of the sect for the present cycle, having uttered the truths by which the cycle is governed. His name is to be found in the Ṛg-Veda, and the story of his life is told in two of the Purāṇas, the Viṣṇu Purāṇa and the Bhāgavata Purāṇa. In all these scriptures he is regarded as a great saint.

[1] It is customary among Western scholars to discover points of similarity between the lives of Mahāvira and Buddha, who were contemporaries, and in consequence of this and of the further fact that both Jainism and Buddhism lay emphasis upon ahiṁsā, or noninjury, they look upon Jainism as an offshoot of Buddhism. But these two religions are really independent of each other, though parallel in their development. Mahāvira is not the founder of Jainism but only, as remarked above, the last in a long succession of sages and seers. Parśwanātha, who lived two centuries before the time of Mahāvira, is another in this succession and also a historical figure.

Mahāvīra, the last one of the twenty-four tīrthaṅkaras, was born in the latter part of the sixth century BC, of kṣatriya parents, near Vaiśāli, the modern village Basrah, about twenty miles north of Patna. He married and had one daughter. From his earliest boyhood he possessed a reflective and inquiring mind. At the age of twenty-eight he renounced the world and thereafter practised austerities and meditation for twelve years, at the end of which time he was spiritually illumined (kevala). Then for thirty years he preached his Jain doctrines to the people, and at the end of his ministry he attained final liberation.

This story, so similar to that of Buddha, adds to Jainism the personal note necessary to the propagation of any religion. Mahāvīra popularized the doctrine of ahiṁsā (doing no harm), and in so doing made his chief contribution to the spread of Jainism. He also organized the community into two classes, monks and householders. Finally, he opened the doors of his religion to all aspirants, irrespective of caste or sex.

With regard to the main precepts of Jainism, all Jains are at one. About the beginning of the Christian Era, however, they divided into two sects, which became known as digambaras and śwetāmbaras because of certain differing regulations regarding the life and conduct of the monks. The most important of these is that the digambara monks, who are supposed to be free from consciousness of their bodies, are allowed to wear no garments whatever, whereas the śwetāmbara monks are enjoined to wear white robes.

The scriptures of the Jains consist chiefly of the Aṅgas, the Pūrvas, and the Prakīrna. There are also other sacred writings, comparatively modern, containing systematic interpretations of Jain philosophy and religion in both Prākrit and Sanskrit.[1]

The Goal of Jainism

Jainism denies the existence of a First Cause, or creator of the universe. In fact it regards the belief that the cosmic universe had a definite beginning in time as illogical and unthinkable, for that belief involves the further belief that a God, noncreative before creation, suddenly changed his mind and became creative. The universe, therefore, consisting of jīvas, or souls, and ajīvas, or beings which are not souls, must necessarily be without beginning and without end. It is not necessary to postulate a deity to explain the nature of the

[1] There are altogether only about one and a half million Jains in all India. They are a peace-loving people, and have no quarrel with other Hindu religions. In fact they look upon themselves as quite within the Hindu fold, and are so regarded by the main body of the orthodox.

cosmos, for the very fact of the eternal existence of jīvas and ajīvas requires a cosmos in which they can be manifested. To the critics of Jainism, who contend that for everything that is there must be a maker, the Jains put the question, How then could the maker exist without another maker who made him, and so on backward without end? And if it is possible for one being to exist self-subsistent and eternal, why is it not possible for many to be likewise self-subsistent and eternal?

This ancient problem of a First Cause is thus solved by Jainism through a flat denial that a problem exists. Neither a theory of a definite origin in time of the universe, nor a theory of a God in the sense of creator and sustainer, is admitted in its metaphysics. It does believe, however, in the divinity of every soul and in the perfected soul as the Paramātman, the Supreme Spirit, who is the object of worship and adoration. And every soul is a potential Paramātman. In this sense the Jain religion, despite its denial of the personal factor in creation, is very far from being purely atheistic, for it posits definitely the divinity of the soul and the possibility of our realizing its divinity.

The ontological argument of the Jainists runs thus: When a man breaks the bonds of his karmas by subduing his passions and realizing the supreme purity of the soul, and there is revealed to him in his own soul infinite knowledge, bliss, and power, he becomes at once a Paramātman, or Perfected Soul. Since all souls are potentially divine, there are many that have achieved perfection and many more that are on the way to achieving it. The following is a typical prayer of a Jain devotee:

'Him who is the revealer of the path to salvation, who is the remover of mountains of karmas, and who is the knower of all reality, him I worship, in order that I may realize his qualities within myself.'

So we come to the conclusion that the Jains are believers in man-God, though the concept is not quite the same as the Hindu avatār or the Christian Son of God. The object of their worship is the man-God, and they consider that the best way to worship him is to become, themselves, Sons of God—Paramātmans, supreme perfected spirits.

It is true that souls rank variously. He who has become perfect by realizing his divine nature, who has so overcome the world that he is not touched by the good and evil in it, is in the highest rank. Such a man is called Siddha Parameṣṭhin. Next in the scale of being is the Arhat, one who has not as yet attained final liberation, but who has received illumination, has a desire to serve humanity, and looks upon his fellows with love and kindness. Such a soul reveals the eternal truths of religion to struggling humanity. Arhats enter into human life at certain cosmic periods for the good of all. The three next gradations are composed of ordinary human teachers. These have gained some conquest over the flesh and some knowledge of the divine nature of the soul. Each of the five stages of individual evolution represents the supreme goal of life at a certain level of illumination.

The highest perfection, Siddha Parameṣṭhin, can be described as a state absolutely unconditional, a state of passionless peace, in which one is released from action and is without desire.

Metaphysically, mokṣa is liberation from the bonds of karma and rebirth. Like all other schools of Indian thought, Jainism accepts karma and reincarnation, but unlike the others, it conceives of karma as something material, which, uniting with the soul, binds a man to the world and its attractions. Though it is regarded as a material substance, karma is yet so subtile that it is unperceivable by the senses. It is in this karma that the soul is bound, and it is for this reason that the soul is embodied in the substance of a being and that it is embodied from a beginningless past. But, though this bondage has no beginning, it may definitely have an end, for the soul is essentially free and divine, and just as soon as its true nature is realized karma disappears. The Vedāntic doctrine of avidyā, or ignorance, also holds that individual ignorance, though it may end, has no beginning.

This bondage of the soul to karma is not caused by anything extraneous, but by karma itself. As the soul comes into contact with the world outside, certain psychic conditions arise, such as the desire for enjoyment, which lead to ignorance of the soul's true nature, and cause the karmic molecules to 'flow in' towards it and in the process to surround it. This 'flowing in' of the subtile matter of karma is peculiar to Jain metaphysics, and is technically known as āsrava, the first stage in karmic bondage. The next stage is the actual bondage, known technically as bandha. In this the molecules become settled and build up a subtile body known as the karmaṇa śarīra, and the soul is weighed down by its own karmas. The physical body dies with death, but the karmana śarīra, which corresponds to the subtile body in Hinduism, lingers on until the final liberation.

Freedom from the weight of karma is gained first by saṁvara, self-restraint, for when this is exercised no fresh karma is attached to the soul. Then by self-discipline, both ethical and spiritual, there is induced a state known as nirjara, or the shedding of all past karmas. At this point rebirth ceases, and a certain preliminary liberation is attained, but the next two (and last) stages must precede mokṣa, the final liberation. The first of these is Arhat, in which the enlightened soul, freed from karmas, continues to live in the world, actively engaged in the service of humanity yet no longer tainted by good and evil. This state is comparable with that of the jīvanmukta, free while living, of the Hindu ideal.

In the next stage of its progress, the soul transcends the world. Here, where there is no more activity, it attains the perfect state, characterized by infinite knowledge and infinite peace. This, the final state, is known as Siddha Parameṣṭhin.

The Way to Fulfilment

Mokṣa is achieved through triratna—the three jewels of right faith, right knowledge, and right conduct.[1] The three together make a single unit. Right faith is unshaken faith in the teaching of the Jains; right knowledge is true understanding of their principles; and right conduct is practical living in accordance with these principles. The first of these, right faith, is the foundation of the ethical and spiritual life. Before one can have right faith, one must be free from ignorant superstitions—the idea, for example, that spiritual merit may be acquired by bathing in a river said to be sacred, or by propitiating imaginary gods, or by observing certain external rites. Freedom from superstitions, as well as from pride or arrogance or conceit, is the primary necessity for developing right faith. With right faith arises right knowledge—enlightened understanding of the truths of religion—which in turn must be united with the third jewel, right conduct.

Right conduct comprises the five vratas, or observances: (1) ahiṁsā, or noninjury—great emphasis being laid on this principle, which requires not only that one do no harm to living creatures but also that one show them kindness; (2) satya, or truthfulness; (3) asteya, or nonstealing—understood to extend to the prohibition of covetousness; (4) brahmacarya, or chastity in word, thought, and deed; and (5) aparigraha, or nonattachment to the world.

When applied without limitation, these vratas are known as the mahāvratas—the supreme vows taken by the monks. Thus Jainism makes a distinction between conduct prescribed for its monks and that prescribed for its lay brethren.

Great emphasis is placed by Jainism, as by all other Indian schools of thought, upon human birth as a means to the attainment of divine perfection. Even the gods and angels, who partake of celestial joys in some kind of heaven, must appear on earth in human form if

[1] Compare the way to salvation through the offices of the Roman Catholic Church: faith, instruction, and works.

they would reach the ultimate goal. Blessed, therefore, is human birth.[1]

Jain Metaphysics[2]

The difficult subject of Jain metaphysics is involved in the Jain view of life. Reality, which is uncreated and eternal, is defined as that which is 'characterized by birth and death in the midst of permanence'. That is, it maintains its identity and permanence through the process of continual change—through birth and death. Changes in appearance are the modifications a substance undergoes, the underlying substance remaining always the same. In gold, for example, the underlying substance remains gold despite the modifications involved in the manufacture from it of various ornaments. In the aspect of modification, called paryāya, there are birth and death; in the aspect of substance, or dravya, there is only permanence. One mode disappears, another appears, but the underlying substance is invariable.

Substance and its qualities, the guṇas, can never be separated—there can be no substance without a quality, and no quality without a substance—but they are distinct from each other in the mind of the observer. This is called the bheda-abheda point of view (bheda—different; abheda—identical), a position fundamentally different from that of the Nyāya-Vaiśeṣika school, which recognizes an absolute distinction between substance and its qualities.[3] The ultimate realities, which are uncreated and eternal and which make up the structure of the cosmos, are six in number. The first five are jīva (soul or spirit), pudgala (matter), dharma (the principle of motion), adharma (the principle of rest), and ākāśa (space). They receive the technical name

[1] Edward Washburn Hopkins (*Religions of India*, p. 297) caricatures Jainism when he says that it is 'a religion in which the chief points insisted upon are that one should deny God, worship man, and nourish vermin'. One can caricature any religion. Jainism denies the existence of an extracosmic God and of an all-pervading Spirit, but it accepts the immortal soul and the kingdom of God within. Moreover, it believes in man-Gods—saints who have realized perfection. Such a man-God was Christ, who is worshipped by many millions of men. Again, Jainism insists upon noninjury. 'Thou shalt not kill'—a commandment very imperfectly observed by the West—is simply extended to protect all living creatures.

Perhaps in this connection it should be pointed out that the Jains, true to the characteristic spirit of Indian religion, do not regard theirs as the only true religion. They believe that non-Jains, if they truly follow the precepts of their respective religions, may in their own way arrive at mokṣa, the goal of all life. The whole truth cannot emerge from any one teaching, and we need, therefore, to be tolerant of ways of salvation not our own. We shall return to the Jain theory of religious tolerance in the section 'Jain Logic and Theory of Knowledge'.

[2] The general reader may wish to omit this section since it is highly technical in nature.

[3] Cf. chap. 10.

pañcāstikāyas, five astikāyas. The word astikāya means an existence capable of spatial relations. To these (the pañcāstikāyas) must be added kāla (time), which is a substance different in nature from the five astikāyas, because time is nonspatial, and 'corresponds to unilateral series in mathematics and hence it is excluded from the class of astikāyas. In Jain metaphysics, nevertheless, it is included under the six dravyas, or realities which compose the universe of beings or things.'[1]

These six dravyas, ultimate realities, fall into two divisions: jīva (spirit), and ajīva (nonspirit), the distinction between them being that jīva is conscious (cetana) and ajīva unconscious (acetana).

The jīva is identified with life and consciousness. Consciousness is not in any way the product of matter but is rather the property of the soul, and is identical with the soul, which exists independently of matter. In fact, the soul may exist independently of the body, beyond material units or space units. And there is an infinite number of souls—uncreated and eternal. Birth and death in the material world are not the guṇas (properties) of the soul, but rather paryāyas, its modifications, while it is in the bonds of karma. In this world of matter and spirit, the souls that are still within the shackles of karma are associated with bodies and have measurements corresponding to the measurements of the bodies which they inhabit.

Four main groups of souls dwell in the cosmos. First there are the devas, or gods, living in the heavens. According to the orthodox Hindus as well as the Jains, gods are embodied beings, higher in the scale of evolution than man but like man subject to birth and death. The heavens are places where men are born as gods to enjoy the fruits of their good deeds but where they die when the effects of such deeds are exhausted. The gods, it is said, have to return to earth as human beings to attain liberation. The second group of jīvas consists of human beings. Third in order come the tiryaks, or lower animals, and the vegetable kingdom. The last group comprises nārakas, or beings inhabiting the hells, or lower regions.[2]

All four classes of beings, since they are subject to the law of karma, are happy or miserable according to their deeds in this or other lives.[3]

[1] *Cultural Heritage of India*, vol. I, p. 198.

[2] We cannot definitely locate the heavens and hells, but the Jains, as well as the Hindus, believe in them as places to which men may go after death. The man of good deeds goes to one of the heavens and there receives his due reward; the man of bad deeds goes to one of the hells and there suffers his due punishment. Each, after his temporary enjoyment or misery, returns to earth.

[3] According to Jain metaphysics, the jīva is a knower, an actor, and an enjoyer. This conception differs somewhat from the Sāṁkhya view of Puruṣa, or the soul. According to Sāṁkhya philosophy, the Puruṣa is distinctly inactive, though he remains the knower and enjoyer.

Ignorant of their pure, conscious, and divine nature, they are subject to birth and death.

Mokṣa consists in freeing oneself from the shackles of karma, thereby escaping the cycle of birth and death and reaching beyond the world of relativity to the realm of infinite knowledge, happiness, and power, where there is no more desire and no more action, for no limitations hold the soul back from its destined liberation.

The jīva who attains this final stage of evolution is the pure jīva, known as the siddha, or perfected soul. The saṁsārī jīva, the soul still bound by karma, is always enclosed within a material body. The primary classification of jīvas has been given. They are also classified according to the number of sense organs they possess.

The lowest class have evolved only one sense organ. They are to be found in the vegetable kingdom in the form of trees and plants endowed with the sense of touch. They also exist, microscopic in size—and these are the next higher class—on the earth, in water, in air, and in light. This part of the theory, concerned with microscopic organisms, is often misinterpreted as animism—the belief that the earth, air, water, and light themselves possess souls. For such a misinterpretation there is really no foundation. Worms, the third class in an ascending scale, possess the senses of touch and taste. Ants, in the fourth class, have touch, taste, and smell, and bees, also in the fourth class, are endowed not only with these three but also with sight. Higher animals compose the fifth class, with hearing as the fifth sense. Man is at the top of the scale, being possessed of mind in addition to the five senses.

The sense organs and the bodies to which they belong are not, however, properties of the jīva. The jīva has indeed but one property—consciousness. This lies dormant in lower beings but progressively unfolds as the jīva journeys through successively higher bodies, until it comes into full expression in the pure jīva, the perfected soul.[1]

It has already been noted that the universe is made up of jīva (spirit) and ajīva (nonspirit). The characteristic of ajīva is that it is inert, nonliving. The ajīva substances, which are uncreated and eternal, are pudgala, matter; dharma, the principle of motion; adharma, the principle of rest; ākāśa, space; and kāla, time. Of these only kāla is nonspatial. Pudgala is corporeal, while the others have no bodily existence.

Pudgala, matter, is a substance associated with the sense properties—colour, taste, smell, touch, and sound—and existing independently

[1] It is interesting to note in this connection that the great Hindu scientist, Sir J. C. Bose, proves through specially constructed scientific instruments that life and consciousness exist not only among the plants but even in the mineral kingdom.

of the perceiver, the jīva. It is the physical basis of the universe, and is composed of entities called paramāṇus (atoms). A paramāṇu has no parts, nor any beginning, middle, or end; it is eternal, uncreated, and ultimate. In itself it has no form, though it is the irreducible basis of pudgala, which has form. When two or more atoms unite, they are called skandha (an aggregate). The aggregate of atoms which constitutes the universe is known as the mahāskandha (the great aggregate). The atoms are subject to modification, producing different substances as they combine differently, though no differences exist in the primary atoms. In this respect the atoms of Jain metaphysics differ from the paramāṇus of the Nyāya-Vaiśeṣika philosophy, which holds that there are as many kinds of atoms as there are primary elements. These are five in number: earth, air, ether, fire, and water.

The movement and combination of atoms are caused by the intervention of ākāśa (space), dharma (principle of motion), and adharma (principle of rest)—uncreated, eternal, and formless substances.

Ākāśa, space, is infinite in extent and possesses objective reality. Its only function is to provide a place in which the other substances can exist.

Dharma (the principle of motion), and adharma (the principle of rest), are the two categories peculiar to Jain philosophy. Both motion and rest are to be found in jīva and pudgala. These two, spirit and matter, though in themselves capable of motion, yet are conditioned by dharma and adharma, which pervade the cosmos. Dharma and adharma remain nonoperative, and yet they serve as prerequisites of movement and the cessation of movement. With respect to dharma, we may use as an illustration the movement of fish in the sea. When a fish swims, the operating cause is present in itself, yet it could not do so without pressure from the water. Water is, therefore, not an operating but a conditioning cause of the swimming of the fish. So also while life and matter are capable of moving under their own impulsion, this movement is determined by causal nonoperating conditions called dharma, or the principle of motion. Similarly, when a moving object comes to rest of its own accord, the opposite principle, or adharma, is present. This also, as we may perceive, is nonoperating but conditioning. A bird, when it ceases to beat its wings, stops its flight and comes to rest. But this cessation of activity depends on a further condition, in this case the branch of a tree upon which it perches. The branch serves as a nonoperative condition of rest, and concretely illustrates the adharma principle. The two principles, of motion and of rest, are necessary for postulating an orderly structure of the world.

The last category is kāla (time). Time is an objective reality but nonspatial. It is a necessary condition of all growth and decay—of the evolution and involution that constitute the life of the universe. The process of change is unthinkable and unintelligible without kāla.

The five ajīva substances, together with jīva, form the six dravyas, or categories, of Jain metaphysics.

Before we consider the subject of Jain logic and its theory of knowledge, we ought to review the Jain classification of substances and categories. This classification includes seven tattwas (principles), nine padārthas (categories), six dravyas (substances), and two further tattwas (ultimate reals)—'according to the point of view adopted and the purpose for which the categories are enumerated'.[1]

A table may facilitate the comprehension of this difficult subject:

Tattwas (Ultimate reals)	1. Jīva (spirit)
	2. Ajīva (nonspirit)

Dravyas (Substances)	1. Jīva (spirit)	
	2. Pudgala (matter)	Ajīva (nonspirit)
	3. Dharma (principle of motion)	Ajīva (nonspirit)
	4. Adharma (principle of rest)	Ajīva (nonspirit)
	5. Ākāśa (space)	Ajīva (nonspirit)
	6. Kāla (time)	Ajīva (nonspirit)

The first five dravyas, called astikāyas, are spatial; kāla is nonspatial.

Tattwas (Principles)	1. Jīva (spirit)
	2. Ajīva (nonspirit)
	3. Āsrava (the flowing in of karmic molecules that bind the jīva)
	4. Bandha (bondage to the karmaṇa body)
	5. Saṁvara (the checking of fresh karmas for the jīva)
	6. Nirjara (the shedding of karmas)
	7. Mokṣa (salvation as the jīva realizes his true nature)

When puṇya (merit) and pāpa (demerit) are added to the seven principles mentioned above, we obtain the nine padārthas (categories) of Jain metaphysics.

Jain Logic and Theory of Knowledge

Since the jīva is by its very nature pure consciousness, infinite knowledge is its inherent possession. But this knowledge is overlaid

[1] Appaswami Chakravarti, 'Jainism', *The Cultural Heritage of India*, vol. I, p. 208.

by ignorance created by the karmic body. While dwelling within the bonds of karma, the jīva can express only finite knowledge; but as the impediments to greater knowledge are removed, infinite knowledge is manifested, and the true nature of the soul is revealed. These impediments are the desires and passions, and as the soul frees itself from these and from its egoism, and learns the lesson of self-restraint, there comes greater and greater knowledge. Five different kinds or types of knowledge appear as the jīva passes through various stages of unfoldment: mati, śruti, avadhi, manaḥparyāya, and kevala.

Mati is ordinary cognition, including sense perception, memory, and inference; and since the soul is dependent for it on the senses and the ordinary operations of the mind, it is known as parokṣa —indirect knowledge. This last is in contradiction to Western psychology, which regards the knowledge obtained from the senses as immediate or direct.

Śruti, testimony, is revelations of the scriptures—also called parokṣa, indirect knowledge, since the revelations were not made to ourselves.

Avadhi is knowledge derived from the psychic power of clairvoyance and clairaudience—the perception of things and events at great distances of time and space. This knowledge, since it is not dependent upon the senses coming into contact with objects, is known as pratyakṣa—direct or immediate knowledge.

Manaḥparyāya is the direct and immediate knowledge of others' minds.

Kevala is the perfect knowledge which the jīva gains when he is completely free from the bonds of ignorance and has realized his inherent purity. This knowledge is direct, immediate, and independent of the senses and the mind, and can only be felt and experienced—cannot be expressed in logical terms. This kevala, knowledge of the soul, is equivalent to the transcendental knowledge of the Upaniṣads and the nirvāṇa of the Buddhists.

Of the five types of knowledge, the first two are in the possession of every normal man, and the third and fourth may be developed in anyone who will practise self-restraint and concentration; but the fifth is granted only to him who in meditation has attained to absolute purity—an illumined soul.

Both jīvas and ajīvas are, as we have already noted, realities. They are not interdependent for their existence. External objects possess reality independently of jīva, the perceiving subject. Appaswami Chakravarti explains the matter in this way:

'The function of jñāna [knowledge] is merely to reveal, on the one hand, the objective reality which is already existing, and also to reveal itself on the other hand. Knowledge, therefore, is like a lamp which on account of its luminosity reveals other objects as well as itself, the objects so revealed being real. The external objects so known are independent, inasmuch as they exist by themselves and yet are related to knowledge as they are revealed by knowledge. Similarly, in the case of the soul, it is both the subject and the object of knowledge in one; this inner experience is able to reveal the nature of chetana [conscious] entity—the soul.'[1]

Jainism may be called pluralistic realism, since it asserts the reality of both spirit and nonspirit as eternal and uncreated substances, these being many in number and existing independently of one another.

Jain logic, and indirectly Jain metaphysics, would not be complete without an explanation of their peculiar system of predication, a system strangely anticipatory of the new doctrine of relativity in Western physics.

This system declares that both positive and negative predication may be made about the same thing. This is known as asti-nāsti—the thing is and is not. The apparent absurdity will reveal, when closely examined, a genuinely logical implication. An affirmative predication about a thing is dependent upon four conditions: sva-dravya (its own substance), sva-kṣetra (its own locality), sva-kāla (its own time of existence or duration), and sva-bhāva (its own modification); and correspondingly the negative predication about the same thing depends upon four conditions: para-dravya (alien substance), para-kṣetra (alien locality), para-kāla (alien time of existence, or duration), and para-bhāva (alien modification).

Let us illustrate by a concrete instance. If you wish to describe an ornament made of gold, you can do so in the following ways:

Substance	The necklace is made of gold. The necklace is not made of any other metal.
Locality	The necklace is in the box. The necklace is not on the table.
Time of existence or duration	The necklace exists today. The necklace did not exist yesterday.
Modification	The necklace is round. The necklace is not square.

Thus it is clear that affirmative and negative statements may be made about the same thing if these are made from different points of view—it would of course be absurd to affirm and negate from an identical point of view. The doctrine is not applicable, however, to

[1] *Cultural Heritage of India*, vol. I, pp. 209–10.

an object that is not real, for no predication of any kind can be made of an absolute nonentity.[1]

According to Jainism, no absolute predication about a thing is possible. Reality does not admit of absolute predication, but is characterized by appearance and nonappearance in the midst of permanence. One can speak neither of an absolutely unchanging permanence nor of absolute change without permanence. The reality, however, maintains its identity and permanence though it expresses itself in multiple forms. Jain philosophy is, therefore, called anekānta-vāda—unity in multiplicity. Out of this concept grew the general theory of a pluralistic universe.

[1] Upon this doctrine of asti-nāsti is based another Jainist doctrine known as sapta-bhaṅgī—the seven modes of predication. The modes are as follows:

(1) Syād asti (perhaps is). An affirmative predication about a thing is in relation to its own substance, locality, time of existence or duration, and modification.

(2) Syād nāsti (perhaps is not). A negative predication about a thing is in relation to its alien substance, locality, etc.

(3) Syād asti-nāsti (perhaps is and is not). Affirmative and negative predications about a thing are in relation to its own substance, etc.

(4) Syād avaktavya (perhaps inexpressible). If one attempts to represent both affirmative and negative in the same predication, language fails; it is therefore inexpressible.

(5) Syād asti avaktavya (perhaps is and is inexpressible). We note the existence of a thing, and yet predication is inexpressible if our attempts to represent both affirmative and negative are in the same predication.

(6) Syād nāsti avaktavya (perhaps is not, and is inexpressible). We note the relation of a thing to an alien substance, etc., as well as its inexpressibility.

(7) Syād asti-nāsti avaktavya (perhaps is, is not, and is inexpressible). We note the inexpressibility of a thing as well as what it is and what it is not.

CHAPTER 8

BUDDHISM

Introduction

In the Bhagavad-Gītā we have read:

> When goodness grows weak,
> When evil increases,
> I make myself a body.
> In every age I come back
> To deliver the holy,
> To destroy the sin of the sinner,
> To establish righteousness.[1]

As if to fulfil this promise of Śrī Kṛṣṇa, Buddha appeared. At the time of his birth spiritual culture in India was at a low ebb. What was then universally recognized as religion consisted wholly in the observance of rituals and sacrifices, for the people had forgotten the simple fact that religion is primarily a matter of experience and realization. When the externals of religion usurp its inner truth, there ceases to be any struggle towards purification of the soul, or any positive effort to know the Brahman within. It was to the end of relighting the flame of religion in the hearts of individual men that Buddha dedicated his life. His protest against the hardening of the outer forms of religion at the expense of its inner light may be compared with the mission of Christ, who sought to purify and revivify the religion of the Jews.

How very much the spirit of religion was misinterpreted at the time of Buddha's ministry may be learned from his own words as recorded in one of the ancient Buddhistic scriptures, the Tevijja Sutta. In it we are told of a young man, Vāseṭṭha by name, who approached Buddha to learn of the path to union with Brahman. Before, however, the Master was able to tell him of this

[1] IV. 7–8.

path, he was obliged to remove his ignorance concerning the way of spirit:

'Then you say, too, Vāseṭṭha, that the brāhmins bear anger and malice in their hearts, and are sinful and uncontrolled, whilst Brahman is free from anger and malice, and sinless, and has self-mastery. Now can there, then, be concord and likeness between the brāhmins and Brahman? . . .

'That these brāhmins, versed in the Vedas and yet bearing anger and malice in their hearts, sinful, and uncontrolled, should after death, when the body is dissolved, become united to Brahman, who is free from anger and malice, sinless, and has self-mastery—such a condition of things has no existence.

'So that thus then, Vāseṭṭha, the brāhmins, versed though they be in the three Vedas, while they sit down (in confidence), are sinking down (in the mire); and so sinking they are arriving only at despair, thinking the while that they are crossing over into some happier land. Therefore is it that the threefold wisdom of the brāhmins, wise in their three Vedas, is called a waterless desert, their threefold wisdom is called a pathless jungle, their threefold wisdom is called destruction!'[1]

Thus did Buddha utter the truth to be found in the Upaniṣads—that Brahman is to be realized, not by much learning but by purity of heart and rightness of conduct. It is easy to misinterpret him as denouncing the Vedic religion, whereas in fact he only brought to light the truth that religion does not lie in mastering the Vedas or other sacred books, but in realizing the spiritual life in one's own soul. This truth, as a matter of fact, is made manifest in the Vedas themselves—that the spiritual life cannot be attained by mere study of the Vedas but by following their teachings, that is, by living righteously, and by becoming aware of the light within one's own heart. This the brāhmins had forgotten, and Buddha came into the world to reveal once more the true spirit of sanātan dharma—the eternal religion. Buddha taught no new religion; rather he restated and reinterpreted the ancient and genuine Vedic faith, infusing new spirit—the eternally new and eternally old spirit—into a religion that existed before man lived upon this earth, and will exist when man is forgotten.

Life of Buddha

Prince Gautama, the name of Buddha before he attained his illumination, was born in 560 BC at Kapilāvastu, in northern India. At his

[1] I. 37–9.

birth wise men prophesied that either he would become the greatest monarch on earth or, stung by the woes of men, would renounce the world and become a great religious leader. King Śuddhodhana, his father, meditated within himself: 'Stung by the woes of men, he will renounce the world. My son shall never know the woes of men.' The king was determined that his son should be the greatest ruler in the world and that there should exist no possibility of his becoming a religious mendicant.

So, legend says, the king built a palace, and beside it laid out a garden opening on a park that stretched for many miles in every direction. In this palace the young prince lived, and there grew to manhood amid beautiful surroundings and in association with youthful, happy companions. He was bright and cheerful, clever at books and games, and always exhibited a loving disposition. From his earliest years he was kind and affectionate towards all living beings, including all dumb creatures. So true was this that even when he was a little boy his friends called him 'the compassionate one'.

When he had grown to be a young man he married the beautiful Yaśodharā, and from that time he seemed to be caught in a network of roses. A son was born to him, whom he named Rāhula. Prince Gautama was then about thirty years old.

One day, during this period of his life, he bade his charioteer drive him through the city that lay beyond the park surrounding the palace, for he desired to view the city of Kapilāvastu and know life as it was lived by the people. As he rode through the streets of the city, he saw many things, among them children playing and men and women carrying on their work. At all this he was pleased, for he cried to his charioteer, 'I see here labour, and poverty, and hunger; yet so much beauty, love, and joy are mingled with them—surely life, after all, is very sweet.'

No sooner had he uttered these words than there came into view, one after another, the three woes of men—weariness, disease, and death. This was the turning point of his life.

First came weariness. Before him appeared an old, old man, tottering on his crutches, which he held with trembling hands. The charioteer explained: 'All men are subject to old age, and old age, if it lasts long enough, will always end thus.'

Then drew near to him a man, ghastly to look upon, suffering from the deadly poison of leprosy. Prince Gautama ran straight to him, and embracing him cried, 'My brother!' Again did the charioteer explain what the prince saw. He said that the man was suffering from a disease and that every man is subject to disease in many forms. 'And this is the life', mused Gautama, 'that I thought so sweet!' For some time he was silent. Then he asked, 'How can one escape from life? What friend has he to release him?' 'Death,' replied the charioteer. 'Look! There come bearers of the dead, carrying one to the riverside to burn.

'But indeed,' he continued, 'men do not wish to die. Death, they think, is their worst enemy. Him they hate and try to escape, though there is no escape.'

'Take me home,' Prince Gautama now commanded the driver. He had been 'stung by the woes of men'. Thenceforth he sought a way to escape misery, not for himself only but for all humanity. His heart melted in sympathy and compassion for all beings.

The life he was living no longer offered him joy or sweetness. Restlessness came upon him, until at last, as he lay on his couch, he heard a voice calling to him, a cry of agony, as it were, from all humanity: 'Awake! Thou the awakened! Arise, and help the world! Sleep no more!' So must he seek a way of salvation.

Thereupon he arose and stole to the bedside of his sleeping wife and bade her good-bye by gently kissing her feet. For he knew that she would bear half the sacrifice he was about to make, and that hers would be half the wisdom he sought, also, and half the glory.

Thus Prince Gautama renounced the world, the world that was his—a kingdom, a beautiful wife, a loving son—in order to heed the call of suffering humanity. For six or seven years he wandered through the land, spending his time in prayer and meditation. He visited many sages and masters, but he never found a reply to his obstinate questioning. At last he seated himself under a Bo-tree in Gaya, and, firmly resolved to realize the truth, fell into deepest meditation. There, under the tree, after prolonged wrestling with his spirit, he discovered the true secret of life and death, and the knowledge that can be found only within oneself. Thenceforth he was no longer known by his family name; he became the Buddha—the Awakened One, the Blessed One.

After he had attained illumination, he went straightway to Banaras, for he was not content to gain eternal peace for himself alone. There, at Sarnath, he preached his first sermon. There also for the first time he called freedom and eternal peace nirvāṇa, and the life of struggle in search of it the Way of Peace.

In no way did he forget Yaśodharā, his beloved wife, who in her palace was living the life of a nun as she did her utmost to share her husband's life. On one occasion, as Buddha in company with his disciple Ānanda entered the palace to meet Yaśodharā, Rāhula approached his father and asked for his inheritance. Ānanda, the chief disciple, with the permission of Buddha, gave the lad the yellow cloth, the emblem of renunciation, and admitted him to the Way of Peace.

Then they saw the mother, behind her son, evidently longing to enter the Order. Thereupon Ānanda asked, 'Master, may a woman not enter the Order? May she not be one of us?'

And Buddha replied: 'Nay, do not the three woes come to women as well as to men? Why should their feet also not tread the Way of Peace? My Truth and my Order are for all. Yet this request, Ānanda, was for you to make.'[1]

For more than forty years thereafter Buddha preached his truth. At the age of eighty he passed from the earth.

He is known by many names: Buddha, The Awakened One; Śākyamuni, the Sage of the Śākyas; Tathāgata, He Who Has Attained the Highest Truth.

After the death of Buddha, his disciples held their first council, at Rājagṛha, near Magadha, and organized the remembered teachings of the Master; and these were orally transmitted until they were finally reduced to writing in the year 80 BC. These original Buddhistic teachings, preserved in three collections called the Tripiṭaka—literally, the three baskets—form the Pāli canon. The three collections are named, individually, the Vinayapiṭaka, which prescribes rules, in the greatest detail, for the conduct of the monks of the Order; the Suttapiṭaka, tales, containing conversations of Buddha which reveal practical methods of spiritual attainment; and the Abhidhammapiṭaka, doctrines, which deals with Buddha's psychology and ethics.

Religion as Realization

We read in one of the Buddhistic scriptures, 'The Tathāgata has no theories.'[2] If anyone came to Buddha with the intent of merely satisfying an idle curiosity with respect to metaphysical problems, he was certain to be disappointed. We hear of an inquirer who came to discuss theories of the soul and the world, and the problem of knowledge. To him Buddha observed that if one has been wounded by a poisoned arrow and refuses to accept help from the physician until he has learned the exact nature of the man who wounded him—to what caste he belonged, his stature and his complexion—such a one would indeed be foolish. Some questions Buddha dismissed as useless and unnecessary, while others, he said, could not be answered in logical terms. Just so do the Upaniṣads admonish us 'to give up vain talk, for it brings weariness to the tongue'; and they further speak of the truth 'which words cannot express'—'the mind', they say, 'comes away baffled, unable to reach it.'[3]

Moreover, Buddha, like the sages of the Upaniṣads, insisted that

[1] See Sister Nivedita, *Śiva and Buddha*, p. 47.

[2] Majjhima Nikāya, I. 486.

[3] Taittirīya, II. 4.

one should experience the truth for oneself. In the Upaniṣads we read: 'I have known, beyond all darkness, that great Person of golden effulgence. Only by knowing him does one conquer death. There is no other way of escaping the wheel of birth, death, and rebirth.'[1] And Buddha says: 'For Brahman I know, Vāseṭṭha, and the world of Brahman, and the path which leadeth unto it. Yea, I know it even as one who has entered the Brahman world, and has been born within it.'[2] And the truth of Brahman is to be known by one's own exertion in one's own soul. For we read in the teachings of Buddha:

'Therefore, O Ānanda, be ye lamps unto yourselves. Be ye a refuge to yourselves. Betake yourselves to no external refuge. Hold fast to the truth as a lamp. Hold fast as a refuge to the truth. . . .[3] And whosoever, Ānanda, either now or after I am dead, shall be a lamp unto themselves and a refuge unto themselves, shall betake themselves to no external refuge, but holding fast to the truth as their lamp, and holding fast as their refuge to the truth, shall look not for refuge to any one besides themselves—it is they, Ānanda, among my bhikkhus, who shall reach the very topmost height! But they must be anxious to learn.'[4]

'But they must be anxious to learn'; and to learn one must experiment—an action demanded by all the great religious teachers of India. For them essential religion does not lie in dogma or creed, nor in doctrines or theories, but in experience alone. From the Vedic age to our own, every leader has declared this primary truth—that one must realize God in one's own soul.

And Buddha, for all his apparent negation, belongs to the group of Indian teachers who have affirmed in this way the life of the spirit. He undertakes to show the way to 'peace of mind, to the higher wisdom, to full enlightenment, to nirvāṇa'[5]—all of them to be realized not in another life but here and now. The late Irving Babbitt, of Harvard University, a deep student and warm admirer of the Hindu saint, remarks:

'One should add that the "Nirvāna here and now" (Samditthakam Nibbanam) of the Buddhist has much in common with the "release in this life" (jivanmukti) of the Hindu philosopher. One may, however, affirm confidently that no religious teacher was ever more opposed than Buddha in his scheme of salvation to every form of postponement and procrastination. He would have his followers

[1] Śvetāśvatara, III. 9.
[2] Tevijja Sutta, I. 43.
[3] Mahā-parinibbāna Sutta, II. 33.
[4] *Ibid.*, 35.
[5] Foundation of the Kingdom of Righteousness, 4.

take the cash and let the credit go—though the cash in this case is not the immediate pleasure but the immediate peace.'[1]

Philosophically, the Buddhist nirvāṇa is identical with the mokṣa of the Hindu philosophers, which is the release from bondage to karma and ignorance and the attainment of the kingdom of heaven within. I have purposely used the phrase 'attainment of the kingdom of heaven within', in order to remind Western readers that in reality there is no difference in the ultimate goal between Hinduism, Buddhism, and Christianity. The mokṣa of the Hindus, the nirvāṇa of the Buddhists, and the 'kingdom of heaven within' of the Christians are really one and the same, though unfortunately the exponents of Christianity would have us believe otherwise. The late G. K. Chesterton, for example, attempts to show the superiority of Christian over Buddhist saints, declaring, 'The Buddhist saint always has his eyes shut, while the Christian saint always has them very wide open. . . . The Buddhist is looking with peculiar intentness inwards. The Christian is staring with frantic intentness outwards.' Irving Babbitt has beautifully met Chesterton's effusion:

'But a saint, whether Buddhist or Christian, who knows his business as a saint is rightly meditative and in proportion to the rightness of his meditation is the depth of his peace. We have it on an authority which Mr. Chesterton is bound to respect that the kingdom of heaven is within us. It would be interesting to hear Mr. Chesterton explain how a saint can find that which is within by "staring frantically outwards." Failing like many others to discriminate between romanticism and religion, Mr. Chesterton has managed to misrepresent both Buddhism and Christianity. The truth is, that though Christianity from the start was more emotional in its temper than Buddhism, and though an element of nostalgia entered into it from an early period, it is at one in its final emphasis with the older religion. In both faiths this emphasis is on the peace that passeth understanding.'[2]

Is Buddhism Pessimistic?

The Four Noble Truths which Buddha taught are these: (1) That there is suffering; (2) that there is a cause of suffering; (3) that suffering can be overcome; and (4) that there is a way to overcome it.[3]

Because Buddha taught that the world is full of suffering, he has often been called pessimistic. But that is a mistake. If he drew attention to the misery in life, it was only in order to direct the soul towards

[1] *The Dhammapadā*, pp. 97–8. [2] *Ibid.*, p. 99.
[3] See Mahā-parinibbāna Sutta, II. 2.

freedom from it. So long as we cling to sense experience, he knew, so long shall we fail to discover the path to happiness; it is therefore well that we should realize as speedily and vividly as possible the sorrow which is at the core of such experience.

Death, for example: let us face that. 'Not in the sky'—so reads the Dhammapāda—'not in the midst of the sea, not if we enter the clefts of the mountains, is there known a spot in the whole world where death could not overcome (the mortal).'[1] And again: 'How is there laughter, how is there joy, as this world is always burning? Do ye not seek a light, ye who are surrounded by darkness?'[2] 'This body is wasted, frail, full of sickness; this heap of corruption breaks to pieces; life indeed ends in death.'[3]

In this recognition of suffering, Buddhism but joins hands with all the religions of the world. Had the joys of the flesh proved entirely satisfactory, the need either of religious consolation or even of inquiry into spiritual truths would not have been apparent. Did not Jesus cry out to her who gave him water from the well: 'Whosoever drinketh of this water shall thirst again?'[4] Thus it is, he meant to say, with the pleasures of the world. And then he continued: 'But whosoever drinketh of the water that I shall give him shall never thirst; but the water that I shall give him shall be in him a well of water springing up into everlasting life.'[5] In like manner the Upaniṣads declare, 'There is no happiness in the finite. In the Infinite alone is happiness.'[6]

If by pessimism, therefore, is meant full acknowledgement of the obvious facts that the world bears a burden of sorrow, that earthly joy is but a momentary experience, that mortal life ends inevitably in death, then Buddhism is clearly pessimistic. And if by pessimism is meant, further, that true unalloyed happiness cannot be achieved in a finite world unless it be achieved by overcoming all worldliness, then is Buddhism clearly pessimistic. But likewise pessimistic, it must be added, are all other religions.

It all amounts to this. If we would steadfastly seek after eternal happiness and peace, we must necessarily look upon the momentary pleasures of the world with indifference, knowing that they end in suffering. Buddha's message was not essentially different from that of Christ when Christ said, 'In the world ye shall have tribulation: but be of good cheer; I have overcome the world.'[7] To overcome the world and its tribulation is to find the peace that passeth understanding. And the desire to overcome the world and attain perfect peace cannot arise in one who still clings to the lusts of the flesh. We read in the Kaṭha Upaniṣad the story of Naciketā, who went to the

[1] IX. 128. [2] XI. 146. [3] *Ibid.*, 148. [4] John iv. 13.
[5] *Ibid.*, 14. [6] Chāndogya, VII. xxiii. 1. [7] John xvi. 33.

King of Death to learn the secret of immortality. But before the King of Death taught him he tested him to discover if it was really a longing for knowledge that filled the heart of the young boy. He offered him, instead of the secret he came for, the worldly objects that men most desire. But Naciketā replied, 'These things endure only till the morrow, and the pleasures they give wear out the senses. Keep thou therefore horses and chariots, keep dance and song for thyself! How shall he desire wealth, O Death, who once has seen thy face?'[1] 'Blessed are they', said Jesus, 'which do hunger and thirst after righteousness, for they shall be filled.'[2]

Buddha's doctrine, then, is not one of despair, since it insists upon perfect happiness as possible for all men. They need only rise above the world of the senses to achieve a blissful peace.

Buddha regards this world of sense experience as a dream world. If we compare our state with that of a Buddha, we are living in a dream. The saying of Goethe, the wise man of the world, that 'error stands in the same relation to truth as sleeping to waking',[3] finds its religious counterpart in the almost identical words of the Gītā: 'What is sleep to the ignorant, that, to the wise, is waking.'[4] The word Buddha, as we have seen, means 'awakened'.

The Philosophy of Flux and Nirvāṇa

With respect to the world of mind and matter, Buddha has very forcefully declared that all things are in a state of constant flux. Nothing in the universe is permanent. It is for this reason that he makes his reiterated declaration that the world is full of suffering. In one of his dialogues he remarks: 'And that which is transient, O monks, is it painful or pleasant? Painful.'[5]

Because of the transitory and changing nature of the world, Buddha does not say that it is either real or unreal, but that it is somewhere between the real and the unreal.

'This world, O Kāccana, generally proceeds on a duality, on the "it is" and the "it is not". But, O Kāccana, whoever perceives in truth and wisdom how things originate in the world, in his eyes there is no "it is not". Whoever, Kāccana, perceives in truth and wisdom how things pass away in this world, in his eyes there is no "it is" in this world. . . . "Everything is"—this is one extreme, O Kāccana.

[1] I. i. 26.
[2] Matt. v. 6.
[3] Quoted by Irving Babbitt, *Spanish Character and Other Essays* (Boston: Houghton Mifflin Co., 1940), p. 154.
[4] II. 69.
[5] Majjhima Nikāya, III. 19.

"Everything is not"—this is another extreme. The truth is the middle.'[1]

Buddhistic literature employs the figure of the torch whirled rapidly round so as to create a circle of fire in order to illustrate the truth that the identity or permanency of anything in our experience is not real, but the illusory result of succession and constant flux. That is to say, an object never remains the same from moment to moment, but there exists the appearance of permanence because of a series of states. Furthermore, an unchanging law, called by Buddha dharma, continues to operate, the law of causation, which accounts for the appearance of continuity and identity. 'I will teach you the dharma,' says Buddha: 'That being present, this becomes; from the arising of that, this arises. That being absent, this does not become; from the cessation of that, this ceases.'[2]

The operation upon one state of this dharma, or law of causation, changes it into a successive state, and thus is created the ceaseless pulsation, or continuous flux. Dr S. Radhakrishnan makes this comment on the doctrine of dharma:

'The causal evolution is not to be viewed as a mechanical succession of movements, in which case the world process becomes a series of extinctions and fresh creations, but is one state working itself up to another state or informing it with a ceaseless pulsation. It is the determination of the present by the past. Buddhism believes in transitive causation, where one state transmits its *paccayasatti*, or causal energy, to some newly conceived germ. Causal relations are of the type of the seed growing into the tree, where the one is necessary for the other.'[3]

Buddha is not concerned with the philosophical explanation of this law of dharma, nor is he interested in explaining the doctrine of the flux. He simply states the psychological experience one has of the universe of flux and proceeds to an analysis of it. 'All are impermanent, body, sensation, perception, saṅkhāras [impressions of past deeds and thoughts], and consciousness—all these are sorrow. They are not self.' Both the world outside and the world within are in a state of constant flux.

Does a being, a reality, something permanent, exist behind this ever-changing flux?[4] The meaning and purpose of all philosophy

[1] Saṁyutta Nikāya. [2] Majjhima Nikāya, II. 32.

[3] *Indian Philosophy*, vol. I, p. 372.

[4] An affirmative answer is not unfamiliar in the West. Plato answers yes in his doctrine of the One and the many; and in the same sense both Shelley and

and all religion alike, and of life, are bound up in the effort to find, in the words of the Upaniṣads, 'the eternal amongst the noneternals, the consciousness of the conscious'.[1] And in the midst of change there is possible, in the words of Buddha, escape from sorrow in the cessation of the flux, as one attains 'peace of mind, higher wisdom, full enlightenment, and nirvāṇa'.[2]

Before we explain the nature of this attainment, let us repeat that Buddha asserts, not a mere philosophy of the flux, but a philosophy that will enable one to escape the flux. And herein lies the fundamental difference, as philosophers of the flux, between Buddha and certain Western writers.

In fact Buddha's teachings have often been mistakenly identified with the philosophy of flux as expounded by Bergson and Croce. This identification is especially urged with respect to Bergson. Superficially indeed, the two appear much alike, but on deeper analysis they prove to be at opposite poles. According to Bergson, the ultimate reality is an incessant flux, a creative evolution, or real duration. Buddha assumes, it is true, that the universe of experience is in constant flux; but he does not admit that this incessant flux is the ultimate reality. The universe of flux, to Buddha, is neither unreal nor real. It is, and it is not. Bergson, on the other hand, revels in the flux, and his intuition, in Babbitt's phrase, 'would ask nothing better than to whirl forever on the wheel of change',[3] or, in Hindu parlance, 'within the bonds of māyā'. To Bergson 'time' or 'duration' is real, and we should accordingly strive to see things not *sub specie aeternitatis* but *sub specie durationis*. Buddha perceives the flux but rises above it, above time, space, and causation.

Wordsworth may be quoted. Shelley, doubtless remembering Plato, says in 'Adonais':

> The One remains, the many change and pass:
> Heaven's light forever shines, Earth's shadows fly:
> Life, like a dome of many-coloured glass,
> Stains the white radiance of Eternity,
> Until Death tramples it to fragments.

And Wordsworth says in *The Excursion*:

> Even such a shell the universe itself
> Is to the ear of Faith; and there are times,
> I doubt not, when to you it doth impart
> Authentic tidings of invisible things;
> Of ebb and flow, and ever-enduring power;
> And central peace, subsisting at the heart
> Of endless agitation.

[1] Śvetāśvatara, VI. 13.

[2] Foundation of the Kingdom of Righteousness, *loc. cit*

[3] *Spanish Character and Other Essays*, pp. 156 f.

Plato, too, points out the weakness in assuming flux and change to be ultimate. If they were, knowledge would be impossible. His impatience with the later Heracleiteans—'All things whatsoever are in change'—is expressed in the *Theaetetus* where he has Theodorus go so far as to call the followers of the doctrine maniacs since they cannot even stand 'still to attend to an argument or a question'.[1] And Plato's words may be justly applied to the modern votaries of the God Whirl. Buddha, like Plato, sought to find the state beyond the flux—Bhāva-nirodha-nibbāṇam. 'To withdraw from the flux', he said, 'is to attain nirvāṇa.'

The philosophers mentioned above—Bergson and Croce—have done great service to Western philosophy by pointing out that the ultimate reality cannot be discovered by the intellect alone, but they have egregiously failed to discover a way whereby one may rise above the intellect and arrive at the very source of knowledge itself. It is true that both Bergson and Croce speak much of intuition, but this intuition of theirs is confined to the realm where 'time' is supreme and a sense of the 'many' prevails. Theirs is essentially a naturalistic interpretation of reality—that is, it issues entirely from the senses and the faculty of cognition. The Bergsonian *élan vital* is merely vital expansion within the universe of relativity and plurality and flux or change—within, that is, the bonds of māyā. Frankly, the use of this word intuition by the modern philosophers of the flux—or rather abuse—can only mean a sinking below the reason and the conscious mind into the realm of instinct which we share with the lower animals.

This pseudo-intuition of Bergson and Croce has of course no relation to the nirvāṇa of Buddha, the samādhi of the yogis, and the turīya, or transcendental consciousness, of the Upaniṣads. Nirvāṇa is in fact the 'state in which both sensations and ideas have ceased to be', in which 'the sage is delivered from time'. It is the state of śunyatā, wrongly translated as 'nothingness', which really means 'the absence of subject-object relation'. The Māṇḍūkya Upaniṣad thus describes turīya, which is identical with the Buddhistic nirvāṇa:

'Turiya is not subjective experience, nor objective experience, nor experience intermediate between these two, nor is it a negative condition which is neither consciousness nor unconsciousness. It is not the knowledge of the senses, nor is it relative knowledge, nor yet inferential knowledge. Beyond the senses, beyond the understanding, beyond all expression, is The Fourth. It is pure unitary consciousness, wherein awareness of the world and of multiplicity is completely

[1] *Theaetetus*, 179c–183c (trans. F. M. Cornford, *Plato's Theory of Knowledge*, Kegan Paul, Trench, Trubner & Co., Ltd., London, 1946).

obliterated. It is the supreme good. It is one without a second. It is the Self. Know it alone.'[1]

The nirvāṇa of the Buddhists and the turīya of the Upaniṣads are not conceptual, since they are beyond the relation of subject and object or of the knower and the object of knowledge, beyond time, space, and causation. In sum, they refer to consciousness itself, without the contents of consciousness—something from the relative point of view unthinkable and inconceivable but yet attainable. They are consciousness itself, beyond all awareness of flux and relativity; they are not attainable within the bounds of our normal consciousness, nor by the submersion of the self below the level of consciousness, but rather by a control of the conscious and the subconscious mind, and by a supreme act of self-restraint and of meditation, a rising above and beyond reason. So long as we remain upon the level of the flux, and experience only the objects within the flux, we are asleep. 'How many people', asks Buddha, 'eat, drink, and get married; buy, sell, and build; make contracts and attend to their fortunes; have friends and enemies, pleasures and pains; are born, grow up, love, and die—but asleep?' To attain nirvāṇa is simply to break this sleep in which we experience only the flux and to wake to the intuition of the One.

Buddha, like all the other philosophers of India, believed in the law of karma and in reincarnation as the working out of this law. He believed that we are bound to the wheel of birth and death until we finally break our chains and attain illumination in nirvāṇa. Then no longer are there birth and death, as we pass into a state of being that is indescribable and unthinkable in concrete terms. Buddha even refused to define concretely what he meant by the word nirvāṇa. To define is to limit, and definition is possible only of something within 'time, space, and causation'.

But though nirvāṇa must remain indefinable, we know the effects it produces in life. 'By their fruits ye shall know them,' said Jesus.[2] And St Paul has enumerated these fruits as follows: 'love, joy, peace, long-suffering, gentleness, goodness, faith, meekness, temperance.'[3] Aśoka, the great Buddhist emperor of India and founder of a Buddhistic canon, carved in stone these fruits: 'compassion, liberality, truth, purity, gentleness, peace, joyousness, saintliness, self-control.'

Thus we may see that however divergent the paths taken by the great religions, and however varied the approach, we may know experimentally that they all lead to the same ultimate goal, the release of the human spirit from the wheel of change and the refining of our individual lives through the development of similar high

[1] 7. [2] Matt. vii. 20. [3] Gal. v. 22–3.

qualities in our several natures. They all lead, in the words of the Upaniṣads, to the attainment of 'infinite knowledge, infinite freedom, and infinite peace'. 'My peace I give unto you,' said Christ. And Buddha said of the awakened soul: 'His thought is quiet, quiet are his word and deed, when he has obtained freedom by true knowledge, when he has thus become a quiet man.'[1]

The Ultimate Reality

There is an ancient charge that Buddha was an atheist, that he disbelieved in the soul and in God, that he denied the existence of anything that is abiding, permanent, unchangeable. But this charge is without any foundation. If it had any foundation, the whole teaching of nirvāṇa—the ideal of Buddhahood—would fall to pieces. Buddha expresses himself very clearly on this point when he says: 'There is an unborn, an unoriginated, an unmade, an uncompounded; were there not, O mendicants, there would be no escape from the world of the born, the originated, the made, and the compounded.'[2]

But Buddha steadfastly refused to define the nature of this unchangeable, uncompounded reality, and he emphatically declared it to be beyond the experience of our senses and our minds. Similarly, the Upaniṣads declare that Brahman, who is identical with the Ātman, is 'beyond speech, and the mind comes away baffled, unable to reach him'.[3] Śrī Rāmakṛṣṇa remarked concerning this ultimate reality:

'What Brahman is, none can define in words. Everything has been defiled, as it were, like the leavings of food. The Vedas, the Tantras, the Purāṇas, the Systems of philosophy, all are defiled; they have been studied and they have been uttered by human tongues. But there is one truth, one substance, that has never been defiled, and that is Brahman. None has ever succeeded in describing Brahman in words.[4]

'True it is that the Vedas and the other scriptures speak of him, but do you know what it is like? When a man returns from seeing the ocean and is asked to describe it, he exclaims in amazement, "Oh, what a vast expanse! How huge the waves are!" Like unto this is the talk of Brahman.[5]

'When one attains samādhi, then alone comes the knowledge of Brahman. One realizes him. In that realization, all thoughts cease; one becomes perfectly silent. There is no power of speech left by which to express Brahman.'[6]

[1] Dhammapāda, VII. 96. [2] Udāna, VIII. 3. [3] Taittirīya, II. 4.
[4] *Kathāmṛta*, vol. III, p. 8. [5] *Ibid.*, p. 9. [6] *Ibid.*, pp. 9–10.

So Buddha held his peace on this subject. He simply stated the fact that within the range of our normal experience there exist only compound and changeable objects—objects pertaining therefore only to the non-Self. To Buddha, as well as to the seers of the Upaniṣads, the mind and the ego are as clearly non-Self as is the body. This is the view, confirmed though it is by the entire Hindu religious tradition, that has been misinterpreted by Western scholars into a denial of the true Self, or God. The misinterpretation is highly significant. It indicates a fundamental divergence between East and West, for it is the tendency of the West to identify thought with being, a tendency that reaches as far back as Parmenides; whereas the East, as represented by both Buddha and the Upaniṣads, declares that the mind and the ego are as much objects of cognition as the external objects of knowledge, and hence not being, the knower, the Self.

One important difference, however, between the teachings of Buddha and those of the Upaniṣads lies in the distribution of emphasis. Buddha stresses the impermanence of the flux—the impermanence of everything within the limits of our sense experience. The Upaniṣads lay their chief emphasis upon the abiding—the permanent and the unchangeable reality behind the flux, beyond the limits of our sense experience.

Buddha did not deny this permanent reality, but he did consistently deny the possibility of positing it so long as we dwell within the limitations of sense experience, because he feared that the element within man which is commonly known as the self, but which is really the ego, dependent on the flux for its character and existence, would be mistaken for the true Self, which does not change.

We read in one of the Buddhistic scriptures how, when a monk asked Buddha if there is a Self, the Master maintained silence. When asked if there is no Self, he again maintained silence. Then, when his disciple Ānanda asked why he maintained silence in the face of these opposing questions, he explained that if he had declared that there is a Self, the monk might have regarded the impermanent element as permanent, and if he had replied in the negative, the monk might have thought that 'belief in annihilation' had been confirmed.

The Upaniṣads declare again and again, as we have seen, that the true Self must not be identified with the body, the senses, or the cognitive mind. To think that they are the same is possible only through ignorance. And this false identification, according to the same authority, gives rise to the concept of the individual soul, or jīva. Buddha, as a great psychologist, recognizes the falseness of assuming the compound and changeable elements of man to be the permanent Self. He first invokes the fact of ordinary experience, and then he points out that nirvāṇa does exist—the way to peace and knowledge—beyond the range of this ordinary experience, and that just so soon as the veil of our ignorance is removed, the truth is revealed.

There is no problem in Buddhism as to the relation of the soul to God. Buddha takes a firm stand upon the reality of the final experience, the turīya of the Upaniṣads, and upon the reality of his own personal experience of nirvāṇa. In these things he clearly finds a nonduality. What is there to relate to whom, when there is but the One?

The Causes of Suffering

Of the Four Noble Truths taught by Buddha, two have already been discussed: that the world is full of suffering and that from this suffering there may be found an escape. It remains to consider the two other Noble Truths: that this suffering has a cause, and that there is a way to peace.

Buddha, 'stung by the woes of men', sought a way out of the suffering that lay heavy on the world. He saw that men are ushered into this earthly existence, that they mature, decay, die, and are born again; and he saw that none knew the way of escape. As he meditated upon this hapless lot of human kind, he learned the root cause of suffering, decay, and death, and discovered the way of escape and of peace. We read in the Mahāvāgga, an early Buddhistic scripture, as follows:

'Then the Blessed One (at the end of these seven days) during the first watch of the night fixed his mind upon the Chain of Causation, in direct and in reverse order: "From Ignorance spring the samkhāras, from the samkhāras springs Consciousness, from Consciousness spring Name-and-Form, from Name-and-Form spring the six Provinces (of the six senses), from the six Provinces springs Contact, from Contact springs Sensation, from Sensation springs Thirst (or Desire), from Thirst springs Attachment, from Attachment springs Existence, from Existence springs Birth, from Birth spring Old Age and Death . . ."'[1]

In this 'wheel of existence' (bhāva-cakra), the first in the series is ignorance (avijjā)—the root cause of all suffering. This ignorance is universal, and how it came into the world is a mystery which neither Buddha nor any other seer or philosopher attempts to explain. For the nature of this ignorance is that it is neither real, nor unreal; it is,

[1] I. i. 2.

and it is not. 'It is', so long as we remain in ignorance; 'it is not' when we attain nirvāṇa—illumination.

Buddha, like all other Indian seers and philosophers, accepts the law of karma and reincarnation. According to the Upaniṣads, karma attaches itself to one who, because of ignorance (avidyā), identifies his true Self with the non-Self. And, according to Buddha, the law of karma operates, there is the chain of birth and death, we remain in the 'wheel of existence', with the direct consequence of suffering, only so long as we attach ourselves to the flux and ignorantly cling to the ego as permanent.

This doctrine of the 'wheel of existence', which we have been discussing, is known in Buddhist terminology also as the 'doctrine of dependent origination'. It leads us straight to the central doctrine of Buddhism, that existence in ignorance is suffering and that the clinging to a false individuality—or, as we should term it, the ego—as something real and permanent, is the root of this ignorance. This central doctrine has often been misinterpreted by Western scholars—by Schopenhauer in particular, who declared that the greatest sin of man is to have been born, that life itself is painful, and that the goal of living is the absence of pain and of life itself. But Buddha declares that only life as we know it, and as we live it in ignorance, is painful. This life in ignorance, as we have seen, is compared by Buddha to sleep and forgetfulness; and once we have awakened from this sleep we can attain nirvāṇa in this very life. The possibility of achieving spiritual rebirth is central also in the Gospel of Christ:

> 'Except a man be born again, he cannot see the kingdom of God. Nicodemus saith unto him, How can a man be born when he is old? Can he enter the second time into his mother's womb, and be born? Jesus answered, Verily, verily, I say unto thee, except a man be born of water and of the spirit, he cannot enter into the kingdom of God. That which is born of the flesh is flesh; and that which is born of the Spirit is Spirit.'[1]

And is not this birth in the Spirit the same as awakening from the sleep of ignorance? What alone distinguishes Buddha from Christ, in this matter, is that he couched the doctrine in different terms, in declaring that by the death of the ego, the life in ignorance, one attains nirvāṇa—where by nirvāṇa is meant, not a mere negation of pain and suffering, but, in Buddha's own words, 'the highest wisdom, the full enlightenment and peace'.

The approaches to the attainment of Christian salvation and Buddhist nirvāṇa are different. Christ said, 'Thy will be done'. And

[1] John iii. 3–6.

Dante expressed the central Christian doctrine in these words: 'In His will is our peace.' Buddha, on the other hand, taught the exercise of the higher will, saying that 'Self is the lord of self . . .'[1] Christ taught us to efface our ordinary will by submitting ourselves to the will of God. Buddha taught elimination of the false self, which wills to desire, by exercise of the will to check, the will to control. As the will to desire is controlled, the false self is eliminated and nirvāṇa is attained.

Christ taught elimination of the ego by surrendering ourselves to the will of God, and Buddha taught achievement of the same end by self-effort. Whichever means may be adopted, the effect is the same—namely, death of the ego and birth in the Spirit.

Buddha and Christ, then, it would seem, set up the same goal, though as regards the path to it they differ. The two paths—the Buddhistic and the Christian—are both adumbrated in the Upaniṣads.

The Way of Peace

We read in the Mahā-parinibbāna Sutta, one of the earliest Buddhistic scriptures, these words:

> 'There the Blessed One addressed the brethren, and said: "It is through not understanding and grasping four truths, O brethren, that we have had to run so long, to wander so long in this weary path of transmigration—both you and I! And what are these four? The noble conduct of life, the noble earnestness in meditation, the noble kind of wisdom, and the noble salvation of freedom. But when noble conduct is realized and known, when noble meditation is realized and known, when noble wisdom is realized and known, when noble freedom is realized and known—then is the craving for existence rooted out, that which leads to renewed existence is destroyed, and there is no more birth.'[2]

The goal is the noble way of freedom, nirvāṇa, wherein there is no more birth, nor suffering, nor old age, nor death. This nirvāṇa, it should be emphasized, may be attained in this present life. 'Be earnest in effort, and you too shall soon be free from the great evils . . .'[3]

The state of attainment is described only in negative terms, a state in which one is 'delivered from time'. It is paralleled by the 'eternal life' of Christian teachings. In general, there exists in the Western world the misconception that eternal life, or immortality, is a continuation of life in time. What, then, is the explanation of Christ's adjuration to his followers to come unto him that in him they might

[1] Dhammapāda, XII. 160. [2] IV. 2. [3] *Ibid.*, V. 35.

find eternal life? The very fact that a being exists implies a continuity of existence, though the existence may be in different forms and under different conditions. Modern science proves conclusively the impossibility of complete annihilation. The 'immortality' of Christ's reiterated plea, and the similar doctrine to be found in all other great religions, cannot, therefore, mean simply a continuity of life after death, but rather, and primarily, the life of realization and perfection while one still lives in this world. To one who achieves this life, there can be no more birth nor death. The Upaniṣads regard the true Self as unborn and undying, the unchangeable reality within us. As we realize that true Self, they say, we realize it as one with Brahman, and then and then only, rising above and beyond time, we attain to immortality. It is then that the experience of the Self as living in time, with a past, a present, and a future, passes like a dream, and the Self is realized as immortal. So Buddha points to the same goal of immortality above time, to be reached by realizing 'the unborn, undying, and changeless'.

The nirvāṇa of Buddha is therefore not a state of annihilation but the attainment of the unchangeable reality, which can be positively described as the eternal peace. But what this peace really is, no words can define; all definition can be only symbol and can offer only a vague suggestion. Buddha employs negative terms for its description, such as freedom from misery and death, freedom 'from sensuality, from the ego, from delusion, from ignorance'.[1]

This state of freedom is attainable by the 'noble kind of wisdom'—a phrase already quoted from the Buddhist scripture and signifying what the Vedānta calls transcendental knowledge. The wisdom meant is not a wisdom of the intellect, which implies a knower and an object of knowledge, but rather a state, śunyatā, in which no subject-object relation exists, and in which one transcends both intellect and mind—these two words representing, in Hindu psychology, separate entities. Christ refers directly to this transcendental wisdom when he says: 'And ye shall know the truth and the truth shall make you free.'[2] It is identical with perfection, the same perfection that Christ has in mind when he says: 'Be ye therefore perfect, even as your Father which is in heaven is perfect.'[3] It is, in brief, the direct, immediate knowledge of that which is timeless, unconditional Existence.

The 'noble kind of wisdom' is attainable by 'the noble conduct of life' and 'the noble earnestness of meditation'.

This 'wisdom' is existent in every being, covered up, in the Vedāntic phrase, by layers of ignorance, and according to Buddha, by avijjā, ignorance. Remove this avijjā, and wisdom shines, nirvāṇa is attained.

[1] Mahā-parinibbāna Sutta, V. 35. [2] John viii. 32. [3] Matt. v. 48.

Christ would seem to have referred to the same truth when he said, 'The kingdom of heaven is at hand.' This wisdom, then, this kingdom of heaven, is for Christ, like the self-luminous sun, already 'at hand'; only, if we would find it, we must 'watch and pray'. And Christ's 'watch and pray' is Buddha's 'right conduct of life and meditation'.

Practising 'right conduct of life' is likened by Śrī Rāmakṛṣṇa to 'using soap on a dirty cloth' and the act of 'meditation' to 'washing the cloth clean'. 'Both are essential,' he says, 'and not until through these means the evils of ignorance and misconception are washed away can spiritual peace be attained.' Ethical conduct is the foundation of all spiritual life, but it does not represent the whole of religion. It has often been said that Buddha's teachings are merely ethical in their import. Similarly Christianity has been mistakenly defined, by Matthew Arnold, as 'morality touched by emotion'. But real Christianity and real Buddhism reach far beyond such tepid doctrine, for the peace of heaven and nirvāṇa transcends morality and transcends emotion. Evil, no doubt, needs to be overcome by good in this realm of human struggle, but there exists a state of attainment that transcends both good and evil—something far different, again, from Nietzsche's 'beyond good and evil'. Both morality and meditation come within the range of Buddha's survey, and one without the other is fruitless. Both of them, however, are but means to the attainment of illumination, or nirvāṇa.

Moral conduct, in Buddha's view, has its genesis in psychology. Right conduct is called right because it is a prerequisite to knowledge of the secret of life, the road to illumination. All conduct, therefore, is moral which has that knowledge in view. As Swami Vivekananda has declared: 'That which leads to illumination is good; that which makes for greater ignorance and greater bondage is evil.'

In order to follow these paths of right conduct and right meditation, we must be earnest and intent upon exercising the will to action—where by 'action' is meant the highest form of activity, the control of the mind. Mere acceptance of religious doctrine is not sufficient unto salvation, it must be reinforced by strenuous spiritual strivings. He who merely acquiesces is compared by Buddha to a 'cowherd who is merely counting others' kine'. On one occasion Buddha begged a rich farmer for alms, but in return was reproached for being an idler. Buddha replied: '"Faith is the seed, penance the rain, understanding my yoke and plough, modesty the pole of the plough, mind the tie, thoughtfulness my ploughshare and goad, . . . exertion my beast of burden." As a result of this spiritual husbandry one achieves the "fruit of immortality".'[1]

To be engaged in spiritual husbandry is to exert one's will. Moral

[1] As quoted by Babbitt, *The Dhammapada*, p. 92.

laziness, failure to be diligent in self-control, is the greatest sin—pamāda; its opposite, appamāda, 'not to be morally lazy, but to be strenuous in exerting one's will, is the greatest virtue'. The entire responsibility for either bondage or freedom is placed directly upon one's self. 'Therefore, O Ānanda,' says Buddha, as we have already seen, 'be ye lamps unto yourselves. Be ye a refuge to yourselves.'[1]

Buddha thus lays extraordinary emphasis upon the will as a psychological phenomenon. The will to satisfy thirst (broadly interpreted), which is formed by previous habits of self-indulgence, leads us to gratification of the senses; the flux within ourselves seeks to remain within the limitations of the flux of the objective world. But another will also exists, within our deepest selves, a higher will, which, though it may be very weak in most of us, seeks to cut loose to freedom from the limitations of the flux and to attain to the permanent, abiding reality. This is the inner check, the will to attain the supreme goal.

Buddha indeed insists upon the continual strengthening of this higher will in order that we may rise above all the flux of life. He does not say, however, that the will is ultimate and permanent, as does Schopenhauer in his interpretation of Buddhistic philosophy. It is, on the contrary, to be of paramount importance only for the sādhaka, or aspirant after spiritual attainment; to the siddha, the perfected one, it is no more of any value, and it is at last dissolved in the flux. For the will is as much a compound substance as any other object within the flux.

The teachings of Vedānta bring out this truth with great clearness in declaring that all scriptural instruction and all spiritual struggles are within the limitations of māyā, or, as Buddha would have said, of the flux. They are, however, a necessary part of our effort to attain the ultimate liberation. The truth is in fact self-luminous, and it is only by ignorance that it is ever veiled from the eyes of men; but the veil is only too universally there, and to remove it the instruction and the struggles are needed. The will to control must be exercised, but when it has done its work by removing ignorance, it becomes superfluous. Śrī Rāmakṛṣṇa was in the habit of illustrating this great truth by the simile of using one thorn to remove another from the body. When the task is completed both thorns may be thrown away. Similarly, we read in the Gītā: 'When the whole country is flooded, the reservoir becomes superfluous. So, to the illumined seer, the Vedas are all superfluous.'[2]

But so long as the spiritual aspirant is still struggling to attain illumination, the higher will is paramount. 'Let small and great exert themselves', taught the great Buddhistic Emperor, Aśoka; and this

[1] Mahā-parinibbāna Sutta, *loc. cit.*

[2] II. 46.

exertion must be directed towards right conduct (śīla) and right contemplation (samādhi).

'Great is the fruit, great the advantage of earnest contemplation, when set round with upright conduct. Great is the fruit, great the advantage of intellect when set round with earnest contemplation. The mind set round with intelligence is freed from the great evils, that is to say, from sensuality, from individuality, from delusion, and from ignorance.'[1]

Right conduct and right meditation have been further analysed and their parts set forth in what is known as the Eightfold Path, which is also referred to by Buddha as the Middle Path or the Golden Mean. It has been explained by Buddha in 'The Foundations of the Kingdom of Righteousness' as follows:

'There are two extremes, O Bhikkus, which the man who has given up the world ought not to follow—the habitual practice, on the one hand, of those things whose attraction depends upon the passions, and especially of sensuality—a low and pagan way of seeking satisfaction, unworthy, unprofitable and fit only for the worldly-minded —and the habitual practice, on the other hand, of asceticism or self-mortification, which is painful, unworthy, and unprofitable. There is a middle path, O Bhikkus, avoiding these two extremes, discovered by the Tathāgata—a path which opens the eyes and bestows understanding, which leads to peace of mind, to the higher wisdom, to full enlightenment, to nirvāṇa.

'What is that middle path, O Bhikkus, avoiding these two extremes, discovered by the Tathāgata—that path which opens the eyes and bestows understanding, which leads to peace of mind, to the higher wisdom, to full enlightenment, to nirvāṇa? Verily, it is this noble eightfold path; that is to say: right view, right aspiration, right speech, right conduct, right livelihood, right effort, right mindfulness, and right contemplation.'[2]

The Eightfold Path

The first step in the path of progress towards infinite peace is right view, or right faith. There is a saying in Bengali that a man is as his faith is, that our actions are guided by our faith. Right faith, according to Buddha, is the faith that nirvāṇa, the eternal peace, can be attained in this life if we cease to cling to the false individual self. Wrong faith is faith that results in clinging to the non-Self as Self, and must be replaced by right faith, or right view.

[1] Mahā-parinibbāna Sutta, I. 18. [2] 1–4.

Right aspiration arises from right faith. It is the aspiration to renounce the false self, to shun all selfishness, and 'to live in love and harmony with all'. Buddha's own aspiration was not merely to attain nirvāṇa for himself but to show the way to it to all mankind. Such also was to be the aspiration of his followers: to live for their fellow men, renouncing all regard for self.

But to aspire is not enough. We must act to fulfil our aspiration, and our actions must necessarily find expression through our speech, our conduct, and our daily work. Right speech, right conduct, and right work are, in effect, the practice of such virtues as truthfulness, noninjury, noncovetousness, and chastity. In the words of the Tevijja Sutta:

'. . . Putting away the murder of that which lives, [the aspirant] abstains from destroying life. . . . he is compassionate and kind to all creatures that have life!

'Putting away the theft of that which is not his, he abstains from taking anything not given. He takes only what is given; therewith is he content, and he passes his life in honesty and in purity of heart! . . .

'Putting away unchastity, he lives a life of chastity and purity, averse to the low habit of sexual intercourse. . . .

'Putting away lying, he abstains from speaking falsehood. He speaks truth, from the truth he never swerves; faithful and trustworthy, he injures not his fellow man by deceit. . . .

'Putting away slander, he abstains from calumny. What he hears here he repeats not elsewhere to raise a quarrel against the people here; what he hears elsewhere he repeats not here to raise a quarrel against the people there. Thus he lives as a binder together of those who are divided, an encourager of those who are friends, a peacemaker, a lover of peace, impassioned for peace, a speaker of words that make for peace. . . .

'Putting away bitterness of speech, he abstains from harsh language. Whatever word is humane, pleasant to the ear, lovely, reaching to the heart, urbane, pleasing to the people, beloved of the people—such are the words he speaks. . . .

'Putting away foolish talk, he abstains from vain conversation. In season he speaks; he speaks that which is; he speaks fact; . . . he speaks, and at the right time, that which redounds to profit, is well-grounded, is well-defined, and is full of wisdom.'[1]

The practice of these virtues involves a double process, one step in which we may term negative and the other positive: first a vice must be abstained from, and then the opposite virtue must be acquired.

[1] II. 1–7.

Right livelihood means earning one's living by acceptable means. Such means do not include the occupations, for example, of slave dealer, butcher, publican, or trafficker in poisons.

After proper external conduct, inner purification must be achieved. So right effort is practice with the purpose of controlling the mind, not allowing it to remain a slave to the passions of lust, anger, greed, envy, and pride, and freeing it from the two extremes of self-indulgence and self-mortification.

This practice of right effort, or self-control, is not possible without right mindfulness and right meditation. It is possible to refrain from passion and the life of the senses only when the mind is engaged in something higher or greater.

Right mindfulness is thinking thoughts concerning the evil effects of clinging to the objects within the flux.

The last stage, right meditation, is keeping the mind occupied in spiritual contemplation, in order ultimately to free it from all thought, and, transcending all thought, to attain nirvāṇa.

Right faith, right aspiration, right speech, right conduct, right livelihood, right effort, right mindfulness, and right contemplation form the Eightfold Path of Buddhism, and lead one to the highest goal—nirvāṇa—the supreme enlightenment and peace.

Later Schools of Buddhism

Before we discuss Buddhism in its development after the death of its founder, we shall do well to point out once more its relation to the Vedic religion. Swami Vivekananda has expressed this relationship in the following words:

'The relation between Hinduism (by Hinduism, I mean the religion of the Vedas) and what is called Buddhism at the present day is nearly the same as between Judaism and Christianity. Jesus Christ was a Jew, and Shakya Muni was a Hindu. The Jews rejected Jesus Christ, nay crucified him, and the Hindus have accepted Shakya Muni as God and worship him. But the real difference that we Hindus want to show between modern Buddhism and what we should understand as the teachings of Lord Buddha, lies principally in this: Shakya Muni came to preach nothing new. He also, like Jesus, came to fulfil and not to destroy. Only, in the case of Jesus, it was the old people, the Jews, who did not understand him, while in the case of Buddha, it was his own followers who did not realize the import of his teachings. As the Jews did not understand the fulfilment of the Old Testament, so the Buddhists did not understand the fulfilment of the truths of the Hindu religion. Again, I repeat, Shakya Muni came not to destroy, but he was the fulfilment, the logical conclusion, the logical development of the religion of the Hindus.'[1]

In just the same way that Christ abhorred crystallized Jewish dogma and Jewish ritual, Buddha abhorred all ceremonials and the ritualistic portion of the Vedas. Even this was nothing new. The Upaniṣads, which comprise the later Vedas, insisted that true religion consists not in rites and ceremonies but in realization of the Self; so also did the Gītā. Once more was the spirit of religion brought to the fore when Buddha preached his gospel of renewed spiritual life. Nowhere does he actually contradict the teachings of the Upaniṣads. In fact, two elements in these he does emphasize, the acosmic aspect of Brahman and monastic discipline. The Hindus therefore readily accepted Buddha as one within their own fold. Later followers of Buddha, however, falsely judged his opposition to the ceremonial portions of the Vedas—the Brāhmaṇas—to be his general attitude towards the Vedic religion, and cut themselves off from the main body of the mother religion. For a few centuries Buddhism flourished in India but then died a natural death, though Buddha himself survives as a living spiritual force. Truly has it been said by Dr Radhakrishnan:

'Buddha today lives in the lives of those Indians who have not given up their past traditions. His presence is felt in all around. Throughout worshipped as a god, he has a place in the mythology which is still alive, and so long as the old faith remains without crumbling down before the corrosive influence of a new spirit, Buddha will have a place among the gods of India. His life and teaching will compel the reverence of mankind, give ease to many troubled minds, gladden many simple hearts, and answer to many innocent prayers.'[2]

After the passing of Buddha, his disciples, who came to be known as the Elders, met together at Rājagṛha to compile the three Piṭakas, the original teachings of Buddha. About a hundred years later a second council met at Vaiśāli, where a split occurred among the delegates. One group, who might be called the progressive party, desired some relaxation in the rigour of monastic vows, but the orthodox party clung to the laws and regulations laid down by the Elders, and they won the day. The progressives, however, gained a large following and proceeded to hold a council of their own, which they called the Great Council and which broke with the main body

[1] *Complete Works of Vivekananda*, vol. I, p. 19.
[2] *Indian Philosophy*, vol. I, pp. 609 f.

of Buddhists. According to Dr Radhakrishnan, this schism was an early effect of that movement which was to find its full expression in Mahāyāna Buddhism, which emerged in the first century AD.

Buddhism, which had been only a local sect within the fold of Hinduism, assumed a wider aspect about three hundred years after Buddha's death, when Aśoka, the great emperor of India (274–232 BC), was converted to Buddhism by Upagupta, a well-known Buddhist monk. Aśoka became actively engaged in spreading his adopted religion throughout his empire, his own transformation from a cruel tyrant into a loving, kind, and compassionate ruler providing a great example. He dispatched missionaries to many countries outside of India, among them Syria, Egypt, Macedonia, and Epirus, and under his influence Buddhism gradually attained the status of a world religion.[1] Within India itself, it became, more than ever before, a part of the life of the people. It inspired, for example, the splendid Mauryān stone sculpture, which is distinguished by its expressive symbolism and technical mastery. In temple and statue and relief the story of the Buddha was repeated, and these monuments still bear witness to one of the happiest periods in the history of India. Thus in the third century before Christ Buddhism reached its greatest power and made its influence most widely felt.

Aśoka particularly stressed the ethical teachings of the Master—self-control and loving service to all living beings. These he popularized throughout the vast empire of India by engraving them on stone pillars and by illustrating them in his own conduct.

Hinduism, however, did not die out. Aśoka, though a Buddhist ruler, showed the same spirit of toleration and the same sympathy in relation to Hinduism that the Hindus had shown in relation to Buddhism. Hinduism regained its vigour during the rule of the Guptas, who came into power in the first century AD.

Coinciding with this revival of Hinduism were the decline of the early Buddhism and the rise of Mahāyāna. Elements of the Mahāyāna, or the Great Way, had been present in Buddhistic thought and practice almost from the beginning, but they coexisted with the original Buddhism, or Hināyāna (the Narrow Way, as it came to be called) until this time, when they were given a definite form. They engendered an extensive literature in Sanskrit—not in Pāli, the language of the canon of the Elders. Generally speaking, the tendency of the Mahāyāna was to popularize the original teachings of the Buddha, giving a mystical and devotional turn to his doctrine. Thus it preached that higher than Arhathood (or personal sanctity, which was the ideal of the Hināyāna), was Buddhahood, the state of supreme perfection which Gautama reached, a state which was accessible to

[1] See S. Radhakrishnan, *op. cit.*, vol. I, p. 582.

all. Instead of the asceticism and monastic seclusion of the Hināyāna, it visualized the attainment of perfection in the midst of the tumult of the world. Instead of the unaided spiritual effort of the Hināyāna, it urged dependence on and worship of Buddha as an incarnation of God. Furthermore, it was responsible for the exalted conception of the Bodhisattva, the compassionate being, who vows from the beginning of his spiritual life to postpone his own salvation until all have attained that cherished goal. This was a marked contrast to the objective of exclusive, personal salvation which is generally attributed to the Hināyānists.

As we have noted, the Hināyāna, under Aśoka's patronage, spread far beyond the boundaries of India, and it remains to this day a dominant religious and cultural influence in countries to the south and east such as Ceylon, Burma, and Siam. The Mahāyāna spread to the north, where it flourished in Tibet, Mongolia, China, Korea, and Japan. In Tibet alone, a mysterious land long closed to travellers from the outside world, it has not only been made into a national religion but has become the ruling power of the state. The lamas, or holy men, are the priests of a theistic religion, for whose God, Buddha, temples have been built and an elaborate ritual has been created. In China, Mahāyāna has exerted a profound influence. There also Buddha has been worshipped, and other Buddhas and Bodhisattvas—or heavenly helpers of the aspirant—have found favour. In the year AD 648 there were approximately four thousand Buddhist monasteries in the country. Zen Buddhism, a peculiar blending of Mahāyāna Buddhism with the native Taoism, by enhancing the tendency to meditation spread throughout China, and was carried to Japan, where it established itself as one of the chief religions of the land. In both China and Japan Buddhism was the inspiration of their greatest artistic triumphs.

SELECTED PASSAGES FROM THE DHAMMAPĀDA

'All that we are is the result of what we have thought: it is founded on our thoughts, it is made up of our thoughts. If a man speaks or acts with an evil thought, pain follows him, as the wheel follows the foot of the ox that draws the carriage.

'All that we are is the result of what we have thought: it is founded on our thoughts, it is made up of our thoughts. If a man speaks or acts with a pure thought, happiness follows him, like a shadow that never leaves him.

' "He abused me, he beat me, he defeated me, he robbed me,"—in those who harbour such thoughts hatred will never cease.

'"He abused me, he beat me, he defeated me, he robbed me,"—in those who do not harbour such thoughts hatred will cease.

'For hatred does not cease by hatred at any time: hatred ceases by love; this is an old rule.'[1]

'If a man is earnest and exerts himself, if he is vigilant, if his deeds are pure, if he acts with consideration and restraint and lives according to law—then his glory will increase.

'By rousing himself, by earnestness, by restraint and self-control, the wise man may make for himself an island which no flood can overwhelm.'[2]

'It is good to tame the mind, which is difficult to hold in and flighty, rushing wherever it listeth; a tamed mind brings happiness.

'Let the wise man guard his thoughts which are difficult to perceive, very artful; they rush wherever they list: thoughts well guarded bring happiness.'[3]

'Like a beautiful flower, full of colour, but without scent, are the fine but fruitless words of him who does not act accordingly.'[4]

'Like a beautiful flower, full of colour and full of scent, are the fine and fruitful words of him who acts accordingly.'[5]

'If a fool be associated with a wise man even all his life, he will perceive the truth as little as a spoon perceives the taste of soup.

'If an intelligent man be associated for one minute only with a wise man, he will soon perceive the truth, as the tongue perceives the taste of soup.'[6]

'Well-makers lead the water (where they like); fletchers bend the arrow; carpenters bend a log of wood; wise people fashion themselves.[7]

'The gods even envy him whose senses, like horses well broken in by the driver, have been subdued, who is free from pride, and free from appetites.'[8]

'Let no man think lightly of evil, saying in his heart, It will not come nigh unto me. Even by the falling of water-drops a water-pot is filled; the fool becomes full of evil, even if he gather it little by little.

'Let no man think lightly of good, saying in his heart, It will not come nigh unto me. Even by the falling of water-drops a water-pot is filled; the wise man becomes full of good, even if he gather it little by little.'[9]

[1] I. 1–5. [2] II. 24–5. [3] III. 35–6. [4] IV. 51. [5] IV. 52.
[6] V. 64–5. [7] VI. 80. [8] VII. 94. [9] IX. 121–2.

'Men who have not observed (religious) discipline, and have not gained (spiritual) wealth in their youth, perish like old herons in a lake without fish.'[1]

'By oneself the evil is done, by oneself one suffers; by oneself evil is left undone, by oneself one is purified.'[2]

'Rouse thyself! Do not be idle! Follow the path of virtue! Do not follow that of sin. The virtuous man rests in bliss, in this world and in the next.'[3]

'Better than sovereignty over the earth, better than going to heaven, better than lordship over all worlds, is the reward of the first step in holiness.'[4]

'Even the gods envy those who are awakened and mindful, who are meditative, who are wise and who delight in the repose of retirement (from the world).'[5]

'Not to commit any sin, to do good, to purify one's own heart—this is the teaching of the Awakened.'[6]

'There is no fire like passion; there is no losing throw like hatred; there is no pain like this body; there is no happiness higher than serenity.'[7]

'Health is the greatest of gifts, contentedness the best of riches; trust is the best of relationships, Nirvāna, the highest happiness.'[8]

'He who possesses virtue and intelligence, who is just, speaks the truth, and does what is his own business, him the world will hold dear.'[9]

'The wise who control their body, tongue, and mind are indeed well-controlled.'[10]

'Make for thyself an island, work hard and promptly, be wise! When thy impurities are blown away and thou art free from guilt, thou wilt not again enter into birth and decay.'[11]

[1] XI. 155. [2] XII. 165. [3] XIII. 168–9. [4] XIII. 178.
[5] XIV. 181. [6] XIV. 183. [7] XV. 202. [8] XV. 204.
[9] XVI. 217. [10] XVII. 234. [11] XVIII. 238.

BOOK IV

THE SIX SYSTEMS OF THOUGHT

CHAPTER 9

THE SIX SYSTEMS OF THOUGHT: GENERAL REMARKS

The spiritual aspirant, as we have read repeatedly in the course of this book, first hears the truth, second, reasons upon it, and, third, meditates upon it. The Six Systems of Hindu philosophy are concerned with the second of these three steps. They have always in view the goal of the aspirant, which is final liberation, but as a means to that goal they seek to give him a complete intellectual grasp of the Self, God, and the universe in which he lives.

The Six Systems of Hindu thought are the Vaiśeṣika of Kaṇāda, the Nyāya of Gotama, the Sāṁkhya of Kapila, the Yoga of Patañjali, the Mīmāṁsā (also called Pūrva Mīmāṁsā) of Jaimini, and the Vedānta (also called Uttara Mīmāṁsā) of Vyāsa. Because of certain metaphysical similarities, these six systems (independent though they were in origin) may for convenience sake be reduced to three, Vaiśeṣika and Nyāya forming one group, Sāṁkhya and Yoga a second, and Mīmāṁsā and Vedānta a third.

The exact dates of the origin of these schools of thought are not known, though it is certain that the general ideas that make up their substance existed prior to Buddhism and even during the Epic Period. Nor is it known just who their founders were: Kaṇāda, Gotama, and the others whose names are associated with them are not their founders. The sūtras in which the views embodied in them were systematically formulated were a series of aphorisms uttered by the sages sometime during the early Buddhistic period—roughly between 600 and 200 BC.[1]

From a time when the art of writing was still unknown, these

[1] Professor Max Müller observes: 'The sūtras or aphorisms which we possess of the six systems of philosophy, each distinct from the others, cannot possibly claim to represent the very first attempt at a systematic treatment; they are rather the last summing up of what had been growing during many generations of isolated thinkers.' (*Six Systems of Philosophy*.)

sūtras were preserved in memory and handed down by word of mouth from teacher to pupil. They are so extremely laconic in form as to be well-nigh unintelligible without commentaries and explanatory notes, and oral supplements of this nature were early associated with the original aphorisms and transmitted with them. More and more commentaries and notes were gradually added, and in time written down, and the custom of composing them persisted even until the sixteenth or seventeenth century of the Christian era.

The Six Systems are regarded as āstika, or orthodox, because, unlike Buddhism and Jainism, they accept the authority of the Vedas on all questions pertaining to the nature of the universe. Moreover, there is nothing unorthodox in expanding, within limits, on the original revelations. For, as has already been explained in the introductory chapter of this book, though reason is given its due part in all the philosophies of India, there is everywhere the assumption that it will be aided by those intuitive perceptions to which the Vedas give the first recorded expression.

Actually the Six Systems of philosophy, reduced to three distinct groups, are not mutually contradictory, though in certain of their theories they would seem to be so. They really represent, not conflicting schools of thought, but a progressive development from truth to higher truth to the highest truth. Nyāya and Vaiśeṣika prepare the mind for philosophic thought and are therefore called the groundwork of philosophy; but passing beyond them through evolving ideas as expressed successively in Sāṁkhya, Yoga, and Mīmāṁsā, we at last arrive at the flower of Indian philosophy in Vedānta. Almost without exception, critics of Indian philosophy perceive the harmony behind the apparent discord, and so would reconcile the Systems as a perception of the same truth from different angles of vision.

The individual systems are variously looked upon. In the estimation of modern students, Vaiśeṣika is not of great importance. Nyāya for its system of logic, and Sāṁkhya for its system of cosmology and certain other metaphysical theories, are popular with scholars, but only as aids to the study of the philosophy of Vedānta. Mīmāṁsā is closely related to Hindu law, and is considered useful in the elucidation of the ritual portion of the Vedas. Yoga and Vedānta are accepted as the chief of the six schools. Yoga is concerned with the practical side of philosophical and religious life and is devotedly studied by aspirants. Vedānta, in one or the other of its various aspects, was the ancient faith of India, and all Hindus now accept it as their living faith.

In the following pages we shall briefly discuss the Vaiśeṣika, Nyāya,

Sāṁkhya, and Mīmāṁsā systems, reserving the fuller treatment for Yoga and Vedānta.[1]

Before entering on this task, however, we should call the attention of Western readers to the fundamental difference between the psychology of India and the psychology of the West. This difference lies in the fact that Western psychology identifies consciousness with mind, being with thought, and thought with the soul, or the Self; whereas Indian psychology distinguishes mind from consciousness. The distinction is due to the fact that Western psychology recognizes only one plane of experience, and gives no consideration to what Hindus call the pure cit, the supreme unconditional consciousness, the Being, which they regard as the real Self, or the soul, different from the rationalizing mind and realized in the superconscious, or transcendental, state. Pure unconditional consciousness cannot be the property of the mind, they believe, for it is the source of the mind's apparent consciousness. Mind is said by the Hindu psychologist to be the 'veiling power' of the pure consciousness, the Self, and it is associated with the Self only as a necessary condition of world experience. All systems of Indian philosophy recognize a Self separate from the mind, and this poses an important problem in each of them. As we proceed with our study we shall learn their notion of the real nature of the mind as well as of the Self.

[1] It should be emphatically stated that all six schools believe in the law of karma, in pre-existence, in rebirth, and in the attainment of mokṣa as the highest goal of human endeavour. All of them are concerned with the nature of the true Self, immediate experience of which makes one free.

CHAPTER 10

NYĀYA-VAIŚEṢIKA[1]

Gotama is the name of the sage who systematized the philosophy of Nyāya in the form of sūtras or aphorisms. In the same way Uluka compiled the sūtras of Vaiśeṣika. Very little is known about either of these men. Tradition has it that Uluka, commonly known as Kaṇāda—literally, he who eats very little—was an austere soul who made his living by picking up the left-over particles of corn from the harvest, and that he attained the grace of the Lord Śiva, who commanded him to systematize the philosophy of Vaiśeṣika. He flourished at some period before the birth of Buddha. Gotama came somewhat later.

The two systems which were embodied in the sūtras composed by these two men are regarded by all authorities as constituting one school of philosophy, though they differ in some details and though in their aphoristic form they were evolved independently of each other. Chronologically, Vaiśeṣika is the older of the two.

The following discussion of the twin philosophies will be divided into three parts: Part I, the first and largest part, will deal with technical ideas that they hold in common; Part II will deal briefly with points in which they differ; Part III will return to the school as such, and supplement, with certain broad considerations, what was said in Part I.

I. Common Doctrine

The Seven Categories

At the very beginning of the Vaiśeṣika sūtras Kaṇāda asserts that the proper object of his philosophy is to expound dharma (virtue), so that men may have abhyudaya (growth or unfoldment in life or character) and attain niśreyasa (the highest good). This niśreyasa is then explained as attainable through immediate perception of the

[1] The general reader may wish to omit this section since it is highly technical in nature—though far less elaborate and detailed than it would need to be if it fully presented its subject.

ultimate realities of Self and the universe. These ultimate realities —padārthas, or categories—are dravya (substance), guṇa (quality), karma (action or motion), sāmānya (genus), viśeṣa (species), and samavāya (relation). To these original six, later philosophers added another category, abhāva (negation).

No attempt is made to reduce the seven padārthas to one; on the contrary, a common-sense scientific position is sought through a perception of the universe as multiple. The padārthas, it should be added, make up the universe of external experience as well as that of the inner man.

A brief characterization of each of the seven categories follows:

(1) Dravya, substance, first and foremost of the categories, is the only one of them that has an independent existence. The remaining six depend upon it.

The substances are nine in number. They are:

The Self—the basis of consciousness and experience—though, according to a doctrine peculiar to the Nyāya-Vaiśeṣika school, its own consciousness is rather an adventitious than an essential characteristic. In reality it is unconscious; it becomes conscious only when it is joined to manas (receiver of sense impressions). The existence of the Self is considered a self-evident fact. The Self is eternal. Its junction with the body is known as birth, and its severance from the body is known as death.

Manas (mind)—the instrument of experience, as of happiness and misery, in the same way that the eyes are the instrument of seeing. Besides being the instrument of experience, the mind is itself an object of experience—quite as much so as the objects of sense. The Self alone is the experiencer. It wields the mind and the body as the fighter wields, according as he wills, the sword in his hand. As the Self associates itself with the mind, it becomes associated with the senses and the body and through them with the external world. This association is the primary cause of bondage and suffering. The manas accompanies the Self in death and is not dissociated from it until the attainment of mokṣa. With rebirth the body and the senses are completely renewed.

Earth, air, water, fire, ether—objective elements, since they are perceived by the external senses, though they are not perceived in their refined, causal states. In their causal states, unperceivable by the senses, conceivable only by the mind, they are called paramāṇus. They are active in the periodic process of creating the universe.

Kāla, time, and dik, space—substances having objective reality.

(2) Guṇa, quality, is distinct from substance, and, like the remaining categories, dependent upon it—since it cannot be known apart from the substance which it modifies. The qualities are broadly

divided into general properties, such as magnitude, which are common to one or more substances, and are perceived by one or more senses, and special qualities, such as taste, odour, colour, which specifically qualify only one substance and are perceivable by one sense only. Time and space, though substances, have no specific qualities.

(3) Karma, motion, is a distinct category, though it is dependent on earth, water, air, fire, and ether. It is of five kinds: upward, downward, contraction, expansion, and movement in general.

(4) Sāmānya, generality, is a category independent of thought. It is also known as jāti, or the that-ness which groups together many individuals into a class. There is a higher and a lower generality. The lower generality signifies a particular quality, such as cowness, common to cows. Being-ness, it may be said, characterizes the largest number of entities. This kind of generality has some resemblance to the Platonic 'idea', but it differs in that the Nyāya-Vaiśeṣika system does not recognize particulars as copies of universals.

(5) Viśeṣa, particularity, enables us to perceive that things differ from each other. It is the distinctive feature in each. (The later philosophers of the school did not admit this as an independent category.)

(6) Samavāya, necessary relation, possesses an objective reality independent of the percipient. It is that which relates a substance to its qualities, a whole to its parts, a cause to its effect. The relation concerned is inherent, as distinguished from ordinary relations, which can be brought about at will. Two or more objects, for instance, can be brought together, related to each other, and then separated; but such a relation would not be samavāya, or necessary relation. A necessary relation is like that between the thread and the cloth made from it, or between genus and species.

(7) Abhāva, negation, is not mentioned by Kanāda, who recognized but six categories. Later commentators added it in order to make the philosophy of the system realistic. They considered that the negation of false knowledge is the cause of the negation of misery and gives rise to niśreyasa, or the highest good.

The Nyāya-Vaiśeṣika philosophy, to sum up the preceding analysis, postulates seven categories—the substances, their properties, and their relations. These taken together compose the universe. In their primordial form they are real and eternal. Of the seven categories, the dravya, with its nine elements, is the most important. Of the nine elements, the Self, as the substratum of consciousness, and the only experiencer, is primary. The others, including mind, are objective realities, but though they possess reality they are dependent upon substance.

The Conception of God

In the Nyāya-Vaiśeṣika system, man's self is called jīvātman—the individual self as distinguished from Paramātman, the Supreme Self.

The proofs of the existence of God as given by this system are neither very convincing nor very important. They bear some similarity to the argument from design as we find it in the teleological side of Christian theology. Briefly, we see in the universe a physical order and a moral order, and these imply a controller, a lawgiver, and a governor who dispenses justice. Moreover, a world which is an effect must have not only its material cause but also its efficient cause. God must therefore exist as the efficient cause. There is, finally, no way to disprove the existence of God, just as, in the words of the Sāṁkhya system, there is no way to prove his existence.

The Law of Causation

The Nyāya-Vaiśeṣika system regards cause and effect, though there must always be the relation between an invariable antecedent and consequence, as two distinguishable conditions of things. Further, its doctrine of causation has this peculiarity, that the effect is regarded as nonexistent before its actual appearance. For example, the world as an effect, which is noneternal, is a production of the eternally pre-existing substances, with their properties and relations, but is also something absolutely new. Every cycle of creation, therefore, is called ārambhavāda—that which admits of an entirely fresh creation.

II. Differences

The two systems, in so far as they differ, do so mainly in their approach to the central problems of philosophy. The Vaiśeṣika begins with the conception of being and develops its ideas from that; the Nyāya begins with knowing. Where Vaiśeṣika has seven categories, Nyāya has sixteen, one of which contains all but one of the Vaiśeṣika seven (the exception being the Self, basis of all experience), and the remaining fifteen of which deal not with the universe, but with the means by which we understand it. The fifteen categories are proof, objects of authentic knowledge, doubt, illustration, conclusion, syllogism, argument, settlement (agreement on the truth), discussion, wrangling, idle contention, fallacy, fraud, baseless objection, and occasion for reproof. The last half-dozen of these are negative in character, calling attention to obstacles on the way to truth.

All Indian philosophy considers that ignorance bars the way to liberation. Nyāya philosophy further indicates that this ignorance results from identification of the Self with the body, the senses, and the mind. Because of this identification we are slaves to rāga (attachment) and dveṣa (hate), and these are the cause of all our sinful acts and the principal cause of suffering and death. And death causes rebirth because of our ignorance of the true Self. When we attain to transcendental knowledge of the true Self, we have no more slavery to rāga and dveṣa, and thus the wheel of birth and death is stopped and there is an end to misery.

III. The Nyāya-Vaiśeṣika: Way to Liberation

According to the Nyāya-Vaiśeṣika system of philosophy, the ignorance which is the cause of bondage and suffering and death is not merely a lack of knowledge of the Self but a positive error, or false knowledge. This false knowledge (moha, or delusion) can be eliminated only by right knowledge, which again is not merely intellectual attainment but a transcendental insight that gives immediate perception of the truth. In order that this immediate knowledge of the transcendental Self may be acquired, we must undergo moral and spiritual disciplines.

One way of liberation, according to the school we are studying, is through understanding the different categories and realizing the true nature of the Self. And how does one realize the true nature of the Self? Udāyana, a well-known ancient student of Nyāya philosophy, declares that one does so, with consequent liberation, through worship of God, devotion, and self-surrender. Philosophical speculation he looked upon as a mode of worship.

God, therefore, is the supreme Self, endowed with blessed attributes and devoid of evil. He is the creator and controller of all beings and all things. Individual selves are separate from God and are related to him as children to their father or as creatures to their creator. Individual souls are eternal—beginningless, and immortal—and are born into this world according to the deeds of their past. Justice and the moral order exist because of the law of karma. Man suffers or enjoys according to his own deeds. By surrender and devotion to God, and by worshipping him and meditating upon him, man, purified, becomes freed from the wheel of birth and death and realizes his true nature.

With respect to moral disciplines, this school would follow the duties of caste and of the orders of life. The rules of the conduct to be followed according to one's station in life prescribe faith, noninjury, compassion, nonattachment, freedom from lust, right motive, freedom from anger, cleanliness, purity, and devotion to God.

Liberation is release from pain and suffering. Consciousness, according to this school, is an adventitious property of the Self, not its inherent nature; inevitably, therefore, the state of liberation is devoid of consciousness—a conception which seems to be identical with complete materialism or with a species of philosophic materialism. In order to avoid such a misconstruction, later philosophers of the Nyāya school describe this state, not as one of mere negation of pain, but as positive bliss.

Liberation comes after release from the body. Jīvanmukti, or freedom while living, is not formally recognized by this school, though it does recognize a stage corresponding to it—a stage in which a person has extricated himself from moha, or delusion, and has found enlightenment. He is not 'free', however, in the strict sense of the word. For such a soul, final liberation comes with death.

CHAPTER 11

THE SĀṀKHYA SYSTEM

Date and Origin

The sage Kapila, who is generally regarded as the founder of Sāṁkhya philosophy, is a historical figure, though many myths have gathered about his personality. In the Gītā, Śrī Kṛṣṇa mentions him thus: 'Of the great sages, I am Kapila.' The Bhāgavata Purāṇa describes him as a partial incarnation of Viṣṇu, born with the knowledge of truth for the good of humanity. It is impossible to assign a definite date to Kapila; it can be safely affirmed, however, that he lived before the time of Buddha.

Two books, Tattwa Samāsa and Sāṁkhya Pravacana Sūtra, have been attributed to Kapila, though a difference of opinion exists among the scholars of India as to whether Kapila actually wrote them. Another book on Sāṁkhya, very popular amongst students of philosophy, is the Sāṁkhya Kārikā of Īśwarakṛṣṇa, a work of the third century A.D. Besides these there exist innumerable commentaries by the followers of this school of thought. Śaṁkara, the great Vedāntist, in the course of his refutation of some of the Sāṁkhya tenets, quotes the Kārikā and ignores the Sūtra. For this reason many hold that the Sūtra was of later origin. However, Vijñānabhikṣu, the well-known commentator on the Sūtra, attributes its authorship to Kapila.

The Purpose and Goal of Philosophy

The Upaniṣads say—as we have already stated—that if a man would have a transcendental experience of the Self, he must first read about it in the scriptures and hear about it from a teacher; second, subject it to rational analysis; and, finally, meditate upon it.[1] According to Vijñānabhikṣu, the philosophy of Sāṁkhya was propounded in relation to the second of these steps. It provides a rational analysis of the truth. And as we study this philosophy, we must agree with the

[1] See Bṛhadāraṇyaka, II. iv. 5.

Western scholar and student of Sāṁkhya, Richard Garbe, who says: 'In Kapila's doctrine, for the first time in the history of the world, the complete independence and freedom of the human mind, its full confidence in its own powers, was exhibited.'[1]

The first aphorism in the Sāṁkhya Sūtra runs thus: 'The supreme goal of life is to put an end completely to the three kinds of suffering.' Thus in common with all Indian schools of thought, and indeed in common with all the religions of the world, the complete cessation of suffering is declared to be the goal of life. The 'three kinds of suffering' are adhyātmika, the pain caused by diseases of the body, mental disturbances, and unrest; ādhibhautika, the pain produced by extraneous causes, such as men or beasts; and ādhidaivika, the pain caused by supernatural agencies, by the planets, and by the elements.

Every living being is in some way subject to pain, yet not one desires it, and man has the power to rid himself of it. The Sāṁkhya system purports to show how he can do this. The usual methods he adopts for this purpose are totally inadequate. Medicine, for instance, may cure a physical ailment but can never get rid of disease permanently, for one may fall ill again. Neither are mere good deeds nor the performance of Vedic rites efficacious. Only by right knowledge arising from right discrimination between the Self and the non-Self—between Puruṣa and prakṛti—can one destroy pain.

Sāṁkhya declares that the cause of misery (and by misery is meant the discontent that arises from uncertainty, aimlessness, and a sense of the fleeting nature of all earthly joy) is wrong knowledge, by which one identifies Puruṣa with prakṛti. Misery is to be found in prakṛti and not in Puruṣa. Our experience of misery is immediate, for our identification of Puruṣa with prakṛti is immediate. Whenever right knowledge dawns, giving immediate experience of Puruṣa as separate and detached from prakṛti, and only then, will come complete cessation of misery.

The Sāṁkhya philosophy is claimed by its followers to be a direct means to the attainment of the immediate experience of the transcendental Puruṣa as separate from prakṛti and thus to a complete freedom from all misery.

Realism

The Sāṁkhya philosopher does not, however, see only misery in the world. On the contrary, it is most explicitly stated that prakṛti (understood in all Indian philosophy to mean the world of thought and matter) is a mixture of happiness, misery, and delusion. Take a beautiful young married woman (an illustration drawn directly from the Sāṁkhya philosophy). She gives happiness to her husband; she

[1] *Philosophy of Ancient India*, p. 20.

creates jealousy among women who are not so beautiful; and she brings delusion to the mind of some lustful man. The same person, then, is the cause of happiness, misery, and delusion. Vācaspati Miśra, a commentator, remarks: 'By this illustration of the girl it is known that all objects in the universe are a combination of happiness, misery, and delusion.'

The above illustration may not, however, be wholly convincing; for happiness, misery, and delusion are subjective. They are not concrete objects. How then can the objective universe be a combination of these feelings? In reply it may be said that feelings or sensations are the subjective experiences produced by those same substances or forces which compose the objective universe. And, according to Sāṁkhya, the world of experience is real in its own right, and what we experience really belongs to the object, though we may only partially see its characteristics and not know it in its completeness. Different people may apprehend the same object differently, and this difference is entirely due to subjective characteristics of individual temperament, character, and education. Our knowledge of the objective universe is, therefore, one-sided, and our prejudices affect our judgments; hence our knowledge is bound to be personal and fragmentary. Nevertheless, what fragmentary knowledge we may acquire does actually correspond to external reality. Thus though Sāṁkhya, in the terminology of the West, may be called realistic, yet its realism avoids the two extremes of Western thought; that things are precisely as they are apprehended, and that the mind makes its own images, independently of any objective reality. Professor M. Hiriyanna offers some very pertinent remarks on the subject. He says:

'Such a view of knowledge is not without its lesson for us. The lesson is twofold: it behoves us to feel less positive than we ordinarily do about the correctness of our own views, and to be more regardful of the views of others. In other words, it teaches us the need for humility and charity in our intercourse with fellow-men, and impresses upon us the need for doing our utmost to see things not only as they appear to us but also as they may appear to others. The differences between one man and another may at first sight appear unbridgeable; but it may be that they can be easily adjusted, if only each tries to learn and appreciate the other's point of view. In one word, it bespeaks toleration which, as a matter of fact, is a striking feature of all Indian thought.'[1]

This passage must not be understood to say that no perfect knowledge is possible. Sāṁkhya maintains that the object of philosophy is

[1] *Cultural Heritage of India*, vol. I, p. 323.

to gain the perfect and complete knowledge of the truth, which is no mere aggregate of all the possible views and experiences of the objective world, but an immediate experience of reality in the transcendental consciousness. This knowledge can be attained only when all impurities of the mind and all prejudices and temperamental peculiarities of individual personality have been transcended and overcome. Then it is that knowledge of all things (as distinct from Puruṣa, the real Self) dawns, and they are seen as they actually are. The attainment of this transcendental knowledge is the climax of philosophic thought.

Dualism

Sāṁkhya is dualistic, for it postulates two ultimate realities, Puruṣa (Self—not the empirical self), and prakṛti, primordial nature. Puruṣa, though independent of prakṛti, inactive and separate from her, is regarded as the prime mover, the first cause of the cosmic process. By the proximity of Puruṣa, and not through its volition in any way, or direct action, prakṛti, which contains within herself the material of the universe, evolves as mind and matter. The nature of prakṛti is to be active, but her activity implies a mover not itself in motion. Puruṣa is like the magnet, and prakrti like the iron as it responds to the magnetic influence. Puruṣa, in relation to prakṛti, may be compared to a lame man seated on the shoulder of a blind man who walks, the lame man serving as the guiding eye, while the actual walking is done by the blind man. Puruṣa is the unchanging principle of intelligence and this, being reflected in prakṛti, creates the visible universe.

Prakṛti

Puruṣa, the unchanging principle of intelligence, is distinct from the physical and mental universe and independent of it. The term mind, as used in the West, corresponds to the Sāṁkhya antaḥkaraṇa, which is composed of the intellect, the ego, and the manas (receiver of sense impressions). The antaḥkaraṇa (the mind stuff), the senses, and matter (the objective universe) are all products of the same material cause, the uncaused cause, prakṛti.

The relation of mind to matter forms one of the most important and intricate problems in Western philosophy. Theories that explain the universe in chemical, mechanistic, or biological terms ignore a conception of mind as a separate entity, for according to Western materialistic conceptions of substance, mind is but a product of matter. Subjective idealism, on the other hand, ignores matter and regards thought or mind as the only reality. Realism regards mind and matter as separate substances and both as real. These Western schools of materialism, idealism, and realism pivot round this central problem of the mind-matter relationship. Indian philosophy, on the contrary, has not this particular problem, simply because it places mind and matter in the same category, neither of them exclusively mind nor exclusively matter but both products of one and the same substance.

To give Eastern philosophy Western names, such as idealism or realism, is fundamentally misleading. To the philosophical Indian mind the only problem is that of the soul. What is the real Self? How is it distinguished from mind and body? What is its nature? How can it be known? These are the only issues and concerns of Hindu schools of thought.

It was stated just above that mind in the West corresponds in Sāṁkhya to antaḥkaraṇa, or mind stuff. Strictly speaking, however, such a statement is hardly justified. Western psychology regards mind as intelligent by its inherent nature; the mind is, therefore, considered to be the thinker, the knower, and to know its own thoughts. But according to Sāṁkhya the antaḥkaraṇa, or mind stuff, comprising intellect, ego, and manas, is in itself nonintelligent. It is the product of prakṛti, which is nonintelligent in character, and it is the instrument which Puruṣa, the unchanging principle of intelligence, the Pure Consciousness, illumines, so that it appears intelligent. In brief, the consciousness of mind is a reflected intelligence, borrowed from Puruṣa, whose inherent nature is pure consciousness.

Let us take an illustration. When a bar of iron is heated in a furnace, the heat is borrowed, not from its own intrinsic nature, but from fire. So the antaḥkaraṇa by its proximity to Puruṣa appears intelligent. The real knower of thoughts or objects is not the mind but Puruṣa, the principle of intelligence. The antaḥkaraṇa is the instrument of knowledge, just as the senses and sense organs are also instruments of knowledge.

Finite experience, or what is commonly called knowledge, is that which is gained through the mind, senses, and body; that is, it is the product of antaḥkaraṇa in proximity to Puruṣa.

Western psychology does not even take up the question of the existence of a supreme unitary consciousness, though in metaphysics the West does have its monistic schools. But the aim of Indian philosophy, which again cannot be separated from Indian religion, is not merely to prove the existence of Puruṣa, the unchanging principle of consciousness, but to realize a transcendental experience of this Puruṣa as distinct from all changing phenomena of mind and body.

Prakṛti, on the other hand, is the uncaused cause of the universe. This universe of mind and matter is a pariṇāma, or transformation, of prakṛti, the primordial nature. Prakṛti may be defined as the sum of three guṇas, or forces, in a state of equilibrium. We do not know the real nature of prakṛti, nor of the guṇas, for our knowledge is limited to phenomena only, the product of prakṛti. Strictly, therefore, prakṛti is a mere abstraction, saṁjñā mātram, a mere name. But its existence is assumed as the primal single substance, the uncaused cause of multiple things. It is not a material substance; nor is it an intelligent principle, since Puruṣa, the Pure Spirit, which alone is intelligent and conscious, exists independently of it and is separable from it. It is not a material substance for the reason that it is the ground of the psychical as well as of the physical universe. All objective existence, including the psychical, is its product.

The Guṇas

The three guṇas, sattwa, rajas, and tamas, the constituents of prakṛti, form the material structure of the universe. That is to say, not only prakṛti but every object in the universe evolved from prakṛti consists of these three guṇas. In the Sāṁkhya view of causality, the effect is essentially identical with the cause; and the universe, which is a product, is therefore only a superficial transformation of prakṛti and is essentially constituted of the guṇas. The principle involved is identical, according to the physicist Joseph Kaplan,[1] with what is known in Western physics as the principle of superposition:

> 'In our modern description of nature, we proceed as follows: Let us say we are describing a molecule of nitrogen. Instead of giving a completely detailed account of its structure, as we might do in describing a chair or a house, we say that the molecule is adequately described for experimental purposes by giving all the possible energy states in which the nitrogen molecule can find itself, and then assigning to each such state a number which gives its relative weight, that is, the relative number of times that state appears compared with other states. Thus the molecule is not something which takes on successive states, but it is the states themselves. So dice are the sum of possible ways in which they can fall. The principle is known as the principle of superposition. So the three guṇas represent the universe, and as the three occur in various relative intensities, so the properties of things are determined.'

The constituent elements of the manifold objects in the universe, physical and psychical, are the same, and Sāṁkhya further declares

[1] Dr Kaplan's statements in this chapter were written specifically for this book.

that it is possible for one element to change into another. With this, modern physics is in agreement.[1]

It is extremely difficult to give an exact English equivalent of the word guṇa. It literally means both quality, and, the rope which binds. But if we take it in its literal meanings, we lose the associative connotation of the term. Quality is a product of the guṇas; but as substance and quality in Sāṁkhya are one, the word guṇa may mean substantive entities.[2]

'The rope which binds' characterizes the guṇa as the cause of the bondage of Puruṣa, but as we shall see later, it also brings freedom to Puruṣa.

Such are the traditional explanations of guṇa. Nevertheless, though it may be presumptuous in me, I prefer to explain it in terms of the modern physicist. Matter has been dematerialized by modern science and reduced to energy. Says Dr Kaplan: 'The fundamental positive and negative charges of the physicist have now been reduced to energy; that is, even the electron (plus or minus) or the proton or the neutron is not as fundamental as energy.'

So the guṇas of Sāṁkhya philosophy can be said to denote energies or forces which are never at rest. They are, in the words of the modern physicist, bundles of energies; three forms which are essentially distinct from each other and in a way antagonistic to each other, but which can never be separated. Each guṇa is a distinct type of energy. Later commentators on Sāṁkhya expressly state that, though three general types exist, the guṇas are in reality infinite in number. They are grouped into three classes, each class representing a type, on the basis of similarities and differences in behaviour.

The three types, sattwa, rajas, and tamas, are, we repeat, the material cause of the psychic and the physical universe, and their characteristics are known from their products. Each of them stands for a distinct

[1] 'The transmutability of the elements has been shown in many ways. For example, it is possible, by bombarding certain elements with extremely rapidly-moving electrical particles, to change them into others, and to even produce elements which do not occur in nature because they are unstable (radioactive). We go even further. It is possible to produce matter, such as electrons, from radiation (light). Thus the ultimate constituent of the universe of the physicist is energy of radiation—that is, light. Thus the Sāṁkhya theory is in absolute agreement with the latest results of physics. It is interesting here to make the following comment. The atomic theory is the product of the Western mind. In his naïve way the Western scientist generalizes the experience that one can subdivide matter until one meets an ultimate particle into an atomic theory assuming many elements. The Hindu philosopher goes much further and reduces everything to one element.'—J. Kaplan.

[2] 'The statement that substance and quality are identical is again in keeping with the point of view of modern physics in that we describe substance by stating all its possible qualities.'—J. Kaplan.

aspect of reality in the physical realm and a distinct characteristic of psychic experiences in the realm of thought and feeling. Though the three guṇas form the material of the universe, both physical and psychic, and though they coexist and cohere, one of them upon any specific occasion predominates over the others. From the dominant characteristic of any phase of a material or psychic object we may learn which of the guṇas has, in that object, the predominance.

In the physical world, sattwa informs all that is pure and fine, rajas informs the active principle, and tamas informs the principle of solidity and resistance. All three are present in everything, but one guṇa always predominates. For example, sattwa predominates in sunlight, rajas in an erupting volcano, and tamas in a block of granite.

The guṇas also represent the different stages in the process of evolution of any particular entity. Sattwa is the essence or the form to be realized, tamas is the inherent obstacle to its realization, and rajas is the power by which the obstacle is removed and it becomes manifest. Sattwa, finally, is that power by which a product manifests itself to consciousness.[1]

In the mind of man, sattwa expresses itself as tranquillity, purity, and calmness; rajas as passion, restlessness, aggressive activity; tamas as stupidity, laziness, inertia. Sometimes one guṇa is predominant, sometimes another; and a man's mood and character vary accordingly. But man can cultivate any one of the guṇas by his actions and thoughts and way of living. We are taught that tamas can be overcome by the cultivation of rajas, and rajas by the cultivation of sattwa. However, the ultimate ideal is to transcend sattwa also and reach the Puruṣa, which is above and beyond the guṇas.

Cosmic Evolution

According to the Sāṁkhya doctrine, this heterogeneous universe is a development (sṛṣṭi) out of homogeneous prakṛti, and to prakṛti it returns. There has been no creation, nor will there be a destruction; the present universe is but one of a series of worlds which have existed in the past and are yet to be. Herbert Spencer, in his *First Principles*, echoed Sāṁkhya when he said: 'And thus then is suggested

[1] 'The arguments in the text about the roles of the three guṇas are well made and in entire accord with the point of view of the modern physicist. By this I mean that if a modern physicist were to discuss the guṇas, he would, in the light of his knowledge and experience, use the same arguments. To put it differently, the thought processes of the Western philosopher are such that he is antagonistic to the physicist whereas the Hindu philosopher is sympathetic. Only in the relatively unimportant realm of classical physics—unimportant as regards its fundamental character—does the Western philosopher have any sympathy.'—J. Kaplan.

the conception of a past during which there have been successive Evolutions similar to that which is now going on; and a future during which successive other such Evolutions may go on.' So also did Thomas H. Huxley corroborate this truth in saying: 'It may be that, as Kant suggests, every cosmic magma predestined to evolve into a new world has been the no less predestined end of a vanished predecessor.'[1]

Thus did Sāṁkhya philosophy propound its own theory of evolution ages before the word evolution was known in the West. And it affirms that in the process of evolution, of sṛṣṭi, nothing is added, but that the effect is a reproduction, a transformation, of the cause; that is, the whole of the effect exists potentially in the cause. So evolution is the gradual unfoldment of what is involved, and the only condition for the fulfilment of the process is the removal of barriers. Patañjali, the founder of Yoga philosophy, following the Sāṁkhya theory of evolution, further explained the process by the illustration of a 'farmer removing the obstacles to the course of water, which then runs down by its own nature'. The water intended for irrigation of the fields being already in the canal, the farmer opens the gates, and the water flows in by itself, by the law of gravitation.

The power to remove obstacles exists in the nature of the guṇas, which are the potential cause of every result. These same guṇas, operating as different aspects of prakṛti, are seen in the evolution of both organic and inorganic matter. For this reason the distinction between organic and inorganic has never troubled the evolutionists in India, though until the discoveries of modern Western physics there had always existed an insurmountable barrier between the two among scientists of the West.

It is the guṇas which are never at rest, ever evolve, not the soul, or Puruṣa. Puruṣa is the Pure Consciousness (cit), never undergoing any change; but in the process of biological evolution it is released more and more. The higher the soul in the scale of evolution, the greater the release. Transcendental consciousness is the full release of the pristine purity and the infinite unchangeable consciousness of Puruṣa, or the Self—a state in which Puruṣa knows itself independent of prakṛti, and in which there is no longer any reflection of its consciousness, or any identification of it with antaḥkaraṇa, or mind stuff, the product of prakṛti.

We must remember, however, that prakṛti does not evolve by itself, single and alone, but rather through its proximity to Puruṣa; and Puruṣa remains entirely unchanged.

This, then, is the process of evolution in prakṛti.

[1] T. H. Huxley, 'Prolegomena', T. H. Huxley and Julian Huxley, *Touchstone for Ethics* (New York: Harper & Bros.), p. 43.

We have already defined prakṛti as the state of equilibrium of the three guṇas, and the beginning of evolution as the loss of this equilibrium. The first product of evolution is mahat. Mahat is the cosmic intelligence, which must not be confused with Pure Intelligence, the Puruṣa. We ought rather to translate mahat as the cosmic apparatus by which the intelligence of Puruṣa, the basis of the individual intelligence, is reflected.

Next comes buddhi, which is the individual apparatus illumined by the intelligence of Puruṣa. Its function is to discriminate, to distinguish objects, enabling Puruṣa to experience them. In the individual, buddhi works directly for Puruṣa, and all other organs function for buddhi. Puruṣa remains unchanged and yet, through buddhi, experiences the objective universe.

Buddhi, being a product of prakṛti, contains all the guṇas as its substantive material, though one or another of them may predominate at different times in an individual, or one or another may be the predominating characteristic of an individual.

In his sattwa state, the individual is characterized by purity, tranquillity, knowledge, freedom from desire, and possession of divine powers. Here may be found the greatest reflection of the pure, intelligent Puruṣa. In his rajas state, the individual is a victim of desires, is restless. In his tamas state, he is lethargic and ignorant. It is the experience of all, therefore, that the buddhi (an aspect of the mind in the Western meaning of the word) does not express an equal degree of intelligence at all times—one of the chief reasons why pure intelligence cannot be inherent in the buddhi. Its intelligence is rather the reflected intelligence of Puruṣa, the unchanging Self, and the amount of intelligence reflected differs at different times in accordance with the predominating guṇa.

According to Vijñānabhikṣu, the well-known commentator, buddhi is the storehouse of all subconscious impressions.

The next product is ahaṁkāra, or self-sense. In its individual psychological aspect, ahaṁkāra is the ego; and the sense of doer or agency (kartā) belongs to the ego and not to Puruṣa. When sattwa predominates, we perform good deeds; when rajas, we act selfishly; and when tamas, we are lazy and indifferent.

The guṇas take three different courses of evolution from ahaṁkāra, according to the preponderance of sattwa or tamas, with rajas aiding in either direction. In their sattwa aspect evolve manas, the five organs of perception, and the five organs of action. In their tamas aspect evolve the five tanmātrās, the subtle elements which by further preponderance of tamas, and by combining and recombining with one another, with the aid of rajas, produce the five gross elements—ether, air, fire, earth, and water. The sattwa element in the gross elements is manifested in so far as they reveal themselves directly to buddhi and indirectly to Puruṣa.

Manas is the organ which receives impressions through the senses and then presents them to the buddhi. It also has the function of carrying out the orders of the will through the organs of action. Manas, therefore, is necessary for both knowledge and action. It is not, however, an undivided entity, but is made up of parts.

Thus Indian psychology makes a distinction between buddhi, ahaṁkāra, and manas according to their functions; and all three together form the antaḥkaraṇa—the inner organ, the mind stuff.

Besides manas, as already stated, from ahaṁkāra, or ego-sense, there evolve the five sources of perception—sight, hearing, smell, taste, and touch; and the five organs of action—the tongue, the feet, the hands, and the organs of excretion and of generation.

As also stated, with the preponderance of tamas there evolve from the ahaṁkāra the tanmātrās, or the subtile principles that form the physical universe—the world as the object of perception. These

---

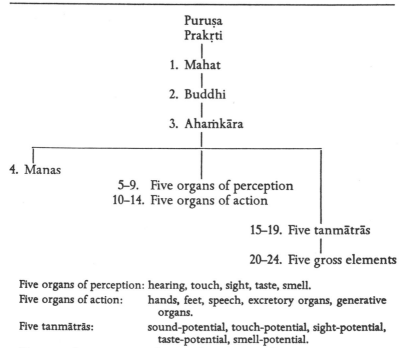

Puruṣa
Prakṛti

1. Mahat

2. Buddhi

3. Ahaṁkāra

4. Manas

5–9. Five organs of perception
10–14. Five organs of action

15–19. Five tanmātrās

20–24. Five gross elements

Five organs of perception:	hearing, touch, sight, taste, smell.
Five organs of action:	hands, feet, speech, excretory organs, generative organs.
Five tanmātrās:	sound-potential, touch-potential, sight-potential, taste-potential, smell-potential.
Five gross elements:	ether, air, fire, water, earth.

The twenty-four numbered categories make up the universe of mind and matter.

tanmātrās (the finer materials of the gross elements) are five, corresponding to the five sense organs—the essences of sound, touch, colour, taste, and smell; and they combine and recombine in different ways to produce the gross universe as perceived through our senses. Through the five senses this physical universe manifests itself to us in five ways as smell, touch, taste, sight, and sound. Out of the tanmātrās are produced the gross elements—earth, water, fire, air, and ether.

The gross elements are combinations of the five tanmātrās, with considerable variety in the combinations. Because of this variety, the universe presents itself to us in manifold aspects. For instance, earth, corresponding to the tanmātrā smell, is composed of one-half smell and one-eighth each of the other four tanmātrās; water, corresponding to the tanmātrā taste, is composed of one-half taste and one-eighth each of the other four tanmātrās; and so on. The tanmātrās—the finer materials of the gross elements—cannot be seen by one of ordinary vision, but only by yogis of high attainment.

The stages of evolution may be thus presented in diagrammatic form (see page 218).

Perception and the Sources of Knowledge

In what we ordinarily call knowledge, three factors are involved: the knower, the object of knowledge, and the process of knowing. Such knowledge is to be distinguished from intuition, or transcendental consciousness, wherein these three factors are transcended to give place solely to what may be called the unitary consciousness. For all forms of knowledge, however, according to Sāṁkhya, the knower is the Puruṣa, the experiencer; the object of knowledge, as experienced by the Puruṣa, is in effect the modification (vṛtti) of the mind stuff; and the process of knowing is the projection in the Puruṣa of the wave of impression (vṛtti) proceeding from the object.

The senses play their part by coming into contact with the objects and by carrying impressions of them to their respective brain centres, or organs.[1] The organs carry these impressions to the manas, which receives them and arranges them in a percept; the ahaṁkāra, or self-sense, refers the percept to the buddhi; the buddhi interprets the percept and the concept is formed. From the buddhi the Puruṣa receives the concept, and perception follows. The buddhi, ahaṁkāra, and manas are the nonconscious inner apparatus for receiving the

[1] Modern physiologists tell us that vision is not in the eyes but in one of the nerve centres of the brain, and so also with respect to the other senses. Sāṁkhya tells us the same things, only from a psychological rather than from the physical point of view.

impressions of the objective world, and they are modified according to the impressions. Then Puruṣa, the unchanging intelligent principle that is reflected and so modified, in the buddhi, appears to assume the modification of the buddhi. And it is this apparent identification with the modification of the buddhi that is known as apprehension. The reflection of the Puruṣa in the buddhi, and its identification with the modifications, is not real, but only apparent, being due to ignorance and a failure to perceive the distinction between Puruṣa and buddhi. It is this association between Puruṣa and buddhi, due to ignorance, which results in a confused notion of their respective true natures; so that Puruṣa, the unchanging reality and the only witness, regards itself as the doer, or active agent, and the buddhi, which is only the instrument of knowledge, appears as conscious and intelligent.[1]

Knowledge derived from the senses and through sense activity is known as perception. Apart from sense perception, Sāṁkhya admits of a kind of perception, called yogic, in which the senses do not have to come into contact with objects; on the contrary, a peculiar power enters an individual's mind which has been disciplined through concentration and meditation, so that it is able to come into contact directly with past and future objects and perceive them.

In memory, perception comes through the activities of manas, ahaṁkāra (self-sense), and buddhi (the faculty of discrimination), and there is no activity of the senses, though there is presupposed the results of their previous activities. Memory is possible only because all our experience leaves impressions in the inner organ, the mind stuff; no thought or action is therefore completely lost. The sum total of these impressions constitutes character. In internal perception, also, no activity of the sense organs occurs. Introspection, or cognition of our thoughts, is possible not because there is another, superimposed cognition, as is asserted in Western psychology, but because the Puruṣa witnesses all changes or modifications of the mind stuff.

Besides perception, Sāṁkhya admits two other sources of knowledge: (1) inference, and (2) āptavākya, or revealed words—the scriptures.

Scriptures are regarded as true only because they have been tested and found true by the seers. Furthermore, revelation must not contradict reason. Aniruddha, an ancient commentator, quotes this

[1] Thus in the so-called knowledge in which the three factors (knower, object of knowledge, and process of knowing) are involved, there is also involved a universal ignorance, or false identification of Puruṣa and prakṛti. True or transcendental knowledge lies beyond the 'three knots of knowledge', for it is the unitary consciousness in which the Puruṣa no longer identifies itself with prakṛti, but exists altogether independently in its transcendental nature.

verse from an ancient text: 'The seers never speak of impossible things, such as huge demons dropping down from heaven. Words which conform to reason should alone be accepted by me and men like you.'

Puruṣa

In the course of our discussion we have learned that Puruṣa is separate and distinct from prakṛti and its products, such as mind stuff, the senses, the body, and so forth, and that therefore it is distinct from the guṇas. Puruṣa is consciousness itself—not that it is conscious, but that it is the unchanging principle of consciousness. As we do not say that 'water is wet', because wetness is its inherent quality, and the two cannot be separated, so we do not say that Puruṣa is conscious, because consciousness is its inherent nature. All knowledge or intelligence manifested either in the mind stuff or in the objective world is a borrowed consciousness, the reflection of the Puruṣa, or the Self. Puruṣa is the unchangeable Reality behind all the changing phenomena of the universe, which in turn are the products of the never-resting guṇas. Hence it is ever free—free from the accidents of finite life, above and beyond the limits of time, space, and causation. It has neither beginning nor end. It is eternal. It is śuddha, buddha, and mukta—that is, purity, consciousness, and freedom.

The following, according to Sāṁkhya, are the proofs of the existence of Puruṣa. First, we may say that every compounded substance exists for a being that is not compounded. The objects of the universe which are compounded exist to serve some purpose of some being who is the eternal subject, never an object. Prakṛti, therefore, exists to serve the purpose of another being, whom we name Puruṣa, and Puruṣa must exist that prakṛti may serve him. Second, all objects of knowledge are composed of three guṇas, whose existence implies a seer independent of them. Mind stuff is also an object of knowledge, and the thoughts of the mind can be cognized only by a seer of thoughts—a being separate from themselves. Third, since prakṛti is nonintelligent, there must be something or someone to experience its operation. Fourth, there must be a supreme background, a centre, to co-ordinate all experience, for our experiences are multiple, and we may have multiple experiences simultaneously. Lastly, there exists a longing in every human being to be free. All of us feel limitations of which we strive to be rid. There exists therefore a reality within us which is by nature free and which possesses the power to escape limitation. In the words of Swami Vivekananda:

'The Soul [identical with Puruṣa] is free, and it is its freedom that tells you every moment that you are free. But you mistake, and mingle that freedom every moment with buddhi and mind. You try to attribute that freedom to the buddhi, and immediately find that the buddhi is not free; you attribute that freedom to the body, and immediately nature tells you that you are again mistaken. That is why there is this sense of freedom and bondage at the same time. The yogi determines what is free and what is bound, and his ignorance vanishes. He finds that the Purusha is free, is the essence of that knowledge which, coming through the buddhi, becomes intelligence, and, as such, is bound.'[1]

To the foregoing five proofs of the existence of Puruṣa, Patañjali, father of Yoga philosophy, adds another: 'The states of the mind are always known because the lord of the mind, the Puruṣa, is unchangeable.'

The fact is that the universe in its various elements is both mental and physical and that in both aspects it is in continual flux. A book or a table or a desk is a group of molecules (guṇas) in continual motion—a whirlpool of infinitesimal objects striking one another with greater or less velocity. But the book or the table or the desk remains the same, possessing substantial unity in itself. The changes it undergoes have an orderly rhythm, and the object sends impressions to the mind that, put together, create an integral picture. This process of integration and change also goes on in the mind. The mind and the body may be likened to two layers of a single substance that move at different rates of speed. Since one layer is slower than the other, the eye can distinguish between the two layers. Let us suppose that three trains are moving in the same direction but at different rates of speed along parallel railroad tracks. Train A is the fastest of the three; Train C is the slowest. Now a passenger who looks at Train A from a window of Train B will say: 'That train is moving. We are standing still.' If, however, he looks out of the opposite window, at Train C, he will correct himself: 'No—I was wrong. We are moving. But *that* train is at rest.' In other words, the motion of a given object, A, can be measured only in relation to another object, B, which has less motion—and so on *ad infinitum*. Universal motion can be recognized only if we know that there is something which is eternally static. All scientists agree that the entire physical universe is moving; and all psychologists agree that the mind is in perpetual flux. To understand our recognition of this physical and mental movement, we must assume the existence of a third factor—unchangeable reality.

So, declares Swami Vivekananda, 'Behind this never-ending chain of motion is the Purusha, the changeless, the colourless, the pure. All impressions are merely projected upon it, as a

[1] *Complete Works of Vivekananda*, vol. I, p. 255.

magic lantern throws images upon a screen without in any way tarnishing it.'[1]

The Puruṣa in many respects resembles the Ātman of the Vedas, but with this fundamental difference, that the Ātman, the unchanging, omnipotent Self, which is one with the all-pervading Brahman, is one, but the Puruṣas are many. They are infinite in number, the Sāṁkhya argues, because if there had been but one Self all men would attain freedom when one attained it.[2] The Puruṣa of Sāṁkhya, like the Ātman of the Vedas, is formless, subtle, omnipresent, beyond mind, senses, and intellect, beyond time, space, and causation. It is unborn, undying, uncreated, without beginning and without end. It is immortal in the sense that it is unchangeable, and perfection and freedom are its inherent nature.

The jīva, the individualized spirit, the empirical self, is distinguished from the Puruṣa by its connection with the buddhi, the manas, and the senses. It is also limited by the body. While Puruṣa is the pure Self beyond the buddhi and the senses, the jīva, with its ahaṁkāra, or ego-sense, is its reflection in buddhi. The ego, which is a product of prakṛti and is not to be confused with the true Self, is the jīvahood, the individualized aspect of man. Through ignorance, which is universal, we do not recognize our true selves, and we do not know that our birthright is purity and knowledge and freedom. In consequence we identify Puruṣa with buddhi and experience limitation and ignorance, pleasure and pain, and bondage to birth and death. But this identification is only temporary, for with true knowledge we at last recognize the Puruṣa for what it is and gain our eternal freedom.

Thus jīva, the individual self, is in reality Puruṣa, the true Self, in association with the buddhi, the manas, the senses, and the body. There exist the gross body and the subtle body. The gross body is the physical body; the subtle body is that which contains within itself the buddhi, the manas, and the senses. The subtle body, still a product of prakṛti, appears conscious, though nonconscious, because of association with Puruṣa; and it is subject to pleasure and pain and to the laws of karma and of rebirth. The Puruṣa, though free, appears subject to the vicissitudes of the subtle body because of ignorance. Forgetting its birthright of eternal peace and freedom, it identifies itself with the forms of finite existence and experiences the bondage and miseries of life and death.

The gross body dies with physical death, but the subtle body continues to exist. In the subtle body are stored all the impressions

[1] *Complete Works of Vivekananda*, vol. I, p. 299.

[2] Nondualistic Vedānta, as we shall see later, insists that there is but one Self, and not many.

of all our experiences, and in accordance with the law of karma, the circumstances of our future birth are determined by these impressions. In Sanskrit the subtle body is known as liṅga śarīra—the distinguishing mark of an individual—that is, his character as it is formed by his own thoughts and deeds.

The subtle body is a composition whose ingredients are the three guṇas. As we have already seen, one or another guṇa predominates in the successive stages of evolution through many lives. In the lowest stage of evolution of animal life, tamas predominates, for this stage is marked by ignorance and stupidity. Since the three guṇas are never separated, rajas and sattwa also appear in these elementary forms, but in them they play but little part. With the predominance of rajas begins the evolution of human life. There occurs not only activity, but also some effort towards freedom from pain and suffering. As this effort is directed into proper channels, sattwa takes charge, and with sattwa appear purity, knowledge, and tranquillity. Ultimately, Puruṣa knows himself as pure being, separate from the gross body—as the eternal witness, free and uncontaminated. This final stage is that of seership. Then, as the gross body dies, Puruṣa attains complete freedom and is detached from the subtle body also. In this condition he exhibits his true nature and his pristine glory. He is now in the final state of absolute liberation.

Thus prakṛti brings one both bondage and freedom. She brings bondage when one identifies oneself with her through ignorance. But as one gathers experience and learns that prakṛti exists for the sake of that experience, one learns detachment from her. One learns that the whole of nature is created for the Self, and not the Self for nature. As the bee comes to suck honey, not to get its feet entangled in it, so one is born to gather experience from nature, not to become entangled in it by identifying oneself with it. Eventually one awakes, for the freedom inherent in Puruṣa ever reasserts itself, and one at last discovers that one is eternally pure and free. Then prakṛti no longer holds one, and one need no longer submit to the bonds of karma. In the words of Swami Vivekananda:

'Nature's task is done, this unselfish task which our sweet nurse has imposed upon herself. She gently took the Self-forgetting soul by the hand, and showed him all that is in the universe, all manifestations, bringing him higher and higher through various bodies till his glory came back and he remembered his own nature. Then the kind mother went back the same way she came, for others who also had lost their way in the trackless desert of life. And thus is she working, without beginning and without end. And thus through pleasure and pain, through good and evil, the infinite river of souls is flowing into the ocean of perfection, or self-realization.[1] Glory unto those who have realized their own nature; may their blessings lie on us all.'[2]

[1] Thus Wordsworth, who sees only one side of the play of Nature—the side which tends to cause forgetfulness in the soul of its true nature, but not the side which leads it back, at last, to its 'imperial palace':

Earth fills her lap with pleasures of her own;
Yearnings she hath in her own natural kind,
And, even with something of a mother's mind,
And no unworthy aim,
The homely nurse doth all she can
To make her foster-child, her Inmate Man,
Forget the glories he hath known,
And that imperial palace whence he came.

[2] *Complete Works of Vivekananda*, vol. I, p. 304.

CHAPTER 12

THE YOGA SYSTEM OF PATAÑJALI

Introduction

Truth is of two kinds: (1) that which is perceived by the five ordinary senses or inferred from the data they provide, and (2) that which is perceived by the subtle, supersensuous power of yoga.

The first kind of truth is called scientific, or empirical, knowledge; the second kind is called transcendental, or yogic, knowledge.

The person in whom supersensuous power is manifested is called a ṛṣi, a seer, a yogi who has achieved union with God.

To develop supersensuous power is to practise genuine religion. So long as a spiritual aspirant does not develop this power, so long is religion a mere empty word to him. He has not yet taken the first step towards his goal.

So we must strive for supersensuous perception, and there exist methods or processes which we may use if we will. These require as a prerequisite, if they are to be effective, a life of lofty ethical attainment, but they are in themselves definite spiritual disciplines. They are known to the Hindus as yogas. The primary meaning of the word yoga, which is related to the English word yoke, is union, and what is referred to is union with the true Self, or God; in its secondary meaning it is a method for achieving that union. Patañjali employs it to signify a striving towards the realization of Puruṣa, or the Divine Self—'an effort to separate Puruṣa from prakṛti'. From the earliest times aspirants have followed the practices of yoga. All the earliest Hindu scriptures and all the subsequent systems of philosophy not only express their conception of spiritual truth but also offer practical methods for realizing the divine consciousness. These methods, however, receive but casual mention in the Vedas, the Upaniṣads, and other early works, and whatever references there are to them deal with the specific and detailed processes of Self-realization handed down orally, generation after generation, from teacher to disciple. The same processes have been followed even to the present day. All aspirants after spiritual things must practise them if they would acquire personal experience of the truth they are seeking.

Patañjali, the author of the Yoga system of philosophy, can therefore scarcely be called the founder or originator of yoga, but he was the first to gather together the spiritual practices known to the yogis and build them into a system.

It is impossible to assign a definite period to the life of this great yogi. One Patañjali, a grammarian, lived in the middle of the second century BC, but it is uncertain whether he and the author of the *Yoga Aphorisms* are one and the same.

Conception of God in Yoga Philosophy

The Yoga system as formulated by Patañjali is a systematized religious discipline providing a means of attaining the highest consciousness, which in turn leads to final release. All spiritual aspirants in India, whatever may be their individual religious preference, accept the discipline of yoga, though, strictly speaking, Yoga philosophy in its metaphysical aspects is closely allied to Sāṁkhya, with one important difference—its acceptance of God. Sāṁkhya, as we have seen, leaves no room for God, either in its system of metaphysics, or in its scheme of salvation. While Sāṁkhya asserts that there can be no proof of the existence of God, Patañjali advances certain proofs, and in his plan of salvation declares that worship of God and meditation upon him are one of the means of attaining supreme knowledge and liberation. He does admit, however, that it is not absolutely necessary to believe in God in order to experience the truth of religion, holding that truth will make itself felt in spite of belief or disbelief provided one follow the practices of yoga. He only says that it is easier to gain the end of spiritual enlightenment through faith in God and through worshipping him and meditating upon him.

For those, however, who cannot believe in a personal deity, other methods are provided that will bring them the same enlightenment. Indeed, religious truths, as we have already pointed out over and over in our account of Indian philosophy and religion, are not mere dogmas, accepted on faith, but facts made visible by an inner light. Belief or no belief, it is Patañjali's claim that if we follow any of the yoga practices faithfully, we shall be led directly to the spiritual goal.

Devotion to God is one of the means, declared Patañjali, to attain liberation and the truth of the spirit. In Sanskrit, God is called Īśwara, interpreted by Bhoja, the well-known commentator, to mean the 'One who by his mere wish has the power to give liberation to all who seek him.'

Patañjali himself has defined Īśwara as a 'special kind of Being'—

distinct from man, inasmuch as 'he is untouched by ignorance and the products of ignorance'. He is 'not subject to karmas or saṁskāras or the results of action'.[1] Unlike man—in other words—he is not bound by the law of karma; he has neither birth nor death; he is eternal, unborn, undying, and unchangeable. And he is free from desires.[2]

But Īśwara, as the yogis look upon him, is not the creator of the universe. Its evolution had been explained by Sāṁkhya without admitting the existence of a creator. Yoga arrives at a proof of God's existence in a peculiar fashion of its own. Patañjali says: 'In God knowledge is infinite; in others it is only a germ.'[3] From this aphorism the commentators have derived their proof of the existence of God. The Puruṣas, they declare, are all endowed with knowledge, some with more and some with less, and the fact of limited knowledge proves the existence of unlimited knowledge. There must therefore exist a Being possessed of infinite knowledge. This argument should be compared with the remark of Kant that the concept of the finite involves the existence of the infinite.

Patañjali also says of Īśwara: 'He was the teacher even of the earliest teachers, since he is not limited by time.'[4] The deduction from this aphorism is that no knowledge can come without a teacher—and that God is the teacher of all teachers. Swami Vivekananda remarks:

> 'It is true, as the modern philosophers say, that there is something in man which evolves out of him; all knowledge is in man, but certain environments are necessary to call it out. We cannot find any knowledge without teachers. If there are men teachers, god teachers, or angel teachers—they are all limited; . . . who was the teacher before them? We are forced to admit, as a last conclusion, [the existence of] one Teacher, who is not limited by time; and that one Teacher of infinite knowledge, without beginning or end, is called God.'[5]

How may one express devotion to God, how worship him and meditate upon him? In spite of all definitions and all descriptions, God remains to the human mind but an abstraction. Patañjali, realizing this fact, offers a definite, concrete way of understanding

[1] Man is subject to unhappiness because of his false identification of himself with the buddhi through ignorance. God has not this ignorance; hence he is free from suffering and unhappiness.

[2] Man identifies himself with the buddhi through ignorance and is therefore controlled by desires arising from impressions of past deeds and thoughts. God is free from identification of himself with the buddhi and has therefore no stored impressions of past deeds or thoughts.

[3] *Yoga Aphorisms*, I. 25.

[4] *Ibid.*, I. 26.

[5] *Complete Works of Vivekananda*, vol. I, p. 217.

God which the mind may grasp and meditate upon. He says: 'The word which expresses him is Om. This word must be repeated with meditation upon its meaning. Hence come knowledge of the Puruṣa and destruction of the obstacles to that knowledge.'[1]

In the Upaniṣads, as we have already noted, the word Om was held sacred by sages and seers, being regarded as a symbol of Brahman. From Vedic times until the present day it has been so understood, and it has been employed as an aid in meditation by all aspirants after God. It is accepted both as one with Brahman and as the medium, the Logos, connecting man and God. It is God, and by its aid man may realize God. The entire history of the syllable is in the revelations of the Vedas and the Upanıṣads, and this history in the hands of the later philosophers developed into what became known as sphoṭa-vāda, or philosophy of the Word. The similar doctrine of the Logos, later also than the Vedas and the Upaniṣads, we discover among Greek metaphysicians—a doctrine which influenced the writer of the Fourth Gospel.

As indicated, the sphoṭa-vāda is not precisely the Logos of the Greek philosophers. The Greeks first conceived of the Logos as a bridge over the gulf that separates man and God, the known and the unknown. The earliest Greek conception was a crude one. The Logos was identified with one or another of the physical elements, according as one or another was thought to be the ultimate substance of the universe. Heraclitus, who lived in the sixth century BC, was the first who tried to break away from a purely physical conception of creation, substituting for the material first cause of his predecessors a principle which he called intelligence. This principle of intelligence was the Logos. The advance Heraclitus made, however, was rendered somewhat equivocal by his identification of the Logos with the physical element fire.

In the hands of Plato the theory of the Logos underwent a complete transformation. He regarded the Logos as the cosmic purpose, the highest idea, the supreme Good, under which all lesser ideas—i.e. eternal archetypes of things, relations, qualities and values—are subsumed. According to him, these ideas are arranged in a logical order, and are governed by the Logos: thus the universe is a unity in diversity, a rational, organic whole.

The Stoics denied the validity of Plato's supersensual archetypes, accepting rather the essential theory of Heraclitus: like Heraclitus, they posited a principle of reason immanent and active in the universe. To them the Logos was this eternal reason, 'made concrete in the endless variety of the physical world'. The fact that this rational principle was regarded by the Stoics as the essence of human nature

[1] *Yoga Aphorisms*, I. 27–9.

is of special significance, as far as their ethical teachings are concerned. A man is free, they believed, insofar as he lives in conformity with his reason, and hence, in harmony with the rational nature of the universe.

The Stoic conception of the Logos as an active principle pervading the universe and determining it was adopted by the Hellenized Jewish philosopher, Philo of Alexandria, a contemporary of Jesus of Nazareth. But whereas the Stoics, by conceiving of the Logos as the principle of reason inherent in all things, endeavoured to escape from the recognition of a divine Creator, Philo was committed from the beginning to the Jewish belief in a supreme, self-existent Deity to whom the reason of the world must be made subservient. Philo also accepted Plato's idea of the Logos as the transcendent Good in which all individual ideas are comprehended, but he made this conception distinctively his own by combining with it the conception of the Logos as the immanent and active reason. All of these theories of Philo regarding the Logos stem ultimately from his view of God as a transcendent Being of whom nothing can be predicated, and from the necessity of explaining how such a pure and perfect Being could have any contact with the finite world.

Philo's descriptions of the Logos as mediator between God and the world reflect the two sources from which he drew—Greek philosophy and Jewish religion. He speaks of an infinite variety of Divine Forces, through which an active relation between God and the world is effected.

'Sometimes he describes these powers as properties of God, as ideas or thoughts of God, as parts of the universal power or reason, sometimes as messengers or servants of God, as souls, angels, or demons—thinking now in terms of Greek philosophy, now in terms of the Jewish religion. All such powers he combines into one, the Logos, the Divine Reason or Wisdom. . . . The Logos is the container or place of all ideas, the power of all powers, the highest of the angels, the first-born son of God, the image of God, the second God, the God-man . . .'[1]

Philo's system contains an unresolved conflict between the Greek and Hebraic conceptions: sometimes, in accord with the Greeks, he represents the Logos as an independent and personal Being, a 'second God', and sometimes, in accord with the Jews, he conceives of it as a distinct and subordinate thing, a mere aspect of the divine activity.

The author of the Fourth Gospel used Philo's Logos theory as the basis for his interpretation of the life of Christ, but gave it new

[1] Frank Thilly, *A History of Philosophy*, p. 148.

expression to serve the theological needs of Christianity.[1] The Logos, that is, which is identical with God, and through which the universe was created, was 'made flesh' in Jesus Christ. Thus Jesus, one with the Logos, became the 'only begotten son of God' and identical with him. 'In the beginning was the Word,' says St John, 'and the Word was with God, and the Word was God.' The verse is almost identical with one in the Vedas: 'Prajāpatir vai idam agre āsīt—In the beginning was Prajāpati (Brahman); Tasya vāg dvītīyā āsīt—with whom was the Word; Vāg vai Paramaṁ Brahma—and the Word was verily Brahman.'

In adapting Philo's doctrine of the Logos to his account of a historical person, St. John altered it in several respects. In addition to the change we have already described, that of attributing a real personality to the Logos, he emphasized, not its creative aspect but its redemptive function, its communication of spiritual power to men. Also, he stressed more than Philo did the Old Testament conception of the Logos as Word, as distinguished from the Greek view of the Logos as Reason; that is, he interpreted it as an expression of the divine will, an outpouring of God's goodness and power, light and love.

The Philonic and Johannean conceptions of the Logos may conceivably owe no debt to Indian thought, for the truth is no monopoly of any race or nation, and with spiritual growth the same truth is often realized by different peoples independently of one another. Yet it is also possible that both Greek philosophers and Christian theologians were in some degree under obligation to India for their initial ideas, since it is a well-known fact that Hindu thought exercised a strong influence upon the minds of early Western thinkers.

Not only, however, are there general points of similarity between the Eastern conception of the Logos and that which took root in the West; there are differences that are quite as great. To a Hindu mind, the expressed sensible universe is the form behind which stands the eternal Sphoṭa, the inexpressible, the Logos or Word. This eternal Sphoṭa, the essential material of all ideas or names, is the power through which God creates all things.[2] Īśwara, Brahman conditioned by māyā, first manifests himself as the Sphoṭa, the inexpressible Word, out of which he then evolves as the concrete, sensible world. The Christian Logos, on the other hand, is not regarded as the material cause of the universe, for God, according to Christianity, is only an efficient cause.

[1] Cf. J. Reville: *La Doctrine du Logos dans le quatrième Evangile et dans les Oeuvres de Philon.*

[2] Patañjali, however, did not agree with this last statement, for the universe was to him a product of prakṛti. The Vedānta accepts the Sāṁkhya-Pātañjali view, and then reduces its dualism to nondualism by regarding prakṛti as māyā, or the power of God—the power to create, preserve, and dissolve the universe.

The Christian Logos, as we read in the Fourth Gospel, 'was made flesh, and dwelt among us (and we beheld his glory, the glory as of the only begotten of the Father), full of grace and truth'. There is here a second interesting difference between the Christian and the Hindu Logos. The Christian Logos was incarnate once, in the person of Jesus, whereas the Sphoṭa of the Hindus was and is and will be incarnate in all persons—and not in persons only but in all other beings, throughout the universe—each of whom may directly realize God through his power, the power of the Sphoṭa. Says Swami Vivekananda:

'This Sphota has one word as its only possible symbol and this is Om. And as by no possible means of analysis can we separate the word from the idea, this Om and the eternal Sphota are inseparable; and therefore it is out of the holiest of all holy words, the mother of all names and forms, the eternal Om, that the whole universe may be supposed to have been created. But it may be said that, although thought and word are inseparable, yet as there may be various word-symbols for the same thought it is not necessary that this particular word Om should be the word representative of the thought out of which the universe has become manifested. To this objection we reply that this Om is the only possible symbol which covers the whole ground. The Sphota is the material of all words, yet it is not any definite word in its fully formed state. That is to say, if all the particularities which distinguish one word from another be removed, then what remains will be the Sphota; therefore this Sphota is called the Nada-Brahman, the Sound-Brahman.

'Now, as every word-symbol intended to express the inexpressible Sphota will so particularize it that it will no longer be the Sphota, that symbol which particularizes it the least and at the same time most approximately expresses its nature, will be the Om, and the Om only; because these three letters A, U, M, pronounced in combination as Om, may well be the generalized symbol of all possible sounds. The letter A is the least differentiated of all sounds. Again, all articulate sounds are produced in the space within the mouth beginning with the root of the tongue and ending in the lips—the throat sound is A, and M is the last lip sound; and the U exactly represents the rolling forward of the impulse which begins at the root of the tongue and continues till it ends in the lips. If properly pronounced, this Om will represent the whole phenomenon of sound production, and no other word can do this; and this, therefore, is the fittest symbol of the Sphota, which is the real meaning of the Om. And as the symbol can never be separated from the thing signified, the Om and the Sphota are one. And as the Sphota, being the finer side of the manifested universe, is nearest to God, and is indeed the first manifestation of Divine Wisdom, this Om is truly symbolic of God.'[1]

More than this, the yogis say that through meditation one may hear this word Om vibrating through the universe.

According to Patañjali, worship of God can be effected by repeating Om and meditating upon its meaning.

What Yoga Is

Patañjali, the father of Indian Yoga philosophy, has defined yoga as 'the control of thought-waves in the mind'. The mind (citta), according to Patañjali, is made up of three components, manas, buddhi, and ahaṁkāra. Manas is the recording faculty, which receives impressions gathered by the senses from the outside world. Buddhi is the discriminative faculty, which classifies these impressions and reacts to them. Ahaṁkāra is the ego-sense, which claims these impressions for its own and stores them up as individual knowledge. The mind seems to be intelligent and conscious. Yoga philosophy teaches that it is not. It has only a borrowed intelligence. Puruṣa is intelligence itself, is pure consciousness. The mind reflects that consciousness and so appears to be conscious. Knowledge, or perception, according to Patañjali, is a vṛtti, a thought-wave in the mind. All knowledge is therefore objective. Even what Western psychologists call introspection or self-knowledge is objective knowledge according to Patañjali, since the mind is not the seer, but only an instrument of knowledge, an object of perception like the outside world. The Puruṣa, the real seer, remains unknown.

Every perception arouses the ego-sense, which says: 'I know this.' But this is the ego speaking, not the Puruṣa, the real Self. The ego-sense is caused by the identification of Puruṣa with the products of prakṛti—the mind, the senses, etc.

When an event or object in the external world impinges on the senses, a thought-wave is raised in the mind. The ego-sense identifies itself with this wave. If the thought-wave is pleasant, the ego-sense feels, 'I am happy'; if unpleasant, it feels, 'I am unhappy'. This false identification is the cause of all our misery; even the ego's temporary sensation of happiness brings anxiety, a fear that the object of pleasure will be taken away—unhappiness in itself and a preparation for possible more acute unhappiness to come. The Puruṣa, in contrast, remains forever outside the power of thought-waves; eternally pure, enlightened, and free, it experiences the only true, unchanging

[1] *Complete Works of Vivekananda*, vol. III, pp. 57–8.

happiness. It follows, therefore, that man can never know his real Self as long as Puruṣa is identified with the products of prakṛti. In order to become enlightened we must bring the thought-waves under control, so that this false identification may cease.

To clarify this matter, the commentators employ a simple image. If the surface of a lake, they say, is lashed into waves, or if the water is muddy, the bottom cannot be seen. The lake represents the mind, and the bottom of the lake the Puruṣa, the Self.

Whenever the mind is made tranquil, knowledge of the Self is revealed.

Subduing the thought-waves that would possess the mind is not a simple act, nor one to be quickly accomplished, for it completely transforms the mind. It is an act, however, made possible by yogic discipline. Doubtless St Paul had reference to a discipline of this kind when he said, 'Be ye transformed by the renewing of your mind.'

In order to achieve this renewal of the mind, Yoga psychology considers not only the actual states of the mind but also the latent states, called the saṁskāras, or potentialities. Before we can hope to restrain the thought-waves successfully, we must endeavour to eradicate the potentialities, the root impressions which control the actual states. For when one mental state passes into another, it is not altogether lost, but leaves behind it an impression—latent state or saṁskāra—which in turn tends to give rise to actual states similar to itself. Thus the actual states cause the saṁskāras, and the saṁskāras cause the actual states. The saṁskāras are deep roots in the soil of the mind from which grow the plants, the actual states, the thought-waves. To destroy the weeds, we must eradicate the roots, and to do this it is not enough to restrain the actual states; it is necessary also, through yoga discipline, to overcome, weaken, and destroy the saṁskāras, the potentialities of the actual states.

Modern Western psychology, particularly Freudian, takes into consideration these potentialities. Freud postulates three 'areas', or states of mind: the unconscious, the preconscious, and the conscious. The unconscious is the receptacle of such of our past experiences as have been definitely forgotten and cannot be recalled by the ordinary method of recollection. The preconscious is that part of the mind in which are stored experiences which, though apparently forgotten, can be recalled by an effort of the will. Modern Western psychologists differ in their explanation of the unconscious mind, some holding that it is the receptacle of our individual past experiences, and of these alone, while others would include with them the common experiences of the race.

Yoga psychology agrees with the Western view that the unconscious is a depository of certain individual past experiences, but as to the extent of our individual past it differs radically. To Patañjali, our individual past is not limited to the present life, as all Western psychologists would assume, but continues indefinitely backward through a succession of incarnations. According to the law of karma, our birth is the result of our past lives, in each of which, and in the present life, we possess the same mind. In the 'unconscious mind', if we may adopt the Freudian term, are stored the impressions and the tendencies which have been formed in our previous existences, and in our present existence up to this moment, and which, taken together, have made us what we are.

The saṁskāras, or potentialities, represent therefore the root impressions received from all our past experiences, including those of our former lives, and they have moulded our characters so that, even though largely forgotten, they still indirectly control or influence our every act and thought. They may also take on fresh life and potency without our conscious effort or will. Now Yoga philosophy—and this is the very core of its doctrine—proposes a discipline whereby these root impressions may first be overcome, and then destroyed, and whereby in consequence a complete transformation of character may in the end be effected. Yoga psychology agrees with Freud that the conscious is controlled and guided by the unconscious, but it insists that there is a power inherent in the mind through which the mind, restraining itself, can overcome the unconscious and all its tendencies, and achieve by so doing a complete renewal. Thus is its original purity restored—a purity that reflects the supreme purity and infinite knowledge of the Puruṣa. Thus at last does the Puruṣa learn his true nature—his utter separateness from prakṛti—and attain to freedom.

Any thought-wave arising in the mind, or any perception apprehended by the mind, is a vṛtti—or what we have called an actual state. The objects of perception and of thought are innumerable: innumerable, therefore, are the vṛttis. These Patañjali has roughly classified into two main divisions: kliṣṭa, painful, and akliṣṭa, not painful. A painful wave, according to Patañjali's use of the term, is not necessarily a wave which *seems* painful when it first arises in the mind; it is a wave which brings with it an increased degree of ignorance, addiction, and bondage. Similarly, a wave which seems painful at first may actually belong to the category of the not painful, provided that it impels the mind toward greater freedom and knowledge. For example, Patañjali would describe a lustful thought-wave as painful, because lust, even when pleasantly satisfied, causes addiction, jealousy, and bondage to the person desired. A wave of pity, on the other hand, he would describe as not painful, because pity is an unselfish emotion which loosens the bonds of our egotism. We may suffer deeply when we see others suffering, but our pity will teach us understanding—and hence freedom.

This distinction between the two kinds of thought-wave is very important in the practice of yoga discipline. For the thought-waves cannot all be controlled at once. First, we have to overcome the painful thought-waves by raising waves which are not painful. To our thoughts of anger, desire, and delusion, we must oppose thoughts of love, generosity, and truth. Only much later, when the painful thought-waves have been completely stilled, can we proceed to the second stage of discipline: the stilling of the not painful waves which we have deliberately created.

The idea that we should ultimately have to overcome even those thought-waves which are good, pure, and truthful may at first seem shocking to a student who has been trained in the Western approach to morality. But a little reflection will show him that this must be so. The external world, even in its most beautiful appearances and noblest manifestations, is still superficial and transient. It is not the basic reality. We must look through it, not at it, in order to see the Puruṣa. Certainly, it is better to love than to hate, better to share than to hoard, better to tell the truth than to lie. But the thought-waves which motivate the practice of virtue are nevertheless disturbances in the mind. We all know instances of admirable, earnest men who become so deeply involved in the cares of a great reform movement or social relief project that they cannot think of anything beyond the practical problems of their daily work. Their minds are not calm. They are full of anxiety and restlessness. The mind of the truly illumined man is calm—not because he is selfishly indifferent to the needs of others, but because he perceives the peace of the Puruṣa within all things, even within the appearance of misery, disease, strife, and want.[1]

Now it is a characteristic of the citta, the mind, that it tends both towards good and towards evil. Vyāsa, an ancient commentator, compares it to a river that should flow at the same time in opposite directions. Though, again, the citta plays this dual role, its tendency towards good, the will to freedom inherent in every man, is the greater of the opposed forces. Having noted this superior strength of the will to freedom, Professor Das Gupta observes, in substance:

This point is rather remarkable. It affirms that there is within us, at bottom, a greater desire for liberation than for what as ordinary human beings we count as pleasure or happiness.

[1] 'A holy man is freed from all saṁskāras, but the thought-wave of compassion stays with him to the last moment of his life.'—Śrī Rāmakṛṣṇa.

Could it be, one wonders, that the will to freedom described in Yoga philosophy is the force which Freud wrongly interprets as the 'death-instinct'? Freud finds within us two innate tendencies: the life-instinct and the death-instinct. But the death-instinct is not, he thinks, to be found in its pure form, but is inextricably mixed with its opposite, the life-instinct—a theory that would explain the strange phenomena of sadism and masochism and the feeling of alternate love and hate towards the same object. We are not concerned, however, with the truth or falsity of Freud's explanation of the phenomena we have just mentioned, but rather with the fact that by his characterization of the two instincts as antithetical he almost arrived at the position taken by Yoga psychology—and yet somehow failed to do so. Yoga mentions the two opposed instincts: the will to live and the will to freedom. The will to liberation exists, according to Yoga, side by side with the will to live (the will to desire), though in some men it is dormant and in others expressed. It is the principal purpose of Yoga psychology to show how the will to freedom, the higher will, may be strengthened and the will to live overcome.

As the will to freedom gains in strength, the will to live, what Freud calls the life-instinct, grows weaker. Evidence of this fact may be seen in the lives of all who check impulse and desire. And, strange though it may seem, impulse and desire can be completely overcome, though the will to freedom cannot.

The concrete means by which spiritual control is exercised Patañjali analyses in considerable detail. Control comes, he says, 'from practice and nonattachment'.

By 'practice' is meant, he tells us, the exercise of the ethical and spiritual disciplines. These are yama, cultivating of moral virtues, such as truthfulness, noninjury, continence; niyama, acquiring regular habits of study and worship; āsana, sitting quietly in order to achieve tranquillity; prāṇāyāma, taking breathing exercises in order to gain control of the mind; pratyāhāra, freeing the mind from the thraldom of the senses; dhāraṇā, concentrating; dhyāna, meditating; and samādhi, rising to the superconscious state.[1]

The eight disciplines we are to practise, and along with the practice, says the yogi, we must sow the seed of nonattachment in our hearts. In fact, practice and nonattachment must go together. Nonattachment, in Patañjali's words, is 'that effect which comes to those who have given up their thirst after objects either seen or heard'.

There are stages of nonattachment through which we pass, the commentators point out, as we practise the yoga disciplines and as we strive to attain to complete renunciation. There are four such stages. The first is yatamāna, during which there arises an inner

[1] These 'limbs of yoga', as they are called, are later explained more fully.

struggle from our not permitting the mind to seek gratification of the senses. The second is vyatireka, during which, through self-analysis, we realize the measure of our own achievement in the field of self-control. We realize what desires we can control and what we as yet cannot. Then with vigour and enthusiasm we must continue to attack all desires that still remain in the way of illumination. The third is ekendriya, during which greater self-control is achieved, and the heart no longer desires the objects of enjoyment, knowing their ephemeral and shadowy nature; yet there may still remain in it a longing curiosity. When this longing also has been overcome, we attain the fourth and highest stage of renunciation. This is known as vaśīkāra.

This, the supreme goal of renunciation, is achieved only by him who has attained complete enlightenment. 'When, through knowledge of the Puruṣa, one ceases to desire any manifestation of prakṛti, then one experiences the highest kind of nonattachment,'[1] says Patañjali. And the Gītā says:

> The abstinent run away from what they desire
> But carry their desires with them:
> When a man enters Reality,
> He leaves his desires behind him.[2]

Again the Gītā, summing up the whole truth of yoga:

> 'When men have thrown off their ignorance, they are free from pride and delusion. They have conquered the evil of worldly attachment. They live in constant union with the Atman. All craving has left them. They are no longer at the mercy of opposing sense-reactions. Thus they reach that state which is beyond all change.'[3]

How to Become a Yogi

Bhoja, the commentator, indicates how rare are the souls who at birth are endowed with minds having an aptitude for yoga. Most men, he says, have to mature slowly as they gradually equip themselves with minds fit for practising it. And the learned commentator proceeds to discover in minds five types.

The first three of these may be grouped together. The first is the scattered mind, which is filled with rajas and impelled by its power to be ever in search of excitement in the external world; never at rest, but ever tossed up and down by the waves that bring to it the manifold experiences of pleasure and pain. The second is the dull

[1] *Yoga Aphorisms*, I. 16. [2] II. 59. [3] XV. 5.

mind, its perceptions veiled by the power of tamas; such a mind revolts from undertaking even the obligatory duties of life and is a slave to low passions. The third is the middling or average mind, restless at times and again momentarily calm and serene. Those possessed of minds represented by one or another of these three types are not suited to higher yoga practices. They must first undergo the preliminary disciplines of habitual ethical conduct.

Bhoja's fourth and fifth types, unlike the others, are one-pointed, concentrated. Whenever sattwa predominates in it the mind is characterized by a natural purity; it is tranquil, never agitated by the rise of passions from below, but possessing the power of control over them, and it rises continually towards higher and higher planes of being. Such is the one-pointed mind. The concentrated mind not only is pure and tranquil, but also is absorbed in the contemplation of Puruṣa, the Self, or God, forgetful of the body.

Attaining the state of absorption, and advancing beyond it to samādhi and illumination, can come only gradually, step by step, and only by following the prescribed rules of conduct and the other practices of yoga. In a general way the necessary discipline has been defined by Patañjali in the following aphorism: 'The concentration of the true spiritual aspirant is attained through faith, strenuousness, recollectedness, absorption and illumination.'[1]

The primary requirement is faith. The word faith, however, must not be understood in its generally accepted meaning of belief in something that reason cannot penetrate. At the very beginning there must be understanding, a conviction in the mind; then comes the effort to have faith—which means response in the heart. Most people, in an abstract sort of way, believe in the existence of God. But as to *realizing* God—few do anything about that. When one has faith, one will *act* on that faith. Bhoja, the commentator, explains the Sanskrit word śraddhā, translated faith, as signifying a condition in which the heart is 'pleasantly inclined towards attaining yoga'.

There must, moreover, be spiritual strenuousness. Buddha pointed out that if there is any sin it is laziness. Strenuousness grows by strenuous acts. As faith increases and strenuousness grows, the mind takes a direction. It becomes *recollected*, in the basic meaning of this word. Our thoughts have been scattered all over the mental field. Now we begin to gather them together and direct them toward a definite goal—knowledge of the Puruṣa. As we do this, we find ourselves becoming increasingly absorbed in the thought of God. And so, at length, absorption merges in illumination, and the knowledge is ours.

Success in yoga depends upon the amount of energy we put forth

[1] *Yoga Aphorisms*, I. 20.

in our struggles for its attainment. Patañjali says: 'Success in yoga comes quickly to those who are intensely energetic'; and to the same purpose: 'Success varies according to the strength of the effort expended to attain it—mild, moderate, or intense.'[1]

Again, in order that we may put forth energy for success in yoga, we must remove certain physical and mental obstacles that stand in the way. 'Sickness, mental laziness, doubt, lack of enthusiasm, sloth, craving for sense-pleasure, false perception, despair caused by failure to concentrate and unsteadiness in concentration: these distractions are the obstacles to knowledge. These distractions are accompanied by grief, despondency, trembling of the body, and irregular breathing. They can be removed by the practice of concentration upon a single truth.'[2]

In order to achieve this concentration, we must calm and purify our minds. Patañjali tells us how to do this.

'Undisturbed calmness of mind is attained by cultivating friendliness toward the happy, compassion for the unhappy, delight in the virtuous, and indifference toward the wicked.'[3]

Hatred, jealousy, fear—in short, the restless, distracted states of mind—are the root causes of most of our physical and mental ills. Every reaction in the form of hatred, or jealousy, or anger, is so much loss to body and mind, and each time we restrain ourselves from such reactions, good energy is stored up in our favour for conversion into higher powers. In order, again, that we may restrain ourselves from the evil reactions to the end that we may establish our minds in tranquillity, Patañjali advises that we assume a mental attitude that will purify our hearts and bring peace of mind. He teaches that we must learn to be happy in the happiness of others; that we must be merciful towards those who are in pain. Let us be glad when others do good deeds and be indifferent to the wicked. By raising opposite waves in the mind, the waves of love and friendliness and mercy, we may overcome offensive mental waves of jealousy, hatred, and anger. By arousing tranquillity in the heart through such transforming practices, we also free ourselves from physical and mental ills.

This consideration of how to gain control over the mind leads us to think of the preliminary disciplines that work towards yoga. In the words of St Paul, which we have already quoted, the spiritual life requires a 'renewing of the mind', and this is achieved by a gradual entire readjustment of outlook and habits; for the impurities of the mind are nothing else than habits of life and thought, and to overcome one set of habits one must form another and contrary set of habits. This process consists in the practice of kriyā yoga, the accessory

[1] *Yoga Aphorisms*, I. 21–2. [2] *Ibid.*, I. 30–2. [3] *Ibid.*, I. 33.

disciplines of yoga: 'austerity, study, and the dedication of the fruits of one's work to God'.[1]

Austerity is the practice of conserving energy and directing it towards the goal of yoga, towards realizing the true nature of the Puruṣa. Obviously, in order to engage in this, we must exercise self-discipline; we must control our physical appetites and passions. In the Gītā, the three kinds of true austerity are defined: 'Reverence for the devas, the seers, the teachers, and the sages; straightforwardness, harmlessness, physical cleanliness, and sexual purity—these are the virtues whose practice is called austerity of the body. To speak without ever causing pain to another, to be truthful, to say always what is kind and beneficial, and to study the scriptures regularly—this practice is called austerity of speech. The practice of serenity, sympathy, meditation upon the Atman, withdrawal of the mind from sense-objects, and integrity of motive, is called austerity of the mind.'[2]

The practice of austerity, as described by commentators on the *Yoga Aphorisms*, may also include the regular performance of ritualistic worship. The observance of ritualism is an excellent training for the wandering mind of the beginner. Each successive act recalls his mind to the thought behind the act. He is too busy to think of anything else. Thought and action, action and thought, form a continuous chain; and it is amazing to find what a comparatively high degree of concentration he can achieve, even from the very first.

'It is of vital importance', said Swami Brahmananda, my master, 'that a man begin his spiritual journey from where he is. If an average man is instructed to meditate on his union with the absolute Brahman, he will not understand. He will neither grasp the truth that lies behind the instructions nor be able to follow them. . . . However, . . . if that same man is asked to worship God with flowers, incense, and other accessories of the ritualistic worship, his mind will gradually become concentrated on God, and he will find joy in his worship.'[3]

'Study' in the context of the *Aphorisms*—it should be noted—means study of the scriptures and of other books which deal with the spiritual life. It also refers to the practice of japa, the repetition of the sacred name of God.

To dedicate the fruits of one's work to God is to work with non-attachment, to practise karma yoga.

[1] *Yoga Aphorisms*, II. 1.
[2] XVII. 14–16.
[3] Swami Prabhavananda, *The Eternal Companion*, p. 115.

The Goal of Yoga

All the great religions hold as a primary article of their faith that the Self is innately pure and divine. 'God made man in his own image.' All of them hold, further, that that original purity and that divinity have somehow been lost. Christianity attributes the fall of man from his pristine state of innocence to the fall of the first man, Adam, and believes that now we are 'born in sin and iniquity' through having inherited his weakness and that we can be saved only through the grace of a merciful heavenly Father as revealed in the sacrifice of his Son, Jesus Christ. The truth in this doctrine would appear to be that man in his original nature is innocent and pure, a perfect image of God, but that as an effect of some inexplicable cause he has lost his pristine attributes. The sin which the story of the Fall of Adam informs us we have inherited cannot, however, be real and permanent, cannot really have altered our original nature. Christianity itself offers us the goal of conquest over sin and the attainment of liberation and a renewed perfection: we are to become perfect—even as the 'Father which is in heaven is perfect'. This goal would be meaningless, because it could never be attained, had we been born in sin. For it is not possible to change the innate character of a substance without destroying the substance itself. One cannot change the nature of fire, which by that very nature must radiate heat, except by destroying fire itself. Nevertheless its inborn nature, its heat, may be smothered by a covering of ash. Remove the ash, fan the fire, and you will again have both fire and heat. The same thing is true of the Self—its innate purity and divinity may be covered by ignorance but not lost. Indian philosophy proclaims: 'You are forever free and divine. Your apparent imperfection is due to ignorance; realize what you are, and be free.' The same truth appears in Christian teachings, although it may not be recognized as such by all theologians, for does not the Bible say: 'The light shineth in darkness; and the darkness comprehended it not'?

We are pure, free, and divine. Suffering, sin, limitations, and all imperfections are due to avidyā, ignorance, which veils the true nature of the Self, causing us to identify ourselves with the non-Self. Patañjali says:

'The obstacles to enlightenment—the causes of man's sufferings—are ignorance, egoism, attachment, aversion, and the desire to cling to life.'

And again:

'To regard the non-eternal as eternal, the impure as pure, the painful as pleasant and the non-Self as the Puruṣa—this is ignorance.'[1]

The ignorance is of course universal, and is the basis of our ordinary, finite lives, the cause of all conditioned experience.

Ignorance, says Patañjali, leads to egoism, attachment, aversion, and the desire to cling to life—the immediate causes of suffering and confusion.

'To identify consciousness with that which merely reflects consciousness—this is egoism.'[2]

The central act of ignorance is the identification of the Puruṣa, which is consciousness itself, with the mind-body—'that which merely reflects consciousness'. This is what Patañjali defines as egoism.

'At whose behest does the mind think?' asks the Kena Upaniṣad. 'Who bids the body live? Who makes the tongue speak? Who is that effulgent Being that directs the eye to form and colour and the ear to sound? The Atman is the ear of the ear, mind of the mind, speech of the speech. He is also breath of the breath and eye of the eye. Having given up the false identification of the Atman with the senses and the mind, and knowing the Atman to be Brahman, the wise become immortal.'[3]

Western philosophy has produced two schools of thought with regard to the problem of consciousness—the materialist and the idealist. The materialists believe that consciousness is the product of a process; that it arises when certain conditions are fulfilled and is lost when these conditions do not exist. Thus, according to the materialist philosophers, consciousness is not the property of any single substance. The idealists, on the other hand, believe that consciousness is the property of the mind, and are therefore faced with the conclusion that it must cease whenever the mind becomes unconscious.

Modern scientists would seem inclined to reject both these hypotheses, and to believe that consciousness is always present everywhere in the universe, even though its presence cannot always be detected by scientific methods. In this they approach the viewpoint of Vedānta. And indeed there are some distinguished scientists and scientific writers whose thinking has brought them to a study of Hindu philosophy. For example, Erwin Schrödinger in his book *What is Life?* writes as follows:

'Consciousness is never experienced in the plural, only in the singular.... How does the idea of plurality (so emphatically opposed by the Upanishad writers) arise at all? Consciousness finds itself

[1] *Yoga Aphorisms*, II. 3, 5. [2] *Ibid.*, II. 6. [3] I. 1–2.

intimately connected with, and dependent on, the physical state of a limited region of matter, the body. . . . Now, there is a great plurality of similar bodies. Hence the pluralization of consciousness or minds seems a very suggestive hypothesis. Probably all simple ingenuous people, as well as the great majority of Western philosophers, have accepted it. . . . The only possible alternative is simply to keep to the immediate experience that consciousness is a singular of which the plural is unknown; that there *is* only one thing and that, what seems to be a plurality, is merely a series of different aspects of this one thing, produced by a deception (the Indian Maya); the same illusion is produced in a gallery of mirrors, and in the same way Gaurisankar and Mount Everest turned out to be the same peak seen from different valleys. . . .

'Yet each of us has the undisputable impression that the sum total of his own experience and memory forms a unit, quite distinct from that of any other person. He refers to it as "I". *What is this "I"?*

'If you analyse it closely you will, I think, find that it is just a little bit more than a collection of single data (experiences and memories), namely the canvas *upon which* they are collected. And you will, on close introspection, find that, what you really mean by "I", is that ground-stuff upon which they are collected. You may come to a distant country, lose sight of all your friends, may all but forget them; you acquire new friends, you share life with them as intensely as you ever did with your old ones. Less and less important will become that fact that, while living your new life, you still recollect the old one. "The youth that was I", you may come to speak of him in the third person, indeed the protagonist of the novel you are reading is probably nearer to your heart, certainly more intensely alive and better known to you. Yet there has been no intermediate break, no death. And even if a skilled hypnotist succeeded in blotting out entirely all your earlier reminiscences, you would not find that he had killed *you*. In no case is there a loss of personal existence to deplore. Nor will there ever be.'[1]

The mind merely reflects consciousness and is the instrument of perception and experience; the identification of the Puruṣa, who is consciousness itself, with the instrument, the mind, is, as we have seen, egoism. We say 'I am happy' or 'I am suffering', but happiness or suffering is but waves of thought arising in the mind. Through egoism the Self, becoming identified with the mind, identifies itself with the waves or thoughts in the mind, and either enjoys or suffers.

Through egoism there arises the desire for pleasurable sense experiences, and there grows attachment to them. Desire for

[1] (New York: Cambridge University Press, 1955), pp. 90 ff.

sensational and emotional experiences and attachment to them cause suffering. Therefore attachment to those experiences and a desire for them must be avoided if we are to obtain tranquillity of mind and heart. Opposed to attachment is aversion, which is also a cause of suffering, and to be avoided. Śrī Kṛṣṇa says in the Gītā,

> When he has no lust, no hatred,
> A man walks safely among the things of lust and hatred.
> To obey the Atman
> Is his peaceful joy:
> Sorrow melts
> Into that clear peace:
> His quiet mind
> Is soon established in peace.[1]

Not a complete withdrawal of the senses from the world, nor a denial of the normal experiences of life, is required for tranquillity of mind, but a freeing of the mind from both attraction and aversion.

The last of the 'pain-bearing obstructions', according to Patañjali, is the desire to cling to life, a feeling which may perhaps be correlated with Freud's life-instinct. Commentators have explained it as fear of death, which exists instinctively in all living beings. This fear of death is another cause of unhappiness.

These five causes of suffering are the chief obstacles in the path of yoga; of them all, ignorance is the root cause. They exist universally in all beings, though in different states and degrees in different people. Patañjali says, 'They may exist either in a potential or a vestigial form, or they may have been temporarily overcome or fully developed.'[2]

In most people these obstacles exist fully developed, in some in a repressed or overpowered condition. Through the practices of yoga and self-discipline, they may be attenuated and finally destroyed.

The goal of yoga is to eradicate these obstacles completely and thus to remove the causes of suffering. The root cause, as we have seen, is ignorance, which is the 'productive field' for all other obstacles; and its removal is possible by means of its opposite, vidyā, or knowledge. Patañjali says, 'Ignorance is destroyed by awakening to knowledge of the Puruṣa, until no trace of illusion remains.'[3] This knowledge that removes the ignorance is not knowledge such as is associated with the intellect, but rather an immediate, direct illumination in one's own soul. 'The experiencer gains this knowledge', says Patañjali, 'in seven stages, advancing toward the highest.'[4]

[1] II. 64.
[2] *Yoga Aphorisms*, II. 4.
[3] *Ibid.*, II. 26.
[4] *Ibid.*, II. 27.

The seven stages are as follows:

(*a*) The realization that the source of all spiritual wisdom is inside ourselves; that the kingdom of heaven is within us. As Swami Vivekananda says:

'After long searches here and there, in temples and churches, in earths and in heavens, at last you come back, completing the circle from where you started, to your own soul and find that He, for whom you have been seeking all over the world, for whom you have been weeping and praying in churches and temples, on whom you were looking as the mystery of all mysteries shrouded in the clouds, is nearest of the near, is your own Self, the reality of your life, body and soul.'[1]

These are stirring words, to which our hearts can immediately respond; but a firm realization of their truth is not so easily achieved. It is not enough to accept it as an intellectual proposition. It is not enough to glimpse it in moments of religious emotion or temporary insight. We cannot claim to have reached the first stage until we are continuously aware of the presence of the Ātman, or Puruṣa,[2] within us. When we are aware of this, we know also, without any doubt, that union with the Ātman is possible, since no external obstacles can arise to prevent it.

(*b*) The cessation of pain. Pain, as we have seen, is caused by our attachment or aversion to the phenomena of the external universe. As the mind turns inward towards knowledge of the Ātman, this attachment or aversion loses its power. We have already quoted the Gītā's phrase: 'Yoga is the breaking of contact with pain.'[3]

(*c*) Samādhi—complete realization of, and union with, the Ātman. The objective universe disappears. The Ātman is experienced as total existence, consciousness, and joy. In this experience all sense of individual separateness and differentiation is lost.

(*d*) The state of consciousness following samādhi. When a man comes out of samādhi, he returns to consciousness of the objective universe; but this consciousness differs from the kind which we all experience. To one who has achieved samādhi, the external world is known to be merely an appearance. In Śaṁkara's phrase, 'it is and is not'. The man of illumination no longer identifies the external world with the Ātman. He sees that it is only a reflection of the Ātman—not, indeed, utterly unreal, since it is projected by the Reality; yet

[1] *Complete Works of Vivekananda*, vol. II, pp. 81–2.

[2] Ātman and Puruṣa are interchangeable terms.

[3] VI. 23.

lacking substance and independent existence, like an image in a mirror.

In this stage, a man knows that he is no longer bound by any worldly duty or obligation. This does not mean, of course, that a man who has achieved samādhi will thenceforward do nothing at all. On the contrary, most of the great saints have been very active, particularly in teaching others. 'They are like big steamships,' said Śrī Rāmakṛṣṇa, 'which not only cross the ocean themselves but carry many passengers to the other shore.' But the actions of the saint differ from the actions of ordinary men, because they are not motivated by any attachment or selfish desire. They are, in the most literal sense of the word, voluntary actions. Action, for the rest of us, is only partially voluntary; it always contains an element of compulsion due to our past karmas and present involvements in the life of the senses. For this reason, the behaviour of a saint is often very hard for us to understand; it seems strange, arbitrary, or capricious, precisely because it is not subject to our familiar compulsions. A great teacher was once asked to explain one of the most seemingly mysterious actions recorded in the Gospels, Christ's cursing of the barren fig tree. 'Become a Christ,' he replied smilingly, 'and then you will know why he did that.'

(*e*) Freedom from need of the mind and the objective world—the realization that the mind and the objective world have both ended their services. The mind has been the instrument, and the world the object of the experience whereby the experiencer has come to know the Ātman, his real nature. The mind has been used to transcend the mind—just as we use a ladder to transcend a ladder: once we have reached the sill of the window against which it rested, the ladder can be kicked away; we do not need it any more.

(*f*) Freedom from impressions and guṇas. Now the stored-up impressions within the mind, and the guṇas themselves, fall away forever, like rocks, to quote one of the classic commentators, 'fallen from the top of the mountain peak, never to return'.

(*g*) Union with the Ātman. And so the final stage is reached—the state of eternal existence in union with the Ātman. Now there is no more returning from samādhi to partial sense-consciousness, no more identification of the Ātman with the mind. We realize, in the words of Vivekananda,

'. . . that we have been alone throughout all time, neither body nor mind was ever related, much less joined, to us. They were working their own way and we, through ignorance, joined ourselves to them. But we have been alone, omnipotent, omnipresent, ever blessed; our own Atman was so pure and perfect that we required nothing else. . . . Throughout the universe there can be nothing that will not become effulgent before our knowledge. This will be the last state, and the yogi will become peaceful and calm, never to feel any more pain, never to be again deluded, never to be touched by misery. He will know that he is ever blessed, ever perfect, almighty.'[1]

The Limbs of Yoga

Two of the yoga aphorisms provide the text for this section:

> 'As soon as all impurities have been removed by the practice of spiritual disciplines—the "limbs" of yoga—a man's spirit opens to the light-giving knowledge of the Puruṣa.
>
> 'The eight limbs of yoga are: the various forms of abstention from evil-doing (yama), the various observances (niyama), posture (āsana), control of the prāṇa (prāṇāyāma), withdrawal of the mind from sense objects (pratyāhāra), concentration (dhāraṇā), meditation (dhyāna), and absorption in the Puruṣa (samādhi).'[2]

Yoga has been aptly compared to a tree bearing luscious fruit. The seed of the yoga-tree is nourished by yama and niyama; as it begins to germinate it is further fed by posture and prāṇāyāma; and as it matures and becomes a full-grown tree it bears flowers in the practice of pratyāhāra, and abundant fruits in concentration, meditation, and samādhi.

So important are the eight limbs that each will be accorded special comment.

Yama, the first, has been analysed in the two following aphorisms:

> 'Yama is the abstention from harming others, from falsehood, from theft, from incontinence, and from greed.
>
> 'These forms of abstention are basic rules of conduct. They must be practiced without any reservations as to time, place, purpose, or caste rules.'[3]

It will be noticed that yama, thus understood, embraces the ethical principles universally taught in all the great religions.

Abstention from harming others is living and acting in such a way as never to cause any pain to a living soul by one's thought, word, or deed. It is said to be the greatest of the virtues. In its positive aspect the injunction is to do good to all and to learn to live in love and harmony with all.

[1] *Complete Works of Vivekananda*, vol. I, pp. 258–9.

[2] *Yoga Aphorisms*, II. 28, 29.

[3] *Ibid.*, II. 30, 31.

'When a man becomes steadfast in his abstention from harming others, then all creatures will cease to feel enmity in his presence.'[1]

When a man has truly and entirely renounced violence in his own thoughts, and in his dealings with others, he begins to create an atmosphere around himself within which violence and enmity must cease to exist, because they find no reciprocation. Animals too are sensitive to such an atmosphere. There is a saying that the tiger and the lamb will play together before a true yogi. 'The test of ahimsa [harmlessness] is absence of jealousy, . . .' said Swami Vivekananda. 'The so-called great men of the world may all be seen to become jealous of each other for a small name, for a little fame, and for a few bits of gold. So long as this jealousy exists in a heart, it is far away from the perfection of ahimsa.'[2]

Abstention from falsehood is truthfulness in thought, word, and deed. In the Gītā we are admonished 'to speak without ever causing pain to another, to be truthful, and to say always what is kind and beneficial'. And thus Patañjali:

'When a man becomes steadfast in his abstention from falsehood he gets the power of obtaining for himself and others the fruits of good deeds, without having to perform the deeds themselves.'[3]

Such a man cannot think or even dream a lie; everything he says is or becomes true. Facts, as it were, follow his words. If he blesses someone, that person becomes blessed.

Abstention from theft has a deeper significance than what the phrase literally means. We must realize that nothing belongs to us; consequently, we may not harbour the idea of possession or own attachment to things of this world. 'When a man becomes steadfast in his abstention from theft, all wealth comes to him.'[4] Swami Vivekananda, commenting upon this aphorism, remarks, 'The more you fly from nature, the more she follows you, and if you do not care for her at all, she becomes your slave.'[5]

Abstention from incontinence is chastity in thought, word, and deed. 'When a man becomes steadfast in his abstention from incontinence, he acquires spiritual energy.'[6] Such energy is indispensable to a religious teacher. With it comes tremendous force and gigantic will to turn humanity into the path of good.

Abstention from greed is freedom from covetousness.

The foregoing are the virtues included under yama.

[1] *Yoga Aphorisms*, II. 35.
[2] *Complete Works of Vivekananda*, vol. III, pp. 67–8.
[3] *Yoga Aphorisms*, II. 36.
[4] *Ibid.*, II. 37.
[5] *Complete Works of Vivekananda*, vol. I, p. 263.
[6] *Yoga Aphorisms*, II. 38.

The second limb of yoga is niyama. Patañjali has defined it thus:

'The niyamas [observances] are purity, contentment, mortification, study, and devotion to God.'[1]

Purity is cleanliness, both physical and mental. Just as a regular habit of bathing is formed for physical cleanliness, in the same way a regular habit is to be formed of bathing our inner organ, the mind, by feeling within it the living presence of God. From the practice of cleanliness, physical and mental, 'one achieves purification of the heart, cheerfulness of mind, the power of concentration, control of the passions, and fitness for the vision of the Puruṣa'.[2]

Commenting on this aphorism, Swami Vivekananda remarks:

'The first sign of your becoming religious is that you are becoming cheerful. When a man is gloomy, his condition may be dyspepsia, but it is not religion. To the yogi everything is bliss, every human face that he sees brings cheerfulness to him. This is the sign of a virtuous man.'[3]

Contentment is the practice of quiet acceptance of whatever comes in the course of our lives, and the maintenance of an inner poise.

The remaining three regular habits have already been discussed in our explanation of kriyā yoga, that is, the preliminary practices for achieving growth towards yoga. We may note, however, that study, which has been interpreted as the chanting of sacred words and prayers, is of three kinds: verbal, semi-verbal, and mental. The first is audible chanting; the second is the moving of the lips from which no sound issues as one repeats the sacred word; and the third is the repetition of the sacred word in the mind. In all these cases repetition must be accompanied by meditation upon the meaning of the word or prayer.

For the effective practice of the virtues mentioned above, Patañjali suggests: 'To be free from thoughts that distract one from yoga, thoughts of an opposite kind must be cultivated.'[4] When a wave of anger, for example, has entered the mind, let it be controlled by raising an opposite wave of love.

Yama and niyama are the first two limbs of yoga; āsana, posture, is the third. A series of exercises, for the most part mental, is to be followed each day until certain of the higher states of consciousness

[1] *Yoga Aphorisms*, II. 32.
[2] *Ibid.*, II. 41.
[3] *Complete Works of Vivekananda*, vol. I, p. 264.
[4] *Yoga Aphorisms*, II. 33.

are reached. It is necessary that we should learn to be seated in a firm position, Patañjali advising that the easiest and most natural one should be chosen. 'Proper posture requires that one be seated in a position which is firm but relaxed.'[1] The Gītā says, 'His posture must be motionless, with the body, head and neck held erect . . .'[2] Swami Vivekananda suggests, 'Let the whole weight of the body be supported by the ribs, and then you have an easy, natural posture, with the spine straight.'[3] In one of the Sāṁkhya Sūtras we read: 'Any posture which is easy and steady is an āsana; there is no other rule.'[4]

With regard to posture Patañjali gives this advice:

'Posture becomes firm and relaxed through control of the natural tendencies of the body, and through meditation on the Infinite.'[5]

The purpose of āsana is to calm the mind; and calm is achieved if when seated we meditate on the all-pervading presence of God, or fix our minds upon some thought concerning vastness or infinitude. 'Thereafter, one is no longer troubled by the dualities of sense-experience.'[6] After a period during which we observe our bodies in a certain posture, we gain in control over them, and then the dualities, heat and cold and the other pairs of opposites in our empirical lives, cease to disturb the equilibrium of our minds.

In this connection it may be interesting to learn what Vedānta

[1] *Yoga Aphorisms*, II. 46.
[2] VI. 13.
[3] *Complete Works of Vivekananda*, vol. I, p. 138.
[4] The posture as taught by Patañjali has nothing to do with the postures and practices mistakenly associated with the word yoga. The West, ignorantly, has connected the word yoga with acrobatic feats, sword-swallowing, lying on spikes, crystal-gazing, and so on. The so-called yogis who are to be met with in the busy streets of Banaras or in the places of pilgrimage are never regarded by the Hindus as genuine yogis. They make a practice of showing their feats, or lie in the public gaze, proclaiming the mortification of their flesh in order to obtain a few cents from the credulous and the ignorant. They are misguided in the same way as are the American pole-sitters and marathon dancers, and their number is correspondingly small. Unfortunately, however, the pictures of these fakirs are printed and reprinted in American newspapers and magazines as pictures of the genuine yogis of India.

In hatha yoga, which is radically different from Patañjali's system, greater importance is attached to the practice of āsanas, or postures. Hatha yoga is a system of physical exercises and can hardly be correlated with systems the purpose of which is the attainment of spiritual freedom. Physical health is its principal objective. Many of the exercises in posture are not dissimilar to the practices recommended by Delsarte and other Western teachers. The hatha-yoga exercises no doubt have definite therapeutic value.

[5] *Yoga Aphorisms*, II. 47.
[6] *Ibid.*, II. 48.

philosophy has to say with respect to posture. The following are aphorisms from Vyāsa:

'Worship is possible in a sitting posture, because this encourages meditation. The meditating person is compared to the immovable earth. There is no law of place; wherever the mind is concentrated, there worship should be performed.'[1]

The fourth limb of yoga is prāṇāyāma. This word means control of vital energy, or of the life-principle. Just what the life-principle really is, no one can tell, but we do recognize its expression. It is the energy that enables us to act, to think, to breathe. Prāṇāyāma is control of this energy, and the word has come to be associated with breathing exercises based on a principle somewhat analogous to that propounded by William James to the Western world. The principle may be stated thus: The mind and the body are closely related, and act and react upon each other; emotions cause characteristic changes in the body, and changes in the body evoke corresponding emotions in the mind. On this principle of experimental psychology, discovered in the West in recent years, but known to the yogis of India from almost a beginningless past, there is taught control of the breath to bring calmness and concentration to the mind. The state of the mind, whether it be lethargic or restless or calm, is first observed in the breathing, for the rise of passions brings about characteristic changes in the way we breathe. If, then, breathing can be made rhythmic, calm is the inevitable result. If, moreover, the mind is in process of concentration, we scarcely breathe, and when the mind is in a state of complete concentration, we do not breathe at all. Prāṇāyāma needs therefore to be practised first in order to win control over the body and mind, and finally to control the very life energy itself. In the words of Swami Vivekananda:

'In this body of ours, the breath motion is the "silken thread"; by laying hold of and learning to control it we grasp the pack thread of the nerve currents, and from these the stout twine of our thoughts, and lastly the rope of prana, controlling which we reach freedom.'[2]

According to Patañjali, the prāṇāyāma consists of three parts: inhalation, exhalation, and pause. This pause may be either internal, when the breath is held in the lungs, or external, when it is prevented from entering them. A fourth kind of prāṇāyāma exists when in the

[1] Vedānta Sūtras, IV. i. 7–9, 11.
[2] *Complete Works of Vivekananda*, vol. I, pp. 143–4.

process of meditation the yogi enters the stage of kumbhaka, or natural cessation of breath.[1]

The fifth in order of the limbs of yoga is pratyāhāra, the practice undertaken to gain detachment of the mind from objects of sense by not permitting the mind to join itself to the centres of perception or the organs of sense. In the words of the Gītā:

> The tortoise can draw in its legs:
> The seer can draw in his senses.
> I call him illumined.[2]

That is pratyāhāra. Swami Vivekananda remarks:

'He who has succeeded in attaching his mind to the centres of perception at will, or in detaching it from them, has succeeded in pratyahara, which means "gathering towards", checking the outgoing powers of the mind, freeing it from the thraldom of the senses. When we can do this we shall really possess character; then alone we shall have taken a long step towards freedom.'[3]

[1] I have purposely refrained from giving the breathing exercises known to the yogis, for they should never be practised without previous instruction from an adept teacher. Many books published in America on the subject of yoga describe breathing exercises which are not the prāṇāyāma as taught by Patañjali, but rather that belonging to the school of hatha yoga. I am certain that those who write indiscriminately of yoga breathing exercises do much unintentional harm. For these exercises are dangerous to the beginner without the proper personal guidance. Furthermore, it is my opinion that the many varieties of breathing exercises taught by hatha yogis are dangerous even when practised under the supervision of teachers skilled in hatha yoga. They may sometimes aid in building the physical body, but they just as often injure the brain. There are instances in India, to my personal knowledge, of men who have become mentally unbalanced by such practices. Unfortunately an interest in breathing exercises that go by the name of yoga has been created in America by irresponsible authors and teachers.

I do not wish, however, to entirely disappoint readers who may wish some healthful exercises for their individual practice. Preliminary to prāṇāyāma there is a breathing exercise which is very easy to practise and quite harmless. As great an authority as Śaṁkara, one of the greatest of all yogis and Vedāntists, recommends it. He says, 'The mind whose dross has been cleared away by prāṇāyāma becomes fixed in Brahman; therefore prāṇāyāma is taught. First, the nerves are to be purified; then comes the power to practise prāṇāyāma. Stopping the right nostril with the thumb, through the left nostril breathe in air, according to capacity; then, without any interval, expel the air through the right nostril, closing the left one. Again, inhaling through the right nostril, expel the air through the left, according to capacity. By practising this three or five times at four periods of the day, before dawn, during midday, in the evening, and at midnight, in fifteen days or a month one may attain purity of the nerves.'

[2] II. 58.

[3] *Complete Works of Vivekananda*, vol. I, pp. 173–4.

How difficult it is to gain control over the mind, which has been aptly compared to a maddened monkey drunk with wine and stung by a scorpion! Like that monkey, the human mind is restless, drunk with the wine of desires and stung by the passions. Control over this restless mind is not an easy task, but through the discipline of yoga it can be attained. In the beginning, the yogi would let the mind run its full course while he learned to become a witness to its action. Let us listen again to Swami Vivekananda, who has the comparison to a maddened monkey in mind:

'The first lesson is to sit for some time and let the mind run on. The mind is bubbling up all the time. It is like that monkey jumping about. Let the monkey jump as much as he can; you simply wait and watch. Knowledge is power, says the proverb, and that is true. Until you know what the mind is doing, you cannot control it. Give it the rein; many hideous thoughts may come into it; you will be astonished that it was possible for you to think such thoughts. But you will find that each day the mind's vagaries are becoming fewer and less violent, that each day it is becoming calmer. In the first few months you will find that the mind will have a great many thoughts, later you will find that they have somewhat decreased, and in a few more months you will find that they are fewer and fewer, until at last the mind will be under perfect control—but we must patiently practise every day.'[1]

Concentration, the sixth limb of yoga, has been defined by Patañjali as 'holding the mind within a centre of spiritual consciousness in the body, or fixing it on some divine form, either within the body or outside it'.[2] We again repeat that the kingdom of heaven is within; that is to say, Puruṣa, or the Divine Self, is within the sanctuary of the body. Thus all the forms of worship or of concentration and meditation taught to aspirants after spiritual life are directed towards the search for this kingdom of heaven within one's own self. The Upaniṣads teach that the Self is to be meditated upon within the cavity of the heart. There are within the body, declare the Indian yogis, different spiritual centres within which one may turn one's mind upon the light of God. Patañjali, in defining concentration, has reference to the turning of the mind intently towards these centres of spiritual consciousness.

But this practice must be undertaken only under the instruction of an adept. Men vary both in capacity and in temperament. A single form of concentration may not suit all men in their search for spiritual realization. Patañjali suggests a few simple forms, however,

[1] *Complete Works of Vivekananda*, vol. I, pp. 174–5. [2] *Yoga Aphorisms*, III. 1.

which everyone may practise. The first two of these are contained in the following aphorisms.

'This word [Om] must be repeated with meditation upon its meaning.'[1]

'Concentration may also be attained by fixing the mind upon the Inner Light, which is beyond sorrow.'[2]

This inner light deserves comment. The ancient yogis believed that there was an actual centre of spiritual consciousness, called 'the lotus of the heart', situated between the abdomen and the thorax, which could be revealed to the aspirant in deep meditation. They said that it had the form of a lotus and that it shone with an inner light. It was said to be 'beyond sorrow', since those who saw it were filled with an extraordinary sense of peace and joy.

From the very earliest times, the masters of yoga emphasized the importance of meditating upon this lotus. According to the Kaivalya Upaniṣad:

'The supreme heaven shines in the lotus of the heart. Those who struggle and aspire may enter there. . . . Retire into solitude. Seat yourself on a clean spot in an erect posture, with the head and neck in a straight line. Control all sense organs. Bow down in devotion to your teacher. Then enter the lotus of the heart and meditate there on the presence of Brahman—the pure, the infinite, the blissful.'[3]

And in the Chāndogya Upaniṣad we read:

'Within the city of Brahman, which is the body, there is the heart, and within the heart there is a little house. This house has the shape of a lotus, and within it dwells that which is to be sought after, inquired about, and realized.

'What, then, is that which dwells within this little house, this lotus of the heart? What is it that must be sought after, inquired about, and realized?

'Even so large as the universe outside is the universe within the lotus of the heart. Within it are heaven and earth, the sun, the moon, the lightning, and all the stars. Whatever is in the macrocosm is in this microcosm also.

'All things that exist, all beings and all desires, are in the city of Brahman; what, then, becomes of them when old age approaches and the body dissolves in death?

'Though old age comes to the body, the lotus of the heart does not grow old. It does not die with the death of the body. The lotus of the heart, where Brahman resides in all his glory—that, and not the body,

[1] *Yoga Aphorisms*, I. 28. [2] *Ibid.*, I. 36. [3] 3, 4, 5.

is the true city of Brahman. Brahman, dwelling therein, is untouched by any deed, ageless, deathless, free from grief, free from hunger and from thirst. His desires are right desires, and his desires are fulfilled.'[1]

And in the Muṇḍaka Upaniṣad:

'Within the lotus of the heart he dwells, where the nerves meet like the spokes of a wheel. Meditate upon him as Om, and you may easily cross the ocean of darkness.[2] In the effulgent lotus of the heart dwells Brahman, passionless and indivisible. He is pure. He is the light of all lights. The knowers of Brahman attain him.'[3]

Meditation in the heart centre is helpful because it localizes our image of the spiritual consciousness towards which we are struggling. If the body is thought of as a busy and noisy city, then we can imagine that in the middle of this city there is a little shrine, and that within this shrine the Ātman, our real nature, is present. No matter what is going on in the streets outside, we can always enter that shrine and worship. It is always open.

Or again—a third form—one may meditate 'upon the heart of an illumined soul, that is free from passion'.[4] In the Upaniṣads we read, 'A knower of Brahman has become Brahman.' By worshipping such a knower, we actually worship God. And such a knower is any one of the God-men—for example, Kṛṣṇa, Buddha, or Christ.

Or—a fourth form—one may substitute 'a dream experience, or the experience of deep sleep'.[5] By 'a dream experience' Patañjali means a dream about a holy personality or a divine symbol. Such a dream can properly be called an experience, because it brings a sense of joy and revelation which remains with us after we have awakened. In the literature of Indian spirituality we find many instances of devotees who dreamed that they received a mantra from some great teacher. Such a dream-mantra is regarded as being just as sacred as one received in the waking state, and the devotee who is blessed by it will continue to use it and meditate upon it throughout the rest of his life.

Or, finally, one may substitute 'any divine form or symbol that appeals to one as good'.[6] One of the most attractive characteristics of Patañjali's philosophy is its breadth of vision, its universality. There is no attempt here to impose any particular cult upon the spiritual aspirant. God is within us, and it is by the light of his presence—no matter how dimly it shines through the layers of our ignorance—that we fashion our own pictures and symbols of goodness and

[1] VIII. i. 1–5. [2] II. ii. 6. [3] *Ibid.*, 9.
[4] *Yoga Aphorisms*, I. 37. [5] *Ibid.*, I. 38. [6] *Ibid.*, I. 39.

project them upon the outside world. Every such picture, symbol, or idea is holy if it is conceived in sincerity. It may be crude and childish, it may not appeal to others; that is unimportant. All-important is our attitude towards it. Whatever we truly and purely worship, we make sacred.

As concentration deepens, we arrive at the next, the seventh limb of yoga, called meditation. 'Meditation (dhyāna) is an unbroken flow of thought toward the object of concentration.'[1]

In other words, meditation is prolonged concentration. The process of meditation is often compared to the pouring of oil from one vessel to another in a steady, unbroken stream. We have seen that Patañjali defines thought as a wave (vṛtti)[2] in the mind. Ordinarily a thought-wave arises, remains in the mind for a moment, and then subsides, to be succeeded by another. In the practice of meditation a succession of identical waves is raised in the mind; and this is done so quickly that no one wave is allowed to subside before another rises to take its place. The effect is therefore one of perfect continuity. If you shoot a hundred feet of film without moving your camera or your object, and then project the result on a screen, the spectator might just as well be looking at a single still photograph. The many identical images are fused into one.

It will be seen that Patañjali's dhyānā does not exactly correspond to our usual understanding of meditation. We commonly mean by it a more or less discursive operation of the mind around a central idea. If, for example, we say that we have been meditating on Christ, we are apt to mean that we have not only tried to fix our minds on Christ's ideal form but have also been thinking about his teachings, his miracles, his disciples, his crucifixion, and so on. All this is very good, but it is a mere preliminary to what may properly be called dhāraṇā and dhyāna.

The final stage of meditation is samādhi, absorption. This is the last, the eighth limb of yoga. This absorption is not precisely samādhi in the sense of transcendental consciousness, which will be explained later; it is rather the door to its attainment. It is the state we achieve when meditation deepens and the mind takes on the form of the object of meditation. Then is the mind entirely freed from any other thought, then there is complete forgetfulness of everything but the object of meditation, and the sense of time is annihilated. 'The mind becomes one-pointed when similar thought-waves arise in succession without any gaps between them.'[3]

[1] *Yoga Aphorisms*, III. 2. [2] *Ibid.*, I. 2. [3] *Ibid.*, III. 12.

Patañjali declares that 'these three—concentration, meditation, and absorption—are more direct aids to spiritual experience than the five limbs previously described.'[1] They represent the three stages of the process of contemplation, of which the third is the culmination, and together they are known as saṁyama, which in turn is to be followed by the lower stage of samādhi, transcendental consciousness. The other five limbs of yoga are preparatory to the practice of contemplation.

When one has passed through saṁyama—that is, when one has attained perfection in meditation—illumination arises in the mind. 'By the practice of saṁyama comes the light of knowledge.'[2] Before, however, we discuss this last victory that rewards the aspirant's efforts, we ought briefly to consider the psychic experiences and occult powers which now may be in his possession.

Yoga and Occult Powers

While engaged in an explanation of concentration and meditation, Patañjali refers to the way in which the mind, while becoming deeply absorbed in any particular object or thought, acquires vibhūtis, or occult powers, and psychic phenomena occur. Different powers are acquired as a result of concentrating upon different objects. If one, for instance, should exercise saṁyama on the peculiar signs or features in another's body, one gains knowledge of his mind. Or, 'if one exercises saṁyama on the form of one's own body, obstructing its perceptibility and separating its power of manifestation from the eyes of the beholder, then one's body becomes invisible.'[3] A yogi, for example, though he may not actually depart from the room in which he is seated, may disappear from the sight of everyone present. He has in reality attained to that power of concentration wherein form and the thing formed have become separated. As he exercises saṁyama on his own form, the power to perceive forms by others is so obstructed that he becomes invisible.

Patañjali describes exercising saṁyama on various objects and concepts, and claims therefrom the acquisition of various occult powers and the appearance of various psychic phenomena. We read in the Bible how Christ performed many miracles—for example, walking on the water, turning water into wine, feeding a multitude with five loaves and two fishes, healing the sick, and raising the dead. According to Indian yogic claims, such miracles are not exceptions; rather can they be performed by every man provided he follows certain practices, and the principal apparatus for testing the validity of these claims is the mind cultivated by the practices of concentration

[1] *Yoga Aphorisms*, III. 7. [2] *Ibid.*, III. 5. [3] *Ibid.*, III. 21.

and meditation. If it is asked whether these powers and phenomena are capable of scientific demonstration, the answer is yes and no. They are demonstrable in the sense that the yogi can exhibit his powers before anybody, but not in the sense that he can explain to just anybody how he does so. To comprehend his demonstration, one must oneself in some degree be a yogi—just as to understand a demonstration in physics or chemistry one must be already, in some degree, a scientist. The educated man will understand the demonstration, but will a boor, or a moron?

The law of cause and effect, as we know it in the world of science, does not apply to the process of meditation upon a particular object or concept and to the development of a particular result therefrom. But that there is here an invariable sequence can be proved through continued experiment. Certain powers are easily attainable, while others are the result of long and strenuous practice. Such powers as clairvoyance, clairaudience, thought-reading, telepathy, are child's play compared with some other yogic powers, such as the power of becoming invisible, of levitation, of walking on water, and the like. All these occult or psychic powers may be developed by an exact application of Patañjali's special instructions, or they may suddenly come to a yogi who is not seeking to acquire them but whose mind is concerned with spiritual illumination through a simple following of yoga practices.

However, the yogi who is true to his ideal of spiritual life pays no heed to the occult powers he may discover in himself, nor does he exercise them. Patañjali proves that these powers are not abnormal phenomena nor magic—that they live within all men and can be developed by all; but he shows at the same time that they have nothing at all to do with spiritual life. On the contrary, they are veritable obstacles, stumbling blocks on the road to spiritual attainment. 'They are powers in the worldly state, but they are obstacles to samādhi.'[1] The greatest power, it is contended by all yogis, is the power to control these other powers when they are present. Just as there are physical obstacles and lusts of the flesh which must be overcome, so there are psychic phenomena—the subtler lusts of the mind, the temptations of power—which one must wholly overcome if one would approach the door to God.

We read in the life of Śrī Rāmakṛṣṇa how when he received occult powers he discarded them as heaps of rubbish. The following simple story that he used to tell illustrates how futile and vain they are.

'There were two brothers. One of them withdrew from the world in his search for truth. After twelve years, years of struggle and self-

[1] *Yoga Aphorisms,* III. 38.

denial, he returned to his brother, who then asked him, "What have you gained in these years of austerity?" "Come and I will show you," answered the first brother. They came to a river bank, and the yogi-brother crossed the river by walking on the water. The lay brother called for a boat, paid the boatman a copper, and was ferried across. Then he said, "Brother, is this all you have gained in twelve long years of struggle—to be able to do something that can be had for the price of a copper piece?"'[1]

Samādhi or Transcendental Consciousness

The knowledge which is gained from inference and the study of scriptures is knowledge of one kind. But the knowledge which is gained from samādhi is of a much higher order. It goes beyond inference and scriptures.'[2]

Here Patañjali describes the two kinds of knowledge: knowledge obtained through the mediation of the reason, and knowledge obtained by direct, superconscious experience. Ordinary knowledge comes to us by way of sense perception, and the interpretation of this by our reason. Ordinary knowledge is therefore necessarily limited to ordinary objects; that is to say, to those objects which are within the grasp of our senses. When ordinary knowledge attempts to deal with what is *extraordinary*, its impotence is immediately revealed.

For example, we have the various scriptures and writings which tell us about the existence of God. We may read these and accept their teachings—up to a certain point. But we cannot claim to know God because we have read them. All that we can say we know is that these scriptures were written by men who claimed to know God. Why should we believe them? True, our reason may suggest to us that the authors of the scriptures were probably honest and reliable, not self-deluded or insane, and that therefore we should believe what they tell us. But such belief can only be partial and provisional. It is very unsatisfactory. It is certainly not knowledge.

So now we have two alternatives. Either we must decide that there is only one kind of knowledge, limited to the objects of sense-contact, and thereby resign ourselves to a permanent agnosticism concerning the teachings of the scriptures. Or we must admit the possibility of another, a higher kind of knowledge which is supersensory and therefore capable of confirming the truth of these teachings through direct experience. Such is the knowledge which is obtained through

[1] Swami Brahmananda, *Śrī Śrī Rāmakṛṣṇa Upadeśa*, p. 78.
[2] *Yoga Aphorisms*, I. 49.

samādhi. And each one of us has to find it for himself. Said Swami Vivekananda:

'Realization is real religion; all the rest is only preparation. Hearing lectures, or reading books, or reasoning, is merely preparing the ground; it is not religion. Intellectual assent and intellectual dissent are not religion.'[1]

Religion is, in fact, a severely practical kind of research. You take nothing on trust. You accept nothing but your own experience. You go forward alone, step by step, like an explorer in a virgin jungle, to see what you will find. All that Patañjali, or anybody else, can do for you is to urge you to attempt the exploration and to offer certain general hints and warnings which may be of help to you on your way.

Patañjali tells us that in the state of nirvicāra samādhi the mind becomes 'pure' and 'filled with truth'. The mind is said to be pure because, in this state, all the minor thought-waves have been swallowed up by one great wave of concentration upon a single object. It is true that 'seeds' of attachment still exist within this wave, but only in a state of suspended animation. For the moment, at least, they can do no harm, and it is very improbable that they will ever become fertile again, because, the devotee having progressed thus far, it is comparatively easy for him to take the final step, which will cause their annihilation.

The mind, in nirvicāra samādhi, is said to be filled with truth because it now experiences direct supersensory knowledge. Those who have meditated on some Chosen Ideal or spiritual personality experience direct contact with the object of meditation, no longer something subjectively imagined, but something objectively known. If you have been meditating on Kṛṣṇa, or on Christ, and trying to picture either of them to yourself in your imagination, you will find that your picture dissolves into the reality of a living presence; and, in knowing that presence, you will see that your picture of it was imperfect and unlike the original. Those who have had this experience liken it to the action of a magnet. In the preliminary stages of meditation, the effort seems to come entirely from oneself; one keeps forcing one's mind to remain pointed at its object. But later one becomes aware of an outside force, a magnetic power, which draws one's mind in the desired direction, so that the effort is no longer one's own. This is what is known as grace.

How can we be sure that the revelations obtained through samādhi are genuine revelations, and not some form of self-delusion or auto-

[1] *Complete Works of Vivekananda*, vol. I, p. 232.

hypnosis? Common sense suggests several tests. For instance, it is obvious that the knowledge so obtained must not contradict the knowledge which has already been obtained in the same way by others; there are many knowers but there is only one truth. Again, it is clear that this knowledge must be something which is not knowable by other means—not knowable, that is to say, by means of our ordinary sense experience. And, finally, this knowledge must bring with it a complete renewal of the mind and transformation of character. 'The right relation between prayer and conduct', wrote Archbishop Temple, 'is not that conduct is supremely important and prayer may help it, but that prayer is supremely important and conduct tests it.' If this is found true in the preliminary phases of spiritual life, it should be even more strikingly demonstrated in the final, unitive state of samādhi. In achieving that, a man becomes a saint. For, as Patañjali says: 'The impression which is made upon the mind by samādhi wipes out all other impressions.'[1] And now he goes on to tell us how to take the ultimate step into complete union with Brahman:

'When the impression made by that samādhi is also wiped out, so that there are no more thought-waves at all in the mind, then one enters the samādhi which is called "seedless".'[2]

It has already been explained that samādhi is achieved by raising one object, one great wave of concentration in the mind by which all other thought-waves, all saṁskāras, or past impressions, are swallowed up. But now even this one wave has to be stilled. When it has subsided, we enter the highest samādhi of all, which is called nirvikalpa in the Vedānta system of philosophy. Nirvikalpa samādhi is said to be seedless because it is nothing but pure, undifferentiated consciousness; it contains no phenomenal impressions whatever, no seeds of desire and attachment. In nirvikalpa samādhi one is no longer oneself, one is literally one with Brahman; one enters into the real nature of the apparent universe and all its forms and creatures.

It is hard to follow Patañjali to such heights, even theoretically; and perhaps it will be well, before concluding this chapter, to go back to its beginning and try to recapitulate in a simple and nontechnical manner what he has taught us.

We have to start, we are told, by training the mind to concentrate, but Patañjali has warned us that this practice of concentration must be accompanied by nonattachment; otherwise we shall find ourselves in trouble. If we try to concentrate while remaining attached to the things of this world, we shall either fail altogether or our newly

[1] *Yoga Aphorisms*, I. 50. [2] *Ibid.*, I. 51.

acquired powers will bring us into great danger, because we shall inevitably use them for selfish, unspiritual ends.

What is the simplest way to acquire nonattachment? We must begin by cultivating attachment to the highest object we can conceive of, to God himself. We can do this, first of all, on the lowest level, the level of gross phenomena. Take some great spiritual teacher, a Buddha or a Christ, or any other major saint of any country or religion. This man actually lived on this earth in human form. You can read about his life. You can approach him as a human being. It is easy to grow to love him, to want to be like him, to try to serve him and spread his message by modelling your life upon his. Through this service and this love, nonattachment to other, lesser loves and objectives comes naturally. It is not that we become indifferent to other people or to our own work and duties. But our love for others is included in our love for our Ideal—it ceases to be exclusive and possessive; and our work, because it is now done as service to that Ideal, takes on a new meaning, and we feel more enthusiasm for it than ever before.

Through devotion to our Ideal and meditation upon his life, we shall come gradually to an understanding of the spirit within the man; and so we pass from the level of gross phenomena to the subtle or spiritual level. We shall no longer admire a Buddha or a Christ as a human being within time, but we shall worship him as an eternal, spiritual being. We shall know him in his divine aspect. That is the second stage.

There is, however, a third stage, a third level of consciousness. For behind Buddha, behind Christ, behind any conception of a personal God, there is Brahman, the central reality of which these figures are only partial, individual projections. When we become united with Brahman, we are united with that which was manifested in Christ and hidden within our unregenerate selves, but which is eternally present in all of us. And this union is the state of nirvikalpa samādhi.

The lower stages of samādhi all contain a vestige of the sense of duality; it is still 'I' who am meditating upon 'my' Ideal; there is a separation between our Ideal and ourselves. And it is natural that even the great saint finds it painful to surrender his intense personal love for his Ideal in order to achieve final, impersonal union. In describing how he first reached nirvikalpa samādhi, Śrī Rāmakṛṣṇa said:

'Every time I gathered my mind together, I came face to face with the blissful form of Divine Mother. However much I tried to free my mind from consciousness of Mother, I didn't have the will to go beyond. But at last, collecting all the strength of my will, I cut Mother's form to pieces with the sword of discrimination, and at once my mind became "seedless", and I reached nirvikalpa. It was beyond all expression.'[1]

Nirvikalpa samādhi has been described by Śaṁkara as follows:

'There is a continuous consciousness of the unity of Atman and Brahman. There is no longer any identification of the Atman with its coverings. All sense of duality is obliterated. There is pure, unified consciousness. The man who is well established in this consciousness is said to be illumined.

'A man is said to be free even in this life when he is established in illumination. His bliss is unending. He almost forgets this world of appearances.

'Even though his mind is dissolved in Brahman, he is fully awake, but free from the ignorance of waking life. He is fully conscious, but free from any craving. Such a man is said to be free even in this life.

'For him, the sorrows of this world are over. Though he possesses a finite body, he remains united with the infinite. His heart knows no anxiety. Such a man is said to be free even in this life.'[2]

While in nirvikalpa Śrī Rāmakṛṣṇa experienced union with the impersonal Brahman. But, on returning to normal consciousness, he would speak of God in the aspect of the Divine Mother, his Chosen Ideal. The Divine Mother did not lose her reality for him because he had known Brahman. It is important to remember this, for, in our ordinary speech, the word real is used vaguely and loosely, and is apt to lead to confusion. When we say that Brahman alone is real, we do not mean that everything else is illusion, but rather that Brahman alone is fundamental. The several aspects of God, the divine incarnations, have their own relative order of reality. The materialists—those who describe themselves as being 'down to earth'—are the ones who are living in an unreal world, because they limit themselves to the level of gross sense perception. The perception of the illumined saint ranges over the whole scale, from gross to subtle and from subtle to absolute; and it is only he who knows what the nature of this universe actually is.

[1] *Līlāprasaṅga*, Sādhak bhāv, pp. 319–20.

[2] *Vivekacūḍāmaṇi*, vss. 427–30.

CHAPTER 13

THE PŪRVA MĪMĀṀSĀ

Jaimini, the compiler of the Mīmāṁsā Sūtras, though some controversial issues have been raised by modern Oriental scholars as to his identity, was long accepted by Indian commentators as a disciple of Vyāsa, the famous author of the Mahābhārata. When the compilation was made cannot be ascertained with any exactness, but many scholars believe it to be one of the earliest collections known to Indian philosophy. One famous commentary upon the aphorisms of Jaimini, by Śavara Swāmi (AD 400), has made them intelligible to a modern reader, although it in turn has been interpreted in two different ways, one by Prabhākara (AD 650) and the other by Kumārilla Bhaṭṭa (AD 700).

The two main objectives of Mīmāṁsā philosophy are to establish the authority of the Vedas as the incontrovertible source of all knowledge and to explain their true meaning. It does not claim to be a commentary upon them.

First, then, by way of accepting the authority of the Vedas as a proof and source of knowledge, the Mīmāṁsā philosophy, not dogmatically but logically, enters the lists of controversy with many subtle arguments respecting the relation of word and thought to each other which we need not concern ourselves with here. Briefly, it declares that the Vedas are apauruṣeya—self-revealed. By saying they are self-revelations Mīmāṁsā denies their authorship even to God, for if self-revealed they are without authorship of any sort, human or divine. In fact, it is not clear whether Mīmāṁsā at all accepts an omnipotent, omnipresent, self-existent God, for nowhere does it discuss the question of his existence. Furthermore, the commentators are also silent upon this matter. Later exponents of the system, however, in defining its purpose, declare that it merely attempts to explain the nature of Vedic rites and ceremonies without any concern whether or not God exists. This system, they assert, has nothing to add concerning God and salvation to what has been exhaustively set forth in Vedānta philosophy.

The word mīmāṁsā denotes the reasoning process to be followed if one would understand the meaning of a word or a sentence in the Vedas. The epithet pūrva indicates that the primary aim of the Mīmāṁsā philosophy is to explain the true meaning of the pūrva, or earlier portion of the Vedas. This philosophy is also known as Karma Mīmāṁsā, since it seeks to explain the karma, the rites and ceremonies taught in the Vedas, and the effects of their performance. It explains the Vedas as essentially injunctions concerning the performance of the sacred rites, and it subordinates the Upaniṣads, the last, philosophical part of the Vedas, to the part giving such injunctions. It attributes so much importance to sacrificial rites that even the deities in whose favour these rites are performed seem to occupy a secondary place. It denies their very existence, in fact, as separate from the mantras, or revealed words of the Vedas.

Adherents of the Mīmāṁsā school cite the following Vedic story to show the importance of ritual sacrifice:

'There was once a famous sage named Bharadvāja. By dint of penance he attained a long life of three hundred years, during which he remained unmarried and devoted himself to performing the ordained Vedic rites and studying the Vedas. At last, crippled with age, he was confined to his bed. One day Indra himself came to him and said, "Bharadvāja, if I extend your life by a hundred years, what will you do with it?" Bharadvāja replied, "I shall continue to do as I have done so far." Whereupon Indra showed him three large mountains that he had never seen and placed before him a handful of dust from each, saying, "Bharadvāja, the three mountains that you see are the three Vedas—Sāma, Ṛk, and Yajur; they are eternal and endless; what you have learned from your teacher and from study of the Vedas, by observing celibacy, is equal only to these three handfuls of dust; the endless remainder lies unexplored before you. Come, learn from me the real import of the Vedas. They are the source of all knowledge." So saying, and wishing to give him the means of attaining Vedic knowledge, Indra initiated the sage into the worship of that fire which is connected with the sun. Bharadvāja worshipped the sun as he had been instructed and obtained eternal life.'[1]

Mīmāṁsā philosophy thus lays most stress upon work, which chiefly denotes the performance of ceremonial rites.[2]

[1] Taittirīya Brāhmaṇa, III. i. 11.

[2] Compare the medieval discussion among Christian divines concerning the relative importance of faith and works, the latter meaning essentially the performance of the offices of the church. Moral conduct, in the Mīmāṁsā

True religious life, therefore, is the observance of dharma, or religious duties and ceremonial rites which lead to heaven in the life hereafter; and the Vedas alone can guide us concerning what is right and what is wrong, so that we may do the one and avoid the other. The performance of dharma gives rise to a peculiar quality called apūrba (literally, never before, or something unexpected), and it is by possessing that that one is entitled to the felicity of heaven.

Mīmāṁās regards the attainment of heaven as the primary objective in life; but no explanation is offered, either in the original work of Jaimini or in the commentaries, of the nature of heaven, whether it is a place of unalloyed happiness, as we find it in popular interpretations of Christianity, or a blissful state of the soul. Certain followers of the school accept it as a place of enjoyment to which we go after death. Others believe it to be the present attainment of a 'happiness which is not mixed with sorrow, or eclipsed by any other mental state, which never ends, and which may be had by merely wishing for it'.

Except for Mīmāṁsā, all schools of Indian thought make of the problem of the Self the main subject of discussion. Mīmāṁsā gives no specific attention to it, but we may gather from careful study that it regards the Self as distinct from the body, senses, and mind—and intelligence, will, and effort as its natural attributes. If one uses these attributes in the right way by following the injunctions of the Vedas, one may in the afterlife attain felicity in heaven.

philosophy, is a necessary condition for the performance of rites, but moral conduct is not regarded as an ideal in itself; rather, right living is a prerequisite for the performance of Vedic rites.

CHAPTER 14

THE UTTARA-MĪMĀṀSĀ OR THE VEDĀNTA SŪTRAS

The word Vedānta means, literally, the end of the Vedas, with specific reference to the Upaniṣads, the last portion or the essential part of each of the four Vedas. The Upaniṣads, as we have already noted, make no attempt to order their contents but merely record the extraordinary experiences of the seers. There accordingly arose the necessity of interpreting them in terms of human reason and organizing them into a systematic philosophy. Bādarāyaṇa is the author of the Vedānta Sūtras in which the systematizing attempt is made. From him we learn of other sages who preceded him in the same attempt but whose writings have not been preserved.

About Bādarāyaṇa little is known, though Indian tradition identifies him with Vyāsa, author of the Mahābhārata, who flourished sometime between 500 and 200 BC.

The Vedānta Sūtras are also known as Brahma Sūtras because they expound the philosophy of Brahman, and as Śarīraka Sūtras because they deal with the nature of the unconditioned Self embodied in human form. Though the Sūtras undertake to interpret and organize the Upaniṣads, they are themselves quite unintelligible without commentaries. The commentaries, moreover, are so diverse and often so conflicting that it is well-nigh impossible to arrive at the precise views held by Bādarāyaṇa. The Vedānta Sūtras are unquestionably of great authority, however, for every important philosopher has written commentaries upon them. They are indeed one of the three great works upon which all the theologies of India rest. The others are the Upaniṣads, of course, and the Gītā.

To understand the place of the three works in modern Indian philosophy, we recall to mind once again the three steps in attaining Self-knowledge prescribed by the Upaniṣads. We must hear of the truth of the Self, we must reason upon this truth, and we must meditate upon the Self.[1] The Upaniṣads speak to us of the truth of

[1] Bṛhadāraṇyaka, II. iv. 5.

the Self. The Vedānta Sūtras aid us to reason and understand. Finally, the Gītā affords us practical ways and means of living and prescribes details of conduct and methods of meditation. Of the many philosophers who have commented upon these fundamental scriptures, the chief are Śaṁkara, Bhāskara, Yādava Prakāś, Rāmānuja, Nimbārka, Keśava, Nīlakaṇṭha, Mādhwa, Baladeva, Vallabha, and Vijñānabhikṣu. Five of these have had a large following: Śaṁkara, the exponent of nondualism; Rāmānuja, the exponent of qualified monism; Nimbārka, the exponent of the philosophy of unity in difference; Mādhwa, the exponent of dualism; and Vallabha, the exponent of the philosophy of devotion. Of these Śaṁkara and Rāmānuja are the most famous.

It is difficult to state with any definiteness which of these philosophers presents the correct view of the original Vedānta Sūtras of Bādarāyaṇa, for opinions differ, and each school of thought believes that it represents the true tradition. Dr G. Thibaut is of the opinion that Rāmānuja is the truest interpreter. My brother monk Swami Vireswarananda, in the learned introduction to his translation of the Vedānta Sūtras, has argued that Saṁkara's interpretation closely follows Bādarāyaṇa. A brief summary of the Vedānta Sūtras and of the points of agreement regarding them may help to clarify what really is a most obscure and complex problem.

The Sūtras contain four chapters in all. The first deals with Brahman, his relation to the world and to the soul of man. An attempt is made to reconcile metaphysically the various Vedic passages on the subject, the recorded experiences of Brahman on the part of the early ṛṣis, or seers. The second chapter meets the objections to the view of Brahman, the soul, and the world expounded in the first, and reveals the fallacious nature of all rival theories on the subject. The third chapter is mainly concerned with methods by which an individual can attain knowledge of Brahman, but incidentally discusses the question of rebirth for those who fail to attain this knowledge, together with some minor psychological and theological topics. The last chapter takes up the fruits of the knowledge of Brahman—these differing in relation to the differing experiences of aspirants and knowers, the deeper the experience, the greater the fruits. It also discusses at length mokṣa and the two paths possible after death—return (rebirth) and nonreturn (gradual liberation).

According to Bādarāyaṇa, perception and inference are the two sources of all knowledge. On the spiritual plane, he identifies perception, direct divine insight, with Śruti, or the revealed scriptures, particularly the Upaniṣads; and inference with Smṛti, the auxiliary scriptures—the Gītā, the Mahābhārata, and the Laws of Manu. Perception in relation to knowledge of Brahman (pratyakṣa upalabdhi) is not sense perception, for nobody sees God with physical eyes—it is supersensuous perception; spiritual inference depends on revelation, for logic independent of revelation is blind and leads nowhere.

Brahman is regarded by Bādarāyaṇa as the material as well as the efficient cause of the universe, its origin and support, himself uncreated and eternal. It is difficult to state with any definiteness, however, what Bādarāyaṇa actually believed concerning the universe, whether that it is a transformation of Brahman or that it is only something superimposed upon him. Nor is it clear how the individual soul is related to Brahman, whether as a part of him or as a mere reflection of him. Because of these obscurities or uncertainties, the various schools of thought have flourished. But all are agreed that the ultimate goal in Vedānta is certainly the knowledge of Brahman and that it can be attained in this life. This knowledge, once attained, burns away all the seeds of karma and gives the promised liberation.

The other various metaphysical, ethical, and psychological aspects of the Vedānta Sūtras will be fully explained when we discuss the philosophers who commented upon them.

BOOK V

VEDĀNTA AND ITS GREAT EXPONENTS

This last section will be devoted to a review of the lives and teachings of certain of the saints and thinkers of India, ancient and modern, who have been followers of Vedānta. These include not merely distinguished commentators upon the Indian scriptures, but others who have influenced philosophical thought and brought spiritual blessings to their fellow men.

CHAPTER 15

GAUḌAPĀDA

To Gauḍapāda, the first historic philosopher of the system of Vedānta, and the expounder of its nondualistic aspect, no definite date can be assigned. There is a tradition that Śaṁkara, who lived in the seventh century AD,[1] met Gauḍapāda and received his blessing. Śaṁkara, in his commentary on the Māṇḍūkya Upaniṣad, makes obeisance to Gauḍapāda as his guru's guru. Thence arose the belief of many scholars that Gauḍapāda and Śaṁkara were contemporaries. Other scholars, on the contrary, consider that Gauḍapāda lived many centuries before Śaṁkara, perhaps even before Buddha. And their contention is that the tradition of Śaṁkara's meeting with Gauḍapāda is true, but that they met each other on the yogic plane, where, the spiritual eye of the aspirant being opened, a direct communion with the great souls of the past may be obtained. Śaṁkara is also said to have met Vyāsa, author of the Mahābhārata; if so, he must have met him too on the yogic plane, for undoubtedly Vyāsa lived many centuries before Śaṁkara. Gauḍapāda's being saluted by Śaṁkara as his guru's guru might be due to the fact he was one of the most important of the early teachers of the Vedāntic order. Scholars quote another tradition to the effect that Gauḍapāda was a disciple of Śuka and therefore a contemporary of the Mahābhārata.

Some Western scholars claim Gauḍapāda as a Buddhist saint, their main argument being that at the beginning of the fourth chapter of his philosophical treatise, the Kārikā, he adores the 'superman', whom they identify with Buddha. But the word superman had been used in the Mahābhārata and the Purāṇas, even before the advent of Buddha, to denote one who has known Brahman, and also to denote God conceived in human form—Nārāyaṇa; and according to Indian tradition Gauḍapāda also used the word superman to denote Nārāyaṇa. Ānandagiri, a disciple of Śaṁkara, mentions that Gauḍapāda

[1] See chap. 16, pp. 279 281

practised austerities and meditation in Badarikāśrama,[1] and that Nārāyaṇa, God in human form, appeared before him and revealed to him the highest truth of Vedānta.

Whatever may have been the period in which Gauḍapāda lived, he is regarded by Indian authorities as the first Vedāntic philosopher and one of the greatest seers of all the ages.

The Kārikā

The advaita Vedānta (Vedānta in its nondualistic aspect) is as old as the Upaniṣads, for, however variously the ancient scriptures have been interpreted, and however much they have supplied the foundations for varying schools, it is the consensus of opinion that their final truth consists in the identification of the Self with Brahman and the absolute reality of one and only one existence. Of the Upaniṣads, the Māṇḍūkya most emphatically declares the truth of advaita. Gauḍapāda made himself famous by writing the Kārikā, a commentary upon this single Upaniṣad. Śaṁkara, who wrote commentaries on the Kārikā of Gauḍapāda, very truly remarked, 'The Māṇḍūkya Upaniṣad, with the Kārikā, embodies in itself the quintessence of all the Upaniṣads or Vedānta.'

The Kārikā is divided into four chapters. The first, the āgama (scripture), glosses the verses of the Māṇḍūkya Upaniṣad. The second, the vaitathya (the nature of sense experience), through an elaborate argument explains the relative and phenomenal nature of the objective universe. The third, the advaita (nondualism), establishes by means of logic and reason the truth of nondualism. The final chapter, the alātaśānti (the quenching of the fire-brand), further establishes the sole reality of the Ātman and the relative nature of our experiences in the ordinary states of consciousness.

The Philosophy of Experience

To arrive at the ultimate truth, philosophy must consider not only our experiences in the waking state but those in other states of consciousness, such as dream and dreamless sleep, and co-ordinate them all by extending its inquiry to the possible source of all consciousness. Gauḍapāda, as well as the Upaniṣadic ṛṣis, meets this requirement. V. Subrahmanya Iyer rightly remarks of Gauḍapāda:

[1] Badarikāśrama, in the Himalayas, is a well-known place of pilgrimage, where devotees from throughout India gather in great numbers every summer. At other times of the year the roads to it are covered with heavy snow. The place has in it a famous temple, dedicated to the worship of Nārāyaṇa. had the privilege of visiting this holy shrine in 1916.

'His distinction lies in the emphasis he lays on the impossibility of reaching the highest truth unless the *totality* of human experience or knowledge be taken into consideration.'[1] This totality Gauḍapāda himself investigates.

Western philosophy, in contrast, seems to have run into a blind alley, not only because it fails to recognize transcendental consciousness, but also because it does not attempt to *co-ordinate* the three other states of consciousness. Says Mr Iyer:

> 'Philosophy, according to Gauḍapāda and Śankara, is an interpretation of the *totality* of human experience or of the *whole* of life from the standpoint of truth. Philosophy, therefore, is the whole, of which Religion, Mysticism (Yoga), Theology, Scholasticism, Speculation, Art and Science are but parts. Such philosophy or Vedānta as ignores any part or parts is no Vedānta. . . . And the object sought by philosophy, as these two pre-eminent Hindu philosophers say, is the happiness (*sukham*) and welfare (*hitam*) of all beings (*sarva sattwa*) in this world (*ihaiva*).'[2]

In analysing the three states of consciousness, waking, dreaming, and dreamless sleep, Gauḍapāda discovers as the witness behind them an unchangeable reality. For in all these states there is the Self ever-present, though remaining unknown. It is the experiencer of all actions and thoughts in all the three states, but it is never affected by them. It forever remains pure, free, perfect.

Through our ignorance, however, the Self becomes identified with experience and appears to be changing, as when it appears first happy and then miserable, or to be born and then to die. But the appearance has no absolute reality. The Self remains unaltered, and when we rise above and beyond the three states to turīya, Pure Consciousness, its absolute oneness with all things, the absolute nonduality, is at last clearly revealed.

It is true that in deep sleep all experience seems to be annihilated. What then is the difference between deep sleep and turīya? In the words of Gauḍapāda, 'Deep sleep (prajñā) does not know anything either of the Self or of the non-Self, either of truth, or of untruth. But turīya is ever existent and ever all-seeing.'[3] Again he says: 'Dream is the wrong apprehension of reality. Sleep is the state in which one does not know what reality is. When the false experience in these

[1] Foreword to *Māṇḍūkyopanishad with Gauḍapāda's Kārikā and Śankara's Commentary* (Swami Nikhilananda trans., Sri Ramakrishna Ashrama: Mysore, 1949), p. v.

[2] *Ibid.*, pp. vi–vii.

[3] Kārikā, I. 7. 12. This and the following passages from the Kārikā have been translated by the author.

two states disappears turīya is realized.'[1] In the following verse he makes a clear distinction between a man who is asleep and a man who is in turīya: 'In deep sleep the mind is withdrawn. But it is disciplined, and not withdrawn, in turīya. One whose mind is disciplined becomes one with Brahman—who is fearless and the light of whose knowledge shines in every direction.'[2]

The real Self, the ultimate reality, remains unknown in the three ordinary states of consciousness. 'When, however,' says Gauḍapāda, 'the individual soul, sleeping under the influence of māyā (ignorance), is awakened, it then realizes nonduality, beginningless and endless.'[3]

The Self (or Ātman), as we know, is immortal, in that it has neither birth nor death. It is nondual, though it appears to be many, just as the one sun, reflected in many lakes, appears manifold. Describing the nature of the Ātman, Gauḍapāda says, 'This Ātman is beyond all expression by words, beyond all acts of the mind. It is peace, eternal effulgence, absence of activity; and it is attainable when the mind becomes pure and tranquil.'[4]

Gauḍapāda, like all the other saintly philosophers of India, points out the way to illumination within one's own soul. With patience and perseverance, he tells us, we should seek to control the vagaries of the mind; then through the practice of discrimination we must learn to renounce the pleasures of the senses; and finally, by the practice of concentration and meditation, when we are quite absorbed in our devotions, we arrive at a kind of bliss, a lower stage of samādhi. We must also, Gauḍapāda insists, give up our attachment to this bliss if we would realize the supreme bliss. My master, Swami Brahmananda, also, used to tell us that we must not stop with the bliss we may find in deep contemplation but go deeper and deeper. In the words of Gauḍapāda:

'The mind should not be allowed to enjoy the bliss that arises out of the condition of absorption. It should be freed from attachment to such happiness through the exercise of discrimination. When the mind does not lose itself in inactivity and oblivion, or is not distracted by desires—that is to say, when the mind achieves quietness and does not give rise to appearances—it verily becomes Brahman. This, the highest bliss, is based upon the realization of Self; it is peace, identical with liberation, indescribable, and unborn. It is further described as the omniscient Brahman, because it is one with the unborn Self, which is the object sought by knowledge.'[5]

Gauḍapāda contends that the waking and the dreaming states are

[1] Kārikā, I. 7. 15. [2] *Ibid.*, III. 35. [3] *Ibid.*, I. 7. 16.
[4] *Ibid.*, III. 37. [5] *Ibid.*, III. 45, 46, 47.

equally real and equally unreal. They are real only in a relative sense, and so they are unreal as compared with the transcendental, in which there is identification with the Reality, the unchangeable Self. The definition of Reality is that it is never contradicted at any time but persists forever. 'Anything which is nonexistent at the beginning, and also at the end, necessarily does not exist in the middle.'[1] By this test, all experience of both dreaming and waking is unreal. And from the standpoint of the ultimate reality, experience of the waking state is but a prolonged dream. Shakespeare seems to have caught the dreamlike quality of this world of appearances in the famous lines:

> . . . These our actors,
> As I foretold you, were all spirits, and
> Are melted into air, into thin air;
> And, like the baseless fabric of this vision,
> The cloud-capp'd towers, the gorgeous palaces,
> The solemn temples, the great globe itself,
> Yea, all which it inherit, shall dissolve,
> And, like this insubstantial pageant faded,
> Leave not a rack behind. We are such stuff
> As dreams are made on, and our little life
> Is rounded with a sleep.

Consistent with his philosophy of nondualism, Gauḍapāda did not believe in the absolute reality of creation. The one absolute, nondual Self, or God, neither created this universe nor did he become this universe. In reality there is no creation, for the one infinite Existence appears to be the manifold universe just as a rope may appear to be a snake. The universe is not a reality but something superimposed upon the Ātman.

'There is no death,' says Gauḍapāda, 'no birth; there is no one in bondage, no one aspiring to knowledge; there is no seeker after liberation, no one liberated. This is the absolute truth.'[2] In evident allusion to expressions such as these, S. Radhakrishnan observes: 'The general idea pervading Gauḍapāda's work, that bondage and liberation, the individual soul and the world, are all unreal, makes the caustic critic observe that the theory which has nothing better to say than that an unreal soul is trying to escape from an unreal bondage in an unreal world to accomplish an unreal supreme good, may itself be an unreality.'[3]

Now if one fails to take into consideration the main contention of Gauḍapāda, the above criticism may apply. What is his main conten-

[1] Kārikā, IV. 31. [2] *Ibid.*, II. 32. [3] *Indian Philosophy*, vol. II, p. 463.

tion? That the highest good, that is, freedom, supreme bliss, is the very nature of the Ātman, an absolute reality which persists. The supreme good, therefore, is not, as Dr Radhakrishnan alleges, unreal, but something you already have. To seek to possess something that you already have is foolish fancy. To think that you do not have something, though you always have it, is delusion. The story is told of a man who had a towel on his shoulder but sought for it everywhere. He but needed to awake to the fact that the towel was where he had placed it. So it is with us. Thinking we are bound, we seek liberation, though the liberation we seek is already within us. We but need to awake from the sleep of ignorance to realize 'I am Brahman.' Either that we are bound or that we seek liberation is false.

Dr Radhakrishnan further remarks: 'If we have to play the game of life, we cannot do so with the conviction that the play is a show and all the prizes in it mere blanks. No philosophy can consistently hold such a view and be at rest with itself. The greatest condemnation of such a theory is that we are obliged to occupy ourselves with objects, the existence and value of which we are continually denying in theory.'[1]

To this one may reply with the question, Can we play the game of life well if we take life itself as a reality? The game is then no longer a game but a burden. Only for a genuine yogi, who has seen life as mere play, is it possible to play with satisfaction the game of life. To him the prizes are not blanks but the bliss of a free soul. We can play the game of life well only when we recognize that it is not everlasting, that joys and sorrows are in their very nature impermanent. The genuine yogi enjoys the game, plays it better than does one who clings to the enjoyments of life and finds to his despair that they elude his grasp at every moment, howsoever he may 'bid the clouds to stay'. Howsoever one may try to fool oneself by asserting the reality of the world, there is no world when life ends in death. As one holds fast to life and its experiences, the prizes in the game become mere blanks. The fact is that Gauḍapāda does not in any way reveal a romantic desire to chase the shadows of life nor does he attempt to hide his head in the sand. Rather does he boldly seize upon naked reality and fearlessly face the facts of life by rising above them, above life and death, above joys and sorrows, into the realization 'I am Brahman.'

[1] *Indian Philosophy*, vol. II, p. 463.

CHAPTER 16

ŚAṀKARA

Introduction

As prophet and as thinker, Śaṁkara stands among the greatest figures in the history of the world. He is, primarily, the unrivalled propounder of advaita Vedānta, the nondualistic aspect of the Vedic teachings. By means of his remarkable clearness, his supreme wisdom, and his profound spirituality he has so stamped himself upon Vedānta that it has remained the paragon of Indian philosophy, and has given solace to the sorrowful heart of a large segment of mankind.

Life of Śaṁkara

Beautiful and fantastic clouds of legend surround the austere, charming, boyish figure of Śaṁkara—saint, philosopher, and poet. But, historically speaking, we know very little about the circumstances of his life.

He was born in or around the year AD 686 of brāhmin parents, at Kālādi, a small village of western Malabar, in southern India.[1] By the

[1] The date is that given by Pandit Rajenrda Nath Ghosh, a noted authority on Śaṁkara. S. Radhakrishnan writes (*Indian Philosophy*, vol. II, p. 447): 'According to Telang, Śaṁkara flourished about the middle or the end of the sixth century AD. (His argument is that Pūrṇavarman referred to in Saṁkara's commentary on the Brahma Sūtras was a Buddhist king of Magadha about that time.) Sir R. G. Bhāndārkar proposes AD 680 as the date of Śaṁkara's birth, and is even inclined to go a few years earlier. Max Müller and Professor Macdonell hold that he was born in AD 788 and died in AD 820. That he flourished in the first quarter of the ninth century is also the opinion of Professor Keith.'

To an Indian scholar, A. V. Sankaranarayana Rao, I owe the following recent statement:

'The date of Śaṅkara has not been definitely arrived at and is still a matter of controversy. It is the consensus of opinion that he lived after Bhagavān Buddha. The dates assigned to him vary from sixth century BC to eighth century AD. The traditional date is Kaliyuga 2593 or 509 BC. It has been generally accepted by many modern historians that he lived between 788 and 820 AD. This has been more or age of ten, he was already an intellectual prodigy. Not only had he read and memorized all the scriptures, but he had written commentaries on many of them, and had held discussions with famous scholars who came to him from every part of the country.

Yet the boy was dissatisfied. At a time when most children are only beginning to study, he was already disgusted by the emptiness of book-knowledge. He saw, moreover, that his teachers did not practise the lofty principles they preached. Indeed, the whole society in which he lived was materialistic and pleasure-seeking. India was passing through a period of spiritual decadence. Śaṁkara, burning with youthful zeal, resolved to make his own life an example which would lead men back to the paths of truth.

The death of his father set him puzzling over the riddle of life and death, and he determined to solve it. He would renounce everything in his search for the meaning of existence. It was then that he wrote the poem called 'Moha Mudgaram'—'The Shattering of Illusion'. Of this the following is a more or less literal translation:

> Who is thy wife? Who is thy son?
> The ways of this world are strange indeed.
> Whose art thou? Whence art thou come?
> Vast is thy ignorance, my beloved.
> Therefore ponder these things and worship the Lord.
>
> Behold the folly of Man:
> In childhood busy with his toys,
> In youth bewitched by love,
> In age bowed down with cares—
> And always unmindful of the Lord!
> The hours fly, the seasons roll, life ebbs,
> But the breeze of hope blows continually in his heart.
>
> Birth brings death, death brings rebirth:
> This evil needs no proof.
> Where then, O Man, is thy happiness?
> This life trembles in the balance
> Like water on a lotus-leaf—
> And yet the sage can show us, in an instant,
> How to bridge this sea of change.

less supported by the investigations made by Prof. Max Müller and Prof. Macdonell as well as by Prof. Keith and Dr Bhandarkar. Prof. Telang, on the basis of a reference to Pūrṇa Varman, the Buddhist king of Magadha, in the *Sūtra Bhāṣya* of Śaṅkara, pleads that he must have lived in the sixth century AD.' (*Prabuddha Bharata*, November, 1957.)

When the body is wrinkled, when the hair turns
 grey,
When the gums are toothless, and the old man's
 staff
Shakes like a reed beneath his weight,
The cup of his desire is still full.

Thy son may bring thee suffering,
Thy wealth is no assurance of heaven:
Therefore be not vain of thy wealth,
Or of thy family, or of thy youth—
All are fleeting, all must change.
Know this and be free.
Enter the joy of the Lord.

Seek neither peace nor strife
With kith or kin, with friend or foe.
O beloved, if thou wouldst attain freedom,
Be equal unto all.[1]

Śaṁkara now persuaded his mother to let him take the monastic vow, promising that he would return to visit her before she died. Then, having made arrangements for her needs, he set out in search of a teacher.

On the banks of the River Narmadā he met Gauḍapāda,[2] a famous philosopher and seer, who had attained knowledge of the Reality. Śaṁkara asked the old man for initiation, but Gauḍapāda refused. He had made a vow to remain absorbed in union with Brahman. However, he sent the boy to his foremost disciple, Govindapāda. Govindapāda initiated him and instructed him in meditation and in the whole process of yoga. Within a very short time, Śaṁkara achieved complete mystical realization, and himself went out to teach.

One morning, when he was on his way to bathe in the Ganges, he met a caṇḍāla, a member of the lowest caste, the untouchables. The man had four dogs with him, and they were blocking Śaṁkara's path. For a moment, inborn caste-prejudice asserted itself. Śaṁkara, the brāhmin, ordered the caṇḍāla out of his way. But the caṇḍāla answered: 'If there is only one God, how can there be many kinds of men? How can there be any distinctions of caste or creed?' Śaṁkara was filled with shame and reverence. He prostrated himself before the caṇḍāla. This incident inspired one of Śaṁkara's finest poems,

[1] Translated by Swami Prabhavananda and Christopher Isherwood.
[2] There is difference of opinion regarding the meeting of Śaṁkara with Gauḍapāda. See chap. 15, p. 273.

the 'Manīṣā Pañcaka'. It consists of five stanzas, each one ending with the refrain:

> He who has learned to see the one Existence everywhere,
> He is my master—be he brāhmin or caṇḍāla.

Śaṁkara began his teaching among the scholars of the country, converting the teachers first, and then their pupils. One of the teachers was the famous philosopher Maṇḍan Miśra. Maṇḍan Miśra held that the life of the householder was far superior to that of the monk, and his opinion was respected and widely shared throughout India. Śaṁkara determined to argue with him, and journeyed to his home. When he arrived, he found the doors locked. Miśra was holding a religious ceremony and did not wish to be disturbed. Śaṁkara, with the mischievous spirit of a boy in his teens, climbed a near-by tree and jumped down from it into the courtyard. Miśra noticed him among the crowd. He disapproved of monks—especially when they were so youthful—and asked sarcastically: 'Whence comes this shaven head?' 'You have eyes to see, sir,' Śaṁkara answered saucily: 'The shaven head comes up from the neck.' Miśra lost his temper, but Śaṁkara continued to tease him, and at length the two of them agreed to hold a debate on the relative merits of the life of the monk and the life of the householder. It was understood that Śaṁkara, if he lost, should become a householder, and that Miśra, if he lost, should become a monk. The debate lasted for several days. Bhārati, the learned wife of Miśra, acted as umpire. Finally, Śaṁkara was able to convince Miśra of the superiority of the monastic life, and Miśra became his disciple. It was he who later annotated Śaṁkara's commentaries on the Brahma Sūtras.

Śaṁkara's life came to an end at Kedarnath in the Himalayas. He was only thirty-two years old. During this brief period, he had established many monasteries, and had founded ten monastic orders. This was the first time that Hindu monasticism had ever been organized in India, and Śaṁkara's system still exists. He was a reformer rather than an innovator. He preached no new doctrine or creed. But he gave a new impulse to the spiritual life of his time. Separated by intervals of a thousand years, Buddha, Śaṁkara, and Rāmakṛṣṇa dominate India's religious history.

Śaṁkara's literary output was enormous. He not only made commentaries on the Vedānta Sūtras, the principal Upaniṣads, and the Bhagavad-Gītā, but produced two major philosophical works, the *Upadeśāsāhasrī* and the *Vivekacūḍāmaṇi* (*The Crest-Jewel of Discrimination*). He was also the author of many poems, hymns, prayers, and minor works on Vedānta.

The Spirit of Śaṁkara's Philosophy

'Brahman—the absolute existence, knowledge, and bliss—is real. The universe is not real. Brahman and Ātman are one.'[1]

In these words, Śaṁkara sums up his philosophy. What are the implications of this statement? What does he mean by 'real' and by 'not real'?

Śaṁkara accepts as 'real' only that which neither changes nor ceases to exist. In making this definition, he follows the teachings of the Upaniṣads and of Gauḍapāda, his predecessor. No object, no kind of knowledge, can be absolutely real if its existence is only temporary. Absolute reality implies permanent existence. If we consider our various experiences during the states of waking and dreaming, we find that dream-experiences are contradicted by waking-experiences and vice versa—and that both kinds of experience cease in dreamless sleep. In other words, every object of knowledge, external or internal (for a thought or idea is as much an object of knowledge as is the external world), is subject to modification and therefore, by Śaṁkara's definition, 'not real'.

What, then, is the reality behind all our experiences? There is only one thing that never leaves us—pure consciousness. This alone is the constant feature of all experience. And this consciousness is the real, absolute Self. In dreamless sleep, even, the real Self persists (as we realize on waking, there being no break in essential continuity), while the ego-sense, which we call 'ourself', or individuality, has become temporarily merged in ignorance (avidyā) and has disappeared.

Vedānta philosophy occupies a central position between realism and idealism. Western realism and idealism are both based on a distinction between mind and matter; Indian philosophy puts mind and matter in the same category—both are objects of knowledge. Śaṁkara should not, however, be regarded as a precursor of Berkeley: he does not say that the world is unreal simply because its existence depends upon our perception. The world, according to Śaṁkara, 'is and is not'. Its fundamental unreality can be understood only in relation to the ultimate mystical experience, the experience of an illumined soul. When the illumined soul passes into transcendental consciousness, he realizes the Self (the Ātman) as pure bliss and pure intelligence, the one without a second. In this state of consciousness, all perception of multiplicity ceases, there is no longer any sense of 'mine' and 'thine', the world as we ordinarily know it has vanished. Then the Self shines forth as the One, the Truth, the Brahman, the basis of the apparent world. The apparent world, as it is experienced in the waking state, may be likened, says Śaṁkara, to an imagined

[1] *Brahmajñānāvalīmālā*, v. 21.

snake which proves, on closer inspection, to be nothing but a coil of rope. When the truth is known, we are no longer deluded by the appearance—the snake-appearance vanishes into the reality of the rope, the world vanishes into Brahman.

Other systems of Hindu philosophy—Sāṁkhya, Yoga, and Nyāya—maintain that the phenomenal world possesses objective reality, even though it may not be apparent to the eyes of an illumined soul. Advaita Vedānta denies this objective reality. The point is a vital one. Mind and matter, finite objects and their relations, Śaṁkara holds, are a misreading of Brahman—and nothing more.

The Nature of the Apparent World

When Śaṁkara says that the world of thought and matter is not real, he does not mean that it is nonexistent. The apparent world is and is not. In the state of ignorance (our everyday consciousness) it is experienced, and it exists as it appears. In the state of illumination it is not experienced, and it ceases to exist. Śaṁkara does not regard any experience as nonexistent as long as it is experienced, but he very naturally draws a distinction between the private illusions of the individual and the universal, or world, illusion. The former he calls prātibhāsika (illusory) and the latter vyavahārika (phenomenal). For example, a man's dreams are his private illusions; when he wakes, they cease. But the universal illusion—the illusion of world-phenomena—continues throughout a man's whole waking life unless he becomes aware of the truth through knowledge of Brahman. Śaṁkara makes, also, a further distinction between these two kinds of illusion and those ideas which are altogether unreal and imaginary, which represent a total impossibility or a flat contradiction in terms—such as the idea of the son of a barren woman.

Here, then, we are confronted by a paradox—the world is and is not. It is neither real nor nonreal. And yet this paradox simply recognizes the existence of what Śaṁkara calls māyā. Māyā, this apparent world, has its basis in Brahman, the eternal. According to Śaṁkara, it consists of names and forms. It is not nonexistent, yet it differs from the Reality, the Brahman, upon whom it depends for its existence. It is not real, since it disappears in the light of knowledge of its eternal basis. The apparent world is māyā; the Self, the Ātman, alone is real.

Superimposition, or Māyā

The most difficult of all philosophical problems is that of the relation between the finite and the Infinite; the problem of how this finite world came into being. If we believe that the finite has an absolute reality of its own, and that it has emerged from the Infinite and is an actual transformation of the Infinite, or if we regard the Infinite as a transcendental first cause of the phenomenal world (a position held by most Christian theologians), then we must admit that the Infinite is infinite no longer. A God who transforms himself into the visible universe is himself subject to transformation and change—he cannot be regarded as the absolute reality. A God who creates a world limits himself by the very act of creation, and thus ceases to be infinite. The question 'Why should God create at all?' remains unanswered.

This difficulty is overcome, however, if we consider the world as māyā; and this explanation of our universe is, moreover, in perfect accord with the findings of modern science.

'A soap-bubble with irregularities and corrugations on its surface is perhaps the best representation of this new universe revealed to us by the theory of relativity. The universe is not the interior of the soap-bubble but its surface—and the substance out of which this bubble is blown, the soap film, is empty space welded into empty time.'[1]

Thus it is only when we analyse the nature of the universe and discover it to be māyā—neither absolutely real nor absolutely nonexistent—that we learn how the phenomenal surface of the soap-bubble safeguards the eternal presence of the Absolute.

The Upaniṣads, it is true, appear to consider Brahman the first cause of the universe, both material and efficient. They declare that the universe emanates from, subsists in, and finally merges in the absolute Brahman. Śaṁkara never directly contradicts the Upaniṣads, although sometimes he appears to interpret them to suit his own views. The universe, he says, is a superimposition upon Brahman. Brahman remains eternally infinite and unchanged. He is not transformed into this universe. He simply appears as this universe to us, in our ignorance. We superimpose the apparent world upon Brahman, just as we sometimes superimpose a snake upon a coil of rope.

This theory of superimposition (vivartavāda) is inseparably linked with the theory of causality. Causal relation exists in the world of multiplicity, which is māyā. Within māyā, the mind cannot function without causal relation. But to speak of cause and effect with reference to the Absolute is simply absurd. To seek to know what caused the world is to transcend the world. To seek to find the cause of māyā is to go beyond māyā—and, when we do that, māyā vanishes, the effect ceases to exist. How, then, can there be a cause of a nonexistent effect? In other words, the relation between Brahman and māyā is,

[1] Sir James Jeans.

by its very nature, unknowable and indefinable by any process of the human intellect.

Māyā: A Statement of Fact as Well as a Principle

Thus, according to Śaṁkara, the world of thought and matter has a phenomenal or relative existence, and is superimposed upon Brahman, the unique, absolute reality. As long as we remain in ignorance (that is, as long as we have not achieved transcendental consciousness), we shall continue to experience this apparent world, which is the effect of superimposition. When transcendental consciousness is achieved, superimposition ceases.

What is the nature of this superimposition? In the introduction to his commentary on the Brahma Sūtras, Śaṁkara tells us that 'Superimposition is the apparent presentation to consciousness, by the memory, of something previously observed elsewhere.'[1] We see a snake. We remember it. Next day we see a coil of rope. We superimpose the remembered snake upon it, and thereby misunderstand its nature.

Śaṁkara foresees an objection to his theory and goes on to anticipate and answer it. We may challenge the theory of superimposition by pointing out that Brahman is not an object of perception. How can we superimpose a snake upon a rope which we do not perceive? How can we superimpose a world-appearance upon a reality which is not apparent to our senses? 'For every man superimposes objects only upon such other objects as are placed before him (that is, as come into contact with his sense organs).'[2] To this, Śaṁkara answers:

> 'Brahman is not, we reply, non-objective in the absolute sense. For Brahman is the object of the ego-idea. We know quite well, by intuition, that the inner Self must exist, since the ego-idea is a presentation of the Self. Nor is it an absolute rule that objects can be superimposed only upon such other objects as are placed before us; for ignorant people superimpose a dark blue colour upon the sky, which is not an object of sense perception.'[3]

This statement needs some further explanation. Although Brahman is never apparent to our everyday sense perception, there is a manner in which we are aware of the Reality, the inner Self. Brahman, it has been said, is absolute existence, knowledge, and bliss. Only in transcendental consciousness can we know this fully. Yet Brahman is partly apparent to our normal consciousness also. Brahman is Existence, and we all know that we exist. In this sense, every one of us has an intuitive knowledge of the inner Self (the Ātman, or

[1] Commentary on I. i. 1. [2] *Ibid.* [3] *Ibid.*

Brahman-within-the-creature). The inner Self, the Reality, is never an object of sense perception, however—because, in our ignorance, we superimpose the idea of a private individuality—of being Mr Smith or Mrs Jones—upon our awareness of Existence. We are unable to understand that Existence is not our private property, that it is universal and absolute. The inner Self is therefore present in our normal consciousness as 'the object of the ego-idea'—a literal translation of Śaṁkara's phrase. The superimposition of the ego-idea upon Existence is our first and most important act as human beings. The moment we have made this central act of superimposition—the moment we have said 'I am I, I am private, I am separate, I am an individual'—we have made further superimposition inevitable. The claim to individuality for ourselves implies individuality everywhere. It automatically superimposes a multiple world of creatures and objects upon the one, undivided reality, the Existence which is Brahman. Ego-idea and world-appearance depend upon each other. Lose the ego-idea in transcendental consciousness, and the world-appearance must necessarily vanish.

When and how did this act of superimposition occur? Was it at our latest individual birth, or in some previous life? Was there a historical moment—corresponding to that in which Adam is said to have fallen—in which the phenomenal world came into being as the result of the ego-idea? The futility of such questions should be self-evident. We merely go round in a circle. What is this world-appearance? Māyā. What causes it? Our ignorance. What is this ignorance? Māyā, also. If there always was, and is, and always will be one unchanging reality, how can we possibly assume that māyā began at some definite historical moment in time? We cannot.

Therefore we are forced to conclude, as Śaṁkara does, that māyā, like Brahman, is without any beginning. Ignorance as the cause and the apparent world as the effect have existed always and will always exist. They are like seed and tree. The 'coupling of the real and the unreal', produced by our ignorance, is a process universally evident in our daily lives. Śaṁkara says: 'It is obvious and needs no proof that the object, which is the nonego, and the subject, which is the ego-idea (superimposed upon the Self), are opposed to each other, like light and darkness, and cannot be identified. Still less can their respective attributes be identified. . . . Nevertheless, it is natural to man (because of his wrong ideas) not to be able to distinguish between these distinct entities and between their respective attributes. He superimposes upon each the nature and attributes of the other, uniting the real with the unreal and making use of such expressions as "I am that," "That is mine".'[1]

[1] Commentary on I. i. 1.

Śaṁkara is speaking here of two stages in the process of superimposition. First, the ego-idea is superimposed upon the inner Self, the existence-reality. Then the ego-idea, reaching outward, as it were, identifies itself with the body and the body's mental and physical attributes and actions. We say, as a matter of course, 'I am fat', 'I am tired', 'I am walking', 'I am sitting down'—without ever stopping to consider what this 'I' really is. We go further. We claim purely external objects and names for our own. We say 'I am a Republican', or 'This house is mine'. As superimpositions multiply, extraordinary statements become possible and normal—such as 'We sunk three submarines yesterday' or 'I carry a good deal of insurance'. We identify our ego, more or less, with every object in the universe. And all the while, the inner Self looks on, utterly detached from these moods and antics, yet making them all possible by lending to the mind that light of consciousness without which māyā could not exist.

That māyā is beginningless can be shown if we return for a moment to the image of the rope and the snake. The superimposition of the snake upon the rope is possible only if we can remember what a snake looks like; a child who had never seen a snake could never superimpose it. How then is it possible for the newborn child to superimpose the world-appearance (the snake) upon Brahman (the rope)? We can answer this question only if we postulate a universal snake-memory that is common to all mankind and that has existed from a time without beginning. This snake-memory is māyā.

Māyā, says Śaṁkara, is not only universal but beginningless and endless. A distinction must be made, however, between māyā as a universal principle and ignorance (avidyā), which is individual. Individual ignorance is beginningless, but it can end at any moment; it is lost when a man achieves spiritual illumination. Thus the world may vanish from the consciousness of an individual and yet continue to exist for the rest of mankind. In saying this, Śaṁkara's philosophy differs essentially from the subjective idealism of the West.

Brahman and Īśwara

In a sense, Brahman is the ultimate cause of the universe, since, by the action of māyā, the world-appearance is superimposed upon him. Brahman is the cause, māyā the effect. Yet Brahman cannot be said to have transformed himself into the world, or to have created it, since absolute Reality is, by definition, incapable of temporal action or change. Another word, Īśwara, must therefore be employed to describe the creative principle. Īśwara is Brahman united with māyā—the combination which creates, preserves, and dissolves the universe in an endless and beginningless process. Īśwara is God personified, God with attributes.

According to the Sāṁkhya system of philosophy, the universe is an evolution of prakṛti—undifferentiated matter, composed of three forces called the guṇas. Creation is a disturbance in the balance of these forces. The guṇas enter into an enormous variety of combinations—somewhat like the atoms in Western physics—and these combinations are individual elements, objects, and creatures. This concept of prakṛti corresponds, more or less, to Śaṁkara's concept of māyā—but with this important difference: prakṛti is said to be other than and independent of Puruṣa (the absolute Reality) while māyā is said to have no absolute reality but to be dependent on Brahman. Therefore, according to Śaṁkara, it is Īśwara, rather than prakṛti, who can be described as the ultimate cause of the universe.

Are there then two Gods—one the impersonal Brahman, the other the personal Īśwara? No—for Brahman appears as Īśwara only when viewed in the relative ignorance of māyā. Īśwara has the same degree of reality that māyā has. God the person is not Brahman in his ultimate nature. In the words of Swami Vivekananda, 'The personal God is the highest possible reading of the Absolute by the human mind.'[1]

The idea is thus ingeniously illustrated by Śrī Rāmakṛṣṇa:

'Brahman may be compared to an infinite ocean, without beginning or end. Just as, through intense cold, some portions of the ocean freeze into ice and the formless water appears to have form, so, through the intense love of the devotee, Brahman appears to take on form and personality.[2] But the form melts away again as the sun of knowledge rises. Then the universe also disappears, and there is seen to be nothing but Brahman, the infinite.'[3]

Although Īśwara is, in a sense, a person, we must beware of regarding him as similar to, or identical with, the jīva, the individual human soul. Īśwara, like the jīva, is Brahman united with māyā, but with this fundamental difference—Īśwara is the ruler and controller of māyā, the jīva is māyā's servant and plaything. We can therefore say, without paradox, that we are, at the same time, God and the servants of God. In our absolute nature, we are one with Brahman; in our relative nature, we are other than the Īśwara, and subject to him.

Devotion to the Īśwara, the Personal God, may lead a man very far along the path of spirituality; it may even make him into a saint. But by itself it does not give the ultimate knowledge. To be completely enlightened is to go beyond Īśwara, to know the impersonal Reality

[1] *Complete Works of Vivekananda*, vol. III, p. 37.

[2] *Kathāmṛta*, vol. V, p. 40.

[3] *Ibid.*, vol. IV, p. 255.

behind the personal divine Appearance. We can become Brahman, since Brahman is present in us always. But we can never become Īśwara, because Īśwara is above and distant from our human personality. It follows, therefore, that we can never become rulers of the universe. To rule it is Īśwara's function, and the desire to usurp this function is the ultimate madness of the ego. It is symbolized in Christian literature by the legend of the fall of Lucifer.

Vyāsa, the author of the Brahma Sūtras, makes the same point when he says that no one will acquire the power of creating, ruling, or dissolving the universe, since that power belongs to Īśwara alone. And Śaṁkara in his commentary discusses the problem as follows:

'If a man, by worshipping the qualified Brahman (Īśwara), achieves knowledge of the Supreme Ruler while still preserving his individual consciousness—is his power limited or unlimited? When this question arises, some will argue that his power is unlimited, and they will quote the scriptural texts (referring to those who achieve knowledge of Īśwara): "They attain their own kingdom", "To them all the gods offer worship", and "Their desires are fulfilled in all the worlds".

'But Vyāsa answers this question when he adds: "Except for the power of creating the universe". The powers of Īśwara can be acquired by the liberated, but that power belongs to Īśwara alone. How do we know this? Because he is the subject of the scriptural texts concerning creation. These texts do not refer to the liberated souls, in any connection whatsoever. That is why he is called "the ever-perfect". The scriptures also say that the powers of the liberated are acquired by worshipping and searching after God; therefore the liberated have no place in the ruling of the universe. Again, because these liberated souls still preserve their individual consciousness, it is possible that their will may differ, and that, while one desires creation, another may desire destruction. The only way to avoid this conflict is to make all wills subordinate to some one will. Therefore we must conclude that the wills of the liberated are dependent on the will of the Supreme Ruler.'[1]

If there is only one consciousness, one Brahman, who is the seer and who is the seen? Who sees Brahman as Īśwara, and who is the jīva? Are they different or one?

As long as man is within the limitations of māyā, the One is seen as many. Ignorance can do no better than to worship Appearance; and Īśwara is the ruler of all appearances—the highest idea which the human mind can grasp and the human heart can love. The human mind can never grasp the absolute Reality, it can only infer its

[1] Commentary on the Brahma Sūtras, IV. iv. 17.

presence and worship its projected image. In the process of this worship, the mind becomes purified, the ego-idea thins away like mist, superimposition ceases, Īśwara and world-appearance both vanish in the blaze of transcendental consciousness, wherein there is no seer, no seen—nothing but Brahman, the single, all-embracing, timeless fact.

The Problem of Evil

Every religion or system of philosophy has to deal with the problem of evil—and unfortunately it is a problem which is usually explained away rather than explained. 'Why', it is asked, 'does God permit evil, when he himself is all goodness?'

One of two answers is usually given to this question by Western religious thought. Sometimes we are told that evil is educational and penal. God punishes us for our sins by visiting us with war, famine, earthquake, disaster, and disease. He employs temptation (either directly or through the agency of the Devil) to test and strengthen the virtue of the good. This is the answer given by the Old Testament. It repels many people today and has become unfashionable—although, according to Vedānta, as we shall see in a moment, it contains a certain amount of truth.

The other answer—now more generally accepted—is that evil does not exist at all. If we view life *sub specie aeternitatis*, we shall know that evil has no reality; that it is simply a misreading of good.

Vedānta philosophy disagrees with both these answers—with the second even more radically than with the first. How, it asks, can evil be changed into good, merely by viewing it in a special manner? Pain and misfortune may be borne more easily than would otherwise be possible, if we fix our minds upon God, but they are very real experiences nevertheless, even though their duration is limited. Vedānta agrees that evil, in the absolute sense, is unreal. But it reminds us that in this sense good is unreal also. The absolute Reality is beyond good and evil, pleasure and pain, success and disaster. Both good and evil are aspects of māyā. As long as māyā exists, they exist. Within māyā they are real enough.

The question 'Why does God permit evil?' is, in fact, most misleadingly phrased. It is as absurd as if one were to ask 'Why does God permit good?' Nobody today would ask why rain 'permitted' a catastrophic flood; nobody would blame or praise fire because it burns one man's house and cooks another man's dinner. Nor can it be properly said that Brahman is 'good' in any personal sense of the word. Brahman is not good in the sense that Christ was good—for Christ's goodness was within māyā. The Reality itself is beyond all phenomena; even the noblest. It is beyond purity, beauty, happiness, glory, or success. It can be described as good only if we mean that absolute consciousness is absolute knowledge, and that absolute knowledge is absolute joy.

But perhaps the question does not refer to Brahman at all. Perhaps, in this connection, 'God' means Īśwara, the Ruler of māyā. If this is granted, can Vedānta philosophy agree with the Old Testament that God is a law-giver, a stern and somewhat unpredictable father, whose ways are not ours, whose punishments and rewards often seem unmerited, who permits us to fall into temptation? The answer is yes and no. The Vedānta doctrine of karma is a doctrine of absolute, automatic justice. The circumstances of our lives, our pains and our pleasures, are all the result of our past actions in this present existence, and in countless previous existences, from a beginningless time. Viewed from a relative standpoint, māyā is quite pitiless. We get exactly what we earn, no more, no less. If we cry out against some apparent injustice, it is only because the act that brought it upon us is buried deep in the past, out of reach of our memory. To be born a beggar, a king, an athlete, or a helpless cripple is simply the composite consequence of the deeds of our other lives. We have no one to thank but ourselves. It is no use trying to bargain with Īśwara, or propitiate him, or hold him responsible for our troubles. It is no use inventing a Devil as an excuse for our weakness. Māyā is what we make of it—and Īśwara simply represents that stern and solemn fact.

Viewed from a relative standpoint, this world of appearance is a bleak place, and as such it often drives us to despair. The seers, with their larger knowledge, tell us otherwise. Once we become conscious, even dimly, of the Ātman, the Reality within us, the world shows itself in a very different aspect. It is no longer a court of justice but a kind of gymnasium. Good and evil, pain and pleasure, still exist, but they seem more like the ropes and vaulting-horses and parallel bars which can be used to make our bodies strong. Māyā is no longer an endlessly revolving wheel of pain and pleasure but a ladder which can be climbed to consciousness of the Reality. From this standpoint, fortune and misfortune are both mercies—that is to say, opportunities. Every experience offers us the chance of making a constructive reaction to it—a reaction which helps to break some chain of our bondage to māyā and bring us nearer to spiritual freedom. Śaṁkara therefore distinguishes between two kinds of māyā—avidyā (evil or ignorance) and vidyā (good or knowledge in a relative sense). Avidyā is that which causes us to move farther away from the Self and obscures our knowledge of the Truth. Vidyā is that which enables us to come nearer to the Self by removing the veil of ignorance. Both vidyā and avidyā are transcended when we pass beyond māyā into consciousness of the absolute reality.

It has been said already that māyā is the superimposition of the ego-idea upon the Ātman, the real Self. The ego-idea represents a false claim to individuality, to being different from, or separate from, our neighbours. It follows, therefore, that any act which contradicts this claim will bring us one step back towards right knowledge, towards consciousness of the inner reality. If we recognize our brotherhood with our fellow men; if we try to deal honestly, truthfully, charitably with them; if we work for equal rights and equal justice, politically and economically, and for abolition of barriers of race and class—then we are in fact giving the lie to the ego-idea and moving towards awareness of the universal, nonindividual Existence. All such actions belong to what is known as ethical goodness—just as all selfish actions belong to ethical evil. In one sense, and in one sense only, goodness may be said to be more 'real', or more valid, than evil: since evil actions and thoughts involve us more deeply in māyā, while good thoughts and actions lead us beyond māyā, to transcendental consciousness.

The words sin and virtue are somewhat alien to the spirit of Vedānta philosophy, because they necessarily foster a sense of possessiveness with regard to thought and action. If we say 'I am good' or 'I am bad', we are only talking the language of māyā. 'I am Brahman' is the only true statement regarding ourselves that any of us can make. St François de Sales wrote that 'even our repentance must be peaceful' —meaning that exaggerated remorse, just as much as excessive self-congratulation, simply binds us more firmly to the ego-idea, the lie of māyā. We must never forget that ethical conduct is a means, not an end in itself. Knowledge of the impersonal reality is the only valid knowledge. Apart from that, our deepest wisdom is black ignorance and our strictest righteousness is all in vain.

The Supreme Goal

It may be objected that Vedānta philosophy, like every other system of religious thought, is based upon a central hypothesis. Certainly, the supreme goal of life is to know Brahman—if Brahman exists. But can we be sure of this? Isn't it possible that there is no underlying reality in the universe? Isn't it possible that life is just a meaningless flux, a dying and a becoming in eternal alternation?

What is so attractive about Vedānta is its undogmatic, experimental approach to truth. Śaṁkara does not tell us that we must accept the existence of Brahman as a dogma before we can enter upon the spiritual life. No—he invites us to find out for ourselves.

Nothing—no teacher, no scripture—can do the work for us. Teachers and scriptures are merely encouragements to personal effort. But, as such, they can be very effective. Imagine that the existence or nonexistence of God is the subject of a lawsuit and that you are the judge. Try to listen impartially to both sides. Consider the witnesses for Brahman—the seers and saints who claim to have known the eternal reality. Consider the circumstances of their lives, their personalities, their words. Ask yourself, Are all these witnesses liars or hypocrites or insane persons, or are they telling the truth? Compare the great scriptures of the world and ask, Do they contradict each other, or do they agree? Then give your verdict.

But mere assent, as Śaṁkara insists, is not enough. It is only a preliminary step towards active participation in the search for Brahman. Direct personal experience is the only satisfactory proof of his existence, and each of us must have it.

Modern science goes a long way towards confirming the Vedānta world-picture. It admits that consciousness, in varying degrees, may be present everywhere. Differences between objects and creatures are only surface differences, varying arrangements of atomic pattern. Elements can be changed into other elements. Identity is only provisional. Science does not yet accept the concept of absolute reality, but it certainly does not exclude it. Śaṁkara knew nothing of science, but his approach is fundamentally scientific. It is based upon the practice of discrimination—a discrimination to be applied to ourselves and to every circumstance and object of our experience, at each instant of our lives. Again and again—thousands and thousands of times a day—we must ask ourselves, Is this real or unreal, is this fact or fancy, is this nature or only appearance? Thus we probe deeper and deeper towards the truth.

We all know that we exist. We are all aware of our own consciousness. But what is the nature of this consciousness, this existence? Discrimination will soon prove to us that the ego-idea is not the fundamental reality. There is something beyond it. We can call this something 'Brahman'—but 'Brahman' is only another word. It does not reveal the nature of the thing we are looking for.

Can Brahman be known as an existing substance or thing? Not in the ordinary meaning of the verb to know. To know something is to have objective knowledge of it, and such knowledge is relative, depending upon space, time, and causation. We cannot know absolute consciousness in this manner, because absolute consciousness is knowledge itself. Brahman is the source of all other knowledge; he comprises the knower, the knowledge, and that which is known. He is independent of space, time, and cause.

In this sense, the practice of discrimination differs from the method of scientific research. The scientist concentrates upon some object of knowledge, and pursues it beyond the range of physical sense-perception, with the aid of mechanical apparatus, chemical analysis, mathematics, and so forth. His research extends like a journey, deeper and deeper into time and space. The religious philosopher, on the other hand, is trying to annihilate time and space, the dimensions of the ego-idea, and thus uncover the Reality which is nearer and more instant than the ego, the body, or the mind. He is trying to be aware of what he already and always is, and this awareness is not an aspect of consciousness, but consciousness itself. The illumined seer does not merely know Brahman; he is Brahman, he is Existence, he is Knowledge. Absolute freedom is not something to be attained, absolute knowledge is not something to be won, Brahman is not something to be found anew. It is only māyā which has to be pierced, ignorance which has to be overcome. The process of discrimination is a negative process. The positive fact, our real nature, eternally exists. We are Brahman—and only ignorance divides us from knowledge of the fact.

Transcendental consciousness, or union with Brahman, can never be investigated by the methods of scientific research, since such research depends ultimately upon sense perception, and Brahman is beyond the grasp of the senses. But this does not mean that we are doomed to doubt, or to blind trust in the experience of the seers, until we have reached the supreme goal for ourselves. Even a little effort in meditation and the spiritual life will reward us with the conviction that this is really the way to truth and peace, that we are not simply deceiving or hypnotizing ourselves, that Reality is accessible. We shall have our ups and downs, of course, and our moments of uncertainty, but we shall always return to this conviction. No spiritual gain, however small, is ever lost or wasted.

By temperament, Śaṁkara inclined towards jñāna yoga, the way of pure discrimination, although he was capable of great devotion also. Renunciation, discrimination, self-control—these are his watchwords. Some may find his austerity too forbidding, but it is precisely this austerity which supplies a valuable corrective to the dangers of an easy sentimentality, an excess of carefree optimism, a confusion of real devotion with mere emotional self-indulgence. Śaṁkara was under no illusions about this world of māyā; he condemns its apparent pleasures and delights with brutal frankness. For this very reason he was able to describe so powerfully the complete transformation of the universe which takes place before the eyes of the illumined seer. When Brahman is experienced, when all creatures and objects are seen in their real relation to the Absolute, then this world is indeed a paradise; it is nothing but Brahman, nothing but utter consciousness, knowledge, and peace.

To quote Śaṁkara, describing the experience of an illumined soul:

'The ego has disappeared. I have realized my identity with Brahman, and so all my desires have melted away. I have risen above my ignorance and my knowledge of this seeming universe. What is this joy that I feel? Who shall measure it? I know nothing but joy, limitless, unbounded!

'The ocean of Brahman is full of nectar—the joy of the Atman. The treasure I have found there cannot be described in words. The mind cannot conceive of it. My mind fell like a hailstone into that vast expanse of Brahman's ocean. Touching one drop of it, I melted away and became one with Brahman. And now, though I return to human consciousness, I abide in the joy of the Atman.

'Where is this universe? Who took it away? Has it merged in something else? A while ago, I beheld it—now it exists no longer. This is wonderful indeed!

'Here is the ocean of Brahman, full of endless joy. How can I accept or reject anything? Is there anything apart or distinct from Brahman?

'Now, finally and clearly, I know that I am the Atman, whose nature is eternal joy. I see nothing, I hear nothing, I know nothing that is separate from me.'[1]

SELECTED PASSAGES FROM ŚAṀKARA'S VIVEKACŪḌĀMAṆI

CREST-JEWEL OF DISCRIMINATION

A man should be intelligent and learned, with great powers of comprehension, and able to overcome doubts by the exercise of his reason. One who has these qualifications is fitted for knowledge of the Atman.

He alone may be considered qualified to seek Brahman who has discrimination, whose mind is turned away from all enjoyments, who possesses tranquillity and the kindred virtues, and who feels a longing for liberation.[2]

Longing for liberation is the will to be free from the fetters forged by ignorance—beginning with the ego-sense and so on, down to the physical body itself—through the realization of one's true nature.[3]

Among all means of liberation, devotion is supreme. To seek earnestly to know one's real nature—this is said to be devotion.[4]

[1] *Vivekacūḍāmaṇi*, vv. 481–5.
[2] *Ibid.*, vv. 16, 17.
[3] *Ibid.*, v. 27.
[4] *Ibid.*, v. 31.

The spiritual seeker who is possessed of tranquillity, self-control, mental poise and forbearance, devotes himself to the practice of contemplation, and meditates upon the Atman within himself as the Atman within all beings. Thus he completely destroys the sense of separateness which arises from the darkness of ignorance, and dwells in joy, identifying himself with Brahman, free from distracting thoughts and selfish occupations.

Those who echo borrowed teachings are not free from the world. But those who have attained samadhi by merging the external universe, the sense organs, the mind and the ego in the pure consciousness of the Atman—they alone are free from the world, with its bonds and snares.[1]

Be devoted to Brahman and you will be able to control your senses. Control your senses and you will gain mastery over your mind. Master your mind, and the sense of ego will be dissolved. In this manner, the yogi achieves an unbroken realization of the joy of Brahman. Therefore let the seeker strive to give his heart to Brahman.[2]

The self-luminous Atman, the witness of all, is ever-present within your own heart. This Atman stands apart from all that is unreal. Know it to be yourself, and meditate upon it unceasingly.[3]

When the mind achieves perfect union with Brahman, the wise man realizes Brahman entirely within his own heart. Brahman is beyond speech or thought. It is the pure, eternal consciousness. It is absolute bliss. It is incomparable and immeasurable. It is ever-free, beyond all action, boundless as the sky, indivisible and absolute.[4]

To taste, within his own heart and in the external world, the endless bliss of the Atman—such is the reward obtained by the yogi who has reached perfection and liberation in this life.[5]

The fruit of dispassion is illumination; the fruit of illumination is the stilling of desire; the fruit of stilled desire is experience of the bliss of the Atman, whence follows peace.[6]

Teachers and scriptures can stimulate spiritual awareness. But the wise disciple crosses the ocean of his ignorance by direct illumination, through the grace of God.[7]

Our perception of the universe is a continuous perception of Brahman, though the ignorant man is not aware of this. Indeed,

[1] *Vivekacūḍāmaṇi*, vv. 355, 356. [2] v. 368. [3] v. 380.
[4] v. 408. [5] v. 418. [6] v. 419. [7] v. 476.

this universe is nothing but Brahman. See Brahman everywhere, under all circumstances, with the eye of the spirit and a tranquil heart. How can the physical eyes see anything but physical objects? How can the mind of the enlightened man think of anything other than the Reality?[1]

[1] *Vivekacūḍāmaṇi*, v. 521.

CHAPTER 17

BHĀSKARA

Still another aspect of Vedānta, known as Bhedābhedavāda, or doctrine of identity in difference, finds its exponent in Bhāskara. Oudulumi originated the system, but his writings are not now available, and we know of him only through mention of him in the Brahma Sūtras of Vyāsa. Bhāskara wrote commentaries upon the Sūtras and in so doing explained his own and Oudulumi's philosophy. In the main he attempted an attack upon Śaṁkara's doctrine of māyā. He therefore lived after Śaṁkara—according to Indian authorities, in the early part of the ninth century.

The Philosophy of Identity in Difference

Brahman is one without a second, the unchangeable reality, endowed with blessed attributes, including the power to create, sustain, and dissolve the universe. He is the formless, personal God who in his causal state is transcendental—beyond time, space, and causation; in his aspect as effect, he has evolved or become transformed into the empirical universe. Since Brahman, the Infinite, has made himself finite, as finite he is real, though he, the Infinite, is not necessarily conditioned by the finitude. Brahman as cause contains the whole universe potentially within himself, and the universe is the cause actualized, though in part only, since the cause has not exhausted itself in the effect.

Again, as effect, Brahman is both jīva, or the individual soul, and the world. He is endowed with power of two kinds: bhogya, the kind which evolves as the objective universe, and bhoktṛ, the kind which evolves as living souls. This power of Brahman is not māyā, but is real in the absolute sense.

Empirical existence therefore consists of (1) the subject, the experiencer, the jīva, and (2) the object of experience, the world of the senses. Though the empirical world of subject and object is not separate from Brahman, for it is Brahman that is evolved as the universe, yet again Brahman is not merely the universe of name and form—he is transcendental as well.[1]

Individual souls are many, and they are parts of Brahman. They are related to him as are the rays of the sun to the sun. They are neither absolutely different from God, nor are they absolutely identical with him. In the state of bondage—that is, ignorance—individual souls are different from God; and in the state of liberation—that is, knowledge—they become one with him. To the self, purified by spiritual discipline, is revealed the knowledge of Brahman, and as the self finally becomes one with Brahman, all consciousness of separation is dissolved. But this union is possible only after death, never at any time during life. In this respect the philosophy of Bhāskara differs from all the other systems we have studied.[2]

Union with Brahman is the supreme goal. As the means of achieving this, Bhāskara, like all other teachers of religion, offers the ideal of nonattachment, the ideal of being *in* the world and yet not *of* it, and the worship of Brahman and meditation upon him.

[1] Na prapañcamātraṁ Brahma.

[2] Compare this philosophy of union with God after death with the Pauline interpretation of the teachings of Christ.

CHAPTER 18

YĀMUNA

Viśiṣṭādvaita Vedānta, the Vedānta in its aspect of qualified nondualism, traces its origin to the period of the Upaniṣads; at least it had gained followers at the time of the composition of the Mahābhārata, being identical with the doctrine of Pañcarātra mentioned in that poem. In the tenth century AD, however, it received greater impetus and a brighter light from the teachings of the saint Yāmuna; and in the eleventh century the great teacher Rāmānuja, who had been influenced by Yāmuna, gave it a sound philosophical basis, and made it a popular religion, particularly in southern India. Yāmuna and Rāmānuja belong to the long line of Vaiṣṇava saints recognized in southern India and generally known as Ālvārs. Ālvār is a Tamil word which means 'he who rules the world by his love of and devotion to God'. Many legends are told of these ancient Ālvārs, and all of them clearly express love of God and devotion and self-surrender to him.

One of the Ālvārs was Nāthamuni, grandfather of Yāmuna. He was known to history as a great saint living in the early part of the tenth century. Born of a well-known brāhmin family, on the death of his son he gave up the life of the world and embraced a life of renunciation. He wrote two books which are regarded as authoritative by the Śrī Vaiṣṇava, the school of qualified nondualism.

Yāmuna, his grandson, was born in AD 953. At the age of twelve he became king of half the kingdom of Pāṇḍu. There is extant an interesting account, though obviously legendary, of how he ascended the throne.

The king of Pāṇḍu, it seems, had a court pundit who was very clever in debate; and it was the custom of the country that whoever challenged the scholarship of the pundit and defeated him in argument was appointed court pundit in turn; and whoever challenged the pundit and was defeated by him must pay him an annual sum as tax. Bhāśya, teacher of the boy Yāmuna, had been defeated by the pundit and had thus become subject to the penalty. Now it so happened that once the tax-collector appeared when Bhāśya was absent from home, and Yāmuna, feeling the humiliation of his master, challenged the pundit to debate. Though the king and his pundit were amazed at the child's temerity, they were obliged to accept the challenge.

The boy was brought to court and accorded due honour and respect. The queen felt sure that he would be crowned victor, for she could see that he was no ordinary child. When she confided her thoughts to the king, he laughed and jokingly offered to lay a wager against him. The queen said, 'If the boy is defeated, I promise to be the slave of Your Majesty's slaves.' To this the king replied, 'If the boy wins, I will offer him half my kingdom.'

So the boy and the pundit entered into debate. To the surprise of all, the boy was victorious, and the pundit was obliged to acknowledge himself beaten at the hands of a child. The king, paying his bet, offered Yāmuna half his kingdom. The boy accepted the gift and ruled for many years at peace with all men.

The news of Yāmuna's elevation to the throne came to the ears of Nāthamuni, his grandfather, who was then living as a monk. Fearing lest his grandson should give himself over to worldliness, Muni charged Nambi, his favourite disciple, to watch over him and see that he did not lose himself in love of the world but that instead he sought the truth.

When Yāmuna was thirty-five years of age, and still reigning over his kingdom, Nambi appeared before him and said, 'Your grandfather has left a vast treasure with me. If it is your desire to find this treasure, you must follow me, and follow me alone.' So Yāmuna left his kingdom and followed Nambi. As he associated closely with his grandfather's disciple, he came to admire his greatness, his love for God, his purity of conduct, and above all the peace and joy that shone in his countenance. And there arose in the heart of King Yāmuna a mighty longing to find God and attain peace. He lost all taste for the enjoyments of the world, even the desire to return to his kingdom. Both king and devotee retired to the temple of Śrī Raṅganātha. Thus Yāmuna became a monk and teacher.

In his later years Yāmuna wrote four famous books. He wished to write, in addition, a commentary on the Brahma Sūtras, but passed away before the fulfilment of this desire. As he lay dying, he expressed a wish that Rāmānuja, whom he loved much, should write the commentary. Hearing of this, Rāmānuja, who had already won fame for himself, hastened to him, but arrived too late. He promised, however, to carry out Yāmuna's wish, and succeeded in doing so.

Briefly—for we shall consider the doctrine of qualified nondualism in some detail in the chapter on Rāmānuja—the philosophy of Yāmuna consists of the following ideas.

God is the Supreme Being. He is the whole, of which individual souls are the parts. We are related to him as are the waves of the ocean to the ocean. The universe is a transformation of God. God is its soul; the visible world is his body.

The ideals of all-consuming love for God, and self-surrender to him, Yāmuna has expressed beautifully in a famous prayer:

'God is beyond the realm of speech and mind. He is the ground of speech and mind, and he is the ocean of mercy. How can we pray to him or praise him, who is worshipped and praised even by the great gods? In the ocean are drowned the high mountain and the small atom. No difference between them is felt by the ocean.

'My beloved, O thou Sweet One, "I" and "me" and "mine" all belong to thee. And if I am conscious of this truth that whatever I have—all—belongs to thee forever, then what can I offer thee?'

'I am Thine': this expresses the attitude of the devotees of Viśiṣṭād-vaita. The Vaiṣṇava devotees of Bengal preach another beautiful truth: 'Thou art mine.'

Elsewhere Yāmuna writes: 'Thou art father, thou art mother, thou art son, thou art daughter, thou art dear friend, thou art guru, thou art the supreme goal and refuge of the whole universe.' According to Yāmuna, the highest ideal is to take refuge in the Lord and surrender oneself completely to him. This ideal of surrendering oneself to God was developed by Rāmānuja, as we shall now see, into a complete philosophy.

CHAPTER 19

RĀMĀNUJA

Since human beings possess widely differing temperaments, they conduct their lives upon different levels. For this reason, no one system of religion can equally well satisfy everyone, and there exist diverse forms of religious truth. And yet, however divergent they may be, they have an underlying unity, and all of them lead men by one path or another to a single goal. The varied scriptures of the world may be likened to a kind mother who cherishes her many children by granting their demands according to their needs.

After Śaṁkara, Rāmānuja ranks first among the greatest interpreters of Vedānta. Śaṁkara's philosophy, though it did afford spiritual comfort to many, yet did not meet the requirements of all aspirants. There are men in every age who hunger for a God whom they can love, whom they can worship. Now the Absolute of Śaṁkara becomes to such men entirely too much of an abstraction to be the object of love and worship. It is true that Śaṁkara does reserve a place in his system for a God of love, and there is room in it for devotion to him; but to many his Īśwara is not wholly satisfying, for they regard him as but a lower aspect of Brahman, the Absolute. The Śaṁkara philosophy touches indeed such dizzy heights of abstraction, and at the same time offers such a surpassing degree of spiritual illumination, that it becomes extremely difficult, if not impossible, for most men either to comprehend it or to accept it. They are therefore inclined to regard this Absolute of Śaṁkara as, in the words of Dr Radhakrishnan, 'a bloodless Absolute dark with the excess of light'.[1]

So the kind mother, the scriptures, spoke once more, this time through the lips of Rāmānuja, and led the people to the bosom of truth.[2] Rāmānuja argues that God and the souls of men are not the

[1] The above remark reminds one, by way of contrast, of the bold, impersonal thinkers of the Vedic age who asked, 'Who has seen the first-born, when he that had no bones bore him that has bones?' (Ṛg-Veda, i. 4. 164, quoted by S. Radhakrishnan, *Indian Philosophy*, vol. I, p. 93.)

[2] Rāmānuja did not originate the philosophy associated with his name, but he is its chief exponent.

same, though they are not separate from each other, and that the highest ideal and the ultimate goal are to love and worship God and surrender ourselves utterly and completely to him. The material world and human beings, though different, have a real existence of their own as the body of Brahman, who is their soul and controlling power. Apart from Brahman they are literally nonentities. So Rāmānuja's philosophy is known as Viśiṣṭādvaita—that is, advaita, nondualism, with viśeṣa, or qualifications—because it admits the plurality both of matter and of souls.

Life of Rāmānuja

Rāmānuja was born at Śrī-perum-budur in southern India in the year AD 1017. His mother was the granddaughter of Yāmuna, the saint and philosopher whom we have already met. In his youth Rāmānuja journeyed to Conjeevaram in order to study Vedānta with a teacher known as Yādava Prakāś.

Yādava Prakāś, a celebrated interpreter of Vedānta, wrote a commentary upon the Brahma Sūtras which has unfortunately been lost. We do know, however, that his interpretation closely followed that of Bhāskara, who, as we have already discovered, believed in the unity of the soul with Brahman in relation to transcendental knowledge, and acknowledged difference from him in relation to ignorance. In the view of Yādava, this difference is as real as is the unity. Like Bhāskara, Yādava interpreted the philosophy of Bhedābheda, or unity in difference.

For a time, the youthful Rāmānuja pursued his studies under the direction of Yādava, but their paths soon parted. The fact was that the young man soon developed his own interpretation of the philosophy of Vedānta, and this seemed more reasonable to the other students gathered about the master than did that of the master himself. Yādava became furiously angry. He accordingly conceived a dislike and a consuming envy of his brilliant pupil.

Matters came to a head when Yādava was requested by the ruler of the country to heal his little daughter supposed to be possessed by demons. When the master failed, Rāmānuja was called upon. The story goes that at the young man's bidding the spirit left the girl, and she became quite well. Yādava now hated Rāmānuja, who was obliged to leave the master's school. But this was not enough. Yādava became so possessed by hate and jealousy that he even attempted to assassinate his young pupil, who was saved by a warning given to him by a hunter and his wife. Many years later, however, Yādava recognized Rāmānuja's greatness, repented, and became his loyal follower.

Rāmānuja now returned to his mother's home, and at her request took upon himself the state of a householder by marrying a girl of her choice.

About this time, Yāmuna, head of the temple of Śrīraṅgam, being old and sick and hearing of Rāmānuja's learning and purity of character, desired to install him as his successor. When the aged saint was about to breathe his last, his disciples sent for Rāmānuja to come to his bedside, but he did not arrive till just as Yāmuna's body was being conveyed to the river bank for cremation. As Rāmānuja viewed the corpse, he remarked that three fingers of the right hand remained closed. The disciples in explanation said that the closed fingers indicated the existence of an unfulfilled desire, which—as already mentioned—was a wish to compose a commentary upon the Brahma Sūtras. When Rāmānuja promised to take upon himself the fulfilment of this task, legend has it that the three fingers forthwith assumed their natural position.

After Rāmānuja's return to Conjeevaram, his spirit grew restless, for he could see no way to fulfil his promise. Accordingly, he sought advice of the head priest of the temple of Śrīraṅgam, who uttered a Sanskrit verse which seemed to be the word of God, and his will: 'I am the Supreme. The Truth is based upon distinction. Self-surrender is the surest way to the door of salvation. Whether man struggles or not, salvation will come in the end. Accept the discipleship of Periā Nambi.' So Rāmānuja set out to meet Nambi at the same time that Nambi was approaching Conjeevaram to meet him. They came together in a temple on the road, and Nambi initiated Rāmānuja into the mysteries of Vedānta.

Rāmānuja was not happy in his marriage, for in his heart he longed for the time when he might devote himself uninterruptedly to a life of worship and meditation. His wife, instead of aiding him to attain the spiritual ideal he desired, constantly irritated him by her thoughtless conduct. At last Rāmānuja, feeling the call of God from within, renounced all worldly ties, took monastic vows, and set out for Śrīraṅgam, where the great saint Yāmuna had desired that he should live.

While he was a monk at Śrīraṅgam, Rāmānuja became extremely popular, and many aspirants gathered round him. But still he remained unsatisfied. Now there was living at that time another saint, whose name was Gosṭhi-pūrna. Rāmānuja went to him and reverently begged to be initiated. Six times he went to him, and six times was refused. At last, however, seeing Rāmānuja's earnest devotion, Gosṭhi-pūrna initiated him with a holy mantra, a name of God, but warned him that he must never give that mantra to anyone, for if he did he would be damned, while whoever heard the sacred words would attain salvation. Upon hearing this, Rāmānuja went at once into the temple, gathered a crowd around him, and uttered the holy mantra 'Om namo Nārāyaṇāya', in the hearing of all. Gosṭhi-pūrna pretended to be very angry and rebuked him for his disobedience, but Rāmānuja replied, 'If by my damnation so many can be saved, damnation is my supreme desire.' Pleased, the saint answered, 'Because of your great love for humanity, the philosophy of Viśiṣṭādvaita shall henceforth be known as the Rāmānuja Philosophy.'

Rāmānuja now made Śrīraṅgam his headquarters, but travelled occasionally to various parts of the country, preaching and gathering many disciples. It was during this period that he wrote his commentary upon the Brahma Sūtras, as he had promised before the corpse of Yāmuna that he would do. This work is known as Śrī Bhāṣya, and is held in great respect by the followers of Śrī Vaiṣṇavism. He also wrote commentaries upon the Gītā and some original philosophical treatises propounding his doctrine. He passed away in the year AD 1137 after a fruitful life of one hundred and twenty years. He is worshipped today by thousands of his followers, and is regarded by all India as one of the greatest saints and philosophers in its history.

Viśiṣṭādvaitavāda of Rāmānuja

At the beginning of our discussion of Rāmānuja's philosophy, we need to make quite clear the distinction between the definition of knowledge given by Śaṁkara and that given by Rāmānuja, for upon this distinction is based the entire difference between these two great philosophers. If properly understood, it will at once make clear in how many different lights the same truth may be viewed.

According to Śaṁkara, knowledge is self-luminous, light itself. It illumines objects of knowledge, and is therefore apart from and beyond the relation of subject and object. Relative knowledge is not true knowledge; it is not pure consciousness, though grounded upon it. Knowledge, by itself, is absolute. It is the Ātman, Light itself. Relative knowledge is infinite knowledge made finite.

Rāmānuja, on the other hand, does not take into consideration knowledge that is self-luminous and absolute. Knowledge, he declares, is always relative, and in it there is always a distinction between subject and object. In short, Rāmānuja does not admit nirvikalpa samādhi, the unitary consciousness, the experience of the Self as one with Brahman. He was at heart a bhakta, a devotee, who preserved his distinction from Brahman in order to enjoy the bliss of divine love. In consequence, his philosophy is one of devotion, although, being based on careful reasoning, it is not merely emotional in its nature.

One other point of difference between the two great philosophers should be noted. What Śaṁkara calls māyā, which is neither real nor unreal, and which, when joined to Brahman, the Absolute, attributeless and impersonal, becomes the personal Īśwara, or God, Rāmānuja calls Śakti, or power, which in its nature is real and eternally coexistent with Brahman. Thus Rāmānuja does not accept the impersonal, attributeless Brahman of Śaṁkara, but rather an eternal personal Brahman, the repository of all blessed qualities.

Theory of Knowledge

Perception, inference, and scripture are valid as sources of knowledge, and also, each on its own level, as an affirmation of reality. Unlike Śaṁkara, Rāmānuja does not admit a distinction between illusory perception and true perception, for he declares that even in illusory perception, so-called, there is some perception of reality. Thus all experience has its validity.

Rāmānuja's theory of dharma-bhūta-jñāna, or consciousness as an attribute and not the thing itself, explains his conception of the threefold function of knowledge: it gives reality; it has the power to reveal the truth; and it can reveal the truth of Brahman.

So long as man, owing to his imperfections imposed by karma, is crippled in knowledge, Brahman may not be revealed to him. But after he has been purified, he may have immediate intuition of God. This immediate intuition, as we have elsewhere remarked, is not the highest transcendental consciousness described in the Upaniṣads and by Śaṁkara as turīya, and as nirvikalpa samādhi by the yogis, but rather it is a transcendental experience of God in which there still remains the ego as distinct from him. The experience is described as savikalpa samādhi by the yogis, and it comes through absorption in meditation and devotion. This revelation of God in meditation possesses a self-certifying character, and, further, the fact that God is so revealed in the heart of man is borne witness to by the seers and saints of the Upaniṣads, as well as by the saints and seers of all ages and in all lands.

Brahman, or God

In the Upaniṣads we read, 'The knower of Brahman attains the highest.'[1] This text expresses the unity of the threefold nature of wisdom, namely: tattwa, or intellectual and philosophic understanding of Brahman; hita, or way to Brahman; and puruṣārtha, direct perception of Brahman as the supreme goal.

Let us first try philosophically to comprehend the nature of

[1] Taittiriya, II. i. 3.

Brahman. This is tattwa. Brahman is determinate and can therefore be defined by a statement of his essential attributes. In the words of the Upaniṣads, 'Brahman is satyaṁ [or real], jñānaṁ [or conscious], and anantaṁ [or infinite]'.[1] Śaṁkara does not consider these as attributes of Brahman. But Rāmānuja accepts them as essential.

Brahman is the basis of all existence, and since he is also the supreme good, he is also the supreme goal. The universe is composed of cit, the sentient, and acit, the nonsentient. Cit and acit have their source in Brahman, and he is the indwelling Self within all and the ruler of all.

Brahman is both the first cause and the final cause of the universe of the sentient and the nonsentient. 'Brahman . . . wills to be many', we read in the Upaniṣads, and he divides himself into the manifold universe of the living and of the nonliving. This fact does not mean, however, that the act of creation had an absolute beginning in time. The universe, as explained by all systems of Indian thought, alternates between the phases of involution and evolution. In the phase of involution it remains latent in Brahman, and creation or evolution is the actualization of the latent. The one becomes the many, not in the pantheistic sense of emanation, but in the sense that Brahman, by exercise of his will, evolves the twenty-four categories and the jīvas, or individual souls. Brahman is the material as well as the efficient cause of the universe. 'From him the universe has emerged, in him it exists, and unto him it returns.'[2] 'As the web comes out of the spider and is withdrawn, as plants grow from the soil and hair from the body of man, so springs the universe from the eternal Brahman.'[3] God, as the source and support of the universe, has transformed himself into the cosmic manifold; and he is the indwelling Self in his creation, the ruler and director of the cosmic process. The evil that the universe contains is the result of the karma of individuals, for whom God is the dispenser of the law. He, himself, remains unaffected by evil, and is forever absolutely good.

God, though he has transformed himself into the universe of sentient and nonsentient forms, remains distinct from them. Matter is the object of experience, individual souls are the experiencing subjects, and God is the lord and ruler of all. He is defined in the Upaniṣads (as we have seen) as satyaṁ, real; jñānaṁ, conscious; and anantaṁ, infinite. Rāmānuja, in commenting on this text, points out that because of these distinctive attributes God is above and beyond matter (which is changing phenomena) and distinct from individual souls caught in its meshes. Thus, though the universe is a transformation of Brahman, he remains by his nature beyond change, and though immanent, he is transcendent.

[1] Taittirīya, II. i. 3. [2] *Ibid.*, III. i. [3] Muṇḍaka, I. i. 7.

So does Rāmānuja define God as the repository of infinite, noble, and blessed qualities, and as one 'not only differentiating himself into the cosmos but remaining absolutely distinct from it'. Yet, again, 'he is its stuff and soul'.

Brahman, then, is related to the cosmos as the soul is related to the body. As a man has a soul and a body, and as the soul, though distinct from the body, yet controls and guides it, lives in it, and uses it as an instrument, similarly Brahman is the soul of the universe, the source and sustenance of all beings within it, and the ruler over all. In this body-and-soul connection between Brahman and the cosmos are included the three relations defined by Rāmānuja: 'ādhāra and ādheya—support and the supported; niyāmaka and niyamya—the controller and the controlled; śeṣin and śeṣa—the Lord and his servant'. Professor P. N. Srinivasachari, a deep student of Rāmānuja, speaks of this triune relationship thus:

'The relation of ādhāra and ādheya [support and the thing supported] is from the point of view of metaphysics which defines Brahman as real (satya), conscious (jñāna), and infinite (ananta). This relation emphasizes the inner unity of Reality. The relation of niyāmaka and niyamya [controller and the controlled] brings out the transcendental goodness of God and his redemptive impulse. The relation of śeshin and śesha [the Lord and his servant] satisfies the highest demands of ethics and aesthetics by defining God as the supreme Lord for whose satisfaction the world of chit [the sentient] and achit [the insentient] lives, moves and has its being. The relation of body and soul combines all the three together and serves as an analogical representation of a spiritual truth.'[1]

God as the controller of the universe is absolutely good and the redeemer of all beings. Evil and suffering, be it repeated, are caused by the individual's karmas. Karmas—good or evil deeds—create happiness or misery; but by karmas alone man cannot redeem himself. Only the grace of God can save him; God is therefore the saviour. In his infinite love, his absolute goodness, he is forever merciful, for he even becomes flesh in human form in order to redeem the prodigal and to rejoice in the ecstasy of communion with his devotee. The Gītā, as we have seen, expounds the idea of avatār, or divine incarnation; Rāmānuja tells us that the central motive of God in descending to earth in human form is his love for humanity and his desire to save it.

[1] *Cultural Heritage of India*, vol. I, p. 567.

Jīvas, or Individual Souls

The finite self is not a separate self-existent entity, but an organ, an element of Brahman. It is a part of Brahman, essentially different from him but inseparably bound to him. The finite self is anu, or atomic like the point of a goad, though it admits of no spatial division from the fact that it is spirit. The finite self, then, is an essential attribute (prākāra) of God; and as substance and attribute, though inseparably associated, are yet absolutely distinct from each other, so God as substance is absolutely distinct from the individual soul. As inseparably associated with God, the individual self is eternal; and as distinct from him, it has a personality of its own and a free will. But God, being also the inner ruler of the cosmos, which forms his body, 'makes the soul act'. Not that man's acts are good or evil as guided or forced by God—for God permits the individual to choose between good and evil. Eventually, however, by his grace God restores all souls to himself. Man's choice of good or evil, in short, is an exercise of his free will that makes him responsible for his actions, while God remains unaffected by them.

Free will, furthermore, is given in order that man may eventually detach himself from the meshes of ignorance and grow into the 'personality of God'. Though Rāmānuja tries to refute the doctrine of māyā as expounded by Śaṁkara, he is obliged to admit in the final analysis the existence of māyā, or ignorance, in man; for the self, he believes, has forgotten its divine origin and its divine destiny, and tends to identify itself with matter, until it becomes subject to the evils of saṁsāra, or empirical existence. The true Self, which is an eternal mode of God, has degenerated into ego by becoming a mode of matter. We free ourselves from this ego when we surrender ourselves to God. Our free will, a gift of God, finds fulfilment of its purpose when we live in conformity with the will of God, who is our divine source and the Self of ourselves.

The poet Tennyson in two lines sums up the implications of free will and self-surrender:

> Our wills are ours we know not how,
> Our wills are ours to make them Thine.

The Supreme Goal

As we have already stated, God is the tattwa, the truth; he is the hita, the ways and means, and he is the puruṣārtha, the supreme goal.[1]

Not only must we give intellectual assent to the truth that we live,

[1] Cf.: 'I am the way, the truth, and the life' (John xiv. 6).

move, and have our being in God, but we must have awareness of this truth. Like all true saints and philosophers, Rāmānuja held that God can be known and realized, that a vision of his being is possible for man, and that man must strive to attain it. And he realized, like all saints, that the vision of God is vouchsafed to man by God himself out of his infinite love and grace.

Self-effort and divine grace are not opposed to each other; neither is divine grace conditional. In the words of Śrī Rāmakṛṣṇa, the breeze of divine grace is blowing, but we must set sail to catch it. In the same way Rāmānuja explains how we must love God, serve him, and meditate on him; and then, as spiritual hunger grows within us, we experience love and divine grace flowing from him and flooding our whole being. The culmination of spiritual experience, he says, is then realizing God's unbounded love and finding complete refuge in him. To find complete refuge in him is the ideal of self-surrender, or prapatti, which is not extinction of self, but rather a union of our will with the will of God.

Rāmānuja did not believe in a complete identity of man with God. For him kaiṅkarya, or living in the service of God, was the supreme ideal. This ideal of service, however, must not be confused with a modern Christian ideal, that of helping God to realize his own fullness. In this Christian ideal there exists a strong element of egotistical pride. The truth is that God does not need our help; we realize our own fullness by loving and serving him.

Rāmānuja did not, however, believe in jīvanmukti, or liberation in this life, but rather in videha mukti, or liberation after death—death, for him, being a passing 'through the path of light' to our permanent home in God. In death the self realizes union with God as his body, his part, his attribute. Never is there a dissolution of jīvahood, or individual personality. Professor P. N. Srinivasachari has beautifully summarized this ideal of freedom in the following words:

'Release is not freedom in embodiment but freedom from embodiment; it refers to the return of the prākāra or mukta [released soul] to his home in the absolute. [Ramanuja's absolute, however, is not the Absolute proper—but the Personal God.] Mukti [freedom] is beyond the range of materialism and mentalism and involves the intuition of the infinite as well as its attainment. The finite has its roots in the infinite and in mukti there is the coalescence of content without the abolition of existence. When the freed self sees God face to face, its logical outlook becomes a spiritual insight, and freed from the nescience of empirical life, it expands into omniscience. It has a sense of the infinite and sees everything with the eye of the all-self. When the self is Brahmanized, it is stripped of its self-hood and sense of separateness, shakes off the shackles of karma based on kāma [desire] and effaces itself in spiritual service and solidarity. The finite remains, but the fetters of finitude and individualism are removed.'[1]

The Ways and Means of Attainment

In explaining hita, the practical aspect of his philosophy, Rāmānuja insists that God is the Lord of Love, and he prescribes bhakti yoga. 'Bhakti yoga', explains Swami Vivekananda, 'is a real, genuine search after the Lord, a search beginning, continuing, and ending in Love. One single moment of the madness of extreme love of God brings us eternal freedom.'[2]

Śaṁkara laid great stress upon jñāna yoga, the path of knowledge, but Rāmānuja laid stress upon bhakti yoga, the path of love. Both these saintly philosophers admit the need of love and devotion as well as the need of knowledge; only Śaṁkara preaches love as a means to knowledge and Rāmānuja preaches love as both means and end. Rāmānuja, on the other hand, admits knowledge as a means to love, whereas Śaṁkara insists that knowledge is both means and end. I do not believe that there exists, after all, any real difference between their explanations of the means. Swami Vivekananda declares, it is a distinction without much difference. When Rāmānuja speaks of knowledge as a means, he has in mind not transcendental knowledge but intellectual analysis; and when Śaṁkara speaks of love as a means, he has reference to an inferior form of worship. 'Each seems', says Swami Vivekananda, 'to lay a great stress upon his own particular method of worship, forgetting that with perfect love true knowledge is bound to come, even unsought, and that from perfect knowledge true love is inseparable.'[3]

As he explains what meditation is, Rāmānuja also explains what true love is, and how with love and devotion we necessarily must meditate upon God. In his commentary upon the first aphorism of the Vedānta Sūtras, he gives an illuminating explanation of this interlocking of love and meditation:

'Meditation is a constant remembering [of the thing meditated upon], which flows like oil poured from one vessel to another. When this kind of remembering has been attained [in relation to God] all bonds break. Thus the scriptures speak of constant recollectedness as a means to liberation. This remembering again is the same as seeing, because it has the same significance, as is evident from the passage, "When He who is far away and near is seen, the bonds of the

[1] *Ramanuja's Idea of the Finite Self*, pp. 98–9.

[2] *Complete Works of Vivekananda*, vol. III, p. 31.

[3] *Ibid.*, vol. III, p. 34.

heart are broken, all doubts vanish, and all effects of karma disappear." He who is near can be seen, but he who is far away can only be remembered. Nevertheless the scriptures say that we have to see Him who is near as well as far away, thereby indicating to us that the above kind of remembering is as good as seeing. This remembrance when exalted assumes the same form as seeing. . . . Worship is constant remembering, as may be seen from the principal texts of the scriptures. Knowing, which is the same as repeated worship, has been described as constant remembering. . . . Thus the memory, which has attained to the level of direct perception, is spoken of in the Sruti [scripture] as a means of liberation. "This Atman is not to be reached through various sciences, nor by intellect, nor by much study of the Vedas. Whomsoever this Atman desires, by him is the Atman attained; unto him this Atman reveals himself." Here, after saying that mere hearing, thinking, and meditating are not the means of attaining this Atman, the passage continues—"Whomsoever this Atman desires, by him the Atman is attained." The extremely beloved is desired; he by whom this Atman is extremely beloved becomes the most beloved of the Atman. So that this beloved may attain the Atman, the Lord himself helps. For it has been said by the Lord: "Those who are constantly attached to Me and worship Me with love—I give that direction to their will by which they come to Me." Therefore it is said, to whomsoever this remembering, which is the same as direct perception, is very dear, because it is dear to the object of such memory-perception, he is desired by the Supreme Atman, by him the Supreme Atman is attained. This constant remembrance is denoted by the word bhakti (love).'[1]

With respect to the method and means of attaining bhakti, Rāmānuja remarks: 'Its attainment comes through discrimination, control of the passions, habitual practice of religious disciplines, sacrificial work, purity, strength, and suppression of excessive joy.'

By discrimination is meant the distinguishing, among other things, of good food from bad. Body and mind being interrelated, purity of food is important, especially for beginners, because it enables them to think pure thoughts.

Control of the passions is the strengthening of the will and its guidance towards meditation on the Lord. 'By practice and non-attachment is it to be attained.'

Sacrificial work refers to the five great sacrifices mentioned in the Vedas.

Purity is both external and internal. In the list of qualities conducive to purity, Rāmānuja enumerates the following: satya, truthfulness;

[1] Vivekananda's translation; *Complete Works of Vivekananda*, vol. III, pp. 34–5.

ārjava, sincerity; dayā, doing good to others; ahiṁsā, noninjury; abhidyā, noncovetousness, not thinking vain thoughts, not brooding over injuries received from others.

Strength is vigour of mind.

Lastly is suppression of excessive joy. Excessive joy fritters away the energies of the mind, and yet we must be cheerful. Swami Vivekananda rightly says:

'The person who aspires to be a bhakta must be cheerful. In the Western world the idea of a religious man is that he never smiles, that a dark cloud must always hang over his face, which, again, must be long-drawn with the jaws about collapsed. People with emaciated bodies and long faces are fit subjects for the physician, they are not yogis. It is the cheerful mind that is persevering. It is the strong mind that hews its way through a thousand difficulties. And this, the hardest task of all, the cutting of our way out of the net of maya, is the work reserved only for giant wills.'[1]

Rāmānuja makes some slight distinction between bhakti, or devotion, and prapatti, or self-surrender. When love for God arises in the heart, the highest attainment comes in the surrendering of our wills to God's will and in our living, literally, in the service of God. But, as we have seen, according to Rāmānuja there never comes complete union of man and God, of the lover and the beloved. And yet the greatest lovers and devotees tell of the ultimate consummation of love in mystic union—'I and my Father are one'—the union which knows neither separation nor distinction.

To the student of Western philosophy, Rāmānuja's ideas concerning God and the soul bear an astonishing resemblance to ideas on the same subjects with which Scholastic philosophy concerned itself during the Christian Middle Ages. The personality and the attributes of God the Heavenly Father, the relation of man to God, the question of free will and divine grace, the submission of the will of man to a higher will than his, the union of human and divine, the relative positions of reason and love in the divine scheme, the vision of divine love and grace, and the release of the soul from bondage after death—it was principally on these topics that the Schoolmen speculated through many hundreds of years, from St Augustine until the final synthesis of faith and reason in St Thomas Aquinas. And Rāmānuja, living in the tenth century, might well have been the spiritual father of the Christian Dante. It is true that medieval Christianity placed far greater emphasis upon the sense of sin than is to be found anywhere in Hindu philosophy, but in the teachings of

[1] *Complete Works of Vivekananda*, vol. III, p. 69.

Rāmānuja all the other mysteries of Christian theology seem to find their counterpart. We may add in this connection that the greatest Christian mystics attained the height of realization by following bhakti yoga, or the path of love and devotion, the same method of attainment that was taught by Rāmānuja.

CHAPTER 20

NIMBĀRKA

There are four chief schools of Vaiṣṇavism (Vedānta in its devotional aspect): Śrī, of which Rāmānuja is the principal exponent; Sanaka founded by Nimbārka in the eleventh century; Brāhma, founded by Mādhwa in the twelfth century; and Rudra, founded by Vallabha in the sixteenth century. To these should be added the Bengal Vaiṣṇavist school, whose founder was Śrī Caitanya, the prophet of Nadiā. We are here concerned with Nimbārka only.

Very little is known of Nimbārka's life, but he is held in reverence as one of the greatest saints of India, and the monastery he is said to have founded is still a celebrated place of pilgrimage.

Nimbārka's philosophy remains unique in that it never attacked other schools of philosophy. Nearly all of those who wrote commentaries on the Brahma Sūtras in the wake of Śaṁkara attempted to refute his doctrine of nondualism, but without much success. In my discussion of certain of these philosophers I have avoided their endless disagreements with Śaṁkara and with one another in favour of points of agreement and harmony. Infinite is God and infinite are the ways to apprehend and comprehend him—and such was the opinion of Nimbārka also as he approached the fundamental problems of God, the universe, and the human soul.

According to Nimbārka's philosophy of Bhedābheda, or dualism in nondualism, Brahman has two aspects, the absolute and the relative, or, in other words, the impersonal and the personal. In his personal aspect, Brahman possesses attributes, and from him as person has issued the universe of name and form. But Brahman has not exhausted himself in the creation of the universe, for he is also transcendental and impersonal, without attributes, and as such he is greater than the universe.

The universe is, however, one with, as well as different from, Brahman, even as the wave is one with but different from the ocean, or a ray of the sun is one with but different from the sun. Such also is the relationship between individual souls and Brahman; they are at once one with him and different from him. It is not merely a distinction between the part and the whole that we have in mind, for they are both a part of Brahman, and one with him.

Thus there exists almost an identity between the philosophy of Nimbārka and that of Bhāskara, but with the important difference that according to Bhāskara the individual soul is a part of Brahman only so long as it remains in ignorance—that in knowledge and emancipation it becomes one with him; whereas Nimbārka declares that the individual soul is a part of Brahman, and is also one with him, both in the state of ignorance and in that of knowledge and emancipation.

In the state of ignorance—according to Nimbārka—the individual soul experiences the empirical world of phenomena, while in the state of liberation it attains the superconscious, transcendental vision of the noumenal, the absolute Brahman, at the same time that it realizes itself as living both in union with Brahman and separate from him.

Nimbārka lays stress upon both knowledge and devotion as means of attaining freedom. Knowledge reveals the true nature of Brahman, and devotion culminates in all-absorbing love for him and in complete surrender of the finite will to the infinite will, although in both the love and the surrender the individual self remains.

For the followers of Nimbārka, Kṛṣṇa and his divine consort Rādhā embody both supreme will and supreme love.

CHAPTER 21

MĀDHWA

Mādhwa, another celebrated commentator upon the Brahma Sūtras, founded the Vaiṣṇava sect known as Brāhma or Sad Vaiṣṇavism.

He was born in the year AD 1199, of brāhmin parents, in the village of Biligram, which is near the modern town of Udipi in the western part of what is now the Madras Presidency. He was sent to the village school but proved himself to be more an athlete than a scholar. Physically strong and swift, he defeated his playmates in running, in jumping, in swimming, and in other athletic feats. But he left school at an early age and continued his studies of the sacred scriptures at home alone. In later years, his learning was shown in his knowledge of these scriptures, especially the Purāṇas, and of the science of logic.

During the period of his study at home, he was seized with a burning desire for renunciation, and at the age of twenty-five he took monastic vows and devoted himself to the Vedānta philosophy under the guidance of a teacher who expounded its nondualistic aspect. Soon, however, Mādhwa began to differ from his guru in his interpretation of Vedānta. He wrote an independent commentary upon the Gītā, revealing scholarly ability and logical penetration. As a result of his studies, he soon developed a school of philosophy of his own.

In the course of extensive travels in the peninsula of India, he encountered the exponents of many systems of thought, discussed ideas with them, and attempted with success to gain a hearing for his doctrines. He passed away at the age of seventy-nine.

Mādhwa wrote commentaries upon the Upaniṣads, in addition to those on the Brahma Sūtras and the Gītā already mentioned, and also many treatises in which he expounded his own views and attacked others, particularly Śaṁkara's theory of māyā. In the following paragraphs are summed up main aspects of his philosophy.

The proposition on which Mādhwa bases his realism is that both the knower and the object of knowledge must be real, for otherwise no knowledge would be possible. Knowledge necessarily implies them. All knowledge is relative. Absolute knowledge, or the transcendental consciousness, in which all distinction between knowledge, knower, and known vanishes—as absolute knowledge is defined in Yoga and by Śaṁkara—cannot be admitted. 'No knowledge can be known', says Mādhwa, 'without the knower and the known.'

Pramāṇas, the means and instruments of knowledge, are perception, scriptural texts, and inference. Whatever is known through these is directly related to the object of knowledge, which has a reality of its own.

On this theory of knowledge, Mādhwa erects his theory of the objective reality of the world. The world is real because it is perceived as such. The objects presented to our perception may be either subject or not subject to change, and the fact that an object is fleeting and changeable does not mean that it is not real.

Our experience is the experience of difference. We see things and things, people and people, and we perceive them to be different from one another. Different from all living beings and nonliving things is God, who exists in order that his law may be fulfilled in the universe, and in order that finite souls, less limited than nonliving things in power and intelligence, may find release from the sufferings and bondage of the world in loving him and surrendering themselves to him.

Mādhwa's whole philosophy is thus based upon the idea of difference or distinction. And distinctions are known to be five in number: (1) God is distinct from individual souls; (2) God is distinct from nonliving matter; (3) one individual soul is distinct from every other; (4) individual souls are distinct from matter; and (5) in matter, when it is divided, the parts are distinct from one another.

The universe is divided into two categories: Swatantra, independent being, and aswatantra, dependent beings. God is the only independent being. He is the one omnipotent, omniscient, and omnipresent being. How God, who is distinct from individual souls and nonliving things, can be omnipresent is explained by saying that he is not limited by time and space and that the dependent beings 'do not form a resisting medium to his presence'.

(1) Matter is distinct from God and human souls and in itself is only a dependent being. (2) God is the ruler of the universe, but the universe is real and eternally existent.

Each soul is distinct from every other, and all souls are distinct from God, though they have dependent existence in him. By nature souls are intelligent. Each soul when born into this world and invested with body and senses is in a state of bondage, but by continued struggle through many lives release from this bondage may be obtained.

Moreover, although souls are distinct from one another, they fall into classes. Of these there are three, differing in their essential nature as well as in their destiny. One class, who are moral and devoted to God alone, will attain salvation and enjoy the eternal felicity of heaven—an abode called Vaikuṇṭha. The second class will never attain salvation but will remain subject to rebirth, experiencing in life after life both happiness and misery. The third class, who revile Viṣṇu and his devotees, will never attain salvation but will be subject to damnation.

This belief of Mādhwa, that only a few attain salvation while the rest cannot, and some even suffer damnation, is contrary to the teachings of all other Indian religious schools. Mādhwa may possibly have been influenced by certain Christian missionaries who during his time may have penetrated into India.

Only such souls as are devoted to Viṣṇu will attain salvation—that is, go to Vaikuṇṭha and enjoy the beloved company of God. But even in Vaikuṇṭha there are gradations of souls and therefore differences between them.

CHAPTER 22

VALLABHA

Vallabha, the founder of the Vaiṣṇava sect known as Rudra, lived during the first half of the sixteenth century. He was celebrated for his saintly character and for his great love of God and of the divine incarnation Śrī Kṛṣṇa. Like most of the other Vedānta philosophers, he wrote commentaries upon the Brahma Sūtras in which he expounded his philosophy. He also commented upon the Bhāgavatam, one of the Purāṇas—a class of scriptures which he held in high esteem. During the latter part of his life he resided in Banaras, where a monastery has been built in his name and where he is worshipped as the greatest teacher of the Rudza sect.

Brahman in his aspect of love is the centre of Vallabha's teaching. Brahman is personal; that is, he is endowed with divine attributes. He also possesses a spiritual body, which is blissful. A lover of God can realize mystic union with him in his spiritual body.

Brahman has projected this universe out of himself. No other motive can be attributed to him for this act of creation than a purely sportive one; that is, it was done as play (līlā)—just for fun. Though Brahman has transformed himself into the universe, he remains unchanged. This act of unchanging change is called avikṛta pariṇāma, unchanged transformation. It may be added that though God has become everything, he remains unaffected by the sinfulness of individual souls. Though an individual soul is atomic, it is yet a part of Brahman, and as such is pure and divine. The soul resides in the heart, though its intelligence is manifested in every part of the being of man, as the fragrance of sandal paste is diffused in the atmosphere though the paste itself occupies but a small portion of space.

The soul is unborn and undying, for it is the body that undergoes birth and death and change. Souls, which differ in their nature because God desires variety for the sake of play, may be divided into three classes: those who are steeped in worldliness, those who follow spiritual injunctions and gradually grow spiritual in their nature, and those who love God for love's sake.

According to Vallabha, the universe is real if it is seen truly, as a creation of God and as one with him. The universe in which suffering and bondage are experienced is not one with God; it is an appearance caused by ignorance of individual souls and therefore is unreal. This ignorance, the cause of the unreal universe, consists of egoism and attachment.

Souls differ in their nature, as we have seen, and the difference is due to the will of God. That there is the ignorance of egoism and attachment is also due to the will of God; he wills it, this too, because he loves variety and play. In all of this no room is left for human responsibility. God is made responsible, as in a jest, for evil and suffering.

Vallabha admits the efficacy of the paths of knowledge, selfless work, and devotion, if one would attain spiritual growth. He also admits the state of absorption in and union with Brahman. But to him to love for love's sake is the supreme path, and living in mystic union with the Beloved Lord is the supreme goal of life. After we have freed ourselves from all egoism, and from all attachment to the unreal world, and have found the real world in God, and after there arises a hunger for God's love like that of the shepherdesses for Kṛṣṇa, then it is that we reach the supreme goal. To love Kṛṣṇa as the Beloved, as this love is depicted in the Bhāgavatam, is regarded by Vallabha as the highest achievement in life.

CHAPTER 23

ŚRĪ CAITANYA

In Śrī Caitanya is to be found the culmination and fulfilment of the philosophy and the religion of love. Through him Vaiṣṇavism, which is the philosophical expression of the ideal of love for God, ushered in a new era in the higher life of Bengal. His ideas have found exquisite expression in a richly emotional collection of hymns which have been a peculiar contribution of Bengal to Indian culture. Every Bengali has in his blood a liberal admixture of Śrī Caitanya's religion of love.

Even more than his philosophy, it is Śrī Caitanya's pure and gentle character—his loving-kindness and his ecstatic love of God—that has ruled, and still rules, the hearts of the people of Bengal. He knew no distinction of caste or creed in his immense love of God and man; all men, whether they were sinners or saints, were to him but creatures of God, and his heart overflowed with sympathy for the lowly, the suffering, and the destitute. So his very name excites genuine spiritual emotions in the hearts of those who know about him. His followers see in him Kṛṣṇa reborn in the flesh.

Śrī Caitanya was born in the year 1485 at Navadwīp, at that time a large city in Bengal and the seat of Sanskrit learning, particularly of grammar and logic. His parents lost their first eight children, all of them daughters, in infancy, and the ninth, a boy named Viśwarūpa, at an early age entered a monastery in southern India. Śrī Caitanya was the youngest son. He was given the name of Viśwambhar and was nicknamed Nimāi. He was also called Gour or Gourāṅga (fair complexioned) because of the exquisite beauty of his person. The name Śrī Kṛṣṇa Caitanya he received when he was admitted to the order of monks.

As a small baby he was afflicted with prolonged fits of weeping, the only remedy for which his mother found to be the chanting of the name of Hari (God). As a boy, he was full of mischief and took pleasure in teasing others and playing pranks. He lost his father when he was eleven years old. It was then that he seriously applied himself to studies in literature and grammar and other branches of knowledge. His master was Vāsudeva, the well-known teacher of Sanskrit and the famous founder, in conjunction with his brilliant pupil Raghunāth, of the Neo-logic (Nabya-Nyāya) of the Bengal school.

An interesting story is told of the relation between Raghunāth and the young Caitanya. The former, a fellow-student, being at work upon his famous treatise on logic, learned that Caitanya was writing a book of the same character. He asked his friend to read a few pages to him, and when he heard them he grew dispirited. 'I cherished a hope', he said in answer to a question from Caitanya, 'of leaving a name behind me, but I realize that my work will not be read if yours is given to the public.' To this Caitanya replied: 'This trivial matter must not disturb you. I will see that your work is recognized.' Thereupon Caitanya threw his own manuscript into the Ganges.

Though he had not yet completed his education, at sixteen he opened a school of his own at Navadwīp, and in that city he gained fame as one of the greatest teachers of grammar and logic of his time. Hundreds of students flocked to him. While he was teaching at Navadwīp, he wrote a book on Sanskrit grammar which was widely used.

At the age of twenty-two or twenty-three he departed on a pilgrimage to Gaya, the site of a famous temple dedicated to Viṣṇu. It was at Gaya that Buddha, centuries before, sat under the Bodhi tree, and here the young Śrī Caitanya, then known as Nimāi Pundit, while worshipping at the feet of Viṣṇu, received a sudden illumination that transformed his being. Tears rolled down his cheeks, and he lost himself in ecstasy. Amongst the pilgrims was a monk, Īśwar Purī, a sannyāsin of the order of Śaṁkara, who had met Caitanya before and knew him as a great scholar. Now, as he witnessed his ecstatic condition, he recognized in him a great devotee. Caitanya asked for blessings from Īśwar Purī, who then initiated him into the worship of Kṛṣṇa.

Nimāi returned to Navadwīp a changed man. The unrivalled scholastic debater, the grammarian, the logician, now disappeared. Instead, there stood before men a serene, exalted person, continually chanting 'Kṛṣṇa, Kṛṣṇa'. His former students gathered about him as had been their custom, but he could no longer teach them. 'Brothers,' he cried, 'I can no longer give you lessons. Whenever I attempt to explain anything to you, I see before me the little boy Kṛṣṇa, playing upon his flute. You had better seek some other teacher.' Thereupon he sang a kirtan (chant), which has come down to this day and is sung by the Vaiṣṇavas of Bengal.[1]

[1] This chant, which is composed of the many names of Kṛṣṇa, together with words describing his various attributes, is sung to the accompaniment of certain

Now there gathered round the master devotees who found joy in the contemplation of God. So did Śrī Caitanya become a great spiritual force in the city of Navadwīp, and the lives of many unbelievers were transformed by the touch of this God-intoxicated man. Some of his disciples in later years played an important part in the religious life of Bengal by preaching his message of love and giving peace and consolation to many a hungry soul.

At the age of twenty-five, but two years after his conversion at Gaya, Śrī Caitanya was seized by a burning desire to forsake the world. Of his renunciation Swami Durga Chaitanya Bharati, a follower of Śrī Caitanya, and his biographer, writes as follows:

'The story of Gouranga's renunciation has few parallels in history. The heart-rending story of his renunciation, when he left his aged mother, loving young wife, and all Navadwip bewailing his separation from them, soon spread in all directions and moved the people in a way that nothing else had done before in Bengal. This story has since been carried to the furthest corners of the country through poetry, songs, ballads, dramas, and discourses, and yet even after these four hundred and forty-four years it has not lost in the least in its original pathos. There is no man or woman, young or old, who even to this day hearing of Gouranga's renunciation is not moved to tears.'

He took monastic vows at the hands of Keśava Bhārati. To him he related how in a dream he had received a mahāvākya—the sacred words Tat Tvam asi[1] (That Thou art) which were revealed to the seers of the Upaniṣads, and which the great saint and philosopher Śaṁkara accepted as containing the very essence of ultimate truth. Keśava Bhārati, in initiating Gourāṅga into the mysteries of the life of a monk, also initiated him into this same mahāvākya.

Whatever his disciples may have set forth in their systems of thought, Śrī Caitanya discovered an essential harmony between love and knowledge. His biographers tell us that he possessed a dual personality. On the one hand, while he was in samādhi, having lost consciousness of the outer world and all sense of 'me and mine', he taught men that he was one with God; on the other, upon his return to normal consciousness, he remained a lover of God, and he could not bear the thought that he was one with him.

In the normal state of consciousness he desired 'to taste the sweet-

musical instruments. The devotees join in the singing and dance in ecstatic joy. The chant begins thus: 'Hari Haraye namaḥ, Kṛṣṇa Jādavāya namaḥ; Gopāla, Govinda, Rāma, Śrī Madhusudana.'

[1] Chāndogya, VI. xiii. 3.

ness of sugar, not to become sugar'. Śrī Rāmakṛṣṇa has explained this attitude of the saint by remarking that like an elephant he had two sets of teeth, one with which to chew his food, the other with which to defend himself against attack. Śrī Caitanya moved in two states of consciousness. While in the normal state, he was a dualist: he was the lover of God, and God was the Beloved. In samādhi, however, he realized the truth of nondualism; the lover and the Beloved became one. To the outside world and for the masses of men, he preached the ideal of love and the philosophy of dualism; but to the chosen few he preached the highest truth, which he dared not reveal to all men since not all men are prepared to receive it—the supreme truth of nondualism. This aspect of his practice is corroborated in his famous conversation with Rāmānanda Roy, which we shall describe later.

Śrī Rāmakṛṣṇa, who fully appreciated the spiritual greatness of Śrī Caitanya, remarked:

> 'Śrī Caitanya used to experience three moods. In the inmost mood he would be absorbed in samādhi, unconscious of the outer world. In the semiconscious mood he would dance in ecstasy but could not talk. In the conscious mood he would sing the glories of God.'[1]

It is interesting to note in this connection that Śrī Caitanya, though he did not accept Śaṁkara's doctrine of māyā, nowhere denounced Śaṁkara, as did most of the philosophers of the doctrine of love who preceded him. On the contrary, he very plainly stated, as is recorded by his disciples, that Śaṁkara wrote his commentary and expounded his philosophy by direct command of God.[2]

But to return to the story of Caitanya.

After his initiation into the monastic order he set out for Puri, the well-known place of pilgrimage. There he resided for many years, with occasional departures for preaching or teaching. At one time he toured southern India, worshipping in many of the temples, but without prejudice against forms or aspects of the one Godhead other than those which they represented. He also visited Brindaban, the holy seat of the Vaiṣṇavas, where Kṛṣṇa had engaged in his divine play with the shepherds and shepherdesses. The present Brindaban owes much to Śrī Caitanya and his disciples for rescuing the holy place from oblivion.

[1] *Kathāmṛta*, vol. IV, p. 223.

[2] Śrī Caitanya did not comment on the Brahma Sūtras as did his predecessors. Once he remarked that the Bhāgavata Purāṇa is the best commentary on the Brahma Sūtras. Valadeva Vidyābhuṣan, one of his followers, wrote a commentary called Govinda Bhāṣya, in which he expounded the Caitanya philosophy.

During most of the last twelve years of his life, Caitanya lived in samādhi and in the state midway between samādhi and normal consciousness. In these states he was like mad in his love of Kṛṣṇa, sometimes enjoying the sweetness of union with him, and suffering the pangs of separation from him. The pangs, too, were sweet.

Śrī Caitanya's last days were spent in Puri. Here his overmastering, consuming love for God transformed the lives of thousands. In the Jagannath Temple of Puri his influence continues to be felt.

The passing of Śrī Caitanya is shrouded in mystery, his biographers giving no certain account of it. Most of them, however, do state that at the age of forty-eight he entered a temple and came out no more, simply disappearing. So there exists the belief that in the image of God in the temple Caitanya lives for eternity.

Śrī Caitanya's Philosophy of Love

Śrī Caitanya gave little care or attention to a theoretical consideration of the problems of God, the human soul, and the universe. Above all things he was a God-intoxicated man. His spiritual experiences transcended the realm of time, space, and causation; his mind plunged into the domain where God is not an abstraction, but a reality in which dwell all joy, all sweetness, all love—a reality situated deep in the loving hearts of his devotees.

God, it is said, is Sat-chid-ānanda—Existence, Knowledge, and Bliss—he is absolute, indefinable, inexpressible. He is the repository of infinite blessed attributes, the one Existence from whom the universe has issued forth, in whom the universe at last dissolves—the omnipresent, the omniscient, the omnipotent.

Such has been the account men have given of God, but to Śrī Caitanya these aspects of the Godhead meant little. For him God was Kṛṣṇa, the God of love—enchantingly beautiful, eternally youthful; and man was the eternal playmate, the eternal companion. For him, however, this Kṛṣṇa was not the Kṛṣṇa of history, who uttered the mighty spiritual discourses of the Gītā, the philosopher and the harmonizer and the avatār. For him he was the Kṛṣṇa of Brindaban, the great lover and the embodiment of love, divested of all the powers of the Godhead, the companion of shepherds and shepherdesses, playing upon his flute and drawing souls unto him by his compelling love; he was the Soul of souls eternally dwelling in Brindaban—not a land one can point to on a map but the heart of man, the Brindaban that is beyond time and space.

Love divine, which is Kṛṣṇa, is not to be acquired by man, for it is already existent in the soul, though covered by ignorance, by attachment to the world of the senses. When the clouds of ignorance have been swept away, this love, forever existing, becomes manifest. Then does man realize himself.

We may remind the reader in this connection of the philosophy of Śaṁkara. Śaṁkara declared that infinite knowledge is identical with the Self, but that this knowledge is covered over by ignorance. What Śaṁkara called infinite knowledge Śrī Caitanya called infinite love. In reality, there is no difference between the two.

To make manifest this infinite love—according to Śrī Caitanya—one must practise sādhan-bhakti, or disciplinary devotion, by chanting the name of God, hearing and singing his praises, meditating upon the divine play and deeds of Kṛṣṇa, and engaging in the rites and ceremonies of worship. He laid special stress on japa—repeating the name of God to the count of beads. Patañjali, also, the father of Yoga philosophy, approved the practice of japa as one of the methods of spiritual attainment, for the name of God and God, he said, are inseparable. In chanting God's name one necessarily meditates upon his presence.

Śrī Caitanya also emphasized the practice of ethical virtues, particularly humility and forbearance.

By the conduct recommended, one causes the divine love to be made manifest in the heart. Of this manifestation there are five stages, corresponding to various expressions of love on the plane of human life.

First there is śānta, the peaceful stage, in which, as he finds joy in the thought of God, the aspirant attains poise and tranquillity. He feels God near him, but still no definite relationship between the two has been established.

Then comes dāsya, the servant stage, in which the aspirant feels that God is the master, or that he is the father, the protector.

The third is sakhya, the stage of friendship. God is now realized as friend and playmate. He is felt to be nearer as the sense of awe vanishes and the God of power and grandeur is forgotten. He is now only the God of love—a cherished friend.

The fourth is vātsalya, the child stage. Now, Kṛṣṇa, God of love, is a child, and the devotee must take care of him. This stage we think of as higher than the preceding stages because in our human relationships a father or mother has a deeper affection for a child than a child has for its parents.

The fifth and last stage is madhura, the sweetest of relationships, the relationship between the lover and the beloved. The strongest of human ties, that between man and wife, finds its ultimate realization in the new tie between man and God, in which God is the beloved, and in which all the elements of love—admiration, service, comradeship, communion—are present.[1] The highest expression of this type of love is to be found in the shepherdesses of Brindaban, above all in Rādhā. When this kind of love possesses the heart, mystic union is attained.

The following famous conversation between Śrī Caitanya and Rāmānanda, one of his principal disciples, epitomizes the philosophy of the Master as this is recorded by his biographers, and which I give here in my own words.

Śrī Caitanya. What is the goal of life?
Disciple. A man must follow the rules and injunctions prescribed in the scriptures.
Śrī Caitanya. This is the external part of religion—only a means, not the goal. Try again.
Disciple. Surrendering the fruits of action to Kṛṣṇa.
Śrī Caitanya. This, too, is external. Try again.
Disciple. Realizing the devotion that arises from self-surrender.
Śrī Caitanya. This, too, is external. Try again.
Disciple. Realizing devotion with knowledge.
Śrī Caitanya. This, too, is external. Try again.
Disciple. Realizing pure devotion, which knows no reason.
Śrī Caitanya. That is good. Go further.
Disciple. Realizing loving devotion, which is the best goal.
Śrī Caitanya. That is good. Go further.
Disciple. Acquiring the spirit of service to Kṛṣṇa.
Śrī Caitanya. That is good. Go further.
Disciple. To love Kṛṣṇa as a friend.
Śrī Caitanya. That is very good. Go further.
Disciple. To love Kṛṣṇa as a child.
Śrī Caitanya. That is also good. Go further.
Disciple. To love Kṛṣṇa as the beloved bridegroom.
Śrī Caitanya. This is no doubt the ultimate goal. But tell me if there is any attainment further than this.
Disciple. My understanding does not reach beyond this. But there is another stage called Prem-Vilās-Vivarta.

The biographers of Śrī Caitanya record that at this point Śrī Caitanya stopped Rāmānanda from speaking, indicating thereby that the highest truth, the highest secret, must not be divulged. Prem-Vilās-Vivarta is the truth of mystic union, wherein there is no longer a distinction between the lover and the beloved. In this is realized the truth of nondualism: Tat Tvam asi—Thou art That.

[1] An analogy may be drawn between this attitude of madhura and the mystic marriages which are performed in certain Christian monastic orders between the nuns and Christ the Heavenly Bridegroom.

A PRAYER[1]

by

Śrī Caitanya

Chant the name of the Lord and His glory unceasingly
That the mirror of the heart may be wiped clean
And quenched that mighty forest fire,
Worldly lust, raging furiously within.
Oh Name, stream down in moonlight on the lotus-heart,
Opening its cup to knowledge of Thyself.
Oh self, drown deep in the waves of His bliss,
Chanting His Name continually,
Tasting His nectar at every step,
Bathing in His Name, that bath for weary souls.

Various are Thy Names, Oh Lord,
In each and every Name Thy power resides.
No times are set, no rites are needful, for chanting of Thy Name,
So vast is Thy mercy.
How huge, then, is my wretchedness
Who find, in this empty life and heart,
No devotion to Thy Name!

Oh, my mind,
Be humbler than a blade of grass,
Be patient and forbearing like the tree,
Take no honour to thyself,
Give honour to all,
Chant unceasingly the Name of the Lord.

Oh Lord and Soul of the Universe,
Mine is no prayer for wealth or retinue,
The playthings of lust or the toys of fame;
As many times as I may be reborn
Grant me, Oh Lord, a steadfast love for Thee.

A drowning man in this world's fearful ocean
Is Thy servant, Oh Sweet One.
In Thy mercy
Consider him as dust beneath Thy feet.

[1] Translated from the Sanskrit by Swami Prabhavananda and Christopher Isherwood, *Vedanta for the Western World* (Christopher Isherwood, ed., New York: Viking Press, 1960; London: Allen & Unwin, 1948), p. 225.

Ah, how I long for the day
When, in chanting Thy Name, the tears will spill down
From my eyes, and my throat will refuse to utter
Its prayers, choking and stammering with ecstasy,
When all the hairs of my body will stand erect with joy!

Ah, how I long for the day
When an instant's separation from Thee, Oh Govinda,[1]
Will be as a thousand years,
When my heart burns away with its desire
And the world, without Thee, is a heartless void.

Prostrate at Thy feet let me be, in unwavering devotion,
Neither imploring the embrace of Thine arms
Nor bewailing the withdrawal of Thy Presence
Though it tears my soul asunder.
Oh Thou, who stealest the hearts of Thy devotees,
Do with me what Thou wilt—
For Thou art my heart's Beloved, Thou and Thou alone.

[1] Govinda is another name of Śrī Kṛṣṇa.

CHAPTER 24

ŚRĪ RĀMAKṚṢṆA

Śrī Rāmakṛṣṇa has appeared frequently in the preceding chapters, at points where he has been invoked to light up some obscure doctrine or to reconcile some apparently conflicting views. He now becomes, himself, the subject of a chapter.

He was born in 1836 in Kāmārpukur, a small village in West Bengal, to a brāhmin family. His parents were of humble means, but extremely pious and devout. When Śrī Rāmakṛṣṇa was five years old, he was sent to the village primary school. Here he learned to read and write, but showed great aversion to arithmetic. His speech was charming, and he was endowed with so wonderful a memory that if he but once heard a song or a play he could perfectly reproduce its text. He loved acting. Instead of attending school and minding his studies, he would run away with some of his schoolfellows to a mango-grove on the outskirts of the village, and there, with boyish exuberance, perform the pastoral drama of Śrī Kṛṣṇa's life.

When he was six or seven years old, he had a striking experience—one which he often related to his disciples in later years. 'I was walking alone in a paddy field,' he would say, 'carrying a small basket of puffed rice. Looking at the sky overhead while eating the rice, I saw that it was covered with rain clouds. Suddenly I noticed snow-white wild cranes flying in a row against that dark background. I was overwhelmed by the beautiful sight. An ecstatic feeling arose in my heart, and I lost all outward consciousness. I do not know how long I remained in that state. When I regained consciousness I was in my home, brought there by some friendly people.'[1]

At the age of nine Śrī Rāmakṛṣṇa was invested, according to brāhmin custom, with the sacred thread, and initiated into the Gāyatrī mantra, a Vedic prayer. He was thenceforward allowed to do the worship of the household deity, Rāma. He manifested religious moods. He would often remain for a long time absorbed in God, losing all outward consciousness. He used to go alone into the woods,

[1] See *Līlāprasaṅga*, Sādhak bhāv, p. 47.

find a solitary place, and there meditate for hours under the shade of a tree.

Many wandering monks would halt and rest at Kāmārpukur on their way to Puri, the well-known place of pilgrimage. A rich man of the village had built a guesthouse for the pilgrims and had also made it a practice to provide them with food. As a young boy, Śrī Rāmakṛṣṇa was often in their company and would do small services for them, and they loved him.

During his early teens, the ideal of a monastic life attracted Śrī Rāmakṛṣṇa, but he soon gave up the idea, thinking to himself, 'To renounce the world just for one's own liberation is selfishness. I must do something that will be of benefit to all mankind.'[1]

Within a short time after his investiture with the sacred thread, there occurred an incident which showed his keen spiritual understanding. An important gathering of pundits took place at the house of a rich man of the village on the occasion of a memorial service. At this meeting there arose a controversy regarding a complicated philosophical question, and the scholars could not arrive at any correct solution. Śrī Rāmakṛṣṇa and other young boys were present to see the fun. While his friends were enjoying themselves mimicking the gestures of the pundits, Śrī Rāmakṛṣṇa was seated silently by an elderly scholar and was listening intently to the discussion. Suddenly he touched the pundit and whispered in his ear. The elderly man listened attentively to Śrī Rāmakṛṣṇa's words, and seeing immediately that the boy had given a cogent solution, he stood up with him on his shoulder and repeated it to the company. All the pundits praised young Rāmakṛṣṇa and blessed him with all their heart. And the villagers marvelled at his understanding.[2]

When he was seven years old, Śrī Rāmakṛṣṇa's father died. Rāmkumār, his eldest brother, who was a great Sanskrit scholar, went to Calcutta and opened a Sanskrit school to earn his living and support the family. When, years later, he learned that young Rāmakṛṣṇa was neglecting his studies in the village, he sent for him, intending to have him study in his Sanskrit school. It is a shame, Rāmkumār thought, that a brāhmin boy of his family should remain ignorant. So Rāmakṛṣṇa, now seventeen, went to Calcutta. But when Rāmkumār asked him to attend his school, the young boy replied with great firmness, 'Brother, I do not wish to waste my life on a mere bread-winning education. I want to acquire that knowledge which would awaken in me consciousness of the eternal Reality and thus make my life blessed forever.' He remained adamant on the subject, and his brother was at a loss what to do with him.[3]

[1] See *Līlāprasaṅga*, Bālya jīvan, p. 140.
[2] *Ibid.*, Guru bhāv, Pt. I, p. 137.
[3] *Ibid.*, Sādhak bhāv, p. 64.

An unexpected event solved the problem. An enormously wealthy woman named Rāṇī Rāsamaṇi built a temple on the bank of the Ganges at Dakṣiṇeśwar, five miles north of Calcutta. It was dedicated to the Mother of the Universe. Rāmkumār was asked to be the priest of this temple, and he took his young brother to help him. Śrī Rāmakṛṣṇa liked the calm, serene atmosphere of the place, and so it came about that here at Dakṣiṇeśwar, by the sacred river, he spent the rest of his life.

Rāmkumār died after serving only a year as temple priest. Rāmakṛṣṇa was now appointed to his brother's place. He performed the daily duties of a priest, but his inquiring mind longed for something more, and he questioned within himself: 'What is all this for? Is the Divine Mother real? Does she listen to my prayers, or is this mere imagination conjured up by human brains?' He began to yearn increasingly for the direct realization of God the Mother. And soon life became unbearable without her. He would rub his face on the ground like one gripped by pain and cry: 'Oh, Mother, another day is gone and still I have not seen you!' Finally, one day, she revealed herself. Śrī Rāmakṛṣṇa later described his first vision of the Divine Mother to his disciples. To quote his words:

'House, walls, doors, the temple—all disappeared into nothingness. Then I saw an ocean of light, limitless, living, conscious, blissful. From all sides waves of light, with a roaring sound, rushed towards me and engulfed and drowned me, and I lost all awareness of outward things.'

When Śrī Rāmakṛṣṇa regained consciousness, he was uttering the words 'Mother, Mother'.[1]

To his disciples he used to say:

'When true yearning for God comes, then follows the sight of him, then rises the sun of knowledge in the heart. Yearn for him, and love him intensely! . . . The mother loves her child, the chaste wife loves her husband, the miser loves his wealth; let your love for God be as intense as these three loves combined—then shall you see him!'[2]

After the first vision of the Mother of the Universe, Śrī Rāmakṛṣṇa longed to see her continuously. A sort of divine madness seized him. And then, to use his own words, he began to see the Mother 'peeping from every nook and corner'. After this he could no longer perform the ritualistic worship. Worldly people thought he had lost his sanity. One day, in the midst of the food offering to the Deity, he gave the offering to a cat which had walked into the temple, recognizing the

[1] See *Līlāprasaṅga*, Sādhak bhāv, p. 124.

[2] *Kathāmṛta*, vol. I, p. 27.

presence of the Divine Mother in the cat. Naturally in the eyes of the world this was either madness or sacrilege.

Śrī Rāmakṛṣṇa's behaviour became stranger and stranger; but it must be noted that whenever persons of genuine spirituality met him they considered him to have attained a blessed state—as we shall see later.

At last rumours of his strange conduct reached the ears of his mother at Kāmārpukur, and she became anxious to see him. So he went to his village to visit her. He was now twenty-three years old. In Kāmārpukur he continued to live in a God-intoxicated state, indifferent as ever to worldly concerns. Finally his mother and brother thought marriage would be just the thing by which to interest him in worldly matters. Accordingly they began to look about for a suitable bride. Śrī Rāmakṛṣṇa did not object, and the search was enthusiastically continued, but with no success. In the end, finding his mother and brother depressed by their failure, Śrī Rāmakṛṣṇa said to them in a semiconscious state: 'It is useless to try here and there. Go to Jayrāmbāṭī [a village three miles from Kāmārpukur] and there you will find the bride, the daughter of Rāmacandra Mukhopādhyāya, providentially reserved for me.' The girl was found, but she was only five years old. Her parents were agreeable to the marriage, but Candrā Devī, mother of Śrī Rāmakṛṣṇa, was somewhat hesitant because of her tender age. However, considering the fact that the girl was the one selected by her son, she assented. So without delay Śrī Rāmakṛṣṇa was married to Sāradā Devī. After the marriage ceremony was over—it was more a sort of betrothal—Sāradā Devī was sent back to her parents' home. Śrī Rāmakṛṣṇa continued to stay at Kāmārpukur for about a year and a half.

When Śrī Rāmakṛṣṇa returned to the temple garden at Dakṣineśwar, he forgot his marriage and its responsibilities and plunged deeper and deeper into spiritual practices.

In 1861, about six months after his return from Kāmārpukur, Śrī Rāmakṛṣṇa one morning noticed a sannyāsinī (nun) with long dishevelled hair alighting from a country boat and entering the courtyard of the temple. He sent for her. As soon as the sannyāsinī met Śrī Rāmakṛṣṇa, she burst into tears of joy and said, 'My son, you are here! I have been searching for you so long, and now I have found you at last.'

'How could you know about me, Mother?' asked Śrī Rāmakṛṣṇa.

She replied, 'Through the grace of the Divine Mother I came to know that I was to meet three of you. Two I have already met, and today I have found you.'[1]

This nun's name was Yogeśwari, but she was known as the

[1] *Līlāprasaṅga*, Sādhak bhāv, p. 204.

Brāhmaṇī. She was a woman of high spiritual attainments and was well versed in Vaiṣṇava and Tāntric literature. Śrī Rāmakṛṣṇa sat beside her like a little boy sitting by his mother, and told her of his spiritual struggles, visions, and attainments. He further mentioned to her that people thought he was mad. Full of motherly tenderness, she said, 'Who calls you mad, my son? This is divine madness. Your state is what is known as mahābhāva. Śrī Rādhā experienced it, and so did Śrī Caitanya. I shall show you in the scriptures that whoever has earnestly yearned for God has experienced this state.'[1]

So far, whatever spiritual advances Śrī Rāmakṛṣṇa had made were the result of his own independent struggles. He saw the Divine Mother of the Universe, and talked with her. Now she commanded him to undergo spiritual disciplines under the direction of the Brāhmaṇī. Śrī Rāmakṛṣṇa accepted her as his first guru. She also, as we have seen, had received the mandate from the Mother to teach this young man.

The Brāhmaṇī, as already stated, was learned in Hindu religious literature. She began at once to teach Śrī Rāmakṛṣṇa the spiritual disciplines recommended in the Tantras. But of this we may hear from Śrī Rāmakṛṣṇa himself:

'After performing the worship of the Divine Mother, I used to meditate according to the Brāhmaṇī's directions. As soon as I began to tell my beads, I would be overwhelmed with ecstatic fervour and enter into samādhi. I cannot describe the wonderful spiritual visions I used to have. They followed one another in quick succession. The Brāhmaṇī made me undergo all the sixty-four kinds of spiritual disciplines mentioned in the principal Tantras. Most of these were difficult practices, but the infinite grace of the Mother carried me through them with ease.'[2]

After attaining the goal aimed at in the Tāntric spiritual disciplines, Śrī Rāmakṛṣṇa took to the practices of Vaiṣṇavism. The Vaiṣṇavas follow the path of devotion, which advocates worshipping God as a Personal Being in his aspect of Viṣṇu. It is Viṣṇu who from time to time appears on earth in human form—an avatār. He once lived as Rāma, the hero of the Rāmāyaṇa, and again as Kṛṣṇa, the avatār of the Bhagavad-Gītā and the Bhāgavata Purāṇa. In following the path of devotion, the worshipper enters into a relation to God in his form of Rāma or Kṛṣṇa. There are five such relations, corresponding to those on the human plane (we have met them before): Śānta, the peaceful attitude, with only an indefinite relation; dāsya, the relation of servant to master or of child to parent; sakhya, the relation of

[1] *Līlāprasaṅga*, Sādhak bhāv, p. 205. [2] *Ibid.*, pp. 220–1.

friend to friend; vātsalya, the relation of parent to child; and madhura, the sweet relationship of lover to the beloved. Vaiṣṇavism is the philosophy propounded and lived by such saints and seers as Rāmānuja, Vallabha, Mādhwa, and Śrī Caitanya.

Śrī Rāmakṛṣṇa entered into the Vaiṣṇava path first by worshipping Rāma as his own child, the relation of vātsalya, for there had come to him a mystic saint, Jaṭādhāri, who had attained the highest spiritual state as a devotee of Rāma, and who initiated him into his own form of worship. Afterwards Śrī Rāmakṛṣṇa took up various relations in his devotion to Kṛṣṇa. Through each of these he achieved union with God.

A few months later Totā Purī came to the temple garden at Dakṣiṇeśwar. Totā Purī was a Vedāntic monk of the order of Śaṁkara, and an illumined soul, a knower of Brahman. As soon as he met Śrī Rāmakṛṣṇa, he recognized in him a highly advanced spirit. He asked him, 'Should you like to learn Vedānta from me?'

Śrī Rāmakṛṣṇa answered, 'I don't know, but I shall ask Mother.'

'All right, go and ask Mother. I shall not be here long!' Śrī Rāmakṛṣṇa went to the temple and received a command from the Divine Mother—'Yes, go and learn of him. It is for this purpose that he has come here.' In a state of semiconsciousness, and with a beaming countenance, Śrī Rāmakṛṣṇa returned to Totā Purī and said that he had received the Mother's permission.[1]

Totā Purī now acquainted him with the Upaniṣadic teaching of the identity of the Ātman with Brahman, and initiated him into the monastic life.

'After the initiation [says Śrī Rāmakṛṣṇa] "the naked one"[2] asked me to withdraw my mind from all objects and to become absorbed in contemplation of the Ātman. But as soon as I withdrew my mind from the external world, the familiar form of the blissful Mother, radiant and of the essence of pure consciousness, appeared before me as a living reality and I could not pass beyond her. In despair I said to the naked one, "It is hopeless. I cannot raise my mind to the unconditioned state and reach the Ātman." He grew excited and sharply said, "What! You say you can't do it! No, you must!" So saying he looked about him, and finding a piece of broken glass picked it up. Pressing its point between my eyebrows, he said, "Concentrate the mind on this point." Then with great determination I began to meditate as directed, and when this time also the blessed form of the Mother appeared before me, I used my discrimination as a sword and severed her form in two. Then my mind soared

[1] *Līlāprasaṅga*, Sādhak bhāv, pp. 311–12.
[2] Śrī Rāmakṛṣṇa used to refer to Totā Purī as naṅgtā, the naked one.

immediately beyond all duality and entered into nirvikalpa, the nondual, unitary consciousness.'[1]

Totā Purī sat for a long time silently watching his disciple. Then he left the room, locking the door behind him. Three days passed, and still he heard no sound. When Totā Purī finally opened the door, he found Śrī Rāmakṛṣṇa seated in the same position in which he had left him. Totā Purī watched him, and wondered, 'Is it really true that this man has attained in the course of a single day what took me forty years of strenuous practice to achieve?' He examined Śrī Rāmakṛṣṇa closely and in joyous bewilderment exclaimed, 'Great God! It is nothing short of a miracle!' It was the nirvikalpa samādhi—the culmination of nondual Vedāntic practice. Totā Purī now took steps to bring his disciple's mind down to the normal plane. Slowly Śrī Rāmakṛṣṇa regained consciousness of the outer world, and seeing his guru before him, he prostrated. And Totā Purī gave his disciple a warm embrace.[2]

After Totā Purī had left Dakṣiṇeśwar, Śrī Rāmakṛṣṇa resolved to remain immersed in nirvikalpa samādhi, and he passed six months in this state without any consciousness of body or of external surroundings. In later years he referred to this period of his life as follows:

'For six months I remained continuously in the bliss of union with Brahman. I was not conscious of day or night. It would have been impossible for the body to survive except that a monk who was present at the time realized my state of mind and regularly brought me food; and whenever he found me a little conscious, he would press it into my mouth. Only a little of it reached my stomach. Six months passed in this way. . . . At last I received the Mother's command: "Remain in bhāvamukha for the good of mankind."'[3]

Henceforward, in general, Śrī Rāmakṛṣṇa lived in bhāvamukha, a state between samādhi and normal consciousness. It is very difficult to understand exactly what this state is. In later years, however, the Master described it. He said it was as if on the ocean of Brahman, that infinite ocean of existence, knowledge, and bliss, a stick was floating, dividing the ocean into two parts. On one side is God, and on the other side his devotee—in this case Śrī Rāmakṛṣṇa. The stick which divides the ocean is the ripe ego,[4] never forgetful that it is a child of God. The ripe ego is not harmful. It is like a sword that has touched the philosopher's stone and turned into gold.

[1] *Līlāprasaṅga*, Sādhak bhāv, pp. 319–20. [2] *Ibid.*, Sādhak bhāv, p. 321.
[3] *Ibid.*, Guru bhāv, Pt. I, pp. 61–2.
[4] The unripe ego is the barrier that separates man from God and makes him forgetful of the divine.

In later years while Śrī Rāmakṛṣṇa would be teaching the word of God he often went into samādhi. This was a daily occurrence.

Now to resume our story. The practice of spiritual disciplines, however, did not stop with the Vedāntic experience in Śrī Rāmakṛṣṇa's case. He had travelled the paths of devotion, yoga, and knowledge, and he had realized the truths taught in Tāntrikism, Vaiṣṇavism, and Vedānta. But his heart longed to enjoy the divine life of those outside the pale of Hinduism.

Buddha he regarded as one of the incarnations of God. He remarked about him: 'People think Buddha was an atheist, but he was not. Only he could not express in words what he had experienced. When one's buddhi [intellect] merges in the absolute, pure consciousness, one attains the knowledge of Brahman, one realizes one's true nature, and that is to become Buddha—enlightened.'[1] So, according to Śrī Rāmakṛṣṇa, Buddha was a Vedāntist—only misunderstood.

Islam and Christianity, however, belonged in a different category. These now attracted Śrī Rāmakṛṣṇa. A Sufi mystic living at Dakṣiṇeśwar initiated him into the Islam faith. In Śrī Rāmakṛṣṇa's own words:

> 'I began to repeat the holy name of Allah, and would recite the Namaz regularly. After three days I realized the goal of that form of devotion.'[2]

First, Śrī Rāmakṛṣṇa had a vision of a radiant person with a long beard and a solemn countenance. Then he experienced Brahman with attributes, which finally merged into the Impersonal Existence, the attributeless Brahman.[3]

It was some years later that Śrī Rāmakṛṣṇa wanted to explore Christianity. One devotee used to explain the Bible to him whenever he came to Dakṣiṇeśwar. Thus Śrī Rāmakṛṣṇa became drawn to Christ and Christianity. Then one day while he was seated in the drawing-room of Jadu Mallick's garden house, he saw a picture of the Madonna and Child. He fell into a deeply meditative mood, and the picture suddenly became living and effulgent. A deep love for Christ filled Śrī Rāmakṛṣṇa's heart, and there opened before him a vision of a Christian church with devotees burning incense and lighting candles before Jesus. For three days Śrī Rāmakṛṣṇa was under the spell of this experience, and on the fourth day, while he was pacing near the Pañcavati grove at Dakṣiṇeśwar, he saw an extraordinary-looking person of serene countenance approaching with his gaze intently fixed on him. From the inmost recesses of Śrī Rāmakṛṣṇa's

[1] *Kathāmṛta*, vol. V, p. 109.

[2] See *Līlāprasaṅga*, Sādhak bhāv, p. 335.

[3] *Ibid.*

heart came the realization: 'This is Jesus, who poured out his heart's blood for the redemption of mankind. He is none other than the ṛṣi Christ, the embodiment of love.' The Son of Man then embraced Śrī Rāmakṛṣṇa and became merged in him. At this the Master went into samādhi. Thus was Śrī Rāmakṛṣṇa convinced that Jesus was an incarnation of God.

Once Śrī Rāmakṛṣṇa was asked why he had followed so many paths; was not one path enough by which to reach the supreme goal? His answer was: 'The Mother is infinite—infinite are her moods and aspects. I longed to realize her in all of them. And she revealed to me the truth of many religions.' Thus, though he did not practise varied spiritual disciplines with the specific purpose of bringing harmony among the many faiths, his life demonstrated that harmony. In this connection let us hear some of Śrī Rāmakṛṣṇa's teachings on the essential identity of the great religions:

'So many religions, so many paths to reach the same goal.[1] I have practised Hinduism, Islam, Christianity, and in Hinduism again, the ways of the different sects. I have found that it is the same God towards whom all are directing their steps, though along different paths.[2]

'The tank has several ghāts. At one Hindus draw water and call it jal; at another Mohammedans draw water and call it pāni; at a third Christians draw the same liquid and call it water. The substance is one though the names differ, and everyone is seeking the same thing. Every religion of the world is one such ghāt. Go with a sincere and earnest heart by any of these ghāts and you will reach the water of eternal bliss. But do not say that your religion is better than that of another.'[3]

To complete the story of Śrī Rāmakṛṣṇa's life, we must now turn our attention to his relationship with his wife. We have already mentioned how when he was twenty-three years old he married Sāradā Devī, then a five-year old girl. Afterwards, for a time, he apparently forgot all about his marriage. But when he was about to take monastic vows, and Totā Purī was ready to initiate him into sannyās, Śrī Rāmakṛṣṇa told him of his marriage.[4] Totā Purī said merely, 'What does it matter? Have your wife near you. That will be

[1] *Kathāmṛta*, vol. II, p. 166.

[2] See *Gospel of Sri Ramakrishna*, Swami Nikhilananda (trans.), p. 35.

[3] *Kathāmṛta*, vol. I, p. 49.

[4] It was on his initiation into sannyās that he received the name Rāmakṛṣṇa—combining the names of two of India's great avatārs; the 'Śrī'—a title of reverence—was added later when his high spiritual gifts became apparent. His original name was Gadādhar Chatterjee.

the real test of your vows and the real proof that you have become a knower of Brahman.'

All these years Sāradā Devī had been living with her parents. From her earlier years she had shown an intensely spiritual temperament. Like her husband she had had divine visions. When she grew to be a young woman she longed to be near Śrī Rāmakṛṣṇa. But there was no call from him. Then during the period of the Master's practice of Islam, people again began to say that he had lost his mind. How could it be that a Hindu priest should worship Allah? The rumour spread and reached the ears of Sāradā Devī—now eighteen years old—and though she did not believe it, she felt it her duty to be by the side of her husband. Accordingly she expressed her wish to her father, who took her to Dakṣiṇeśwar. Śrī Rāmakṛṣṇa welcomed his wife and made arrangements for her to stay near him. But he asked her, 'Tell me, have you come to drag me down to worldly ways?' Her prompt reply was, 'Oh, no. I have come to help you in your chosen path.' Śrī Rāmakṛṣṇa initiated her into the mysteries of spiritual life and supervised her progress. She became his first disciple.

Within six months of his wife's arrival, on an auspicious night, Śrī Rāmakṛṣṇa made special preparations for worshipping the Divine Mother in his own room and instructed Sāradā Devī to be present. The altar, the seat for a worshipper, and all the paraphernalia for worship were ready. There was, however, no image on the altar. Śrī Rāmakṛṣṇa seated himself on the worshipper's seat and beckoned to Sāradā Devī to be seated on the altar. In an ecstatic mood she obeyed him. Śrī Rāmakṛṣṇa invoked the presence of the Mother of the Universe in his wife and began to worship. Sāradā Devī, in the meanwhile, entered into samādhi, and Śrī Rāmakṛṣṇa likewise became absorbed. Thus they remained for a long time. When partial outer consciousness came to Śrī Rāmakṛṣṇa, he laid, with appropriate mantra, the fruits of all his spiritual struggles, together with his rosary, at the feet of the Mother of the Universe in the form of his wife.

Sāradā Devī lived in her husband's company for fourteen years and served him and his disciples until Śrī Rāmakṛṣṇa's death. In later years known as the Holy Mother, she became the guiding spirit of the Order founded in her husband's name.

Śrī Rāmakṛṣṇa, speaking of his wife, used to say: 'After marriage I earnestly prayed to the Divine Mother to root out all consciousness of physical enjoyment from her mind. That my prayer had been granted, I knew from my long association with her.'

Among the sayings of Śrī Rāmakṛṣṇa is this: 'When the lotus blossoms, the bees come of their own accord to seek the honey. So let the lotus of your heart bloom, realize God seated within it, and the bees, the spiritual aspirants, will seek you out.' Of the moment of Śrī Rāmakṛṣṇa's readiness for aspirants, Swami Vivekananda, his chief disciple, speaks thus:

'All the struggles which we experience in our lives [Śrī Rāmakṛṣṇa] had passed through. His hard-earned jewels of spirituality, for which he had given three-quarters of his life, were now ready to be offered to humanity, and then began his mission.'[1]

Many noted intellectuals of the day soon began to visit Śrī Rāmakṛṣṇa, among them Keshab Sen, who was the first man of Western education to recognize his spiritual genius. Keshab, one of the great religious leaders in India at the time, had a large following, and both in his sermons and in his magazines he spread the name and fame of the new saint. As a result, many men and women were attracted to religion—including college professors, actors, and scientists. Some of them became Śrī Rāmakṛṣṇa's disciples.

But Śrī Rāmakṛṣṇa's real work took root when there came to him a number of young men, mostly in their teens, untouched by worldly ways. Some of them began to live at Dakṣiṇeśwar, associating with him intimately. Among them was Rakhal, who later became known as Swami Brahmananda, and who was regarded by Śrī Rāmakṛṣṇa as his spiritual son.

During Śrī Rāmakṛṣṇa's fatal illness, when he was removed to Cossipore garden house, most of these young men remained with him to serve and nurse him. Of these, Naren, later known as Swami Vivekananda, was chosen as the leader. It was Naren that Śrī Rāmakṛṣṇa taught how to organize an order of monks to propagate his message.

Śrī Rāmakṛṣṇa died in August, 1886. After his death his young disciples banded together and dedicated their lives 'to our own salvation and to the good of mankind'. This is the order known today as the 'Ramakrishna Math and Mission', whose headquarters is located at Belur, near Calcutta.

Since the founding of the Order in 1886, participants in the Rāmakṛṣṇa movement, or Vedāntic revival, have gradually increased in numbers, strength, and influence, both in India and in foreign countries. Vedānta societies, so called, founded in Śrī Rāmakṛṣṇa's name and presided over by monks trained in the Math at Belur, have been established in many parts of the world, especially in Western Europe and in North and South America.

Easily the most characteristic aspect of Śrī Rāmakṛṣṇa's doctrine can be summed up in the words tolerance, reconciliation, harmony.

[1] *Complete Works of Vivekananda*, vol. IV, pp. 172–3.

The ideas the words stand for are not of course new to Indian religion, which, from its remote beginnings, as we have seen, has seldom been narrowly exclusive or dogmatic; but in Śrī Rāmakṛṣṇa they found a comprehensive and seemingly definitive embodiment. He not only brought into agreement the diverse views of Hinduism, but also managed somehow to include in his native faith all the faiths of the outside world. The idea of the unity of the religious sentiment could hardly be carried further.

In the ultimate reaches of Hinduism, there were, to be sure, no diverse views to be reconciled. When the aspirant attained his ultimate goal, views, of whatever kind, ceased to exist. He was absorbed in turīya, the transcendental consciousness, he had become one with God. But at lower levels, where the mind tried to determine the nature of God and the universe, differences early arose. Some said that God was personal, some that he was impersonal; some said that he was with form, some that he was without form. Śrī Rāmakṛṣṇa, bringing to bear his own mystic experiences, dissolved, in his simple way, all such oppositions:

'Infinite is God and infinite are his expressions. He who lives continuously in the consciousness of God, and in this alone, knows him in his true being. He knows his infinite expressions, his various aspects. He knows him as impersonal no less than as personal.'[1]

'Brahman, absolute existence, knowledge, and bliss, may be compared to an infinite ocean, without beginning or end. As through intense cold some portions of the water of the ocean freeze into ice, and the formless water appears as having form, so through intense love of the devotee the formless, absolute, infinite Existence manifests himself before him as having form and personality. But forms and aspects disappear before the man who reaches the highest samādhi, who attains the height of nondualistic philosophy, the Vedānta.'[2]

'So long as there is yet a little ego left, the consciousness that "I am a devotee", God is comprehended as personal, and his form is realized. This consciousness of a separate ego is a barrier that keeps one at a distance from the highest realization. The forms of Kāli or of Kṛṣṇa are represented as of a dark-blue colour. Why? Because the devotee has not yet approached them. At a distance the water of a lake appears blue, but when you come nearer, you find it has no colour. In the same way, to him who attains to the highest truth and experience, Brahman is absolute and impersonal. His real nature cannot be defined in words.'[3]

Following the teachings of Śrī Rāmakṛṣṇa, the highest vision of God

[1] *Kathāmṛta*, vol. I, p. 71. [2] *Ibid.*, vol. I, p. 69. [3] *Ibid.*, pp. 71–2.

can be described in the following words: He indeed has attained the supreme illumination who not only realizes the presence of God, but knows him as both personal and impersonal, who loves him intensely, talks to him, partakes of his bliss. Such an illumined soul realizes the bliss of God while he is absorbed in meditation, attaining oneness with the indivisible, impersonal Being; and he realizes the same bliss as he comes back to normal consciousness and sees this universe as a manifestation of that Being and as a divine play.

What is the relation of God to the universe? In our discussion of the Upaniṣads we have seen that in the nondual unitary consciousness the universe disappears and there remains only Brahman—the absolute existence, knowledge, and bliss. Again, the universe is seen as Brahman when the divine sight opens up. In the Bhagavad-Gītā we read about the illumined soul:

His heart is with Brahman,
His eye in all things
Sees only Brahman
Equally present,
Knows his own Atman
In every creature,
And all creation
Within that Atman.[1]

Śrī Rāmakṛṣṇa reconciled the two views of the universe, the one in which it dissolves in illusion, and the other in which it is one with God, in the following words:

'In turīya, the universe of plurality becomes annihilated—there is attained oneness with Brahman.

'When, having attained the nondual Brahman in samādhi, one comes back to the plane of the ego, one realizes that it is Brahman who has become this universe of plurality. To get to the flesh of the fruit you discard its skin and seeds. But when you want to know the total weight of the fruit, you must weigh them all together. The skin, the seeds, the flesh—all belong to one and the same fruit. Similarly, having realized the unchangeable reality—the one absolute Existence—one finds that he who is the absolute, formless, impersonal, infinite God is again one with the relative universe. He who is absolute in one

[1] VI. 29. To see God in the universe, to see Brahman in all, was considered by Śrī Rāmakṛṣṇa to be the highest spiritual attainment. Once when a young disciple came to him, the Master asked him what his goal of life was. When he received the reply 'To see God everywhere', Śrī Rāmakṛṣṇa remarked, 'Well, my boy, that is the last word of religion.'

aspect is relative in another aspect, and both aspects belong to one and the same substance. . . .

'The sacred syllable Om is explained in the scriptures as a combination of the sounds A, U, M, representing creation, preservation, and dissolution respectively. I compare the sound of Om to the sound of a bell that dissolves in silence. The relative universe dissolves in the imperishable absolute—the great silence. The gross, the subtle, the causal—everything visible and invisible dissolves in the Great Cause. Waking, dreaming, and dreamless sleep, the three states of consciousness, are dissolved in the turīya, the transcendental. Once more the bell rings. The sound Om is heard and as it were a heavy weight falls on the bosom of the calm, infinite ocean; immediately the ocean becomes agitated. From the bosom of the absolute rises the relative; from the Great Cause issues forth the causal, the subtle, the gross universe; from the transcendental come the three states of consciousness—waking, dreaming, and dreamless sleep. Again the waves dissolve in the ocean, and there is the great calm. From the absolute comes the relative, and into the absolute the relative dissolves. I have experienced this infinite ocean of bliss and consciousness; and Mother has shown me how innumerable worlds issue from the ocean and go back into it. I do not know, of course, what is written in books of philosophy.'[1]

'I see the truth directly: what need have I to philosophize? I see how God has become all this—he has become the individual beings and the empirical world. There is nothing but he. But this truth cannot be experienced until the heart is illumined. It is not a matter of philosophy, but of experience. Through the grace of God the light must first shine in one's own soul. When that comes to pass, one attains samādhi. Then, though one comes back to the normal plane, one loses the material sense, one loses all attachment to lust and gold. One then loves only to hear and speak the word of God.'[2]

'To reason out the truth of God is one thing, and to meditate on God is another. But again, when illumination comes through the grace of God, then only is the truth of God known and experienced. Just as a dark room is lighted up when you strike a match, so is the heart lighted up by the grace of God. Then alone are all doubts dissolved away.'[3]

The three main schools of thought in Vedānta—dualism, qualified monism, and nondualism—Śrī Rāmakṛṣṇa reconciled in the following

[1] *Kathāmṛta*, vol. I, pp. 213, 214, 215.

[2] *Ibid.*, p. 239.

[3] *Ibid.*, p. 240.

manner. Quoting an ancient verse from the Hindu scriptures, he told how Rāma, who was worshipped as a divine incarnation, asked his faithful devotee Hanumān how he looked upon him. Hanumān replied: 'When I consider myself as a physical being, thou art the master, I am thy servant. When I consider myself as an individual being, thou art the whole, I am one of thy parts. And when I realize myself as the Ātman, I am one with thee.'[1] Thus Śrī Rāmakṛṣṇa pointed out that dualism, qualified monism, and nondualism are not mutually exclusive and contradictory concepts but successive steps in realization—the third and last being attained when the aspirant loses all consciousness of self in union with God.

Thus, in a way more or less peculiar to himself, through attention mainly to the mystic experience, Śrī Rāmakṛṣṇa harmonized conflicting notions of God and the universe and of their relations to each other. But this was not his only way. Another, still more peculiar to him, might be called, in current terms, pragmatic. Any idea of God, any mode of worshipping him, that *worked*—that led the aspirant to the ultimate goal—must be valid and true. But how could one be sure that an idea or a method is really thus effective? Clearly, by trying it oneself. And that, in all simplicity and sincerity, is what Śrī Rāmakṛṣṇa did. He practised the teachings of many divergent sects within Hinduism, and through each of them achieved the same supreme realization. But even this was not sufficient. What of the Mohammedanism that had long been alive in India? What of Christianity? The story of his experimental contacts with these religions we have already told. In the end he arrived at the grand conclusion with which the ancient ṛṣis began, and which we have more than once recalled: Ekaṁ sat viprā bahudhā vadanti—in Śrī Rāmakṛṣṇa's words, 'So many religions, so many paths to reach one and the same goal.'

In defining this goal Śrī Rāmakṛṣṇa was of course at one with all his spiritual ancestors. It was simply to realize God within one's own soul. Śaṁkara declared that 'Study of the scriptures is fruitless so long as Brahman has not been experienced'; and 'He is born to no purpose,' says Śrī Rāmakṛṣṇa, 'who, having the rare privilege of being born a man, is unable to realize God.'

Continuing, Śrī Rāmakṛṣṇa emphasized the importance of means:

'Adopt adequate means for the end you seek to attain. You cannot get butter by crying yourself hoarse, saying, "There is butter in the milk!" If you wish to make butter, you must turn the milk into curd, and churn it well. Then alone you can get butter. So if you long to

[1] *Kathāmṛta*, vol. III, p. 13.

see God, practise spiritual disciplines. What is the use of merely crying "Lord! Lord!"'[1]

To an aspirant who should ask about particular means to adopt, we can easily anticipate Śrī Rāmakṛṣṇa's answer. Pursue sincerely and diligently any spiritual path, he would say, and you will ultimately achieve realization.

As to what the basic paths are he accepted the Hindu belief that for all religions they can be reduced to the four yogas: jñāna yoga, the path of discrimination between the Real and the unreal; bhakti yoga, the path of loving devotion; karma yoga, the path of selfless work; and rāja yoga, the path of concentration and meditation. In our study of the Bhagavad-Gītā we have seen that Śrī Kṛṣṇa advocated a harmonious combination of all the yogas. The spiritual aspirant should cultivate discrimination and devotion as well as concentration and meditation. Śrī Rāmakṛṣṇa stressed this again and again in his teachings. He did not want anyone to be one-sided.

To be sure, special emphasis should be placed on one or another path according to the temperament of the devotee. Śrī Rāmakṛṣṇa advocated emphasis on jñāna yoga, however, only for an exceptional few, pointing out that if this path is followed without the necessary unfoldment of certain virtues, such as dispassion, meditation on the unity of Ātman and Brahman will be misunderstood and misapplied. For most spiritual aspirants he recommended emphasis on bhakti yoga, because the path of devotion is a natural one leading to realization. Everyone has love in his heart—it merely needs to be directed towards God; and for a follower of bhakti yoga discrimination, dispassion, and all the other virtues unfold easily and naturally. Śrī Rāmakṛṣṇa used to say: 'The more you move towards the light, the farther you will be from darkness.' He told his disciples how he himself prayed for devotion during a period of intense spiritual disciplines:

'O Mother, here is sin and here is virtue; take them both and grant me pure love for thee. Here is knowledge and here is ignorance; I lay them at thy feet. Grant me pure love for thee. Here is purity and here is impurity; take them both and grant me pure love for thee. Here are good works and here are evil works; I lay them at thy feet. Grant me pure love for thee.'[2]

But whatever path the aspirant chiefly follows, according to Śrī Rāmakṛṣṇa, meditation is the most important aspect of his spiritual life. Somehow or other he must keep his mind fixed on God. Meditation is performed not merely with closed eyes but with eyes open as well.

[1] *Kathāmṛta*, vol. II, p. 185. Cf. Matt. vii. 21. [2] *Ibid.*, vol. I, p. 54.

There are many ways to meditate and many forms of meditation. For the jñāna yogi, for example, there is the meditation on the identity of Ātman and Brahman; he tries to live in that identity. There are many means to achieve this end, the one best for a particular aspirant depending on his temperament.

For the bhakti yogi there is meditation on a chosen ideal of God, which may be with or without form. To those who preferred to meditate on God with form, Śrī Rāmakṛṣṇa said:

'Wash away all the impurities of your mind; then let the Lord be seated within the lotus of your heart. Meditate on him as a living presence. Tie your mind to the feet of your Chosen Ideal with a silken thread, but remember not merely to think of him while you are formally meditating: keep recollectedness at other times. Don't you know that in the shrine of Mother Durgā a light burns continually before the image, and the housewife sees to it that the light never goes out? Keep the light of awareness always burning within your heart. Keep your thoughts awake. While engaged in your daily activities, occasionally gaze inward and see if the light is burning.'[1]

To those who preferred to meditate on God in his formless aspect, he said:

'Think of him as an infinite, shoreless ocean. You are like a fish swimming in that ocean of existence, knowledge, and bliss absolute, or like a vessel dipped in it with that Presence inside, outside, and everywhere.'[2]

'Some devotees approach God by going from the aspect without form to that with form; others by going from the aspect with form to that without form. To realize that he is both with form and without form—that is best.'[3]

Two watchwords Śrī Rāmakṛṣṇa set before mankind were renunciation and service.

Spiritual aspirants can follow either the way of the monk or the way of the householder, but renunciation is an ideal which the two ways have in common. The monk's renunciation must be external, however, as well as mental. The householder renounces mentally.

But what, really, does renunciation mean? It is deification—which means seeing God everywhere and in everything, knowing for oneself the truth expressed in the Īśa Upaniṣad: 'In the heart of all things, of whatever there is in the universe, dwells the Lord. He

[1] *Līlāprasaṅga*, Guru bhāv, Pt. I, pp. 89–90.
[2] *Kathāmṛta*, vol. III, p. 256.
[3] *Līlāprasaṅga*, Guru bhāv, Pt. I, p. 90.

alone is the reality. Wherefore, renouncing vain appearances, rejoice in him.'

Śrī Rāmakṛṣṇa used to tell his householder disciples to live in the world in a spirit of detachment, keeping their minds on God. Gradually they would begin to realize that all objects and persons are parts of him. The aspirant, he said, must serve his parents, his wife, and his children as manifestations of God. He who lives in the world in this manner, renouncing all sense of possession, is the ideal householder. He overcomes all fear of death. But in order to reach this ideal the aspirant must occasionally go into solitude, practise contemplation, and yearn to realize God.

In connection with the ideal of service taught by Śrī Rāmakṛṣṇa, I shall mention a very interesting incident from his life. One day, in a state of ecstasy, he was recalling the precepts of another great saint. One of these preached compassion for mankind. Śrī Rāmakṛṣṇa repeated several times the word compassion. Then he exclaimed: 'Compassion! Who am I to be compassionate! Isn't everyone God? How can I be compassionate towards God? Serve him, serve him, serve him!' In this way Śrī Rāmakṛṣṇa elevated the ideal of philanthropy to the worship of God in every being.

He considered the attainment of liberation for oneself to be a low ideal. Swami Turiyananda, one of his disciples, used to say that nirvāṇa was the highest state of realization and was rebuked for what his master called a 'mean conception'. Naren, later known as Swami Vivekananda, one day was asked by Śrī Rāmakṛṣṇa what his ideal was. When Naren answered that he wanted to remain immersed in samādhi and return to normal consciousness only in order to keep his body alive, Śrī Rāmakṛṣṇa exclaimed: 'Shame on you! I thought you were greater than that!' And he taught him the twin ideal on which Vivekananda later founded the monastic Order of Rāmakṛṣṇa: liberation for oneself and service to God in man.

Concerning this same Swami Vivekananda a story is told which illustrates the extraordinary means to which Śrī Rāmakṛṣṇa sometimes resorted in order to advance the spiritual welfare of his disciples. When young Naren first came to Śrī Rāmakṛṣṇa, he was a member of the Brāhmo Samāj, an Indian reform movement which believed in the ideal of theism. Recognizing in his new disciple an aspirant with the capacity to follow the difficult path of jñāna yoga, Śrī Rāmakṛṣṇa asked him to read treatises on advaita Vedānta and made him sing a song expressing the nondual conception. Naren complied with his master's wishes, but he could not accept the doctrine of nondualism, for to him it seemed blasphemous to look on man as one with his Creator. One day he laughingly remarked to a friend: 'How impossible! This vessel is God! This cup is God! Whatever we see is God!

And we ourselves are God!' At this moment Śrī Rāmakṛṣṇa came out of his room, smiling, and touched Naren. The effect of this touch Naren described as follows:

'That strange touch immediately caused a complete revolution in my mind. Wherever I looked I saw Brahman and Brahman alone. I lived in that consciousness the whole day. I returned home, and that same experience continued. When I sat down to eat I saw that the food, the plate, the server, and I myself—all were Brahman. I took one or two morsels of food and again was absorbed in that consciousness. . . . All the time, whether eating or lying down, or going to college, I had the same experience. While walking in the streets I noticed cabs plying but did not feel inclined to move out of the way. I felt that the cabs and myself were made of the same substance. . . . When this state changed a little, the world began to appear to me as a dream. While walking in Cornwallis Square I struck my head against the iron railings to see if they were real or only a dream. After several days, when I returned to the normal plane, I realized that I had had a glimpse of nondual consciousness. Since then I have never doubted the truth of nondualism.'[1]

To sum up the message of Śrī Rāmakṛṣṇa, especially in its relation to practice, we perhaps could do no better than quote the following words of the distinguished swami to whom we have just listened:

'Do not depend on doctrines, do not depend on dogmas, or sects, or churches, or temples; they count for little compared with the essence of existence in man, which is divine; and the more this divinity is developed in a man, the more powerful is he for good. Earn that spirituality first, acquire that, and criticize no one, for all doctrines and creeds have some good in them. Show by your lives that religion does not mean words, or names, or sects, but that it means spiritual realization. Only those can understand who have perceived the Reality. Only those who have attained to spirituality can communicate it to others, can be great teachers of mankind. They alone are the powers of light.'[2]

[1] *Līlāprasanga*, Divya bhāv, pp. 161, 162, 163.
[2] *Complete Works of Vivekananda*, vol. IV, pp. 182–3.

SELECTED PRECEPTS OF ŚRI RĀMAKṚṢṆA

Know yourself and you will know God. What is your ego? Is it your hand or foot or flesh or blood or any other part of your body? Reflect well and you will find that the ego has no real existence. Just as, if you peel off the skin of an onion layer after layer, in search of a kernel, for a while more and more skin appears, and then nothing at all, so it is if you go looking for the ego. There is no kernel within the onion; there is no ego within yourself. In the last analysis what is within you is only the Ātman—Pure Consciousness. When the illusion of the ego disappears, then appears the Reality—God.

There are two kinds of ego—one ripe, and the other unripe. The unripe ego thinks, 'This is *my* house, *my* son, *my* this, *my* that.' The ripe ego thinks, 'I am the servant of the Lord, I am his child; I am the Ātman, immortal, free; I am Pure Consciousness.'[1]

The light of the sun shines equally on all surfaces, but it reflects clearly only on bright surfaces like water, mirrors, and polished metals. In like manner, although God dwells in the hearts of all, he is clearly manifest only in the hearts of the holy.[2]

How long does one argue about the meaning of the scriptures? Only until the Sat-chid-ānanda becomes revealed in one's own heart. The bee buzzes only so long as it does not sit on the flower. As soon as it sits on the flower and begins to drink of the honey, all noise stops—there is complete silence.[3]

Useless is the study of the scriptures if one has no discrimination and dispassion. One cannot find God unless one is endowed with these. Discrimination is knowledge of what is eternal and what is noneternal, and devotion to the eternal, which is God; it is knowledge that the Ātman is separate from the body. Dispassion is nonattachment to the objects of sense.[4]

The true hero is he who can discipline his mind by devotional exercises while living in the world. A strong man can look in any direction while carrying a heavy burden on his head. Similarly, the perfect man can keep his gaze constantly fixed on God while carrying the burden of worldly duties.[5]

[1] Swami Brahmananda, *Śrī Śrī Rāmakṛṣṇa Upadeśa*, pp. 1 f.
[2] *Ibid.*, p. 24.
[3] *Ibid.*, p. 35.
[4] *Ibid.*, pp. 37 f.
[5] *Ibid.*, p. 46.

A boy holds on to a pillar and circles round it with headlong speed. While he is spinning, his attention is constantly fixed on the pillar. He knows that if he lets go his hold upon it he will fall and hurt himself. Similarly, the wise householder holds on to the pillar of God: keeps his mind fixed on him, and performs his worldly duties. Thus is he free from all dangers.[1]

Let the boat stay on the water: there is no harm. But let not water get into the boat, lest the boat sink. Similarly, there is no harm if the devotee lives in the world, provided he lets not worldliness enter into his mind.[2]

Clay in its natural state can be moulded into any form, but burnt clay cannot. Similarly, spiritual truths cannot be impressed upon hearts that have been burnt by the fire of lust.[3]

To bring one's heart and one's speech into accord is the goal of all spiritual discipline. If you say, 'O Lord, Thou art my all in all,' while in your heart you believe the objective world to be all in all, your devotional exercises are bound to be fruitless.[4]

Countless are the pearls lying hidden in the sea. If a single dive yields you none, do not conclude that the sea is without pearls. Similarly, if after practising spiritual disciplines for a little while you fail to have the vision of God, do not lose heart. Continue to practise the disciplines with patience, and at the proper time you are sure to obtain grace.[5]

Strike a match, and the light disperses all at once the darkness of a room, even though accumulated for centuries. Similarly, a single gracious glance of the Lord disperses the accumulated sins of innumerable births.[6]

The magnetic needle always points towards the north, whatever the direction in which the ship is sailing; that is why the ship does not lose her course. Similarly, if the mind of man is always turned towards God, he will steer clear of every danger.[7]

There is only one God, but endless are his aspects and endless are his names. Call him by any name and worship him in any aspect that pleases you, you are sure to see him.[8]

[1] Swami Brahmananda, *Śrī Śrī Rāmakṛṣṇa Upadeśa*, pp. 49 f.
[2] *Ibid.*, pp. 50 f. [3] *Ibid.*, p. 65. [4] *Ibid.*, p. 68. [5] *Ibid.*, p. 101.
[6] *Ibid.*, p. 118. [7] *Ibid.*, pp. 124 f. [8] *Ibid.*, p. 132.

CHAPTER 25

EPITOME

Although in the course of its long history, reaching far back into an unrecorded past, Indian religion has had its share of sects and doctrines, of reformations and revivals, it has nevertheless preserved at its core, unchanged, four fundamental ideas. These may be very simply expressed: God is; he can be realized; to realize him is the supreme goal of human existence; he can be realized in many ways.

God is. This tremendous proposition, though variously interpreted, is of course common, not only to the religions of India, but to all the religions of the world. In every age God-men have proclaimed it, each according to his own spiritual vision, and in every age people have asked for proofs that it is true. Many plausible demonstrations have been devised by philosophers, establishing God as a logical necessity. However, there is not a single argument substantiating God's actuality on the basis of reason which has not been contradicted by equally plausible arguments of opposing philosophers. The only real proof that God *is* must be sought elsewhere.

God can be realized. That is to say, he can be known, felt, experienced, immediately, in the depths of one's own soul. Upon this awe-inspiring fact the religions and philosophies of India, without exception, have been founded. From the dim ages of the Vedic seers, down through the many centuries to our own day, it has been consistently declared that the ultimate reality of the universe can be directly perceived—though never in normal consciousness. To the unique, transcendent state in which the miracle happens, various names have been given—turīya, samādhi, nirvāṇa—names that have occurred over and over again in the pages of this book.

To realize God is the supreme goal of human existence. In this all Indian religions and philosophies have at all times been agreed. 'Arise, awake, approach the feet of the master and know That,' says the ṛṣi of the Kaṭha Upaniṣad. 'Study of the scriptures is fruitless,' says the great Śaṁkara, 'so long as Brahman has not been experienced.' 'He is born to no purpose,' says Śrī Rāmakṛṣṇa, 'who, having the rare privilege of being born a man, is unable to realize God.' A thousand voices have proclaimed what is for pious Hindus the one basic rule of life.

God can be realized in many ways. 'Truth is one,' declares the Ṛg-Veda, most ancient of Hindu scriptures, 'sages call it by various names.' 'So many religions, so many paths', declares Śrī Rāmakṛṣṇa, 'to reach one and the same goal.'

It will be observed that the call for tolerance, harmony, universal consent, applies only to the paths to the goal, not to the goal. This, once realized, admits no diversity of opinion—admits indeed no opinion. For not only is it beyond the senses; it is beyond all thought. The Upaniṣads say 'neti, neti, Ātmā'—the Ātman, or Brahman within, is 'not this', 'not that'. 'In that ecstatic realization', says Śrī Rāmakṛṣṇa, speaking out of his own abundant experience, 'all thoughts cease. . . . No power of speech is left by which to express Brahman.' If this were all, there could of course be no religious doctrines, no religious philosophies. But it is not all. The mystics sooner or later emerge from transcendental consciousness, and then, it sometimes happens, they talk—not for their own sake (they have nothing to gain that they do not already possess) but for the good of their fellow men.

And in talking they may express variously the same ultimately inexpressible truth.

The seers and sages and philosophers of India, as elsewhere, have defined God in many ways, often apparently contradictory. They have, for example, pronounced him impersonal, beyond attributes, and again personal, the repository of infinite blessed qualities; they have pronounced him with form, and again without form. Hence have arisen divergent sects, but what is to be noted is that seldom if ever did differences in doctrine lead to intolerance, let alone to persecution. On the rare occasions when one system of philosophy or religion tried to prove and establish its own truth at the expense of others (this was likely to be some system other than nondualistic), it could not get very far. It could never dominate the minds of the people of India as a whole, so thoroughly ingrained in their hearts was the spirit of understanding and sympathy. For after all, they felt, it was the saintly life that counted. Saints and sages have been produced by following the order of Śaṁkara, but also by following the order of Rāmānuja, of Mādhwa, of Vallabha, or of Śrī Caitanya; and they are recognized as such, not only by their particular followers, but by the whole of India. Moreover, by a natural extension of their liberal attitude, Hindus revere the saints and sages of religions other than their own.

The first systematic attempt to harmonize the many doctrines of Hinduism is to be found in the teachings of the Bhagavad-Gītā—the Bible of the Hindus. By the time of the Epics many schools of thought, with varied ideas of God and the Godhead, as well as varied paths, called yogas, had come into existence. These were all incorporated in the teachings of the Gītā like 'pearls in a necklace'. Śrī Kṛṣṇa says:

> Whatever path men travel
> Is my path:
> No matter where they walk
> It leads to me.[1]

After many centuries, when Hinduism came for the first time into contact with a foreign religion, attempts were made by two great teachers, Guru Nānak and Kabir, to harmonize the new Mohammedanism with the native faith; and more recently, when confronted by Christianity, Hinduism has once more, especially by the precepts and practices of Śrī Rāmakṛṣṇa, continued its role of peacemaker among the creeds.

It is perhaps natural in closing this book to emphasize strongly the age-old effort of India to reconcile differing faiths. For it is probably by continuing this effort on an international scale that she is doing most to advance the spiritual welfare of mankind. To bring together against rampant evil the great religions of the world is no doubt a gigantic task, but it is one for which India has the special qualification that she strives for unity, not by calling for a common doctrine, but only by pointing to a common goal, and by exhorting men to its attainment. The path, she assures us, matters little; it is the goal that is supreme. And what is the goal? It is only—once again—to realize God.

[1] Gītā, IV. 11.

BIBLIOGRAPHY

PART I

Works Significantly Referred to in This Book[1]

Babbitt, Irving. 'Buddha and the Occident', *The Dhammapada*. New York: Oxford University Press, 1936.

Bhāgavatam. *See* Prabhavananda, Swami (tr.). *The Wisdom of God.*

Brahmananda, Swami. *Śrī Śrī Rāmakṛṣṇa Upadeśa*. Calcutta: Udbodhan Office, 15th ed.

Ghose, Sri Aurobindo. *Essays on the Gita*. First Series, 1926; Second Series, 1928. Calcutta: Arya Publishing House.

Gītā. *See* Prabhavananda, Swami, and Isherwood, Christopher (trs.). *Bhagavad-Gita.*

Hiriyanna, M. *Outlines of Indian Philosophy*. London: Allen & Unwin, 1932.

Kamaleswarananda, Swami. *Śruti Sangraha*. Calcutta: Gadadhar Āśrama.

Kathāmṛta. See M. *Śrī Śrī Rāmakṛṣṇa Kathāmṛta.*

Līlāprasaṅga. See Saradananda, Swami. *Śrī Śrī Rāmakṛṣṇa Līlāprasaṅga.*

M. *Śrī Śrī Rāmakṛṣṇa Kathāmṛta*. Vol. I, 10th ed.; vol. II, 5th ed.; vol. III, 4th ed.; vol. IV, 2nd ed.; vol. V, 1st ed. Calcutta: Pravas Chandra Gupta.

Mahābhārata. *Śrīman-Mahābhāratam*. Gorakhpur: Gita Press.

Müller, Max (ed.). *Buddhist Suttas*. (*Sacred Books of the East*, vol. VII.) New York: Charles Scribner's Sons, 1900.

—— (tr.). *The Dhammapada*. (*Sacred Books of the East*, vol. XII.) New York: Charles Scribner's Sons, 1901.

Nivedita, Sister. *Śiva and Buddha*. Calcutta: Udbodhan Office, 1946.

Prabhavananda, Swami (tr.). *The Wisdom of God* (*Srimad Bhagavatam*). Hollywood: Vedanta Press, 1943.

Prabhavananda, Swami, and Isherwood, Christopher. *How to Know God: The Yoga Aphorisms of Patanjali*. (Tr. with new commentary.) New York: Harper & Bros., 1953. London: Allen & Unwin.

—— (trs.). *Bhagavad-Gita: The Song of God*. New York: Harper & Bros., 1951. London: Phoenix House.

—— (trs.) Shankara's *Crest-Jewel of Discrimination* (*Viveka-Chudamani*). Hollywood: Vedanta Press, 1947.

Prabhavananda, Swami, and Manchester, Frederick (trs.). *The Upanishads*. Hollywood: Vedanta Press, 1947.

[1] Bibliographical data for works only incidentally referred to are given in the footnotes.

Radhakrishnan, S. *Indian Philosophy*. Vol. I, 1923; vol. II, 1927. New York: The Macmillan Co. London: Allen & Unwin.

Sri Ramakrishna Centenary Memorial. *The Cultural Heritage of India*, Vol. I. Belur Math. Calcutta: Sri Ramakrishna Centenary Committee, 1936.

Saradananda, Swami. *Śrī Śrī Rāmakṛṣṇa Līlāprasaṅga*. Calcutta: Udbodhan Office, 1955.

Srinivasachari, P. N. *Ramanuja's Idea of the Finite Self*. Calcutta: Longmans, Green & Co., 1928.

Thibaut, George (tr.). *The Vedānta Sūtras with the Commentary by Saṅkarākārya*, Pt. I. (*Sacred Books of the East*, ed. Max Müller, vol. XXXIV.) Oxford: Clarendon Press, 1890.

Upaniṣads. *See* Prabhavananda, Swami, and Manchester, Frederick (trs.).

Vivekacūḍāmaṇi. *See* Prabhavananda, Swami, and Isherwood, Christopher (trs.). Shankara's *Crest-Jewel of Discrimination*.

Vivekananda, Swami. *The Complete Works of Swami Vivekananda*. Vol. I, 1950; vol. II, 1948; vol. III, 1948; vol. IV, 1932; vol. V, 1947; vol. VI, 1947; vol. VII, 1947; vol. VIII, 1955. Mayavati: Advaita Ashrama.

Woodroffe, Sir John (Arthur Avalon). *Śakti and Śākta*. Madras: Ganesh & Co., Ltd., 1959.

Yoga Aphorisms. *See* Prabhavananda, Swami, and Isherwood, Christopher. *How to Know God*.

PART II

Other Works Pertaining to Indian Philosophy

General

Bhattacharyya, Haridas (ed.). *The Cultural Heritage of India*. Vol. III, The Philosophies; vol. IV, The Religions. Calcutta: Ramakrishna Mission Institute of Culture, 1953.

Brahma, Nalini Kanta. *The Philosophy of Hindu Sadhana*. London: Kegan Paul.

Chatterjee, S. C., and Datta, D. M. *An Introduction to Indian Philosophy*. Calcutta University.

Dasgupta, Surendranath. *A History of Indian Philosophy*. Four vols. Cambridge University Press, 1922–49.

Gambhirananda, Swami. *History of the Ramakrishna Math and Mission*. Calcutta: Advaita Ashrama, 1957.

—— *Holy Mother, Sri Sarada Devi*. Madras: Sri Ramakrishna Math, 1955.

Maitra, Sushil Kumar. *The Ethics of the Hindus*. Calcutta University.

Müller, Max. *Six Systems of Indian Philosophy*. London: 1899.

Nikhilananda, Swami. *Hinduism: Its Meaning for the Liberation of the Spirit.* New York: Harper & Bros., 1958.
—— (tr.). *The Gospel of Sri Ramakrishna*, by M. New York: Ramakrishna-Vivekananda Center, 1952.
Prabhavananda, Swami. *The Eternal Companion.* (Life and Teachings of Swami Brahmananda.) Hollywood: Vedanta Press, 1947.
Saradananda, Swami. *Sri Ramakrishna, the Great Master.* Swami Jagadananda (tr.). Madras: Sri Ramakrishna Math, 1956.
Tapasyananda, Swami. *Sri Sarada Devi, the Holy Mother.* (Conversations translated by Swami Nikhilananda.) Madras: Sri Ramakrishna Math, 1958.
Zimmer, Heinrich. *Philosophies of India.* Edited by Joseph Campbell. New York: Pantheon. Bollingen Series XXVI, 1951. London: Routledge & Kegan Paul, Ltd.

Sāṁkhya

Colebrooke, H. T., and Wilson, H. H. *Samkhya-karika* (with the Bhasya of Gaudapada). Text and translation. Bombay, 1887.
Garbe, R. *Die Samkhya Philosophie.* Translated by R. D. Vadekar. Poona.
Jha, Ganganath. *The Samkhya-karika of Isvarakrishna* (with Tattvakaumudi of Vacaspati Misra). Text and translation. Bombay.

Yoga

Coster, Geraldine. *Yoga and Western Psychology.* Oxford University Press.
Dasgupta, Surendranath. *The Study of Patanjali.* Calcutta University.

Nyāya-Vaiśeṣika

Chatterjee, Satish Chandra. *The Nyaya Theory of Knowledge.* Calcutta University.
Gough, A. E. *Vaisesika-Sutras of Kanada* (with comments from Sankara Misra's Upaskara and Jayanarayana's Vivriti). Text and translation. Banaras.
Madhavananda, Swami. *Bhasa-pariccheda* (with Siddhanta-muktavali). Text and translation. Calcutta: Advaita Ashrama.

Pūrva Mīmāṁsā

Keith, A. B. *The Karma Mimamsa.* Oxford University Press.
Madhavananda, Swami. *Mimamsa-paribhasa.* Translated and annotated. Belur Math: Ramakrishna Mission Sarada Pitha.

Advaita

Deussen, Paul. *Outlines of the Vedanta System of Philosophy according to Shankara.* Translated by J. H. Woods and C. B. Runkle. New York.

Jagadananda, Swami. *Upadesasahasri of Shankaracharya*. Text and translation. Madras: Sri Ramakrishna Math.

Madhavananda, Swami. *Brihadaranyaka Upanishad*. Text with translation of Shankara's commentary. Calcutta: Advaita Ashrama.

—— *Vedantaparibhasa*. Text and translation. Calcutta: Advaita Ashrama.

—— *Vivekachudamani*. Text and translation. Calcutta: Advaita Ashrama.

Mahadevan, T. M. P. *Gaudapada: A Study in Early Advaita*. Madras University.

Müller, Max. *Three Lectures on Vedanta Philosophy*. London.

Nikhilananda, Swami. *Atmabodha*. Text and translation. Madras: Sri Ramakrishna Math.

—— *The Upanishads*. Translation. Four vols. New York: Harper & Bros.

Nityaswarupananda, Swami. *Ashtavakra Samhita*. Text and translation. Calcutta: Advaita Ashrama.

Sharvananda, Swami. *Isha, Kena, Katha, Prasna, Mundaka, Mandukya, Aitareva, and Taittiriya Upanishads*. Text and translation with notes. Madras: Sri Ramakrishna Math.

Tyagisananda, Swami. *Svetasvatara Upanishad*. Text and translation with notes. Madras: Sri Ramakrishna Math.

Vimuktananda, Swami. *Aparokshanubhuti*. Text and translation. Calcutta: Advaita Ashrama.

Vireswarananda, Swami. *Brahma-Sutras*. Text and translation with notes. Calcutta: Advaita Ashrama.

Viśiṣṭādvaita

Adidevananda, Swami. *Yatindra-mata-dipika*. Text and translation Madras: Sri Ramakrishna Math.

Srinivasachari, P. N. *The Philosophy of Vishishtadvaita*. Madras: The Adyar Library.

Dvaita

Maitra, Sushil Kumar. *Madhva Logic*. Calcutta University.

Rau, S. Subba. *Purnaprajna-darsana* (Vedanta-Sutra with the commentary of Sri Madhvacharya). Translation. Madras.

Bhedābheda and Śuddhādvaita

Chaudhuri, Mrs. Roma. *Doctrine of Nimbarka and His Followers*. Calcutta: Asiatic Society.

Majumdar, Sridhar. *The Vedanta Philosophy on the Basis of the Commentary by Nimbarkacharya*. Bankipur.

Srinivasachari, P. N. *The Philosophy of Bhedabheda*. Madras: The Adyar Library.

Bhagavad-Gītā

Nikhilananda, Swami (tr.). *The Bhagavad-Gita*. New York: Ramakrishna-Vivekananda Center, 1952.

Radhakrishnan, S. (tr.). *The Bhagavad-Gita*. New York: Harper & Bros.

Swarupananda, Swami (tr.). *Srimad-Bhagavad-Gita*. Calcutta: Advaita Ashrama, 1956.

Vireswarananda, Swami (tr.). *Srimad-Bhagavad-Gita*. Text and gloss of Sridhara Swami. Madras: Sri Ramakrishna Math, 1948.

Tantra

Woodroffe, Sir John (Arthur Avalon). *The Great Liberation* (Mahanirvana *Tantra*). Text and translation. Madras: Ganesh & Co., Ltd.

—— *The Principles of Tantra*. Two vols. Madras: Ganesh & Co., Ltd.

—— *The Serpent Power*. Madras: Ganesh & Co. Ltd.

—— *Varnamala (Garland of Letters)*. Studies in the Mantrasastra. Madras: Ganesh & Co., Ltd.

—— *The World as Power*. Six vols. Madras: Ganesh & Co., Ltd.

Jainism

Chakravarti, Appasvami (ed. and tr.). *Kundakundacharya's Pancastikayasara* (*Sacred Books of the Jainas*). Allahabad: 1920.

Jacobi, Hermann. 'Jainism', in Hastings, *Encyclopaedia of Religion and Ethics*, vol. VII, pp. 465–74. New York: Charles Scribner's Sons.

—— *Jaina Sutras*. (*Sacred Books of the East*, vols. XXII and XLV.) Oxford, 1884 and 1895.

Jaini, Jagmandar Lal. *Outlines of Jainism*. Cambridge: 1916.

—— (ed. and tr.). *Tattvarthadhigama Sutra*. (*Sacred Books of the Jainas*.) Arrah.

Buddhism

Conze, Edward. *Buddhism: Its Essence and Development*. Oxford: Bruno Cassirer, Ltd., 1951.

Evans-Wentz, W. Y. (tr.). *Tibetan Yoga and Secret Doctrines*. London: 1935.

Müller, Max (ed.). *The Sutta Nipata*. (*Sacred Books of the East*, vol. XII.) New York: 1901.

Pratt, James Bissett. *The Pilgrimage of Buddhism*. New York: 1928.

Rhys Davids, T. W. *Buddhist India*. Calcutta: Susil Gupta (India) Ltd.

Warren, H. C. *Buddhism in Translations*. Cambridge: Harvard University Press.

INDEX